Web–Based Multimedia Advancements in Data Communications and Networking Technologies

Varadharajan Sridhar
*Management Development Institute, India
& Sasken Communication Technologies, India*

Debashis Saha
Indian Institute of Management-Calcutta, India

Information Science
REFERENCE

Managing Director:	Lindsay Johnston
Editorial Director:	Joel Gamon
Book Production Manager:	Jennifer Romanchak
Publishing Systems Analyst:	Adrienne Freeland
Assistant Acquisitions Editor:	Kayla Wolfe
Typesetter:	Henry Ulrich
Cover Design:	Nick Newcomer

Published in the United States of America by
Information Science Reference (an imprint of IGI Global)
701 E. Chocolate Avenue
Hershey PA 17033
Tel: 717-533-8845
Fax: 717-533-8661
E-mail: cust@igi-global.com
Web site: http://www.igi-global.com

Library of Congress Cataloging-in-Publication Data

Web-based multimedia advancements in data communications and networking technologies / Varadharajan Sridhar and Debashis Saha, editors.
     p. cm.
 Includes bibliographical references and index.
 ISBN 978-1-4666-2026-1 (hbk.) -- ISBN 978-1-4666-2027-8 (ebook) -- ISBN 978-1-4666-2028-5 (print & perpetual access) 1. Ad hoc networks (Computer networks) 2. Computer networks. 3. Data transmission systems. I. Sridhar, Varadharajan. II. Saha, Debashis, 1965-
 TK5105.5.W43 2013
 004.6--dc23
                              2012009912

British Cataloguing in Publication Data
A Cataloguing in Publication record for this book is available from the British Library.

The views expressed in this book are those of the authors, but not necessarily of the publisher.

Table of Contents

Detailed Table of Contents

Chapter 1

    Alan D. Smith, Robert Morris University, USA

Although online trading has its benefits, such as convenience and the ability to compare prices online, there are still many concerns about the integrity of the buyer, the seller and/or the online action service provider (OASP). This paper investigates these relationships via multivariate statistical analysis of a stratified sample of working professionals, resulting in 198 useable questionnaires from an initial sampling frame of over 550 professional personnel from five relatively large Pittsburgh, Pennsylvania, firms. The author found that buyers that felt feedback systems were viable were more willing to engage in online trading activities and pay a premium price for merchandise being sold by a seller with a better reputation, regardless of gender. Customers were especially concerned with the total price, including shipping cost, regardless of gender. In terms of the convenience of payment method, electronic forms were preferred in transacting online trading activities, regardless of age and gender.

Chapter 2

    Amin Shaqrah, Alzaytoonah University of Jordan, Jordan

This paper investigates the relationship between internet security and e-business competence at banking and exchange firms in Jordan. The proposed conceptual model examines the antecedents and consequences of e-business competence and tests its empirical validity. The sample of 152 banking and exchange firms tests the posited structural equation model. The results consistently support the validity of the proposed conceptual model, the results also found that organizations realize the importance of e- business and are willing to proceed further with e-business. Beyond concerns about internet security, their awareness of security hazards and internet performance is minimal. The author concludes that the public awareness of ICT in general is low. In light of the data collected, the author makes recommendations for the interested authorities to improve e-business in Jordan.

Chapter 3

A Novel Dynamic Noise-Dependent Probabilistic Algorithm for Route Discovery in MANETs........ 52

Hussein Al-Bahadili, Petra University, Jordan
Alia Sabri, Applied Sciences Private University, Jordan

In mobile ad hoc networks (MANETs), broadcasting is widely used in route discovery and other network services. The most widely used broadcasting algorithm is simple flooding, which aggravates a high number of redundant packet retransmissions, causing contention and collisions. Proper use of dynamic probabilistic algorithm significantly reduces the number of retransmissions, which reduces the chance of contention and collisions. In current dynamic probabilistic algorithm, the retransmission probability (p_t) is formulated as a linear/non-linear function of a single variable, the number of first-hop neighbors (k). However, such algorithm is suffers in the presence of noise due to increasing packet-loss. In this paper, the authors propose a new dynamic probabilistic algorithm in which p_t is determined locally by the retransmitting nodes considering both k and the noise-level. This algorithm is referred to as the dynamic noise-dependent probabilistic (DNDP) algorithm. The performance of the DNDP algorithm is evaluated through simulations using the MANET simulator (MANSim). The simulation results show that the DNDP algorithm presents higher network reachability than the dynamic probabilistic algorithm at a reasonable increase in the number of retransmissions for a wide range of noise-level. The effects of nodes densities and nodes speeds on the performance of the DNDP algorithm are also investigated.

Chapter 4

Semantic Mobile Applications for Service Process Improvement 69

Markus Aleksy, ABB AG, Germany
Bernd Stieger, ABB AG, Germany
Thomas Janke, SAP Research Dresden, Germany

The ongoing evolution of industrial field service is mainly driven by demographical changes, increasing complexity of products, and tremendous amounts of product information from enterprise information systems as well as from the emerging Internet of Things. To cope with these challenges, a combined approach utilizing semantic and mobile technologies fosters the provision of the right information, at the right time, in the right place, and to the right people. This paper investigates the exploitation potential of semantic mobile applications to support industrial service processes. Based on identified application scenarios, the authors developed concepts for process improvement and, thus, derived requirements. The necessary semantic data federations are considered in the presented architecture, which enables an integrated approach for tailored information retrieval from heterogeneous information sources.

Chapter 5

Acquiring the Gist of Social Network Service Threads via Comparison with Wikipedia 85

Akiyo Nadamoto, Konan University, Japan
Eiji Aramaki, The University of Tokyo, Japan
Takeshi Abekawa, National Institute Informatics, Japan
Yohei Murakami, National Institute of Information and Communications Technology, Japan

Internet-based social network services (SNSs) have grown increasingly popular and are producing a great amount of content. Multiple users freely post their comments in SNS threads, and extracting the gist of these comments can be difficult due to their complicated dialog. In this paper, the authors propose a system that explores this concept of the gist of an SNS thread by comparing it with Wikipedia. The granularity of information in an SNS thread differs from that in Wikipedia articles, which implies that the information in a thread may be related to different articles on Wikipedia. The authors extract target articles on Wikipedia based on its link graph. When an SNS thread is compared with Wikipedia, the focus is on the table of contents (TOC) of the relevant Wikipedia articles. The system uses a proposed coverage degree to compare the comments in a thread with the information in the TOC. If the coverage degree is higher, the Wikipedia paragraph becomes the gist of the thread.

Chapter 6

Vânia M. P. Vidal, Federal University of Ceará, Brazil

José A. F. de Macêdo, Federal University of Ceará, Brazil

Marco A. Casanova, Pontifícia Universidade Católica do Rio de Janeiro, Brazil

Fábio Porto, Laboratório Nacional de Computação Científica, Brazil

João C. Pinheiro, Federal University of Ceará, Brazil

In this paper, the authors present a three-level mediator based framework for linked data integration. In the approach, the mediated schema is represented by a domain ontology, which provides a conceptual representation of the application. Each relevant data source is described by a source ontology, published on the Web according to the Linked Data principles. Each source ontology is rewritten as an application ontology, whose vocabulary is restricted to be a subset of the vocabulary of the domain ontology. The main contribution of the paper is an algorithm for reformulating a user query into sub-queries over the data sources. The reformulation algorithm exploits inter-ontology links to return more complete query results. The approach is illustrated by an example of a virtual store mediating access to online booksellers.

Chapter 7

Bessam Abdulrazak, University of Sherbrooke, Canada

Patrice Roy, University of Sherbrooke, Canada

Yacine Belala, SAP Labs, Canada

Sylvain Giroux, University of Sherbrooke, Canada

Charles Gouin-Vallerand, University of Sherbrooke, Canada

Context-aware software provides adapted services to users or other software components. On the other hand, Autonomic Pervasive Computing uses context to reduce the complexity of pervasive system utilization, management and maintenance. This paper describes two context-awareness models, the macro and micro approaches, that define and integrate contextual views of individual pervasive components (micro level) and global knowledge of the system (macro level), and provides a more detailed overview of a micro Context-aware programming model for open smart space problems. These models are presented and compared with respect to their ability to meet the requirements of the Autonomic Pervasive Computing concept of the four selves.

Chapter 8

Matthias Wauer, Technische Universität Dresden, Germany

Johannes Meinecke, SAP Research Dresden, Germany

Daniel Schuster, Technische Universität Dresden, Germany

Andreas Konzag, BMW Group, Germany

Markus Aleksy, ABB Corporate Research, Germany

Till Riedel, Karlsruhe Institute of Technology, Germany

Product-related information can be found in various data sources and formats across the product life-cycle. Effectively exploiting this information requires the federation of these sources, the extraction of implicit information, and the efficient access to this comprehensive knowledge base. Existing solutions for product information management (PIM) are usually restricted to structured information, but most of the business-critical information resides in unstructured documents. We present a generic architecture for federating heterogeneous information from various sources, including the Internet of Things, and argue how this process benefits from using semantic representations. A reference implementation tailor-made to business users is explained and evaluated. We also discuss several issues we experienced that we believe to be valuable for researchers and implementers of semantic information systems, as well as the information retrieval community.

Chapter 9

Kevin Curran, University of Ulster, UK

Kevin O'Hara, University of Ulster, UK

Sean O'Brien, University of Ulster, UK

This paper examines the services people seek out on Twitter and the integration of Twitter into businesses. Twitter has experienced tremendous growth in users over the past few years, from users sharing to the world what they had for lunch to their opinions on world events. As a social media website, Twitter has become the third most popular behind only Facebook and YouTube. Its user base statistics ensure a wide audience for business to engage with. However, many find this a daunting prospect as there are no set guidelines as to how business might use the service. The ability to post quick short messages for the whole of the social network to see has encouraged people to use this microblogging platform to comment and share attitudes on company brands and products. The authors present how the business world is using the social network site as a new communication channel to reach customers and examine other possible uses for Twitter in a business context. This paper also discusses how Twitter plans to move forward and evolve with its service, ensuring that personal, business and third party developers' best interests are catered to.

Chapter 10

A. Raghunathan, Bharat Heavy Electricals Limited, India

K. Murugesan, National Institute of Technology, Tiruchirappalli, India

In order to improve the QoS of applications, clusters of web servers are increasingly used in web services. Caching helps improve performance in web servers, but is largely exploited only for static web content. With more web applications using backend databases today, caching of dynamic content has a crucial role in web performance. This paper presents a set of cache management schemes for handling dynamic data in web clusters by sharing cached contents. These schemes use either automatic or expiry-based cache validation, and work with any type of request distribution. The techniques improve response by utilizing the caches efficiently and reducing redundant database accesses by web servers while ensuring cache consistency. The authors present caching schemes for both horizontal and vertical cluster architectures. Simulations show an appreciable performance rise in response times of queries in clustered web servers.

P. Venkateswaran, Jadavpur University, India

Mousumi Kundu, SAMEER, Kolkata Centre, India

Kanika Orea, Jadavpur University, India

R. Nandi, Jadavpur University India

Srishti Shaw, Jadavpur University, India

Mobile ad-hoc network, (MANET) is a collection of wireless mobile nodes dynamically forming a temporary communication network without using any existing infrastructure or centralized administration. To reduce routing overhead, computational complexity and overcome the problem of low bandwidth utilization, MANET is divided into several clusters. The authors propose a fuzzy logic based mobility metric for MANET that had been utilized as the basis of cluster formation in the algorithm viz., FUZZY CLUSTERING. This algorithm leads to more stable cluster formation compared to the existing MOBIC algorithm as evidenced by significant reduction in the number of clusterhead changes. As the frequency of cluster reorganization is a significant attribute, the proposed algorithm is expected to yield improved performance for MANETs.

Fernando Beltrán, University of Auckland, New Zealand

Jairo A. Gutiérrez, Universidad Tecnológica de Bolívar, Colombia

José Luis Melús, Universidad Politécnica de Cataluña, Spain

This paper examines some of the key problems users encounter when accessing current generation wireless networks. Using a case study of a hypothetical user, the authors explore the emerging services and the new broadband wireless network technologies necessary to carry them out. This paper analyses the issues associated with an observed trend in the industry that exposes potential changes to the long-term, rigid commercial relation between wireless providers and users: as a result of a range of evolved broadband wireless access standards and technologies, autonomic communications and policy-based management, and new pricing schemes, consumers will likely face new opportunities to enter short-term and spot contracts with the new wireless providers. This new landscape also allow multiple competing Access Providers (APs) to dynamically assign prices, and poses new and interesting challenges to the regulatory function. The paper also discusses a framework for the integration of heterogeneous technologies and management policies based on the network context that make up this emerging, hybrid wireless landscape, and describes the economic characteristics of new markets likely to arise.

M. Umaparvathi, Anna University of Technology, India

Dharmishtan K. Varughese, Karpagam College of Engineering, India

Mobile Adhoc Networks (MANETs) are open to a wide range of attacks due to their unique characteristics like dynamic topology, shared medium, absence of infrastructure, and resource constraints. Data packets sent by a source node may reach destination through a number of intermediate nodes. In the absence of security mechanism, it is easy for an intermediate node to intercept or modify the messages, thus attacking the normal operation of MANET. One such attack is Black hole attack, in which, a malicious node called Black hole node attracts all the traffic of the network towards itself, and discards all the packets without forwarding them to the intended recipients. This paper evaluates the performance of Adhoc on-demand Distance Vector (AODV) and its multi-path variant Adhoc On-demand Multi-path Distance Vector (AOMDV) routing protocols under black hole attack. Non-cryptographic solutions Secure Blackhole AODV (SBAODV) and Secure Blackhole AOMDV (SBAOMDV) have been proposed to mitigate the effect of black hole attack. Through NS-2 simulations, the performance of the proposed protocols with video streaming is analyzed. The results show that the proposed solutions provide better performance than the conventional AODV and AOMDV.

Chapter 14

Femi A. Aderohunmu, University of Otago, New Zealand

Jeremiah D. Deng, University of Otago, New Zealand

Martin K. Purvis, University of Otago, New Zealand

While wireless sensor networks (WSN) are increasingly equipped to handle more complex functions, in-network processing still requires the battery-powered sensors to judiciously use their constrained energy so as to prolong the elective network life time. There are a few protocols using sensor clusters to coordinate the energy consumption in a WSN, but how to deal with energy heterogeneity remains a research question. The authors propose a modified clustering algorithm with a three-tier energy setting, where energy consumption among sensor nodes is adaptive to their energy levels. A theoretical analysis shows that the proposed modifications result in an extended network stability period. Simulation has been conducted to evaluate the new clustering algorithm against some existing algorithms under different energy heterogeneity settings, and favourable results are obtained especially when the energy levels are significantly imbalanced.

Chapter 15

Mohamed Aissa, University of Nizwa, Oman

Adel Ben Mnaouer, Dar Al Uloom University, Saudi Arabia

Rion Murray, University of Trinidad and Tobago, Trinidad and Tobago

Abdelfettah Belghith, HANA Research Group University of Manouba, Tunisia

Multimedia applications are expected to guarantee end-to-end quality of service (QoS) and are characterized by stringent constraints on delay, delay-jitter, bandwidth, cost, and so forth. The authors observe that Kruskal's algorithm is limited to minimal (maximal) spanning unconstrained tree. As such, the authors extend Kruskal's algorithm to incorporate the delay bound constraint. Consequently, a novel algorithm is proposed, called EKRUS (Extended Kruskal), for constructing multicast trees. The EKRUS' distinguishing features consists of a better management of Kruskal's priority queues, and in the provision of edge priority aggregation. Preliminary results show that the proposed EKRUS algorithm performs as well as the best-known algorithms (such as the DDMC, DMCTc algorithms) while exhibiting reduced complexity. The authors conducted an intensive analysis and evaluations of different strategies of assigning edges into the classes of the queue as well as edge selection. As a result, the EKRUS algorithm was further extended with different edge assignment and selection strategies. Through extensive simulations, the authors have evaluated various versions of the EKRUS and analyzed their performance under different load conditions.

Chapter 16

Much like the financial crisis that precipitated a new world order, a quiet revolution of some sorts is happening in the telecom industry worldwide. The bankruptcy of stalwarts such as Nortel and the impregnation of Google and Apple into the mobile phone space at an amazing alacrity are changing the world order once dominated by the likes of biggies such as AT&T. What are these changes and what can we expect in the future? We explore in this article, the emerging technologies, market evolution, business models and regulatory interventions and indicate possible research directions in the area of data communications and networking in the coming days.

Preface

INTRODUCTION

The chapters in this volume examine the impact of data communications and networking technologies, policies, and management on business organizations, capturing their effect on IT-enabled management practices. This book includes analytical and empirical research articles, business case studies, and surveys that provide solutions and insight into challenges facing telecommunication service providers, equipment manufacturers, enterprise users, and policy makers. The goal is to disseminate practical and theoretical information, which will enable readers to understand, manage, use, and maintain business data communication networks more effectively. This is why this volume addresses key technology, management, and policy issues for utilizing data communications and networking in business and the current best practices for aligning this important technology with the strategic goals of the organization.

OVERVIEW OF THE BOOK

The first chapter is "Linking the Popularity of Online Trading with Consumers' Concerns for Reputation and Identity Theft," by Alan D. Smith. Although online trading has its benefits, such as convenience and the ability to compare prices online, there are still many concerns about the integrity of the buyer, the seller and/or the online action service provider (OASP). This paper investigates these relationships via multivariate statistical analysis of a stratified sample of working professionals, resulting in 198 useable questionnaires from an initial sampling frame of over 550 professional personnel from five relatively large Pittsburgh, Pennsylvania, firms. The author found that buyers that felt feedback systems were viable were more willing to engage in online trading activities and pay a premium price for merchandise being sold by a seller with a better reputation, regardless of gender. Customers were especially concerned with the total price, including shipping cost, regardless of gender. In terms of the convenience of payment method, electronic forms were preferred in transacting online trading activities, regardless of age and gender.

"Antecedents of Security Pillars in E-Commerce Applications," by Amin A. Shaqrah investigates the relationship between internet security and e-business competence at banking and exchange firms in Jordan. The proposed conceptual model examines the antecedents and consequences of e-business competence and tests its empirical validity. The sample of 152 banking and exchange firms tests the posited structural equation model. The results consistently support the validity of the proposed conceptual model, the results also found that organizations realize the importance of e- business and are willing to proceed further with e-business. Beyond concerns about internet security, their awareness of security hazards and internet performance is minimal. The author concludes that the public awareness of ICT in general is low. In light of the data collected, the author makes recommendations for the interested authorities to improve e-business in Jordan.

The next chapter is "A Novel Dynamic Noise-Dependent Probabilistic Algorithm for Route Discovery in MANETs," by Hussein Al-Bahadili and Alia Sabri. In mobile ad hoc networks (MANETs), broadcasting is widely used in route discovery and other network services. The most widely used broadcasting algorithm is simple flooding, which aggravates a high number of redundant packet retransmissions, causing contention and collisions. Proper use of dynamic probabilistic algorithm significantly reduces the number of retransmissions, which reduces the chance of contention and collisions. In current dynamic probabilistic algorithm, the retransmission probability (pt) is formulated as a linear/non-linear function of a single variable, the number of first-hop neighbors (k). However, such algorithm is suffers in the presence of noise due to increasing packet-loss. In this paper, the authors propose a new dynamic probabilistic algorithm in which pt is determined locally by the retransmitting nodes considering both k and the noise-level. This algorithm is referred to as the dynamic noise-dependent probabilistic (DNDP) algorithm. The performance of the DNDP algorithm is evaluated through simulations using the MANET simulator (MANSim). The simulation results show that the DNDP algorithm presents higher network reachability than the dynamic probabilistic algorithm at a reasonable increase in the number of retransmissions for a wide range of noise-level. The effects of nodes densities and nodes speeds on the performance of the DNDP algorithm are also investigated.

"Semantic Mobile Applications for Service Process Improvement" by Markus Aleksy, Bernd Stieger, and Thomas Janke, holds that the ongoing evolution of industrial field service is mainly driven by demographical changes, increasing complexity of products, and tremendous amounts of product information from enterprise information systems as well as from the emerging Internet of Things. To cope with these challenges, a combined approach utilizing semantic and mobile technologies fosters the provision of the right information, at the right time, in the right place, and to the right people. This paper investigates the exploitation potential of semantic mobile applications to support industrial service processes. Based on identified application scenarios, the authors developed concepts for process improvement and, thus, derived requirements. The necessary semantic data federations are considered in the presented architecture, which enables an integrated approach for tailored information retrieval from heterogeneous information sources.

Chapter 5

Internet-based social network services (SNSs) have grown increasingly popular and are producing a great amount of content. Multiple users freely post their comments in SNS threads, and extracting the gist of these comments can be difficult due to their complicated dialog. In "Acquiring the Gist of Social Network Service Threads via Comparison with Wikipedia," Akiyo Nadamoto, Eiji Aramaki, Takeshi Abekawa, and Yohei Murakami propose a system that explores this concept of the gist of an SNS thread by comparing it with Wikipedia. The granularity of information in an SNS thread differs from that in Wikipedia articles, which implies that the information in a thread may be related to different articles on Wikipedia. The authors extract target articles on Wikipedia based on its link graph. When an SNS thread is compared with Wikipedia, the focus is on the table of contents (TOC) of the relevant Wikipedia articles. The system uses a proposed coverage degree to compare the comments in a thread with the information in the TOC. If the coverage degree is higher, the Wikipedia paragraph becomes the gist of the thread.

In "Query Processing in a Mediator Based Framework for Linked Data Integration," Vânia M. P. Vidal, José A. F. de Macêdo, João C. Pinheiro, Marco A. Casanova, and Fábio Porto present a three-level mediator based framework for linked data integration. In the approach, the mediated schema is represented by a domain ontology, which provides a conceptual representation of the application. Each relevant data source is described by a source ontology, published on the Web according to the Linked Data principles. Each source ontology is rewritten as an application ontology, whose vocabulary is restricted to be a subset of the vocabulary of the domain ontology. The main contribution of the paper is an algorithm for reformulating a user query into sub-queries over the data sources. The reformulation algorithm exploits inter-ontology links to return more complete query results. The approach is illustrated by an example of a virtual store mediating access to online booksellers.

Chapter 7

Context-aware software provides adapted services to users or other software components. On the other hand, Autonomic Pervasive Computing uses context to reduce the complexity of pervasive system utilization, management and maintenance. "Micro Context-Awareness for Autonomic Pervasive Computing," by Bessam Abdulrazak, Patrice Roy, Charles Gouin-Vallerand, Yacine Belala, and Sylvain Giroux, describes two context-awareness models, the macro and micro approaches, that define and integrate contextual views of individual pervasive components (micro level) and global knowledge of the system (macro level), and provides a more detailed overview of a micro Context-aware programming model for open smart space problems. These models are presented and compared with respect to their ability to meet the requirements of the Autonomic Pervasive Computing concept of the four selves.

In "Semantic Federation of Product Information from Structured and Unstructured Sources, " the authors present a generic architecture for federating heterogeneous information from various sources, including the Internet of Things, and argue how this process benefits from using semantic representations. Product-related information can be found in various data sources and formats across the product lifecycle. Effectively exploiting this information requires the federation of these sources, the extraction of implicit information, and the efficient access to this comprehensive knowledge base. Existing solutions for product information management (PIM) are usually restricted to structured information, but most of the business-critical information resides in unstructured documents. A reference implementation tailor-made to business users is explained and evaluated. The authors also discuss several issues they experienced that they believe to be valuable for researchers and implementers of semantic information systems, as well as the information retrieval community.

"The Role of Twitter in the World of Business," by Kevin Curran, Kevin O'Hara, and Sean O'Brien, examines the services people seek out on Twitter and the integration of Twitter into businesses. Twitter has experienced tremendous growth in users over the past few years, from users sharing to the world what they had for lunch to their opinions on world events. As a social media website, Twitter has become the third most popular behind only Facebook and YouTube. Its user base statistics ensure a wide audience for business to engage with. However, many find this a daunting prospect as there are no set guidelines as to how business might use the service. The ability to post quick short messages for the whole of the social network to see has encouraged people to use this microblogging platform to comment and share attitudes on company brands and products. The authors present how the business world is using the social network site as a new communication channel to reach customers and examine other possible uses for Twitter in a business context. This chapter also discusses how Twitter plans to move forward and evolve with its service, ensuring that personal, business and third party developers' best interests are catered to.

The next chapter is "Performance-Enhanced Caching Scheme for Web Clusters for Dynamic Content," by A. Raghunathan, and K. Murugesan. In order to improve the QoS of applications, clusters of web servers are increasingly used in web services. Caching helps improve performance in web servers, but is largely exploited only for static web content. With more web applications using backend databases today, caching of dynamic content has a crucial role in web performance. This paper presents a set of cache management schemes for handling dynamic data in web clusters by sharing cached contents. These schemes use either automatic or expiry-based cache validation, and work with any type of request distribution. The techniques improve response by utilizing the caches efficiently and reducing redundant database accesses by web servers while ensuring cache consistency. The authors present caching schemes for both horizontal and vertical cluster architectures. Simulations show an appreciable performance rise in response times of queries in clustered web servers.

Mobile ad-hoc network, (MANET) is a collection of wireless mobile nodes dynamically forming a temporary communication network without using any existing infrastructure or centralized administration. To reduce routing overhead, computational complexity and overcome the problem of low bandwidth utilization, MANET is divided into several clusters. In "Fuzzy Logic-Based Mobility Metric Clustering Algorithm for MANETs," by P. Venkateswaran, Mousumi Kundu, Srishti Shaw, Kanika Orea, and R. Nandi, the authors propose a fuzzy logic based mobility metric for MANET that had been utilized as the basis of cluster formation in the algorithm viz., fuzzy clustering. This algorithm leads to more stable cluster formation compared to the existing MOBIC algorithm as evidenced by significant reduction in the number of clusterhead changes. As the frequency of cluster reorganization is a significant attribute, the proposed algorithm is expected to yield improved performance for MANETs.

"How Evolving Network Access and Network Management Technologies are Redefining the Competitive Wireless Markets," by Fernando Beltrán, Jairo A. Gutiérrez, and José Luis Melús, examines some of the key problems users encounter when accessing current generation wireless networks. Using a case study of a hypothetical user, the authors explore the emerging services and the new broadband wireless network technologies necessary to carry them out. This chapter analyses the issues associated with an observed trend in the industry that exposes potential changes to the long-term, rigid commercial relation between wireless providers and users: as a result of a range of evolved broadband wireless access standards and technologies, autonomic communications and policy-based management, and new pricing schemes, consumers will likely face new opportunities to enter short-term and spot contracts with the new wireless providers. This new landscape also allow multiple competing Access Providers (APs) to dynamically assign prices, and poses new and interesting challenges to the regulatory function. The paper also discusses a framework for the integration of heterogeneous technologies and management policies based on the network context that make up this emerging, hybrid wireless landscape, and describes the economic characteristics of new markets likely to arise.

Mobile Adhoc Networks (MANETs) are open to a wide range of attacks due to their unique characteristics like dynamic topology, shared medium, absence of infrastructure, and resource constraints. Data packets sent by a source node may reach destination through a number of intermediate nodes. In the absence of security mechanism, it is easy for an intermediate node to intercept or modify the messages, thus attacking the normal operation of MANET. One such attack is Black hole attack, in which, a malicious node called Black hole node attracts all the traffic of the network towards itself, and discards all the packets without forwarding them to the intended recipients. "Secure Video Transmission Against Black Hole Attack in MANETs," by M. Umaparvathi and Dharmishtan K. Varughese, evaluates the performance of Adhoc on-demand Distance Vector (AODV) and its multi-path variant Adhoc On-demand Multi-path Distance Vector (AOMDV) routing protocols under black hole attack. Non-cryptographic solutions Secure Blackhole AODV (SBAODV) and Secure Blackhole AOMDV (SBAOMDV) have been proposed to mitigate the effect of black hole attack. Through NS-2 simulations, the performance of the proposed protocols with video streaming is analyzed. The results show that the proposed solutions provide better performance than the conventional AODV and AOMDV.

The authors of the chapter "Enhancing Clustering in Wireless Sensor Networks with Energy Heterogeneity," Femi A. Aderohunmu, Jeremiah D. Deng, and Martin Purvis, propose a modified clustering algorithm with a three-tier energy setting, where energy consumption among sensor nodes is adaptive to their energy levels. While wireless sensor networks (WSN) are increasingly equipped to handle more complex functions, in-network processing still requires the battery-powered sensors to judiciously use their constrained energy so as to prolong the elective network life time. There are a few protocols using sensor clusters to coordinate the energy consumption in a WSN, but how to deal with energy heterogeneity remains a research question. A theoretical analysis shows that the proposed modifications result in an extended network stability period. Simulation has been conducted to evaluate the new clustering algorithm against some existing algorithms under different energy heterogeneity settings, and favorable results are obtained especially when the energy levels are significantly imbalanced.

The next chapter is, "New Strategies and Extensions in Kruskal's Algorithm in Multicast Routing," by Mohamed Aissa, Adel Ben Mnaouer, Rion Murray, and Abdelfettah Belghith. Multimedia applications are expected to guarantee end-to-end quality of service (QoS) and are characterized by stringent constraints on delay, delay-jitter, bandwidth, cost, and so forth. The authors observe that Kruskal's algorithm is limited to minimal (maximal) spanning unconstrained tree. As such, the authors extend Kruskal's algorithm to incorporate the delay bound constraint. Consequently, a novel algorithm is proposed, called EKRUS (Extended Kruskal), for constructing multicast trees. The EKRUS' distinguishing features consists of a better management of Kruskal's priority queues, and in the provision of edge priority aggregation. Preliminary results show that the proposed EKRUS algorithm performs as well as the best-known algorithms (such as the DDMC, DMCTc algorithms) while exhibiting reduced complexity. The authors conducted an intensive analysis and evaluations of different strategies of assigning edges into the classes of the queue as well as edge selection. As a result, the EKRUS algorithm was further extended with different edge assignment and selection strategies. Through extensive simulations, the authors have evaluated various versions of the EKRUS and analyzed their performance under different load conditions.

The last chapter is "Emerging Areas of Research in Business Data Communications," by Debashis Saha and Varadharajan Sridhar. Much like the financial crisis that precipitated a new world order, a quiet revolution of some sorts is happening in the telecom industry worldwide. The bankruptcy of stalwarts such as Nortel and the impregnation of Google and Apple into the mobile phone space at an amazing alacrity are changing the world order once dominated by the likes of biggies such as AT&T. What are these changes and what can we expect in the future? The authors in this chapter explore the emerging technologies, market evolution, business models, and regulatory interventions and indicate possible research directions in the area of data communications and networking in the coming days.

Varadharajan Sridhar
Management Development Institute, India & Sasken Communication Technologies, India

Chapter 1
Linking the Popularity of Online Trading with Consumers' Concerns for Reputation and Identity Theft

Alan D. Smith
Robert Morris University, USA

ABSTRACT

Although online trading has its benefits, such as convenience and the ability to compare prices online, there are still many concerns about the integrity of the buyer, the seller and/or the online action service provider (OASP). This paper investigates these relationships via multivariate statistical analysis of a stratified sample of working professionals, resulting in 198 useable questionnaires from an initial sampling frame of over 550 professional personnel from five relatively large Pittsburgh, Pennsylvania, firms. The author found that buyers that felt feedback systems were viable were more willing to engage in online trading activities and pay a premium price for merchandise being sold by a seller with a better reputation, regardless of gender. Customers were especially concerned with the total price, including shipping cost, regardless of gender. In terms of the convenience of payment method, electronic forms were preferred in transacting online trading activities, regardless of age and gender.

INTRODUCTION

Growth of the Online Trading Industry

Online trading has become an increasingly popular source of income used by consumers as well as businesses. However, many factors need to be

considered in order to determine the success of the auction including security and fraud safeguards, convenience, selling and buying points, reputation and feedback, and competitive forces surrounding pricing structures. Since 1995, online auctions have been one of the major success stories of the Internet with over 1,600 significant web-based auction websites and still growing (Armes, 2006). The largest online auction website for business-to-

DOI: 10.4018/978-1-4666-2026-1.ch001

consumers (B2C) is undoubtedly eBay, which was formed in 1995 by Pierre Omidyar. It has been on a major force in the expanding online auction service provider (OASP) industry since the beginning on the Internet, initially not concerned with banner advertising in its formative years. Coincidentally, the first major business-to-business (B2B) online auction was conducted by FreeMarkets Inc. in 1995, with the company experiencing a slow start for the first two years, but in 1998 they grew at a much higher rate raising US$172.8 million in capital (Emiliani, 2000). FreeMarkets Inc. manufactured industrial parts, raw materials, and commodities. The primarily reasons for their growth in capital was due, in part, to their contracts with General Motors and United Technologies Corp. Ariba, Inc., a company headquartered Sunnyvale, CA, which made its name by providing software and network services to assist corporations in managing their capital, bought TradingDynamics, Inc. in 1999. This acquisition helped make Ariba, Inc. one of the fastest rising companies in the early dotcom era. Ariba acquired a privately-held procurement Business Process Outsourcing provider called Alliente, Inc. and Freemarkets, Inc., which is now the home of the Ariba Pittsburgh, PA office. Ariba has continued to be successful today thanks largely to their partnerships with 40 of the top 100 companies, as well as many other partnerships with smaller companies.

As B2C transactions are the traditional way most consumers view online auctions are utilized and transacted, the growth of e-tailing tied to B2C has been extensive and the B2C auction website, eBay, has become a generic term for e-tailing (Smith, 2009a, 2009b, 2010), as eBay is already a household name for online auctions. Whether management takes advantage of B2B or B2B online auctions, such auctions are rapidly becoming an essential tool that organizations are using to reduce costs and improve margins with a wider supply base. There are different approaches to e-procurement marketplaces, similar to the make or buy options for materials and finished products; namely, one is to establish in-house auction teams and the other is seeking external assistance from specialist auction consultants, namely OASP (Armes, 2006; Hu, Wang, Fetch, & Bidanda, 2008; Jain, Benyoucef, & Deshmukh, 2008; Scherrer-Rathje, Boyle, & Deflorin, 2009).

Typically the B2B online auction process begins with the formation of a cross-functional team, as this team's responsibility is to analyze a commodity and gather data from existing sources to establish the current condition of the commodity (Smith, 2006). Such team members usually identify suppliers that are capable of performing the work and eventually create a bid list. The bid list typically consists of suppliers that currently do business with the buyer as well as the new suppliers and usually contains 50 to 60 suppliers (Emiliani, 2000). After the bid list is created, a comprehensive request for quote is sent to the suppliers, which usually contains important information concerning the commodity as well as the bid time and date as related information. Suppliers are usually given 15 to 45 days to evaluate the request for quote to develop pricing. By this time, the bid list is down to 25 to 30 interested suppliers, which is dependent on the type of product and initial capital outlays to acquire it. After all interested suppliers have communicated with the cross-functional team about all parts of the commodity, the auction is ready to begin as interested suppliers are instructed to log into the auction on a certain day and time and begin to bid on each commodity. The number of suppliers who actually participates in the auction may be quite small, typically between 10 and 20. In online auctions, the buyer is not obligated to accept a bid, as most may have a reserve price or there are certain exceptions in place, which may complicate the process as the highest bidder may not always win.

In B2B auctions, there is a buyer and a seller, where the seller will post an item and initiate a length of time interested parties can bid on the item. The buyer will then bid on the item during the allotted time limit. When the auction closes, the person with the highest bid usually wins the item. The buyer and the seller then arrange payment options and shipping details; online auctions then provide many attractive benefits for both sellers and buyers. The buyer experiences a disciplined process, while the seller gains a fair opportunity to win the materials and learning much from the involvement of an intermediary that brings valuable experience. The seller benefits because an expanded market comes right to their fingertips. According to Emiliani (2000), buyers benefit from the opportunity to directly evaluate other capable suppliers that might not be considered under regular business conditions. Suppliers that participate in these auctions are able to see the market price as well as validate various components before bidding starts. For both buyers and sellers, online auctions save time and effort due to compressed price negotiations and to set marketplace values for these commodities, allowing both parties to concentrate on corporate core competencies. Depending on payment schedules, savings can be instantaneously realized and many engaged parties receive multi-year long-term agreements through online auctions.

Purpose of Present Study

Selected driving forces behind the OASP industry and the acceptability of using B2B and B2C online auctions, as illustrated in Figure 1, have significant and long-term influences on consumer spending and related behavioral patterns. Within the backdrop of current global recession, consumer trust is relatively low and bankruptcy rates are relatively high, although not close to the rates experienced during the Great Recession. It is important for companies to understand these forces and their influences on consumer behavior if management is to formulate successful strategies. These strategies should integrate financial, accounting, and security safeguards against identity theft, control program-costs, provide both tangible and intangible benefits to all stakeholders of online

auctions, as well as rebuilding customer trust. In the empirical analysis, an attempt is made to provide at least some informal linkage between financial markets and governmental efforts to improve the transitions inherent in a recessional economy, such as job loss, less disposal income, credit crunch, and depreciation of property values. To accomplish this task, the empirical examination will use specific research hypothesis-testing procedures to help determine if appropriate reputation and feedback systems, convenience, selling and shipping price concerns and related safeguards are important and customers are willing to pay a premium for such services. In terms of the data reduction or exploration portion, via cluster and hypothesis-analysis techniques, it was decided to perform an analysis of selected customer relationship management (CRM)-based initiatives (Anton & Petouhoff, 2002; Smith, 2006, 2007) and perceived protection against identity theft to promote consumer mutual trust in business transactions (Ba & Pavlou, 2002; Pathak, 2003). Figure 1 highlights the major elements of the present study, in terms of discussion and generation of actual hypotheses that were eventually tested. The next section provides a belief discussion of the major constructs from a clockwise direction, starting with the construct, Security and Fraud Concerns.

CONSUMER CONCERNS ASSOCIATED WITH ONLINE AUCTION SERVICE PROVIDERS (OASP)

Security and Fraud Concerns

Security has been a major issue when considering the future of the OASP industry and its overall popularity and acceptance (Lin & Daim, 2005). Typically, many OASP companies and governmental agencies are working in concert to limit the opportunities of hackers and computer

Figure 1. Conceptual or activity map on the basic forces driving the acceptability associated with online auction programs (numbers refer to specific sections for more discussion)

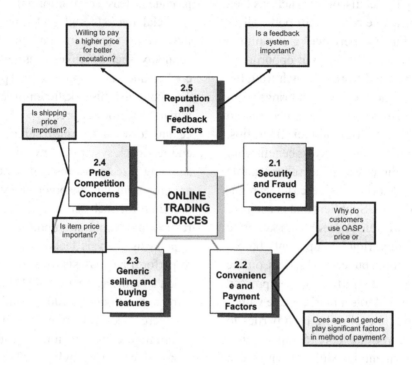

criminals (crackers) to commit fraud and other faceless crimes. Corporate websites and its management must continue to upgrade their security measures to help guarantee an acceptable level of customer safety and ensure repeat business and customer retention. Cybercrime is a serious issue regarding web-enabled services and such security safeguards are especially important for those engaged in online-auctioning and/or other financial exchanges online as compared to simple informational websites. New provisions have been made in both domestic and international laws that have significantly increased penalties for such computer-related offenses, especially identity theft, as a deterrent to those who may be considering or perpetrating this type of crime. Crimes are prosecuted when malicious intent is proven. In general, the perpetrator does not need to complete the crime and cause damage if malicious intent exists.

According to a recent survey (Huang, Radkowski, & Roman, 2007), security is more important when picking a website to those earning less than US$20,000 per year than it is for those earning over that amount. However, virtually all those that engage in web-based transactions are very concerned that they may become the victim of computer crime in an online auction, which can be anything from not receiving an item paid for or an incident of personal identity theft. Hence, most consumers feel that online security is important when picking websites and state the fear of identity theft as their number one concern (Smith, 2005; Smith & Lias, 2005).

One of the most common methods used by hackers in identity theft scams is sending e-mails directly to consumers asking for account updates of personal information. The largest B2C online auctioning website, eBay, and is one of the most well-known OASP currently in operation. After reviewing their website, they have posted easily-accessible security policies on their homepage; by clicking the security link, a list of proactive techniques for online auction users to safeguard their activity on websites is provided. Microsoft has also compiled a top-ten list of ways to prevent identity theft and computer crime, which is linked to their homepage. These can be helpful to read for those considering the use of online auctions as many proactive measures are provided. Following these steps can result in limited liability on behalf of the consumer. If the consumer is still negatively affected by such personal identity attempts, it will not only cause considerable inconvenience, but management of the OASP may be held at least partially liability if they failure to follow the proper procedures from their business end of the transaction.

OASP industrial leaders have made considerable improvements in security that decrease the risk faced by the user of the website. As previously discussed, conspiracy to commit Internet crime is prosecuted and sentenced the same as if the crime was successfully completed. Many websites will have a security policy readily available on their homepage, which states the privacy agreement, security policy, and requires an e-signature as acknowledgement of reading the terms (for example, this concept is directly measured in the empirical section). The e-signature process is usually initiated in the form of a small box which is clicked on before the option is given to move to the next screen. Security contracts and disclosures are often not read by the web users, who merely give their e-signature in hopes of saving time, but are still held accountable for its content. This action may demonstrate that the user either trusts the website or merely signing without knowing what the policy actually states in order to save a few minutes required to read and officially agree to the policy or terms. Bank identification numbers and personal information that are stolen can cause considerable problems for both OASP and end users in terms of fraud

compensation and/or reimbursement of funds lost. With such a low-reading rate of security contacts, many consumers risk agreeing to very one-sided terms. Even as the OASP industry continues to make improvements and have been somewhat successful in slowing the occurrence of cybercrime, the weak links tends to be customers.

There are a number of independent websites which rate OASPs on a basis of price, security, and many other factors; typically eBay is ranked high as they currently are the largest and most-trusted e-auction web website in operation. Their reputation and name recognition has continued to improve as the company has continually remained at the top of the highly competitive OASP industry, especially in terms of sales, visits, and profits. The integrity of these websites can be questionable if third-party audits and sound security safeguards are not in place. Following proper industrial procedures, policies, and practices as well as becoming familiar with preventative measures will help to safeguard online auction users. These procedures are the first line of defense, especially for newcomers that have yet to familiarize themselves to these numerous safeguards that are designed to protect their personal information and exchanges of finances online. Using more popular and highly reputable websites can help as they usually take the most conservative approaches regarding security due to the sheer traffic volume that they experience on a daily basis. Online auctions are generally as safe as the user will allow, as previously mentioned, risk assessment and its management is at its weakest link in the security chain with the consumer.

Convenience and Payment Factors

As an efficient and flexible sales channel, online auction businesses are becoming an internationally successful phenomenon (Dholakia & Simonson, 2005; Li, Ward, & Zhang, 2007; Smith & Potter, 2010). Customers typically use auction websites as a marketplace to conduct online sales; companies use auction websites to liquidate unwanted inventory, as well as to assist in pricing new products, acquire new markets for low-margin items, and reaching markets that would otherwise be too expensive in the past. All participants using online auctions can get their products in front of millions of people spanning the globe for a fraction of the cost and time of traditional methods. In today's online market, companies like eBay, Yahoo, and Amazon are the major players, with eBay leading the industry with over 50 million users at the time of the present study. This trend is projected to continue to grow, perhaps due to the convenience of the online consumer marketplace. Convenience is becoming an increasingly important issue in modern society as people are attracted to new technologies that trade a small amount of their privacy for greater convenience and speed. A major function of B2B, B2C, and P2P (peer-to-peer) transactions are driven by the convenience in information gathering and processing, ultimately ensuring the success of e-commerce. Another major successful factor when dealing with online auctions is the convenience of payment method.

Payment methods have various levels; for example, a credit card is more convenient for a buyer than a money order or a cashier's check. A credit/debit card can be electronically passed, which makes the transaction quicker and smoother for all partners of the transactions, especially the customer. For the seller, credit/debt cards are also more convenient, since the buyer's payments are automatically collected and forwarded to the seller's bank quickly via electronic transmission. Electronic payment systems such as PayPal™ are emerging as the easiest and most popular method of payment online. From a user's standpoint, when dealing with electronic payment systems, it has been found that ease-of-use, convertibility of funds, and security and trust are among the most important features (Adams, Nelson, & Todd, 1992; Bruner & Kumar, 2005; Burton-Jones &

Hubona, 2005; Chau, 1996; Novak, Hoffman, & Yung, 2000).

An important convenience factor for the OASP industry is achieved by strategically positioning themselves within the supply chain (Summers & Scherpereel, 2008; Vinodh, Sundararaj, Devadasan, & Maharaja, 2008). As many OASPs are operationally designed to primarily provide services have little direct connection to manufacturing process, their supply chains encompass only some of the traditional supply stage. Service provides like eBay, on-the-other-hand, provide sellers with the wholesaler-to-distributor-to-retailer stages as primary contributions to the selling process. The customers, as end users, are the final link in the supply chain. To demonstrate this further, a typical supply chain may be composed of a supplier-to-manufacturer-to-distributor-to-retailer-to-customer model; while the eBay supply chain may be better described as seller-to-OASP-to-bidder model, which further demonstrates the simplicity and convenience that OASPs offer the bidding public.

Generic Selling and Buying Features

The OASP industry has had a significant presence in the global economy as demonstrated by eBay, which in 2004 made sales through 48 million people resulting in US$32 billion in merchandise; this is more than the GDP of half the world's countries (Black, 2005). Many frequent bidders are turning towards strategic marketing tools such as eBay pulse™ and other the marketing research tools provided for buyers and sellers on eBay websites in order to help maximize profits and reach (broadcasting to capture a larger share of the potential marketplace) online (Great tools to help eBay sellers …", 2007). Hence, there are many factors that must be considered concerning successful strategies of buying and selling of merchandise through online auctioning.

One of the most important strategic metric is the reputation of the seller (Dholakia, 2004;

Dholakia & Simonson, 2005; Smith, 2010; Smith & Potter, 2010; Smith, Synowka, & Smith, 2010). The peer-evaluation system in which the management at eBay has set in place lets an individual rate another on how well they conducted business on a variety of consumer issues, including shipping cost, clarity of communications, description accuracy, and customer value. Whether it measures how quickly the seller processes the order and ships the items or how quickly the buyer provides the payment for the item, the peer-evaluation system is designed to inform potential and existing future buyers and sellers of the trustworthiness of conducting business online. A high reputation plays a very important role in ensuring the integrity of the online auctioning process by allowing the various stakeholders in the eBay community a direct measure of trustworthiness (as defined by the willingness to purchase products and/or services and to engage in financial transaction with bank accounts, debit/credit instruments) and efficiency concerning online transactions. According to Melnik (1997), Melnik and Alm (2005), and Snijders and Zijdeman (2004), a higher reputation leads to better sales and higher profits online. The reputation system is touched upon briefly here, but is described in further detail in the next section titled feedback and reputation.

An equally important factor is how well the item is described on the auction website. Many OASPs, including eBay, gives each seller a textbox in which they are limited in the number of words to describe their items and provide their selling points. It is similar in traditional practice of many publishers of scholarly journals to limit an abstract to 100 words or less, which can be a severe limitation in search engines' ability to locate an article in an online search of related subject matter. It is important that a seller touches upon not only the basic transactional information, but particular key aspects as well that a potential buyer would want to know. For example, such details as mentioning smoke-free or pet-free environments when selling clothes or providing the actual model number or serial number when selling electronic equipment are essential information that should be provided to potential customers. Often actual pictures play an important role of describing the item by giving the buyer a visual aid, such as providing a relative poor quality or amateur photograph is usually acceptable, while if the product is new and more expensive, a professional catalogue-style photograph would be considered the norm. In general, the better the item is described and presented, the better the item should sell online.

The method of payment provided for the transaction plays an important role in the success of the OASP. PayPal™ is an online company, for example, that works hand-in-hand with eBay. When the auction is completed and the two exchange their information, the buyer can directly deposit money into the seller's financial account. This method of payment is most preferred by eBay, as management runs both companies, and the money is exchanged quickly between the two parties, if both buyer and seller are registered. PayPal™ has the required banking information, which greatly reduces the possibility of a seller not being paid for their sold item through its verification and insurance programs. When using PayPal™, the process will establish an easily available online credit system and leads to more sales and profits. When using conventional checks, no exchange of online credit information is established and considerable time to clear the check; hence, this lack of verifiable information would increase the probability of counterfeiting or insufficient funds. Writing conventional checks is a method of payment that is still very popular, but is not the preferred payment in the online action scenario as the lack of simultaneously available information on the trading partners generally leads to less sales and profits.

The traditional appeals of buying through online auctions include the attraction of discounted merchandise, which is made possible through economies of scale and disintermediation, eliminating the middle man, and dealing direct with customers without the typical overhead of maintaining a physical outlet. Items may be extremely marked down from their original price, allowing for the sale of used or damaged merchandise; even new items can average marked down prices of about 30 to 40% ("eBay's bid to win back buyers", 2007). An appeal for the seller is the chance of selling through online auctions items that are overstocked, outdated, unwanted, or unattractive to customers in a limited geographical area and market them to the global economy. Unfortunately, the transactions' door moves in both directions as it allows for both the various forms of fraud and personal freedom in the conduct of business.

Price Competition Concerns

In response to customer needs, the OASP industry is revamping websites to make it easier to find items to purchase. Many web-empowered buyers are choosing websites like Amazon or simply relying exclusively on search engines to find the products they want to purchase at the lowest price. Managers at OASPs, such as eBay, have certainly realized that customers are probably trying various tools to reduce search time and to perform better price-quality-shipping matches. OASPs are improving shopping logistics by returning better searches, easier-to-view screens with relevant information, personalizing experience, and streamlining the overall buying process. Management is trying to make shopping more enjoyable by launching a "neighborhoods" feature that allows users with a common interest to unite and chat in a virtual community. Many OASPs are basically rebuilding their searching infrastructure and redeveloping the way departments worked together within the organization to communicate more effectively and work more efficiently. As most OASP-related customer bases are extremely diverse, which has made it difficult to know what direction to take in improving websites; they must

appeal to the new convenience shoppers and its old standby auction-loving shoppers.

Academics and practitioners have been analyzing customer behaviors of these very different kinds of shoppers; as noted by Gaylord (2007, p. 13), "Behind the millions of online auctions lies a virtual mini-economy flush with raw data." One phenomenon that is especially interesting is bidder's heat, which refers auction bidders that are so engrossed in the auction and motivated to win, that they lose a sense of reality as the price goes above the "buy it now" price in order to purchase the item. Basically, anyone could have originally obtained the product by clicking on the "buy it now" button, but this is ignored during an intense bidding war. Frequently, there is a disconnection between the shipping price and item price, as some online auctions offered identical items, but with different price dynamics. The total price would be equal, but in one situation the shipping price was very low and in the other auctions, the item price was lower. As noted by Gaylord (2007), the low-cost, high-shipping auction attracted more bids, more bidders, and 255% greater profits. This tendency may cause some sellers to try to bury the cost of shipping in the description of the product, a practice that eBay is trying to curtail.

Unfortunately there have been some that have tried to exploit some customers' willingness to spend more money for the things they really want. For example, a fairly recent OASP auction fraud was committed by Dweck and the employees at EMH Group, LLC, where employees were directed by Dweck to place more than 232,000 fake bids over the course of a year in order to drive of the prices of online auctions, which led to customers being defrauded to an average amount of US$5 each. The company, for example, sold jewelry on eBay and would usually lure customers in by offering no reserve auctions, and then employees were instructed to place fake bids in order to artificially increase the prices of the items up for bid. The EMH Group, LLC were prosecuted and required to pay US$400,000 in penalties and were banned from the online auction industry for four years ("Attorney General Cuomo...", 2007). If the company chooses to resume business, then they will be closely monitored by the U.S. Attorney General's office.

Reputation and Feedback Features

Numerous studies have been conducted about the use of feedback forums to promote trust, to determine whether or not trust leads to higher auction prices and the role that trust plays in relation to risk and the purchase of more expensive products (Bland & Barrett, 2006; Bolton, Katok, & Ockenfels, 2004; Boyd, 2002; Prasad, Bryan, & Reeves, 2007; Roman, 2007; Smith, 2002; Smith & Potter, 2010). Consumer trust measures and security protocols are needed to decrease the temptation for a seller to lure a buyer into a fraudulent transaction. Trust is critical when risk is involved, as buyers have to rely on electronic information without being able to physically inspect the product. One of the aims of the empirical section of the present research effort is to measure this potential impact via the implementation of an online feedback system has on aspects of consumer trust, trustworthiness of financial transactions, trading efficiency, and price. Trust is defined, for the purposes of the present study, as the expectation of payment (seller) and the expectation of delivery of the promised good (buyer); trustworthiness is generally defined as deserving trust and confidence (seller and buyer) within the transaction procedure. Trust is placed by a buyer by bidding on an auctioned item and following through with payment whereas trust is placed by a seller by shipping the auctioned item. The primarily sources of trust that are important may be classified as familiarity, calculativeness, and mutually shared values; familiarity stems from repeated transactions, calculativeness stems from an assessment of the other party's cost and benefits of cheating and values are the structures that encourage trustworthy behavior (Bland & Barrett, 2006; Bolton, Katok, & Ockenfels, 2004; Boyd, 2002; Prasad, Bryan, & Reeves, 2007; Roman, 2007). The types of trust are usually centered in both benevolence and credibility; where benevolence is the belief that one party is genuinely interested in the other party's welfare, credibility is the belief that the other party is honest, reliable and competent. The use of feedback systems are composite attempts, perhaps flawed, at measuring the various sources and types of trust.

Depending on the auction website, buyers and sellers can leave feedback regarding their experience. This feedback is compiled by a scoring mechanism and results in a reputation score or feedback rating. Although there are inherently many factors to be considered when determining trustworthiness and reading the scores or ratings, such as the number of positive scores, the timing of the feedback, the inclusion of comments, to name a few, the interaction of seller reputation with buyer reputation has an affect on trustworthiness. If a buyer leaves negative feedback for a seller, then the seller can retaliate by doing the same, whether truthful or not. Currently eBay tries to reduce this retaliation by reducing the types of negative feedback a seller can post on a buyer. There are several major characteristics to be considered when determining the risk involved for the buyer, such as the perceived value, age, and complexity of the merchandise, while variables such as payment method, bid increments, reserve price, shipment costs, experienced versus inexperienced buyers may have little affect on trustworthiness or consumer and procedure risk.

One study based on reputation found that "the incentive to earn a positive rating decreases as his reputation increases" (Snijders & Zijdeman, 2007, p. 164). This means, for example, if a seller has a positive score of 1,000 or greater, one negative rating will not significantly affect his/her score. The potential may exist for some sellers to purposely achieve high ratings to set the stage for fraud when the value of the sale goes up. Another factor that coincides with this point is to consider whether or not the negative feedback is recent, indicating an ongoing trend in the last several transactions. A seller may have had high scores in the past, but is now showing a trend of negative scores; which, in turn, could mean that the seller is no longer trustworthy.

It may be more difficult to recognize trustworthiness in computer-mediated communication than in face-to-face communication. Online trading allows buyers and sellers to choose a trader identity, different from their true identity, and allows this identity to be easily changed and as often as needed. This can promote distrust and dishonesty in an online trading environment, primarily on the seller's part. In a typical online trading transaction, the seller posts an offer along with a description of the item, its condition, and the item's asking price. A buyer, the person that accepts the offer, sends the money to the seller at which time the seller is supposed to ship the item to the buyer. If the seller chooses the dishonest route and decides not to ship the item, the buyer is out the money, but can respond by submitting appropriate feedback that will be damaging to the seller's trader identity. However, if the seller changes his trader identity, this feedback may not be associated with the new identity.

The buyer's social concerns may not be major driving force in online trading; perhaps the driving force is the sellers' social motives. Most traders care about their own reputation, but sellers' are more likely to be more critically judged than buyers, as most people tend to respond to kind acts with kindness as well as to respond to unkind acts with unkindness. Therefore, a seller will ship the item because the buyer was kind enough to purchase the item. In return, the seller expects to receive positive feedback from the buyer regarding the entire transaction process, which includes confirmations, delivery, quality and timeliness, to name a few. Buyers are at risk whether the item is shipped and lost or damaged in the mail or not shipped at all. How much risk a buyer is willing to

take based on the morals of the sellers verses the amount of risk a buyer would take in a lottery of random-shipping? Bolton, Katok, and Ockenfels (2004) found that "individuals are much more willing to take risks when the outcome is due to chance, as opposed to an equivalent-odd situation where the outcome depends on whether another player is trustworthy" (p. 192). Many buyers who are made aware that they may or may not receive the item already have an expectation that the item may not be shipped. However, buyers that expect to receive an item and the item is not shipped, not only must deal the monetary loss, but the cost of betrayal in business transactions as well.

A seller's rating also may include brief comments as to the reason for the rating, particularly if the rating is negative. There are many reasons that a buyer may not be happy with a transaction and some of these reasons may not be entirely the fault of the seller. For instance, if a seller has promised shipment by a certain date, has shipped the item to meet that deadline, but the shipment is not received by the buyer in time, this can result in the buyer leaving a negative feedback rating. However, the delay in the shipment may have been caused by extenuating circumstances, such as an error by the shipping company or unfavorable weather. The buyer can put this is the comment section and the seller can reply by explaining the circumstances. The comment lets other potential buyers know that the negative rating is not because the seller is untrustworthy or trying to purposely commit fraud.

Negative ratings are important to all transactions, regardless of price, but particularly for items that are more expensive. A buyer is generally going to be more critical of expensive transactions and should look for the more reputable seller. While the seller's reputation may not be as important for transactions involving less money, negative feedback can always be a deal-breaker. The strategic leveraging of feedback systems is similar to the power of traditional word-of-mouth (WOM) networks that encourage trust and trustworthiness.

Many businesses post their feedback profiles on their own websites independent of the OASP; for instance, a company that uses eBay and has an eBay profile will also post this profile on their own commercial website. This allows buyers to view the company's reputation on eBay and may help complete the transaction if they are considering buying directly from the company's website, creating a spillover effect of consumer confidence. If a buyer is skeptical of buying from a particular company but can see that the company has a favorable rating overall, this may result in the buyer completing the transaction. This apparent increase in consumer confidence could put the company in an economic advantage.

Is the usefulness of a bidder's reputation ratings to sellers as important to the more common topic of the usefulness of sellers' reputation ratings to buyers? Most bidder-based reputations may not be useful to most sellers, primarily because most sellers do not ship the merchandise until after they have received payment, resulting in little risk for the seller. There are several new measures that will make the bidders' reputations more useful to sellers by providing a way to track a bidder's multiple-transaction relationship, average purchase amount, bidding intensity and, bidding caution. In addition, sellers will be able to create a profile of bidders that they have done business with in the past. These profiles can be used to notify potential bidders of upcoming auctions or offer discounts on shipping. It can also be used to offer the second-highest bidder, the one who did not win the item, a chance at another item of equal value or to reduce their marketing costs by orienting towards the bidders in their database.

For both buyers and sellers that use online auctions regularly, a bidder's database should be beneficial. Many sellers use online auctions as a primary source of income in a small business or startup situation, with this situation comes the usual expenses associated with running a company, such as keeping customer records, marketing, advertising, to name a few. A seller may find that keeping a bidder profile would be useful when promoting items or offering discounts, much like many brick-and-mortar retailers do today. Instead of offering discounts and coupons to preferred customers through the slow mail, an online seller can offer the same type discounts and coupons to their preferred customers through e-mail. There might be a number of implications for bidders if such systems are introduced. Bidders may find that these measures have a negative tone on their bidding practices, especially if they are rated as transactional-oriented (a bidder that a seller cannot form an ongoing relationship with) or as having a low potential for bidding/buying. If this is the case, then a bidder may change their habits, making their reputation less than accurate, or refrain from the online auction website all together. Many sellers do not generally find the bidder's reputation of any use, as previously mentioned, and they do not have ample time to check a bidder's reputation if the bidder is a sniper (referring to a bidder that waits until the last minute to place a bid), leaving the seller little time for research prior to the closing of the auction. Conversely, there is little risk involved for the seller because a seller will not ship the item until payment has been received.

METHODOLOGY

Sample Characteristics

The current global recession has placed a number of negative consequences in regards to eroding consumer trust, as previously discussed, forcing many customers to significantly change spending and fiscal policies. Ultimately, these negative impacts can have long-term affects on an economy built on consumer confidence and spending. To explore the concepts of customer trust and confidence with the OASP industry, a basic survey instrument was developed for exploratory purposes. This instrument contained 27 items that were grouped on the basis of perceptions of the importance of OASP-related factors tied to building consumer confidence, including reputation and feedback, security and fraud concerns (especially identity theft), convenience, selling and buying promotional points, and pricing concerns, as well as demographic information. A study among working professionals should provide value-added insights concerning such coping strategies in the current economic downturn; hence, a number of specific hypotheses will be tested.

With this in mind, a survey instrument was pre-tested for minimum execution time and confusion and maximum accuracy of the concepts developed from the conceptual activity map originally presented in Figure 1 and previously discussed. The survey was created primarily from a review of business practitioner literature in order to try to understand how relatively well-educated working professionals felt about these driving forces in the online trading industry (note, the research instrument is available upon request). The goal for the research instrument was to better understand customer perceptions of these issues in relationship to the basic constructs of customer relationship management (Anton and Petouhoff, 2002; Potter and Smith, 2010). A conceptual framework, via a conceptual activity map, not a model, was used in the study, which outlined the basic terms and hypotheses tested. The beginning sections discussed the concepts outlined in Figure 1, which lead to the hypothesis testing and data reduction methods.

A series of paper-based questionnaires were distributed via a stratified sample of employed professionals, representative of the service industry located in the metropolitan area of Pittsburgh, PA, a major corporate headquarters. This procedure resulted in 198 useable questionnaires from an initial sampling frame of over 550 professional personnel from five large area firms. The surveyed personnel, primarily service representing marketing and financial services, were conducted over a three-month period. Pittsburgh was chosen as a classical representative of many rustbelt areas most hit by the global recession and, in part, due to accessibility by the present author.

Statistical Techniques

Using a variety of graphical and data reduction techniques, it was hoped that the constructs and propositions discussed in the precious sections dealing with the professional intellect could be validated. Mostly scale and a few nominal-based scales were used to develop graphs and perform the relevant statistical analyses. The dominant statistical techniques used in the present study were multiple regression and Chi-square analyses for the formal hypotheses testing processes and principal-components analysis (PCA) for the exploratory or data reduction portion of the present study. PCA is a classical linear transform statistical method, which has been widely used in data analysis and compression (Bishop, 1995; Cumming, 1993). In general, if the data are concentrated in a linear subspace, this provides a way to compress data without losing much information and simplifying the representation. Hence, by picking the eigenvectors having the largest eigenvalues, little information as possible in the mean-square sense is lost. The survey questions that were used may be at least partially derived from the frequencies, cross-tabulations, and data reduction techniques found in Table 1 through 10 and Figure 2, Figure 3, Figure 4, and Figure 5, which are the bulk of the survey questions contained in the data-collection process and ultimately used in the analysis portion of the present study.

RESULTS AND DISCUSSION

Descriptive Comparisons

Table 1 displays frequencies of selected variables to determine intrinsic and extrinsic motivations behind the extensive use of online trading websites and what their concerns or preferences are in regards to online trading. The specific hypothesis-testing section was designed to answer questions concerning selected major forces promoting the acceptability of online trading as found in Figure

Table 1. Selected frequencies of selected variables that measured the constructs identified in Figure 1 and some used as dependent variables in the hypothesis-testing phase

A. Willing to pay higher price if seller has better reputation.				
Coding Scheme	**Frequency**	**Percent**	**Valid Percent**	**Cumulative Percent**
Strongly Disagree	26	13.1	13.1	13.1
Disagree	28	14.1	14.1	27.3
Neutral	42	21.2	21.2	48.5
Agree	80	40.4	40.4	88.9
Strongly Agree	22	11.1	11.1	100.0
Total	198	100.0	100.0	
B. Feedback systems are important.				
Coding Scheme	**Frequency**	**Percent**	**Valid Percent**	**Cumulative Percent**
Strongly Disagree	8	4.0	4.0	4.0
Disagree	10	5.1	5.1	9.1
Neutral	37	18.7	18.7	27.8
Agree	102	51.5	51.5	79.3
Strongly Agree	41	20.7	20.7	100.0
Total	198	100.0	100.0	
C. Seller concerned with Buyer's reputation.				
Coding Scheme	**Frequency**	**Percent**	**Valid Percent**	**Cumulative Percent**
Strongly Disagree	10	5.1	5.1	5.1
Disagree	10	5.1	5.1	10.1
Neutral	58	29.3	29.3	39.4
Agree	79	39.9	39.9	79.3
Strongly Agree	41	20.7	20.7	100.0
Total	198	100.0	100.0	
D. Buyer concerned with seller's reputation.				
Coding Scheme	**Frequency**	**Percent**	**Valid Percent**	**Cumulative Percent**
Strongly Disagree	6	3.0	3.0	3.0
Disagree	11	5.6	5.6	8.6
Neutral	30	15.2	15.2	23.7
Agree	91	46.0	46.0	69.7
Strongly Agree	60	30.3	30.3	100.0
Total	198	100.0	100.0	
E. Fear of identity theft with online auctions.				
Coding Scheme	**Frequency**	**Percent**	**Valid Percent**	**Cumulative Percent**
Strongly Disagree	7	3.5	3.5	3.5
Disagree	30	15.2	15.2	18.7

continued on following page

Table 1. Continued

Neutral	49	24.7	24.7	43.4
Agree	70	35.4	35.4	78.8
Strongly Agree	42	21.2	21.2	100.0
Total	198	100.0	100.0	

F. Method of payment.

Coding Scheme	Frequency	Percent	Valid Percent	Cumulative Percent
PayPal™	79	39.9	39.9	39.9
Credit Card	100	50.5	50.5	90.4
Check	13	6.6	6.6	97.0
Other	6	3.0	3.0	100.0
Total	198	100.0	100.0	

G. Sold in a year on online auctions (US$).

Coding Scheme	Frequency	Percent	Valid Percent	Cumulative Percent
0 to 20	110	55.6	55.6	55.6
21 to 50	17	8.6	8.6	64.1
51 to 100	31	15.7	15.7	79.8
101 to 500	24	12.1	12.1	91.9
500+	16	8.1	8.1	100.0
Total	198	100.0	100.0	

H. Days of week shop online.

Coding Scheme	Frequency	Percent	Valid Percent	Cumulative Percent
Monday	23	11.6	11.6	11.6
Tuesday	13	6.6	6.6	18.2
Wednesday	27	13.6	13.6	31.8
Thursday	20	10.1	10.1	41.9
Friday	45	22.7	22.7	64.6
Saturday	45	22.7	22.7	87.4
Sunday	25	12.6	12.6	100.0
Total	198	100.0	100.0	

I. Consider shipping price in bidding.

Coding Scheme	Frequency	Percent	Valid Percent	Cumulative Percent
Strongly Disagree	11	5.6	5.6	5.6
Disagree	19	9.6	9.6	15.2
Neutral	52	26.3	26.3	41.4
Agree	74	37.4	37.4	78.8

continued on following page

Table 1. Continued

Strongly Agree	42	21.2	21.2	100.0
Total	198	100.0	100.0	
J. Pay higher shipping price for higher value.				
Coding Scheme	**Frequency**	**Percent**	**Valid Percent**	**Cumulative Percent**
Strongly Disagree	15	7.6	7.6	7.6
Disagree	29	14.6	14.6	22.2
Neutral	63	31.8	31.8	54.0
Agree	68	34.3	34.3	88.4
Strongly Agree	23	11.6	11.6	100.0
Total	198	100.0	100.0	

1; namely are buyers are willing to pay a higher price if the seller has a better reputation, is shipping price is equally important as item price, and are customers using online auctions for price and/or reach as their primary motivations. The survey instrument originally consisted of the categories of reputation and feedback, security and fraud, convenience, selling and buying points, price factors, and demographics.

Table 1 displays frequencies of selected variable of the 198 professionals' responses to the survey instrument. As evident from an inspection of the table, for example, the majority of respondents were willing to pay higher price if seller has better reputation (51.1%), feedback systems are important (only 9.1% disagreed), seller concerned with buyer's reputation (only 10.1% disagreed), buyer concerned with seller's reputation (only 8.61% disagreed), consider shipping price in bidding (only 15.2% disagreed), pay higher shipping price for higher value (only 22.2% disagreed), and used electronic methods of payment (PayPal™ 15.2%, credit card, 50.5%, check, 6.6%). The fear of identity theft while engaged in online trading was felt by the majority of respondents (only 18.7% disagreed and 21.2% strongly agreed). Many of the respondents have engaged directly while selling transactions, with

44.4% selling at least US$21 worth, while 8.1% sold over US$500 annually. Figure 2 illustrates the cross-tabulations of method of payment with reasons for using online auctions and age level. As evident by the figures, electronic payments are vastly preferred, especially by younger professionals, and although price is a dominant factor, the value or reach or broadcasting to greater accessibility to other domestic and international markets is very significant as well.

Due in part to this diversity of behavioral and attitudinal patterns, the next two section deals with individual hypotheses as well as cluster analysis and data reduction techniques, with specific hypothesis-testing procedures. These statistical procedures were employed in order to determine existing patterns from a working professional's confidence perspective in terms of the online trading process, general, and, in particular, an OASP's ability to safeguard its clientele against the thereat of identity theft.

Hypothesis-Testing Results

From the research propositions and business literature on the development of the growth of online trading and the major forces driving its acceptability (namely feedback systems, price

Figure 2. Cross-tabulation of method of payment with selected variables

A. Reasons for using online auctions.

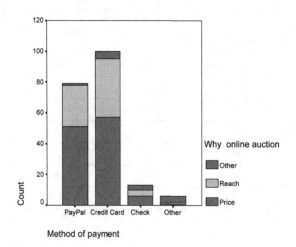

B. Age level (years).

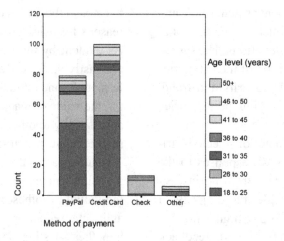

competitiveness, and payment method) both hypothesis-testing and exploratory research procedures were developed to test these relationships. The three specific research hypotheses that were tested are listed below:

H1: Buyers, especially working professionals, that find the feedback systems important are willing to engage in online trading activities and may be willing to pay a higher price for merchandise being sold by a seller with a better reputation, regardless of gender.

H2: Customers, especially working professionals, are concerned with selling price as well as shipping cost or total price, regardless of gender.

H3: In terms of the convenience of payment method, electronic forms are preferred by working professionals in transacting online trading activities, regardless of age and gender.

Specific-Research Hypothesis (H1) Results

Based on the derivation of the inherent value of reputation and feedback systems, it was hypothesize those buyers that find the feedback systems important may willing to pay a higher price for an item being sold by a seller with a better reputation. Table 2 is cross-tabulation statistics of willing higher price if seller has better reputation with feedback systems are important with gender status was found to be highly significant at the 0.01 level of a two-tailed test (for males, Chi-square $= 60.512$, $p = 0.000$; for females, Chi-square $= 62.886$, $p = 0.000$). As demonstrated in Table 2, 72.2% of those that find that a feedback system to be important agree or strongly agree that they are willing to pay a higher price if the seller has a better reputation. It was decided to cross-tabulate willingness to pay a higher price if the seller has a better reputation with gender status, as shown in Table 3. The results were equally impressive with males and females equally agreeing on paying a higher price for a better reputation. This relationship was found to be highly significant at the 0.01 level of a two-tailed test (for males, Chi-square $= 153.577$, $p = 0.000$; for females, Chi-square $= 107.282$, $p = 0.000$). Slightly more males (2.1%) strongly agree that they are willing to pay a higher price for a better reputation over that of females, but that difference is not statistically significant. Figure 3 presents a cross-tabulation of seller's concern with buyer's reputation with buyer concerned with seller's reputation, while Figure 4 displays the cross-tabulation with degree of importance of feedback systems and gender. Hence, H1 was formally accepted, suggesting the strategic leverage value of reputation and feedback systems is very powerful.

Specific-Research Hypothesis (H2) Results

The second hypothesis deals with the construct of competitive pricing structures, which includes the total price and shipping costs. As the results from Table 4 indicates, there is overwhelming evidence and highly significant that buyers that consider the selling price before bidding also consider the shipping price of the item they are bidding on (Chi-square $= 101.915$, $p = 0.000$). There are also a significant number of buyers who strongly agree that they consider both the selling price before bidding as well as the shipping price of the item; the numbers were significantly lower for those buyers that disagreed on both aspects. Hence, most customers, especially working professionals, who are concerned with the selling price before bidding are also consider the total price, including shipping costs; therefore H2 is formally accepted.

Specific-Research Hypothesis (H3) Results

This hypothesis was in the area of convenience of payment methods, especially in terms of gender and age. The results summarized in Table 5 indicated that the most significant use of payment was PayPal™ and credit cards and its was significantly related to the reason for use, namely price and/or reach (the extent of accessibility to other marketplaces), with price the most important factor (Chi-square $= 45.740$, $p = 0.000$). In terms of age, Table 6, of the 105 respondents that were from the age 18 to 25 years, 46% used PayPal™ and 50% used credit cards; the 59 in the age level of 26 to 30 years, 30% used PayPal™ and 50% used credit cards; while the older age groups predominately used credit/debit cards. These relationships between age and use of electronic means, with

Table 2. Cross-tabulation statistics of willing higher price if seller has better reputation with feedback systems are important with gender status

A. Actual count.

Gender status			Feedback systems are important					Total
Coding Scheme			Strongly Disagree	Disagree	Neutral	Agree	Strongly Agree	
Male	Higher price if seller has better reputation	Strongly Disagree	3	3	4	1	2	13
		Disagree	1	1	3	6	0	11
		Neutral	0	0	7	8	4	19
		Agree	0	0	4	30	6	40
		Strongly Agree	0	0	1	4	8	13
	Total		4	4	19	49	20	96
Female	Higher price if seller has better reputation	Strongly Disagree	2	4	2	3	2	13
		Disagree	1	2	4	9	1	17
		Neutral	0	0	8	13	2	23
		Agree	1	0	4	27	8	40
		Strongly Agree	0	0	0	1	8	9
	Total		4	6	18	53	21	102

B. Chi-square test results.

Gender status	Statistics	Value	df	Asymptotic Significance (two-tailed test)
Male	Pearson Chi-Square	60.512	16	0.000 (HS)
	Likelihood Ratio	55.696	16	0.000 (HS)
	Linear-by-Linear Association	30.253	1	0.000 (HS)
	N of Valid Cases	96		
Female	Pearson Chi-Square	62.886	16	0.000 (HS)
	Likelihood Ratio	53.970	16	0.000 (HS)
	Linear-by-Linear Association	25.208	1	0.000 (HS)
	N of Valid Cases	102		

C. Symmetric measures.

Gender status	Statistics		Value	Approximate Significance
Male	Nominal by Nominal	Contingency Coefficient	0.622	0.000 (HS)
	N of Valid Cases		96	
Female	Nominal by Nominal	Contingency Coefficient	0.618	0.000 (HS)
	N of Valid Cases		102	

HS denotes highly significant at the 0.01 level for a two-tailed test.

Table 3. Cross-tabulation statistics of seller concerned with buyer's reputation with buyer concerned with seller's reputation with gender status

A. Actual count.									
Gender status			Buyer concerned with seller's reputation					Total	
Coding Scheme			Strongly Disagree	Disagree	Neutral	Agree	Strongly Agree		
Male	Seller concerned with buyer's reputation	Strongly Disagree	3	3	0	0	0	6	
		Disagree	0	2	0	3	0	5	
		Neutral	0	1	11	11	2	25	
		Agree	0	0	1	35	6	42	
		Strongly Agree	0	1	0	1	16	18	
	Total		3	7	12	50	24	96	
Female	Seller concerned with buyer's reputation	Strongly Disagree	2	1	0	0	1	4	
		Disagree	0	1	0	4	0	5	
		Neutral	0	1	17	12	3	33	
		Agree	1	0	1	22	13	37	
		Strongly Agree	0	1	0	3	19	23	
	Total		3	4	18	41	36	102	

B. Chi-square test results.					
Gender status	Statistics		Value	df	Asymptotic Significance (two-tailed test)
Male	Pearson Chi-Square		153.577	16	0.000 (HS)
	Likelihood Ratio		112.503	16	0.000 (HS)
	Linear-by-Linear Association		55.597	1	0.000 (HS)
	N of Valid Cases		96		
Female	Pearson Chi-Square		107.282	16	0.000 (HS)
	Likelihood Ratio		87.434	16	0.000 (HS)
	Linear-by-Linear Association		34.730	1	0.000 (HS)
	N of Valid Cases		102		

C. Symmetric measures.				
Gender status	Statistics		Value	Approximate Significance
Male	Nominal by Nominal	Contingency Coefficient	0.784	0.000 (HS)
	N of Valid Cases		96	
Female	Nominal by Nominal	Contingency Coefficient	0.716	0.000 (HS)
	N of Valid Cases		102	

HS denotes highly significant at the 0.01 level for a two-tailed test.

Figure 3. Cross-tabulation of seller's concern with buyer's reputation with buyer concerned with seller's reputation

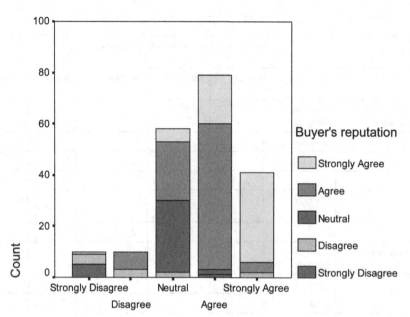

Seller concerned with buyer's reputation

younger professionals preferring PayPal™ over credit/debit cards, were found to be statistically significant, regardless of gender, although less strong for females (for males, Chi-square = 36.884, p = 0.005; for females, Chi-square = 27.331, p = 0.073). Figure 2 previously illustrated some of these important relationships.

Although PayPal™ and credit cards are the most popular methods of payment through all age groups; younger professionals tend to use them more frequently and without much hesitation.

Factor-Analysis and Exploratory Results

In the search for validation of the major constructs that are most likely to be associated with fear of identity theft when engaged in online auctions and the basic constructs outlined in Figure 1, namely considerations of reputation and feedback features, convenience, price competition, security and fraud, payment methods, and generic selling and buying features (other factors). CRM-based aspects and the concerns of professional workers' eroded consumer trust due to the current global recession, principal components and factor analyses techniques were selected as the dominant multivariate statistical procedures to be used in the exploratory segment of this research effort. Principal component analysis (PCA) is a classical linear transform statistical method, which has been widely used in data analysis and compression (Bishop, 1995; Cumming, 1993; Oja, 1989). Factor analysis using PCA techniques computed the communalities and common grouped factors in terms of shared variance. The analysis was done by separating the variables into independent factor-based constructs, then completing the PCA techniques, followed by appropriate hypothesis-testing procedures with degree identity theft fears are affected by the major driving forces of acceptability of online trading among the working professional crowd.

Figure 4. Cross-tabulation of willingness to pay higher prices if greater reputation of seller with selected variables

A. Degree of importance of feedback systems.

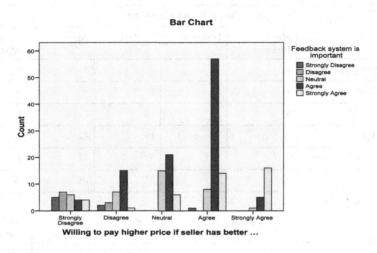

B. Gender.

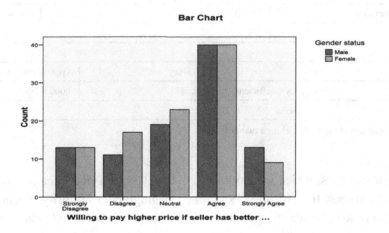

It was the basic research assumption of the present study that there are positive steps that management in the OASP industry can undertake to minimize the negative aspects of global recession to rebuild consumer trust, especially in the integrity of online trading. Table 8, Part C, displays the communalities among factor loadings results for the creation of the independent-variable factor-based constructs, indicating that there are eight statistically significant groupings of data

clusters at the 0.05 level among the independent variables for data-reduction purposes. Figure 5 presents cross-tabulation of fear of identity theft conducting online auctions with selected variables.

In terms of the independent-variable constructs (Table 7), Table 8 displays evidence that the total explained variance from data-reduction techniques of eight major constructs that was statistically significant. The independent factor groups were renamed to suit their description

Table 4. Cross-tabulation statistics of consider shipping price in bidding with consider selling price before bidding

A. Actual count.

Coding Scheme		Consider selling price before bidding					Total
		Strongly Disagree	Disagree	Neutral	Agree	Strongly Agree	
Consider shipping price in bidding	Strongly Disagree	9	1	0	1	0	11
	Disagree	1	5	4	9	0	19
	Neutral	4	5	18	14	11	52
	Agree	3	7	10	42	12	74
	Strongly Agree	2	3	5	17	15	42
Total		19	21	37	83	38	198

B. Chi-square test results.

Statistics	Value	df	Asymptotic Significance (two-tailed test)
Pearson Chi-Square	101.915	16	0.000 (HS)
Likelihood Ratio	71.353	16	0.000 (HS)
Linear-by-Linear Association	34.550	1	0.000(HS)
N of Valid Cases	198		

C. Symmetric measures.

Statistics		Value	Approximate Significance
Nominal by Nominal	Contingency Coefficient	0.583	0.000 (HS)
N of Valid Cases		198	

HS denotes highly significant at the 0.01 level for a two-tailed test.

of the independent variables, which loaded into the groupings with at least 0.5 (Bishop, 1995; Cumming, 1993) and were similar to the labels generated by theoretical constructs from the literature review. As evident from the results, there are eight or less major groupings or data clusters; Table 8, Part A, displays the total explained variance from data reduction techniques of these eight major constructs was 66.955%. The significant variable loadings defining each major factor are highlighted in bold print for easy recognition in Table 8, Parts B (rotated component matrix) and C (component transformation matrix). Table 8, Part A lists these factor-based constructs as, in order of the greatest explained variance; namely Reputation and Feedback Features, Online Auc-

tion Usage, Price Factors, Bidding Preference, Demographic Maturity, Security Factors, Convenience Factors, and Other Factors, resulting in eight factor-based scores.

Factor-Analysis Hypothesis-Testing Results

In the testing of these factor-based constructs to determine the most important considerations for management of OASP-related industry in characterizing the impact of eroded consumer trust, especially due to the fears of identity theft while engaged in online trading, Table 9 presents the relevant statistics associated with testing these independent constructs derived from PCA results

Table 5. Cross-tabulation statistics of method of payment with reason for using online auctions

A. Actual count.

Coding Scheme		Reason for using online auctions			Total
		Price	Reach	Other	
Method of payment	PayPal™	51	27	1	79
	Credit Card	57	38	5	100
	Check	6	4	3	13
	Other	1	1	4	6
Total		115	70	13	198

B. Chi-square test results.

Statistics	Value	df	Asymptotic Significance (two-tailed test
Pearson Chi-Square	45.740	6	0.000 (HS)
Likelihood Ratio	24.498	6	0.000 (HS)
Linear-by-Linear Association	16.348	1	0.000 (HS)
N of Valid Cases	198		

C. Symmetric measures.

Statistics		Value	Approximate Significance
Nominal by Nominal	Contingency Coefficient	0.433	0.000 (HS)
N of Valid Cases		198	

HS denotes highly significant at the 0.01 level for a two-tailed test.

found in Table 8, with the dependent variable, consumer belief that the credit crunch has contributed to consumer insolvency. As displayed Part A, the model summary, a total variance in predicting the dependent variable was a respectable 28.1%. In terms of the hypothesis-testing results, the overall results were not found to be statistically significant (F = 9.294, p = 0.000). While, as shown in Part C that inspects specific contributions of each component in the hypothesis and four independent factor-based constructs were found to be statistically associated with the dependent variable, fear of identity theft with online auctions.

The Reputation and Feedback Features factor-based construct, compositing of highly significant independent variables shown in Table 8 of seller concerned with buyer's reputation (0.860), feedback systems are important (0.789), buyer concerned with seller's reputation (0.757), and higher price if seller has better reputation (0.745), was found to be highly significant and positively related to the dependent variable, fear of identity theft with online auctions as expected (t = 6.317, p = 0.000), suggesting that reputation of both buyers and sellers are important safeguards in dealing with the fear generated from potential identity theft problems while engaging in online auction activities. The other independent variable constructs of Online Auction Usage (t = 1.734, p = 0.084), Price Factors (t = 5.027, p = 0.000), and Demographic Maturity (t = 1.810, p = 0.072) were found to be at least marginally significantly related to fears of identity theft. The other independent variable constructs of Bidding Preference (t = 0.155, p = 0.877), Security Factors (t = 1.646, p = 0.101), Convenience Factors (t = 0.211, p = 0.833), and

Table 6. Cross-tabulation statistics of method of payment with age level (years) with gender status

A. Actual count.										
Gender status			**Age level (years)**							**Total**
Coding Scheme			18 to 25	26 to 30	31 to 35	36 to 40	41 to 45	46 to 50	50+	
Male	Method of payment	Pay-Pal™	32	6	0	3	0	1	0	42
		Credit Card	30	9	2	1	2	0	1	45
		Check	0	2	0	0	1	1	1	5
		Other	2	1	0	0	0	0	1	4
	Total		64	18	2	4	3	2	3	96
Female	Method of payment	Pay-Pal™	16	13	2	1	3	1	1	37
		Credit Card	23	21	2	1	2	5	1	55
		Check	1	7	0	0	0	0	0	8
		Other	1	0	0	0	0	0	1	2
	Total		41	41	4	2	5	6	3	102

B. Chi-square test results.				
Gender status	**Statistics**	**Value**	**df**	**Asymptotic Significance (two-tailed test)**
MaleFemale	Pearson Chi-Square	36.884	18	0.005 (HS)
	Likelihood Ratio	31.009	18	0.029 S)
	Linear-by-Linear Association	9.237	1	0.002 (HS)
	N of Valid Cases	96		
	Pearson Chi-Square	27.331	18	0.073 (MS)
	Likelihood Ratio	18.121	18	0.448 (NS)
	Linear-by-Linear Association	0.308	1	0.579 (NS)
	N of Valid Cases	102		
C. Symmetric measures.				

continued on following page

Table 6. Continued

Gender status	Statistics						Value	Approximate Significance				
Male	Nominal by Nominal		Contingency Coefficient				0.527	0.005 (HS)				
	N of Valid Cases						96					
Female	Nominal by Nominal		Contingency Coefficient				0.460	0.073 (MS)				
	N of Valid Cases						102					

NS denotes not statistically significant at the 0.05 level for a two-tailed test, MS denotes marginally significant at the 0.05 level for a two-tailed test; S denotes significant at the 0.05 level for a two-tailed test, HS denotes highly significant at the 0.01 level for a two-tailed test.

MS denotes marginally significant at the 0.05 level for a two-tailed test, HS denotes highly significant at the 0.01 level for a two-tailed test.

Other Factors (t = 0.344, p = 0.731) were found not to be significantly related to identity theft fears while engaging in online auction activities. Table 10 displays a summary of the hypothesis-testing results associated with both the original testing phase and the exploratory analysis.

GENERAL CONCLUSIONS AND IMPLICATIONS

Basic Summary

After reviewing the results of the present study, it was quite evident that many people use online trading websites for price and convenience based on the accuracy of good measures of reputation through feedback systems; at the same time, customers, especially working professional in the current economic downturn, have many concerns regarding security and fraud safeguards, with identity theft ranked highest among those most concerned issue among those engaged with online trading activities. All specific research hypotheses were found to be highly significant. Buyers, especially working professionals that find the feedback systems important, are more willing to engage in online trading activities and more willing to pay a higher price for merchandise being sold by a seller with a better reputation, regardless of gender. Customers, especially working professionals, are concerned with the total price, including shipping cost, regardless of gender. Finally, in terms of the convenience of payment method, electronic forms are preferred by working professionals in transacting online trading activities, regardless of age and gender. Interestingly, those with a bachelor's degree rank importance of security the highest out of all levels of the sample of professional workers. This demonstrates that identity theft is a serious concern with online auctioning and it is important for websites to have proper policies and procedures in place to prevent computer crimes. Risk of security breaches in online auctions can be greatly reduced if proper procedures are followed by the user to protect themselves.

Managerial Implications

Presently, there is little doubt that the global economy is in the midst of a total transformation in the management of information flows in the

Figure 5. Cross-tabulation of fear of identity theft conducting online auctions with selected variables

A. Method of payment.

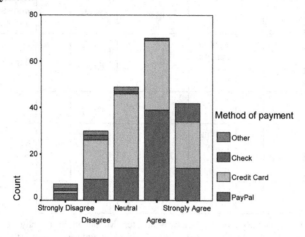

Fear of identity theft with online auctions

B. Gender.

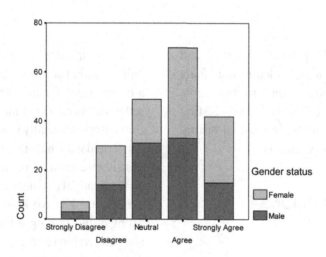

Fear of identity theft with online auctions

decision-making process for both consumers and businesses. The management of both manufacturing and services that strategically leverages its information technologies of IT is all about linking the various strategic components that add value as defined by its end users. Overall, management must link products to orders and orders to shipments and shipments to payments through proper supply chain management, which has strongly been demonstrated by the OASP industry. The use of the web-enabled and automatic identification and data capture (AIDC)-related systems serve

as foundation for management of data flows for strategic purposes and basic transactions that both cause transactions and result from these informational and material flows. OASP industry is characterized by significant strategic efforts concerning customer relations and technological innovations, which points executives toward developing a sustainable competitive advantage. A classic short article by Colvin (1997) lays out his argument that information technology (IT) has revolutionized most industries to the point that

Table 7. Communalities among factor loadings results for the creation of the independent-variable factor-based constructs

Variables used to create Independent Variable Constructs	Initial	Extraction
Higher price if seller has better reputation	1.000	0.640
Feedback systems are important	1.000	0.652
Seller concerned with buyer's reputation	1.000	0.812
Buyer concerned with seller's reputation	1.000	0.711
Involvement in an online auction	1.000	0.671
Likelihood to visit eBay	1.000	0.676
Likelihood to visit UBid	1.000	0.698
Likelihood to visit Amazon	1.000	0.712
Likelihood to visit Yahoo	1.000	0.661
Frequency online auction hours per week	1.000	0.618
Security is important when picking a website	1.000	0.568
Read security policies prior to online signature	1.000	0.713
Compare prices, options and features	1.000	0.500
Spend in a year on online auctions (US$)	1.000	0.670
Sold in a year on online auctions (US$)	1.000	0.777
Number of days shop online	1.000	0.625
Check shipping price before bidding	1.000	0.749
Consider shipping price in bidding	1.000	0.716
Pay higher shipping price for higher value	1.000	0.574
Consider selling price before bidding	1.000	0.599
Paid more in auction than fixed price from other website	1.000	0.659
Education level	1.000	0.710
Age level (years)	1.000	0.785
Income level (US$)	1.000	0.810
Time of day shop online	1.000	0.431

Extraction Method: Principal Component Analysis.

what was originally considered an impenetrable advantage is no longer.

Colvin suggested that in order to distinguish one's company from others, the manager must shift his focus to the less defined and harder to understand concepts of people management and culture manipulation due to the revolutionary impact of IT on the equalization of businesses around the global. Communication sharing has been established to such an intense level that IT can no longer be looked to as a source of competitive advantage. In order to survive, It-based initiatives must be at least as current as their competitors', but management cannot rely on it for an advantage because it is so widely available and inexpensive as well. This phenomenon plays itself out in most industries these days, and undoubtedly has an enormous impact, which Colvin eventually concludes will require companies looking to create a sustainable competitive advantage to manipulate some other form of company asset that is difficult

Table 8. Total explained variance from data reduction techniques for creation of independent-variable constructs

Part A. Total explained variance.

Factor-based Components	Initial Eigenvalues			Rotation Sums of Squared Loadings			
	Total	% of Variance	Cumulative %	Total	% of Variance	Cumulative %	
Reputation and Feedback Features	5.088	20.351	20.351	3.177	12.710	12.710	
Online Auction Usage	2.903	11.614	31.965	3.126	12.505	25.215	
Price Factors	1.841	7.362	39.327	2.274	9.095	34.310	
Bidding Preference	1.715	6.859	46.186	2.068	8.271	42.581	
Demographic Maturity	1.482	5.928	52.114	1.726	6.903	49.484	
Security Factors	1.338	5.354	57.468	1.531	6.123	55.607	
Convenience Factors	1.218	4.873	62.341	1.494	5.976	61.583	
Other Factors	1.153	4.614	66.955	1.343	5.372	66.955	

Part B. Rotated component matrix.

Independent Variables	Factor-based Components							
	Reputation and Feedback Features	Online Auction Usage	Price Factors	Bidding Preference	Demographic Maturity	Security Factors	Convenience Factors	Other Factors
Higher price if seller has better reputation	**0.745**	0.069	-0.123	0.045	-0.037	0.245	0.038	0.035
Feedback systems are important	**0.789**	0.063	0.108	0.109	0.030	-0.012	-0.013	0.034
Seller concerned with buyer's reputation	**0.860**	0.184	0.161	-0.051	-0.078	-0.015	0.053	0.028
Buyer concerned with seller's reputation	**0.757**	0.028	0.173	0.291	0.039	-0.074	0.095	-0.078
Involvement in an online auction	0.149	**0.768**	0.091	0.016	-0.135	0.017	0.056	-0.173
Likelihood to visit eBay	0.120	0.133	0.005	**0.789**	0.004	-0.066	0.100	-0.089
Likelihood to visit UBid	0.015	0.307	-0.394	0.136	0.163	0.024	0.183	**0.608**
Likelihood to visit Amazon	0.057	-0.086	0.173	0.116	0.018	0.038	**0.809**	-0.052
Likelihood to visit Yahoo	0.101	0.094	0.003	0.017	-0.007	-0.034	**0.795**	0.091
Frequency online auction hours per week	0.031	**0.707**	-0.107	-0.084	0.079	0.118	0.003	0.280
Security is important when picking a website	**0.564**	-0.116	0.405	0.112	0.132	0.161	0.133	0.002
Read security policies prior to online signature	0.143	-0.039	0.161	-0.243	0.026	**0.766**	0.032	0.132
Compare prices, options and features	0.034	0.313	0.392	0.443	-0.074	0.083	0.173	-0.095
Spend in a year on online auctions (US$)	0.095	**0.619**	0.176	0.354	0.192	-0.283	-0.065	-0.020

continued on following page

Table 8. Continued

Sold in a year on online auctions (US$)	0.011	**0.864**	0.039	0.027	-0.016	0.095	-0.058	-0.130
Time of day shop online	-0.031	0.067	**0.596**	0.039	0.037	-0.112	0.206	-0.112
Number of days shop online	0.046	**0.703**	0.126	0.166	0.203	-0.059	0.068	0.190
Check shipping price before bidding	0.296	0.072	**0.780**	0.162	-0.036	0.114	-0.050	0.076
Consider shipping price in bidding	0.292	0.140	**0.683**	0.251	-0.059	0.192	-0.006	0.202
Pay higher shipping price for higher value	0.286	-0.006	0.149	0.472	-0.024	0.430	-0.186	0.168
Consider selling price before bidding	0.165	-0.028	0.324	**0.668**	0.075	0.065	0.067	0.076
Paid more in auction than fixed price from other website	-0.014	0.122	-0.067	0.339	-0.042	**0.692**	0.003	-0.208
Education level	-0.015	0.086	-0.174	0.095	0.258	0.014	0.037	-0.771
Age level (years)	-0.028	-0.080	0.025	0.009	**0.881**	-0.009	0.035	0.005
Income level (US$)	0.045	0.265	-0.054	0.019	**0.841**	-0.011	-0.030	-0.164

Part C. Component transformation matrix.

Factor-based Components	Online Reputation	Online Auction Usage	Price Factors	Bidding Preference	Demographic Maturity	Security Factors	Convenience Factors	Other Factors
Reputation and Feedback Features	0.627	0.423	0.448	0.424	0.057	0.157	0.135	0.047
Online Auction Usage	-0.359	0.830	-0.269	0.028	0.278	-0.174	-0.031	-0.025
Price Factors	-0.376	-0.263	0.343	0.457	0.415	-0.265	0.264	-0.389
Bidding Preference	0.501	-0.165	-0.405	-0.200	0.699	-0.090	0.022	-0.142
Demographic Maturity	-0.111	-0.036	0.006	0.231	0.179	0.541	-0.733	-0.267
Security Factors	-0.233	-0.080	-0.191	0.157	0.237	0.650	0.470	0.424
Convenience Factors	-0.141	0.033	0.626	-0.530	0.397	0.011	-0.164	0.349
Other Factors	-0.007	0.166	0.130	-0.461	-0.109	0.390	0.355	-0.673

A. Extraction Method: Principal Component Analysis.

B. Extraction Method: Principal Component Analysis, rotation method was Varimax with Kaiser Normalization; rotation converged in 9 iterations.

C. Extraction Method: Principal Component Analysis, Rotation Method was Varimax with Kaiser Normalization.

to understand and employ: namely, culture and people.

Hence, as evident from the empirical section, the future of competitive advantage in the OASP industry is housed within people, not machines or processes. As demonstrated by Kennedy and Widener (2008), Scherrer-Rathje, Boyle, and Deflorin (2009). Shah, Chandrasekaran, and Linderman (2008), and Sprovieri (2008), there is a fallacy of relying solely on modern production techniques, IT, and incremental process improvements as distinguishing factors for a firm. Since essentially all competitive firms are developing these operational features, such advances cannot be considered to be strategically unique or defendable. Rather, it is intangibles, such as trust

Table 9. Relevant statistics associated with exploratory testing results. Part A displays the model summary, Part B the overall results, and Part C inspects specific contributions of each component in the hypothesis (Dependent variable: Fear of identity theft with online auctions) .

Part A: Model summary.			
R	R Square	Adjusted R Square	Std. Error of the Estimate
0.531	0.282	0.252	0.944

Part B: ANOVA results.					
Source of Variation	Sum of Squares	df	Mean Square	F-ratio	Significance
Regression	66.315	8	8.289	9.294	0.000 (HS)
Residual	168.574	189	0.892		
Total	234.889	197			

Part C: Coefficients-testing results.					
Independent Factor-based Constructs	Un-standardized Coefficients		Standardized Coefficients	t-test	Significance
	B	Std. Error	Beta		
(Constant)	3.556	0.067		52.976	0.000
Reputation and Feedback Features	0.425	0.067	0.389	6.317	0.000 (HS)
Online Auction Usage	0.117	0.067	0.107	1.734	0.084 (MS)
Price Factors	0.338	0.067	0.310	5.027	0.000 (HS)
Bidding Preference	0.010	0.067	0.010	0.155	0.877 (NS)
Demographic Maturity	0.122	0.067	0.112	1.810	0.072 (MS)
Security Factors	0.111	0.067	0.101	1.646	0.101 (NS)
Convenience Factors	0.014	0.067	0.013	0.211	0.833 (NS)
Other Factors	0.023	0.067	0.021	0.344	0.731 (NS)

A. Predictors: (Constant), Reputation and Feedback Features, Online Auction Usage, Price Factors, Bidding Preference, Demographic Maturity, Security Factors, Convenience Factors, and Other Factors.

B. Dependent Variable: Fear of identity theft with online auctions. HS denotes highly significant at the 0.01 level for a two-tailed test.

C. Dependent Variable: Fear of identity theft with online auctions. NS denotes not statistically significant at the 0.05 level for a two-tailed test, MS denotes marginally statistical significant at the 0.05 level for a two-tailed test, HS denotes highly significant at the 0.01 level for a two-tailed test.

and trustworthiness that differentiates the various competitors in the OASP industry. Management should consider the source of future competitive advantage to be somehow contained within the uniqueness within each company, or the ideas and skills their people have, as well as the culture and how it contributes to innovation and service. For example, the speed of reaction in online trading that now required due to the influence of IT on the marketplace is generally taken for granted. Management must strategically position their

companies based on good service, as well as being competitive on pricing, using feedback systems, dealing successfully with security and fraud concerns, emphasizing convenience in payment methods, and providing value to their customers.

As there are numerous literature sources and articles are written about the requirements of nimbleness and quick reaction for modern companies, IT and related technologies have had an enormous impact on this newer marketplace dynamic. The sheer speed and volume of infor-

Table 10. Summary of hypothesis-testing results associated with the exploratory analysis

Hypothesis Number	Description Of Hypothesis	Present Study's Results
H1	Buyers, especially working professionals, that find the feedback systems important are willing to engage in online trading activities and may be willing to pay a higher price for merchandise being sold by a seller with a better reputation, regardless of gender.	HS, accepted (expected)
H2	Customers, especially working professionals, are concerned with selling price as well as shipping cost or total price, regardless of gender.	HS, accepted (expected)
H3	In terms of the convenience of payment method, electronic forms are preferred by working professionals in transacting online trading activities, regardless of age and gender.	HS, accepted (expected)
H4	In terms of exploratory research, there will be a significant predictive relationship between the dependent variable, fear of identity theft with online auctions, with the factor score-based independent construct of Reputation and Feedback Features, a perceived measure of employment experience and knowledge.	HS, accepted (expected)
H5	In terms of exploratory research, there will be a significant predictive relationship between the dependent variable, fear of identity theft with online auctions, with the factor score-based independent construct of Online Auction Usage, a perceived measure of economic support, especially employer-based.	MS, rejected (expected)
H6	In terms of exploratory research, there will be a significant predictive relationship between the dependent variable, fear of identity theft with online auctions, with the factor score-based independent construct of Price Factors, a perceived measure of job experience and respect for education and its affects on employee confidence.	HS, accepted (expected)
H7	In terms of exploratory research, there will be a significant predictive relationship between the dependent variable, fear of identity theft with online auctions, with the factor score-based independent construct of Bidding Preference, a perceived measure of the importance of pursuing educational and/or training opportunities for enhanced economic security and stability on employee confidence.	NS, rejected (expected)
H8	In terms of exploratory research, there will be a significant predictive relationship between the dependent variable, fear of identity theft with online auctions, with the factor score-based independent construct of Demographic Maturity, a perceived measure of job experience and respect for education and its affects on employee confidence.	MS, rejected (expected)
H9	In terms of exploratory research, there will be a significant predictive relationship between the dependent variable, fear of identity theft with online auctions, with the factor score-based independent constructs of Security Factors, a perceived measure of current job satisfaction and employee confidence.	NS, rejected (not expected)
H10	In terms of exploratory research, there will be a significant predictive relationship between the dependent variable, fear of identity theft with online auctions, with the factor score-based independent construct of Convenience Factors, a perceived measure of job experience and respect for education and its affects on employee confidence.	NS, rejected (not expected)
H11	In terms of exploratory research, there will be a significant predictive relationship between the dependent variable, fear of identity theft with online auctions, with the factor score-based independent constructs of Other Factors, a perceived measure of current job satisfaction and employee confidence.	NS, rejected (expected)

NS denotes not statistically significant at the 0.05 level for a two-tailed test, MS denotes marginally statistical significant at the 0.05 level for a two-tailed test, S denotes significant at the 0.05 level for a two-tailed test, HS denotes highly significant at the 0.01 level for a two-tailed test.

mation available for consumers and businesses has had a huge influence on business practices. As customers are web-empowered, comparison shopping goes beyond mere pricing structures. When new innovations are found or patent filed for, the information is readily available for almost anyone who wants it. Hence, providing almost limitless access to data and information that has made a huge impact on how quickly companies now need to react and IT-related technologies are at the core of this changing marketplace dynamic on online actions. Online trading websites must couple their technology initiatives with sound CRM-base strategies that are designed to alleviate fears of identity theft through proper protection of personal and financial information through related software to provide not only a direct contact between the organization and its customers, but also present an opportunity for innovation in both the delivery and selling of these products and services online.

ACKNOWLEDGMENT

I wish to thank most heartedly for the valuable contributions by the reviewers for their input into the final paper. Peer reviewing and editing are commonly tedious and thankless tasks.

REFERENCES

Adams, D. A., Nelson, R. R., & Todd, P. A. (1992). Perceived usefulness, ease of use, and usage of information technology: a replication. *Management Information Systems Quarterly, 16*(2), 227–247. doi:10.2307/249577

Anton, J., & Petouhoff, N. (2002). *Customer Relations Management: the Bottom Line to Optimizing Your ROI*. Upper Saddle River, NJ: Prentice Hall.

Armes, D. (2006). Online auctions prove their staying power. *Strategic Direction, 22*(7), 6–7. doi:10.1108/02580540610669008

2007 *Attorney General Cuomo cracks down on Internet auction fraud* (p. 4). New York: Beacon.

Ba, S., & Pavlou, P. A. (2002). Evidence of the effect of trust building technology in electronic markets: price premiums and buyer behavior. *Management Information Systems Quarterly, 26*(3), 243–268. doi:10.2307/4132332

Bishop, C. M. (1995). *Neural Networks for Pattern Recognition*. Oxford, UK: Oxford University Press.

Black, G. (2005). *Socio-economic determinates of participation in on-line auctions*. Retrieved from http://reddog.rmu.edu:2079/pqdweb?index=32 &did=994410521&SrchMode=1&sid=1&Fmt= 6&VInst=PROD&VType=PQD&RQT=309&V Name=PQD&TS=1194354264&clientId=2138

Bland, E., & Barrett, R. T. (2006). A measure of the factors impacting the effectiveness and efficiency of eBay in the supply chain of online firms. *The Costal Business Journal, 18*(2), 1–15.

Bolton, G. E., Katok, E., & Ockenfels, A. (2004). Trust among Internet traders: a behavioral economics approach. *Analyse & Kritik, 26*(1), 185–202.

Boyd, J. (2002). In community we trust: online security communication at eBay. *Journal of Computer-Mediated Communication, 7*(3).

Bruner, G. C. II, & Kumar, A. (2005). Explaining consumer acceptance of handheld internet devices. *Journal of Business Research, 58*(5), 553–558. doi:10.1016/j.jbusres.2003.08.002

Burton-Jones, A., & Hubona, G. S. (2005). Individual differences and usage behavior: Revisiting a technology acceptance model assumption. *The Data Base for Advances in Information Systems*, *36*(2), 58–77. doi:10.1145/1066149.1066155

Chau, P. Y. K. (1996). An empirical assessment of a modified technology acceptance model. *Journal of Management Information Systems*, *13*(2), 185–204.

Colvin, G. (1997). The changing art of becoming unbeatable. *Fortune*, *136*(10), 299–300.

Cumming, S. (1993). Neural networks for monitoring of engine condition data. *Neural Computing & Applications*, *1*(1), 96–102. doi:10.1007/BF01411378

Dholakia, U. M. (2004). The usefulness of bidders' reputation ratings to sellers in online auctions. *Journal of Interactive Marketing*, *19*(1), 31–40. doi:10.1002/dir.20029

Dholakia, U. M., & Simonson, I. (2005). The effect of explicit reference points on consumer choice and online bidding behavior. *Marketing Science*, *24*(2), 206–217. doi:10.1287/mksc.1040.0099

eBay's bid to win back buyers. (2007). *BusinessWeek*. Retrieved from http://www.businessweek.com/print/technology/content/sep2007/tc20070917_75070.htm

Emiliani, M. L. (2000). Business-to-business online auctions: key issues for purchasing process improvement. *Supply Chain Management*, *5*(4), 176–193. doi:10.1108/13598540010347299

Gaylord, C. (2007). Why we do what we do on eBay. *The Christian Science Monitor*, pp. 13-14. Retrieved from http://www.csmonitor.com/2007/0716/p13s02-wmgn.html

Great tools to help eBay sellers; expert recommends five tools to determine what items to sell on eBay. (2007). *PS Newswire*. Retrieved from http://reddog.rmu.edu:2079/pqdweb?index=1&did=1195547291&SrchMode=1&sid=6&Fmt=3&VInst=PROD&VType=PQD&RQT=309&VName=PQD&TS=1193760199&clientId=2138

Hu, G., Wang, L., Fetch, S., & Bidanda, B. (2008). A multi-objective model for project portfolio selection to implement lean and Six Sigma concepts. *International Journal of Production Research*, *46*(23), 6611–6648. doi:10.1080/00207540802230363

Huang, X., Radkowski, P., & Roman, P. (2007). Computer crimes. *The American Criminal Law Review*, *44*(2), 285–335.

Jain, V., Benyoucef, L., & Deshmukh, S. G. (2008). What's the buzz about moving from 'lean' to 'agile' integrated supply chains? A fuzzy intelligent agent-based approach. *International Journal of Production Research*, *46*(23), 6649–6678. doi:10.1080/00207540802230462

Kennedy, F. A., & Widener, S. K. (2008). A control framework: insights from evidence on lean accounting. *Management Accounting Research*, *19*(4), 301–319. doi:10.1016/j.mar.2008.01.001

Lansing, P., & Hubbard, J. (2002). Online auctions: the need for alternative dispute resolution. *American Business Review*, *20*(1), 108–115.

Li, H., Ward, R., & Zhang, H. (2007). Risk, convenience, cost and online payment choice: a study of eBay transactions. *Commerce Center od DuPree College of Management*, *8*(4), 1-36.

Lin, L., & Daim, T. U. (2005). Platform strategy framework for internet-based service development: case of eBay. *International Journal of Services Technology and Management, 11*(4), 334–354. doi:10.1504/IJSTM.2009.024565

McPherson, K. (2007). Using eBay as a collection development tool. *Teacher Librarian, 34*(5), 71–73.

Melnik, M. (2005). *Seller reputation, information signals, and prices for heterogeneous coins on eBay.* Retrieved from http://reddog.rmu.edu:2079/pqdweb?index=34&did=911359041&SrchMode=1&sid=2&Fmt=3&VInst=PROD&VType=PQD&RQT=309&VName=PQD&TS=1193075203&clientId=2138

Melnik, M. I., & Alm, J. (2005). Seller reputation, information signals, and prices for heterogeneous coins on eBay. *Southern Economic Journal, 72*(2), 305–315. doi:10.2307/20062113

Novak, T. P., Hoffman, D. L., & Yung, Y. F. (2000). Measuring the customer experience in on-line environment: a structural modeling approach. *Marketing Science, 19*(1), 22–42. doi:10.1287/mksc.19.1.22.15184

Oja, E. (1989). Neural networks, principal components, and subspaces. *International Journal of Neural Systems, 1*(1), 61–68. doi:10.1142/S0129065789000475

Pathak, J. (2003). Assurance and e-auctions: are the existing business models still relevant? *Managerial Auditing Journal, 18*(4), 292–294. doi:10.1108/02686900310474307

Potter, J. A., & Smith, A. D. (2010). Performance appraisals and the strategic development of the professional intellect within non-profits. *International Journal of Management in Education, 3*(2), 188–203. doi:10.1504/IJMIE.2009.025275

Prasad, N., Bryan, D., & Reeves, D. (2007). Pennies from eBay: the determinants of price in online auctions. *The Journal of Industrial Economics, 25*(2), 223–233.

Roman, S. (2007). The ethics of online retailing: a scale development and validation from the consumers' perspective. *Journal of Business Ethics, 72*(2), 131–148. doi:10.1007/s10551-006-9161-y

Scherrer-Rathje, M., Boyle, T. A., & Deflorin, P. (2009). Lean, take two! Reflections from the second attempt at lean implementation. *Business Horizons, 52*(1), 79–85. doi:10.1016/j.bushor.2008.08.004

Shah, R., Chandrasekaran, A., & Linderman, K. (2008). In pursuit of implementation patterns: the context of Lean and Six Sigma. *International Journal of Production Research, 46*(23), 6679–6698. doi:10.1080/00207540802230504

Smith, A. A., Synowka, D. P., & Smith, A. D. (2010). Exploring fantasy sports and its fan base from a CRM perspective. *International Journal of Business Innovation and Research, 4*(1-2), 103–142. doi:10.1504/IJBIR.2010.029543

Smith, A. D. (2002). Loyalty and e-marketing issues: customer retention on the Web. *Quarterly Journal of E-commerce, 3*(2), 149–161.

Smith, A. D. (2005). Accountability in EDI systems to prevent employee fraud. *Information Systems Management, 22*(2), 30–38. doi:10.1201/1078/45099.22.2.20050301/87275.4

Smith, A. D. (2006). Supply chain management using electronic reverse auction: a multi-firm case study. *International Journal of Services and Standards, 2*(2), 176–189. doi:10.1504/IJSS.2006.008731

Smith, A. D. (2009a). The impact of e-procurement systems on customer relationship management: a multiple case study. *International Journal of Procurement Management*, 2(3), 314–338. doi:10.1504/IJPM.2009.024814

Smith, A. D. (2009b). Leveraging concepts of knowledge management with total quality management: case studies in the service sector. *International Journal of Logistics Systems and Supply Management*, 5(6), 631–653. doi:10.1504/ IJLSM.2009.024795

Smith, A. D. (2010). Retail-based loyalty card programs and CRM concepts: an empirical study. *International Journal of Innovation and Learning*, 7(3), 303–330. doi:10.1504/IJIL.2010.031949

Smith, A. D., & Lias, A. R. (2005). Identity theft and e-fraud as critical CRM concerns. *International Journal of Enterprise Information Systems*, 1(2), 17–36. doi:10.4018/jeis.2005040102

Smith, A. D., & Potter, J. A. (2010). Loyalty card programs, customer relationships, and information technology: an exploratory approach. *International Journal of Business Innovation and Research*, 4(1-2), 65–92. doi:10.1504/IJBIR.2010.029541

Snijders, C., & Zijdeman, R. (2004). Reputation and Internet auctions: eBay and beyond. *Analyse & Kritik*, 26(1), 158–184.

Sprovieri, J. (2008). A Modest Increase. *Assembly*, 51(13), 22–41.

Summers, G. J., & Scherpereel, C. M. (2008). Decision making in product development: are you outside-in or inside-out? *Management Decision*, 46(9), 1299–1314. doi:10.1108/00251740810911957

Vinodh, S., Sundararaj, G., Devadasan, S. R., & Maharaja, R. (2008). DESSAC: a decision support system for quantifying and analyzing agility. *International Journal of Production Research*, 46(23), 6759–6678. doi:10.1080/00207540802230439

Chapter 2
Antecedents of Security Pillars in E-Commerce Applications

Amin Shaqrah
Alzaytoonah University of Jordan, Jordan

ABSTRACT

This paper investigates the relationship between internet security and e-business competence at banking and exchange firms in Jordan. The proposed conceptual model examines the antecedents and consequences of e-business competence and tests its empirical validity. The sample of 152 banking and exchange firms tests the posited structural equation model. The results consistently support the validity of the proposed conceptual model, the results also found that organizations realize the importance of e- business and are willing to proceed further with e-business. Beyond concerns about internet security, their awareness of security hazards and internet performance is minimal. The author concludes that the public awareness of ICT in general is low. In light of the data collected, the author makes recommendations for the interested authorities to improve e-business in Jordan.

INTRODUCTION

Several studies suggested that the internet has become a popular delivery platform for electronic business (Sheshunoff, 2000; Oyegoke, 1999; Birch, 1999; Evans & Wurster, 1997). Electronic business offered an easy access to their accounts 24 hours per day, seven days a week. Regardless of this convenience, adoption rates of electronic business in most developed countries have been very low. Therefore, of interest to ascertain and understand the factors that drive using e-business applications. Jordan, over a long historical period, is a country of commerce and its people are famous for their trading and business activities. When the internet project entered Jordan, the Jor-

DOI: 10.4018/978-1-4666-2026-1.ch002

danian business organizations faced challenging competition to have a pronounced presence on the web. The aims behind this growing attendance are commercial and for reducing communication costs. Most of the companies in Jordan started to build their own websites on the web and started using them to communicate with both current and potential customers.

Saeed et al. (2005) illustrated that firms with high electronic commerce competence exhibit superior performance and that customer value generated through Web site functionality partially mediates this relationship. Additionally, firms have now started to realize the danger that comes from using this modern method of business, which is the difficulty of having a secure business. Laudon and Traver (2008) explained that the e-commerce environment holds threats for both consumers and merchants; therefore, unsecure operations can cause a firm to lose successful business. There are misconceptions must be overcome before it can be deemed suitable for electronic commerce. A few of the commonly expressed concerns include reliability, security, scalability, ease of use and payment (Ambrose & Johnson, 1998). Hence, security is one barrier but there is the real underlying factor.

HISTORICAL BACKGROUND

The internet as an information and entertainment technology has affected on education, government, publishing, the retail industry, banking, broadcast services, and health care delivery. Therefore, the scope of internet applications and forces is to deliver the internet resource to business utility. Thus, the core indicators on accept and usage of internet by households and individuals should be used in parallel with flourish e-business activities as a starting point of Jordan that planning to implement the information society. In Jordan,

the ICT sector has grown rapidly during the last years and enormous investments recently have made. Jordanian governments, ICT companies are also making efforts to involve more people in the adoption of their products and services. Current Jordanian stakeholders such as the government, internet Service Providers (ISPs), are making a lot of efforts and resources to speed up the adoption of e-commerce applications.

In general, most Jordanian business companies are subscribers to the internet service but the uses of the internet for business purposes are limited to one aspect of internet interaction facilities i.e., communication. Active internet services in the business affairs of Jordanian banks and exchange companies has not reached the necessary level at which the Jordanian business sector can benefit from participating in e-commerce activities. Although the internet can also be a source of significant dangers and risks, most Jordanian business users today feel they will suffer a greater loss by not connecting to the internet than they will face with security issues. The advances in internet technology should go along the same lines as security. The banks in Jordan are covering behind other geographical regions in the areas of technological interaction. Table 1 shows the increased number of subscribers along the eight years.

In January 2008, the Government completed the sale of its Jordan Telecom shares. Such that 51% of company shares became own by France Telecom, and the rest of the shares distributed between the Social Security Corporation, the Nor Financial Investment Company (Nor), the armed forces and security agencies, leaving 7% available for exchange in Amman Stock Exchange market. In June 2008, telecommunication regularly commission "TRC" announced its intention to introduce 3G services in Jordan. Mid August 2009: TRC granted a third generation (3G) license to Orange Mobile Company.

Table 1. Telecom market (Adapted from TRC site)

Number of Subscribers: (000)	2001	2002	2003	2004	2005	2006	2007	2008
Fixed Phone	660	674	623	638	628	614	559	519
Mobile & Trunking	866	1200	1325	1624	3138	4343	4772	5,314
Internet (Subscribers)	66	62	92	111	197	206	228	229
Internet (Users)	238	279	399	537	720	770	1,163	1,500
Penetration Rate per 100 inhabitants (%)	2001	2002	2003	2004	2005	2006	2007	2008
Fixed Phone	13.1	13.4	11.3	11.9	11.6	11	10	8.9
Mobile & Trunking	16.7	22.9	24.2	30.4	57	78	83.3	91
Internet (Subscribers)	1.32	1.16	1.67	2.07	3.6	3.7	4	4
Internet (Users)	4.8	5.5	7.7	10	13.2	13.7	20	26
Volume of Investments: (Million JD)	2001	2002	2003	2004	2005	2006	2007	2008
Fixed Phone	90.1	38.2	11.5	10	12.3	12.7	12.2	23
Mobile & Trunking	89.2	93.3	91.9	100.3	137	139	92.5	65
Internet	5.5	3.5	1.5	0.7	5.6	2.3	11.1	22
Other Services	0.1	2.6	1.1	0.4	0.4	1.5	0.5	5
Total	184.9	137.6	106.0	111.4	155.3	155.4	116.3	115.0
Number of Employees:	2001	2002	2003	2004	2005	2006	2007	2008
Fixed Phone	4792	4548	3663	3048	2701	2432	2303	2212
Mobile & Trunking	1044	1168	1249	1641	2124	2251	2283	2079
Internet	457	408	294	353	450	415	498	644
Telephone Prepaid Calling Service	25	53	45	52	50	294	135	345
Total	6318	6177	5251	5094	5325	5392	5219	5280
Demography, Economy:	2001	2002	2003	2004	2005	2006	2007	2008
Population (000)	4,978	5,098	5,230	5,350	5,473	5,600	5,723	5,849
Households (000)	823	874	897	946	980	1037	1060	1104
Gross Domestic Product (GDP,Million JD) (Current Price)	6364	6794	7229	8081	9012	10109	11225	15058

LITERATURE REVIEW

The use of the internet in business organizations has continuously increased because the facilities that the internet provides push many organizations to replace some of their traditional communications and methods for conducting business methods (Laudon & Traver, 2008). For example, many Jordanian organizations now communicate with their customers using internet facilities such as e-mail services, communities, forum etc. In addition, the internet and web technology turned into the channel for publishing organizations websites whereas organizations use it for promotion and offering online services and participating in e-commerce, including all operations concerning the selling of products and services over the internet. Moreover, the internet enables organizations to deliver an online catalogue and messages to a huge number of target consumers. A few steps should consider to use the internet or to establish online business: First, business organizations must recognize how it will use the internet. Second, they should be able to assess the risks involved. Third, perform a cost/benefit analysis to determine if the benefits prevail over the potential costs. Fourth, know very well the capabilities of their auditor and systems administrator in controlling online change. Fifth, appropriated budget for security purposes. Sixth, management must view its computer system as it would any other company asset.

Booker (2000) noted that with appropriate caution, organizations should be able to use the internet full potential. Jordanian organizations should make sure they are involved in the process because their uses of the internet are more sensitive and in the short-term can cause bottom line loss. It is what marketers are most concerned about when it comes to protecting online property rights; the logo of any e-business will be a vulnerable target too and many may be 'sniffed', especially those successful online business websites. If they fail to sniff, they will try to cause trouble for the owner and users of these sites. More specifically, the company's response time following a security related event is an indication of the organizational readiness towards external threats. Furthermore, when multiple sites suffer synchronously from advanced attacks, the response and recover time is a very important differentiator.

Cross (2001) stated website host must also operate servers that can support the technology with which a website developed. Website host should have its own firewalls and other security technologies in place to protect hosted websites and customers' data from hackers and viruses. According to Zolait et al. (2009), internet security applies to organizations that conduct online business operations over the internet just like a national border. Ahmed et al. (2006) summarized three factors contributing to the growth of internet commerce. First, is the constant decline in the prices of hardware and software? Second, is the expansion of different platforms of internet browsers? Third, is the commercialization of the web itself with media-rich content and electronic commerce? Information sent via computer might route through many different systems before reaching their destination (Forcht & Richard, 1995). Each different system introduces unwanted individuals

who can access data; therefore, security is vital to protect organizations from unwanted damage, copying, or eavesdropping (Zolait et al., 2009). Consequently, gaining access to information on a website or eavesdropping on data, which is supposed to be restricted, can lead to misrepresentation of the organization and loss of information and open the door of vulnerability to many threats. Therefore, each organization is required to secure the content of its website.

The application of security policy must place in easy-to-reach locations, without requiring the user to consume considerable time to track down the links to these statements. Although the procedures and security mechanisms of the systems must be transparent in order not to discomfort the legitimate user, from a trust perspective the presence of the security mechanisms is essential. For example, the existence of a password policy could success with a respective web page educating the user about the password rules (e.g. minimum number of characters, denial of use of names, etc.).

SECURITY HAZARD

There are two types of security mechanisms for conducting online business. First, apply physical security mechanism to minimize the hazard. The second type are the intangible protective security measures of the system acting as the second line of defense, which are a way to enhance the capability of companies' security, enabling them to conduct a successful business over the internet. For example, firewalls with specialized software are placed between the organization LAN or WAN and the internet, preventing unauthorized access to proprietary information stored on the intranet (Jessup & Valacich, 2008). Email is a security hazard and many bad things can happen to an individual's computer by simply previewing the message in a preview window without even opening it (Zolait et al., 2009). Although there are advances in terms of securing the networks against hackers, there are also advances developing in break-in and hacking tools too. It is very simple sometimes to break into other peoples and company's e-mails or sites and know everything available about them (Zolait et al., 2009).

Hackers can use very simple methods to reach you; some of these methods do not require people experienced in programming. Hackers can use ready-made software produced by experts to enable them to reach organization's information by breaking into organization e-mail, company account, and web site. This ready-made software is widespread on the market, for example, spy log software and net pass. There is a lot that organizations should do to strengthen the security requirements to face the anticipated threat that cause company resources. They should think in advance, what will happen if someone gains access to any aspect of the company's resources (Garfinkel, 1997). According to Totty (2001), "companies must stay one-step ahead of the hackers". Users of the organization online system should train to understand what hackers do and how they do it; because that is the only way, they can protect themselves and know their enemy (Nelson, 2000). Aldridge (1997) recommended setting some preventive conditions to enforce. Furthermore, Savage (2000) pointed that the learning from the security crises solutions of others. In addition, Totty (2001) noted that organizations must use authentication software. Organizations must find certifying tools to measure the level of security (Verton, 2000), make sure that they have the skills and time to keep the round-the-clock vigils the software requires (Messmer, 2000), and establish an e-mail policy and enforce members to use it (Parker, 1999).

Assuring the physical security of a website is similar to assuring the physical security of any other computer at any location (Zolait et al., 2009). Restricting physical access to the machine is a preventative strategy that plays a useful role in securing the sensitive information from internal attackers. Business organizations should be eager

to understanding the elements of internet security. Totty (2001) and Jessup and Valacich (2008) classified four strategies necessary to prevent online security breaches in the organization which are First, Authentication; Second, Encryption; Third, Integrity; Fourth, Firewalls. Internet security is a combination of partial components that combine to form a strong internet security for doing business online. Lane (1998) concluded that internet security for business as a group effort to securing the whole set of related contributing parties, which are security of privacy, system privacy, user privacy, commerce transaction privacy and authentication of data. Although there are, risks associated with the use of the internet as the enabling technology for doing business, most of them can mitigate with an organized and systematic security investment, including both technology and organization. Since these risks depend on the security awareness and responsibility of the underlying e-business organization, it follows that trust should refer to the organization rather the internet itself.

PROTECTION MEASURES

Protection measures implemented to protect organizations from different security attacks. To guarantee the security requirements of a given organization, it is essential to be able to evaluate the current security demands of an organization as well as the measures taken to achieve such requirements. Security weaknesses cause a negative impact on organizations such as financial loss, reputations, and loss of customer confidence (Kumar, 2008). Protection measures used in banking and exchange services to protect information security objectives. These measures will assist an evaluator to measure the security level. For example, the security level is high when an organization implements the most proper, updated measures, policies, and countermeasures to protect its security objectives. Organizations are required to take appropriate protection measures based on their requirements. Protection measures can group into three major groups: physical, personal, and network security measures. Each group employs several means for security protection. Within each group, security measures can classify into measures aimed at securing the confidentiality, integrity, and availability of the data and system. Banks, on the other hand, have high demand for data confidentiality.

Hence, the measures required to protect confidentiality are essential for banks. In essence, an organization may have different security requirements for information security objectives. Similarly, an organization may have different security requirements at different times. Some protective options available today are very easy and inexpensive, while others are more complicated and expensive. One inexpensive option is awareness; simply being more aware of the dangers out there and how to avoid them. More expensive and complicated measures include choosing more secure operating systems, imposing access restrictions and enforcing authentication procedures (Zolait et al., 2009). Information systems assets are tangible and intangible. Assets vary from one organization to another. Protecting information systems from breaches and preventing information theft done by defining the information systems assets. Each organization's information assets evaluated to determine their information security.

Dhillon (2006) mentioned that the purpose of defining and characterizing the organization's assets allows for better determination behind the threat. Documentation of the assets will be beneficial to an organization because it will know what to secure, and it will ensure updates of assets in the case of changes (Schou & Shoemaker, 2006). Security breaches appear due to the lack of documenting and characterizing the information system assets within organizations. According to Ciampa (2005), an organization not only protects its information by classifying its assets in order to protect them from any threat caused by crackers and hackers, but it also identifies its vulnerabilities. Automated measurements systems cannot measure the subjective elements. However, the

objective elements measured successfully with the proper automated tools. When working from policy toward automated checks, a key intermediate deliverable is the platform specific checklist. Sometimes these documents, often called 'security cookbooks' are already prepared and in use by systems administrators.

INTERNET PERFORMANCE

Drennan and McColl-Kennedy (2003) summarized that the internet has affected significantly in the services sector such as banks, insurance providers, and government organizations. Ahmed et al. (2006) identified some key challenges to do business over the internet in Arab countries for Saudi's organizations are the continuing relying on face-to-face contact principles, information overload problems, expensive charges, technical support and expertise, management commitment and understanding the potential role of information technology (IT), and older people were more reluctant to use IT. Drennan and McColl-Kennedy (2003) concluded that organizations eager to offer specialized services and develop an innovative customer-focused strategy employing the new technologies to increase customer loyalty.

Web page download delay is a major factor affecting the performance of a site and ultimately a sites success can depend on how quickly a user can navigate its pages (Saiedian & Naeem, 2001). It is important for banking and exchange services to make every effort to ensure their sites are of a high quality with download times kept to a minimum to prevent surfers moving on elsewhere. This will do two things, compress it in size and ensure its colors are web safe (can be displayed properly). Compressing an image gets rid of redundant data from the image. For example, if a company is selling products online and they have not compressed their images, the extra download time required can distance a user. There needs to be a tradeoff between quality and download time if the company is to succeed.

TRUST

Mayer et al. (1995) defined trust as "the willingness of a party to be vulnerable to the actions of another party." Trust based on the expectation performs a particular action important to the trust or, irrespective of the ability to monitor or control that other party. Internet security generally relied on users' mutual respect and honor, as well as their knowledge of conduct considered appropriate on the network. Trust based on the potential use of the technology to increase online business. Trust increases the probability of a trading partner's willingness to expand the amount of information sharing through EDI and explore new mutually beneficial arrangements (Hart & Saunders, 1997). Trust, especially among the banking and exchanges services in electronic commerce reinforces the prospect of continuity in a relationship and a commitment to extend an inter-organizational relationship. It implies that the online business is dependable and follows their promises, thus developing high levels of cooperation that will in turn reinforce trust (Cummings & Bromiley, 1996).

Both reliability and security are impaired when inconsistencies between words and actions among the trading partners increase. This decreases trust due to the lack of consistent and reliable behavior. Thus, trust only occurs when the trading partners assured of others willingness and ability to deliver on their obligations. Trust is vital not only in the pre-transaction and transaction phase (that is advertising, providing information about the product, ordering, purchasing, paying, and delivering the product), but also in the post-transaction phase in the form of warranties and refunds. internet security is depend on trust not only in the EC systems that provide efficient services and guarantee delivery of the messages, but also more importantly, that the message in actual fact came from an authorized person thus being authentic, having integrity, confidentiality and unable of being repudiated. Hence, high levels of trust will likely result in high levels of security.

CIA TRIAD

To protecting banking online business, an information security professional must establish and maintain a strict security defense that ensures three requirements: The information keep confidential, integrity of the information is high, and the information is available when needed for authorized users. Bishop (2002) noted that confidentiality related to privacy, which means the sender, and its respective receiver should only share information, but unfortunately, TCP/IP has its own deficiencies. It is not able to guarantee data confidentiality while it flows in the system. This can easily lead us to logins, passwords deviation during a telnet session, for instance, data interception during a home-banking, commercial or even a personal transaction may result in serious hazards, and this kind of interference observed easily in e-mail operations, Web commercial transactions, and many other important data exchange. Such banking systems use long sequences of characters and complex algorithms to encode and decode information exchanged between computers with the appropriate application installed.

Integrity related to the verification performed by the internet security system against any kind of data loss, modification, and/or damage, which caused by intentional or casual reasons, such as prejudicial actions of hackers or normal electrical interference during data transference. Thus, the internet security system expected to assure that data received exactly the same way. Regardless of the original cause of losing data integrity, this loss will certainly be catastrophic in many ways. According to Ackermann (2001) "Data integrity may be affected without being noticed during storage or transmission, i.e. data may be altered due to inadequate access controls while located in one system, being then sent without any problem detection to the other end of the connection." Another fact considered is the possibility of intercepted during its transference, putting its integrity and/or confidentiality in doubt. Such tools detect non-authorized and/or unexpected data modification on those specific parts of the system.

Authenticity verification is directly related to the procedures the security system performs in order to establish how and where the data package was created, thus trying to assure the message or data received was really originated where it says it is coming from and sent by the one mentioned on its label (Brown,1999). The organization and coordination of operations in a net connection ruled by protocols - or a group of them, which may unfortunately add some problems as far as system security, is concerned. The most common group of protocols used in internet transactions is the TCP/IP. Brown (1999) elaborated that some security techniques, such as SSL, which stands for Secure Sockets Layer, include as part of their normal routines, procedures that try to provide some enhanced protection to lower layers of TCP/IP. Netscape SSL tries to protect all TCP/IP stack and provides a security structure in which application protocols may be executed safely. Actually, SSL gathers two protocols together. One specifically designed for real data transmission registry and other dedicated to handshake tasks, which supervises the duties accomplished, including authenticity and confidentiality.

METHODOLOGY

The objective of the study is First, to be familiar with attraction factors that will improve the use of the internet for business, the benefit from this technology and avoidance of its serious problems. Second, is to categorize the main obstacle to the acceptance of e-business that hinder Jordanian business organizations "banking sectors and exchange services" from conducting online business activities, as well as the challenges facing the use of e-business by those organizations surveyed. Third, to investigate the role of security in the adoption of online business -how secure is the internet for the investigated organizations? In

other words, how does the business community consider the security of the internet in their work over the internet? How do Jordanian organizations "banking sectors and exchange services" treat the security aspect when they work online?

The current study uses the quantitative approach whereby data collection attained by a survey questionnaire. In addition, individual interviews with the IT department officers of five banks' head offices, ISP "Jordan telecom, Tedata, Mada", and the related public sector Telecommunications Regularly Commission "TRC" were are one of the methods used to collect data. The focal population of the present study are "IT units and computer divisions" of the Arab bank, Cairo Amman bank, Housing bank, Islamic bank, Commercial bank, Al-alami for exchange, Jawdat for exchange, Abu-Allaban for exchange, and Jamal for exchange. The questionnaire items are mainly adapted from a review of previous literature. Pilot test performed and the feedback used in finalizing the survey format. The questionnaire format selected covered three parts -care of the basic demographic information, investigate the willingness/usefulness to do business over the internet and probe the expected problem of conducting online business by selected Jordanian organizations. There were 200 questionnaire forms self-administrated and distributed to the purposive sample. The responses received were 152 usable and completed forms from business organizations. IT professionals and executive managers who considered the decisions makers in these IT departments of both banks and trading organization interviewed.

DATA ANALYSIS

Table 2 displays the percentages of internet usages in five business activities performed by surveyed organization. The companies that use internet facilities totally for their internal business affairs represent only 6.0%, while, 35% of the surveyed

Table 2. Internet usage in business activities

Usage	0%	10%	25%	50%	75%	100%
Activity	%	%	%	%	%	%
Internal Business	17.9	35	20.5	12.8	7.7	6
External Business	17.6	24.4	25.2	9.2	11.8	11.8
Market-ing	56.8	33.2	19.5	10.2	10.2	2.5
Job achieve-ment	35.7	8.7	3.5	6.1	6.1	40
Online Activity	72.5	6	23.2	4.2	9	2.5

organizations agree that the internet assists them to do 10% of their organization's internal daily business. About 52% of surveyed agree on the range rate, from 10% to 25%, of their organization's external daily business affairs assisted by the internet. For marketing activity, 56.8% of the respondents agree that they do benefit 10% from using internet for marketing activities. While 33.2% of the surveyed organizations agree that, there is no use for the internet to support marketing activities. For assistance in online activities, 72.5% of the surveyed organizations agree that they have no use for the internet to do online business activities, while 23.2% of them agree that they have benefited 25% from using the internet to do online business. Online business inclination through the individual interviews with the Jordanian executives and their executives' researchers gained a very positive feeling concerning how interested they are in doing e-business and how willing they are to accept and use the new concept.

MAIN OBSTACLES OF E-BUSINESS ADOPTION

The acceptance of online business in Jordanian society needs the cooperation of all related parties to take it to a level where all participants are satisfied with internet performance. Therefore, Table

3 illustrates some obstacles to the acceptance of e-business should be considered to find suitable solutions.

There are 50.6% of the surveyed organizations didn't use the web for business purposes because of the lack of expertise, while 18.5% of the surveyed organizations didn't use the web for business purposes because it is costly. 55.4% of the surveyed organizations did not use the web for business because infrastructure is not available. 66.5% of the surveyed organizations did not use the web for business because organizations believe it is unsafe technology. 85.0% of them did not use the web for business because government support for online business is not available. And 60.0% of the surveyed organizations didn't use the web for business because they think that the internet is not a trustworthy medium to do online business, while 21.0% of them think that undesired information on the internet minimizes the use of the internet. 82.5% of the organizations think the absence of cyber law (law on the internet) is minimizing the use of the internet further. The undesirable beliefs and thought that the internet can bring are minimizing the use of the internet for business represented by 33.0% of the surveyed organizations. 35.4% of them think that non-literate people are minimizing the use of the internet further.

Security is one of the hindering problems that prevent the further adoption of e-business even in the advanced countries and sometimes leads to a stop in any further online activities. The following low ratio for security tools use proves that security is a common reason preventing the adoption of e-business (see Table 4).

Results displayed in Table 4 revealed that only 32.5% of the surveyed organizations use a firewall as a security tool, and only 25.3% of them use encryption technology. In addition, 72.0% of surveyed organizations do not use a firewall and 50.8% of them do not use encryption technology to enhance the security of data and systems. In addition, that 37.7% of the surveyed organizations

Table 3. Obstacles of e-business adoption

Factors	Major concern
	%
Expertise	50.6
Cost	18.5
Infrastructure	55.4
Security	66.5
Government support	85.0
Not a trustworthy tool	60.0
Fraudulent	21.0
Lack of cyber law	82.5
Undesired believed (Cyber terrorism)	33.0
Internet illiteracy	35.4

rely on proxy technology to scrutinize incoming and receiving e-mails, while 66.2% of them do not use proxy. The table showed that 70.0% of the surveyed organizations do not use any sort of filtering for securitizing incoming and receiving e-mails, while 17.0% of them are using filtering to enhance the security of data and systems.

ASSESSING THE MEASUREMENT MODEL

A confirmatory factor analysis (CFA) using EQS conducted to test the measurement model. The overall goodness-of-fit of the measure-

Table 4. Security methods activated by organization

Security Technology	Technology Activated	Technology Not Activated
	%	%
Firewall	32.5	72.0
Encryption	25.3	50.8
Proxy server	37.7	66.2
Filtering	17.0	70.0

ment model examined using the following eight common model fit measures: X^2/DF ratio, GFI, AGFI, NFI, NNFI, CFI, RMSR, and RMSEA. The measurement model in the CFA revised by removing items, one at a time had large standardized residuals and/or weak correlations with other items. After removing items, as summarized in Table 1, the measurement model exhibited an overall good model fit, with the data collected from the respondents by meeting the acceptance levels commonly suggested by previous research. The exception was for the GFI level. GFI at 0.861 was slightly below but closer to the recommended level 0.90. Although the GFI level could improve by dropping additional items, it decided to stop the dropping procedure by considering the content of the measurement. Recognizing the good model fit for the measurement model, further analysis was conducted to assess the psychometric properties of the scales; that is, for the construct validity of the research instruments. The construct validity has two important dimensions: convergent validity and discriminant validity (Table 5).

The convergent validity assessed by three measures, as shown in Table 6: factor loading, composite construct reliability, and average variance extracted (Fornell & Larcker, 1981). In determining, the appropriate minimum factor loadings required for the inclusion of an item within a construct, factor loadings greater than 0.50 considered highly significant (Hair et. al. 1998). A stricter recommendation of factor loading greater than 0.70 was also proposed (Fornell & Larcker, 1981). All of the factor loadings of the items in the measurement model were greater than 0.60, with most of them above 0.80. Each item loaded significantly ($p<0.01$ in all cases) on its underlying construct. The composite construct reliabilities were also within the commonly accepted range greater than 0.70 (Gefen et al., 2000). As a stricter criterion, the guideline with a minimum of 0.80 suggested by Nunnally and Bernstein (1994) applied to determine the adequacy of the reliability coefficients obtained for each construct.

Table 5. Fit indices

Fit	Recommended		Measurement	Structural
index	value		model	model
X^2	N/A		1401.89	388.17
Df	N/A		657	221
X^2/df	<	3.00	2.133	1.756
GFI	>	0.90	0.861	0.929
AGFI	>	0.80	0.835	0.912
NFI	>	0.90	0.971	0.980
NNFI	>	0.90	0.983	0.990
CFI	>	0.90	0.985	0.991
RMSR	<	0.10	0.043	0.046
RMSEA	<	0.08	0.051	0.041

Finally, AVE measures the amount of variance captured by the construct in relation to the amount of variance due to measurement error (Fornell & Larcker, 1981). AVE was all above the recommended level of 0.50 (Hair et al., 1998) which meant that more than fifty percent of the variances observed in the items explained by their underlying constructs. Therefore, all constructs in the measurement model had adequate convergent validity.

The discriminant validity examined in two ways: comparing the inter-construct variances and average variances extracted and comparing the X^2 statistic of the original model against other models with every possible combination of two constructs. The shared variances between constructs compared with the average variance extracted of the individual constructs (Fornell & Larcker, 1981). To confirm discriminant validity, the average variance shared between the construct and its indicators should be larger than the variance shared between the construct and other constructs. As shown by comparing the inter-construct variances and average variances extracted in Table 7, all constructs share more variance with their indicators than with other constructs. Discriminant validity of the constructs was validating by combining the items between

various constructs and then re-estimating the modified model (Segars, 1997). That is, comparing the X^2 statistic of the original model with its all constructs against other models with every possible combination of two constructs conducted. Significant differences in the X^2 statistic of the original and alternative models imply high discriminant validity. As reported in Table 7, the X^2 statistic of the original model was significantly better than any possible combination of any two constructs, confirming discriminant validity. Therefore, these results revealed no violation of the criteria for the discriminant validity of the constructs in the research model. To confirm the multidimensionality for the constructs of organizational commitment and attitude toward change, a second order CFA for these constructs conducted. All of coefficients and the factor loadings of the items were greater than 0.60, with most of them above 0.80, and all the paths are significant ($p<0.01$ in all cases). In addition, the second order factor model exhibited an overall good model fit with the data collected from the respondents, by meeting the commonly recommended levels. These results confirmed the multidimensionality of the above two constructs.

ASSESSING THE STRUCTURAL MODEL

A structural equation modeling technique called Partial Least Squares (PLS) chosen for analyzing the research model (Wold, 1985). PLS is a technique that uses a combination of principal components analysis, path analysis, and regression evaluated theory and data simultaneously (Wold, 1985). The path coefficients in a PLS structural model are standardized regression coefficients, while the loadings can interpret as factor loadings. PLS is ideally suited to the early stages of theory development and testing - as is the case here - and has been used by a growing number of researchers from a variety of disciplines (e.g.

Table 6. Convergent validity test

Constructs*	Items	Factor loading	Composite reliability	AVE
SH	SH1	0.798	0.862	0.612
	SH2	0.650		
	SH3	0.786		
	SH4	0.879		
PM	PM1	0.735	0.848	0.583
	PM2	0.851		
	PM3	0.753		
	PM4	0.707		
IP	IP1	0.802	0.835	0.560
	IP2	0.775		
	IP3	0.758		
	IP4	0.649		
T	T1	0.727	0.868	0.687
	T2	0.893		
	T3	0.858		
CIA	CIA1	0.822	0.904	0.701
	CIA 2	0.864		
	CIA 3	0.822		
	CIA 4	0.840		

*SH: Security Hazard, PM: Protection Measures, IP: Internet Performance, T: Trust, CIA: Confidentiality; Integrity; Availability

Birkinshaw et al., 1995; Green et al., 1995; Higgins et al., 1992). The explanatory power of the model tested by examining the size, sign, and statistical significance of the path coefficients between constructs in the model. The predictive capacity of a PLS model can also be evaluated by examining the variance explained (i.e. R^2) in the dependent (or endogenous) constructs. The objective of a PLS analysis is to explain variance in the endogenous constructs, rather than to replicate the observed covariance matrix as is the case with covariance structure techniques (such as LISREL). One consequence of using a variance-minimization objective is the absence of overall fit t statistics for PLS models (Hulland, 1999).

The model explained 32% of the variance in the use of online business construct. Overall, the amount of variance explained by the model appeared reasonable. The exogenous variables would likely be only some of many things affecting the endogenous construct, resulting in the relatively modest R^2 value as can be seen in Figure 1. All three exogenous variables have direct effect correlate statistically significant to doing online business; security hazard (path coefficient=0.55), protection measures (path coefficient =0.61), internet performance (path coefficient =0.57), trust (path coefficient =0.72), and CIA Triad (path coefficient =0.65) .The construction of the model by induction from quantitative data may set a limit to its applicability. A more accurate verification of the model by using our qualitative data from conducted in-depth interviews is included in Figure 1. Another limitation of this model is that its data derived from one sample, and has not tested with different organization groups. While non-users and users differ in many parts, the factors

Table 7. Discriminant validity test using AVE comparison

Constructs	SH	PM	IP	T	CIA
SH	0.612				
PM	0.513	0.583			
IP	0.444	0.349	0.560		
T	0.162	0.078	0.124	0.687	
CIA	0.277	0.156	0.166	0.674	0.701

in the model may have quite different loadings for different segments.

CONCLUSION

This study provides a unique contribution to the Internet security and online business literature by substantiating several key propositions. Our study was one of the empirical evidence about the influence of security hazard, protection measures, Internet performance, Trust, and CIA triad on online business activities at banking & exchange firms in Jordan. It offers insights to practitioners on the value of internet security and reasons why firms are or are not willing to engage in online business. Our study provides an illustration of the use of structural equation modeling technique for testing the validity of conceptual models as building blocks to theory development. One of the

advantages of using SEM is inherent capability to test the measurement and structural models simultaneously which derived from the conceptual model. We found that trust and CIA triad are the most critical factor in applying online business. Since it is more convenient for banking & exchange firms to reinforce these dimensions.

Most of companies and banks are still unfamiliar with security hazard and most of them do not use firewalls to protect the information assets that they possess. On other word, protective and preventive tools of security are not widely adapted by business organization in the Jordan. Researcher concluded that there are a company affiliated with international business, to facilitate their business affairs this arranges of company is adopting computerized systems. In addition, there are companies affiliated with national business, these variety of trade companies own their computerized system, which enables them to drive the internal business. Some of them are connecting to the net and others do not feel that the internet has any importance for their business.

RECOMMENDATIONS

The work would like to make some recommendations that considered important for government authorities, interested organizations and users of Internet technology in Jordan. The purposes of

Figure 1. Testing the research model

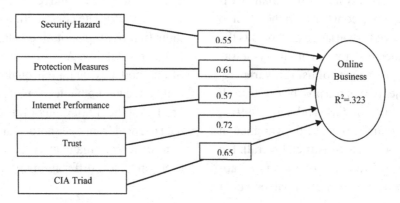

these recommendations are to make the Internet a meaningful way of doing business for companies and banks located in Jordan. The recommendations are:

- Increasing awareness by offering opportunities to businesses interested in attending seminars on the internet, e-business, and training session courses. Encourage the presence of Jordan companies to participate in community service projects intended to increase internet awareness and usefulness for improving the business.
- Reduce the cost of the telephone and internet subscription fees, taxes on the internet and e-business hardware equipment and software. Also, offer national expertise to those who can undertake to build local capacity in IT security, especially for the business sector and those demanding security on the internet and provide consultancy at a low price.
- Adopt e banking through offering some online services, adoption of digital signature and e contracting and encourage the creation of e-commerce companies.

REFERENCES

Ackermann, R., Schumacher, M., Roedig, U., & Steinmetz, R. (2001). Vulnerabilities and Security Limitations of Current IP Telephony Systems. In *Proceedings of the Conference on Communications and Multimedia Security* (pp. 53–66).

Ahmed, A., Zairi, S., & Alwabel, S. (2006). Global benchmarking for Internet and e-commerce applications. *Benchmarking International Journal, 13*(2), 68–80. doi:10.1108/14635770610644583

Aldridge, A., White, M., & Forcht, K. (1997). Considerations of doing business via the internet: Cautions to be considered. *Internet Research: Electronic Networking Applications and Policy, 7*(1), 9–15. doi:10.1108/10662249710159809

Ambrose, P., & Johnson, G. (1998). A Trust Model of Buying Behavior in Electronic Retailing, Association for Information Systems. In *Proceedings of the Americans Conference,* Baltimore, MD (pp. 263-265).

Birch, D. (1999). Mobile finance services: the Internet is not the only digital channel to consumers. *Journal of Internet Banking and Commerce, 4*(1), 20–29.

Birkinshaw, J., Morrison, A., & Hulland, J. (1995). Structural and competitive determinants of a global integration strategy. *Strategic Management Journal, 16*(8), 637–655. doi:10.1002/smj.4250160805

Bishop, M. (2002). *Computer Security: Art and Science.* Reading, MA: Addison-Wesley.

Booker, E. (2000). Protect online brand from unauthorized use. *B to B., 85*(18), 12-39.

Brown, F., Divietri, J., Diaz, G., & Fernandez, E. (1999). The Authenticator Pattern. In *Proceedings of PLoP*.

Ciampa, M. (2005). *Security+ Guide to network security fundamentals* (2nd ed.). Boston: Course Technology.

Cross, M. (2001). Set strategy before selecting a web site host. *Internet Health Care Magazine,* 42-43.

Cummings, L., & Bromiley, P. (1996). The Organizational Trust Inventory (OTI): Development and Validation . In Kramer, R. M., & Tyler, T. R. (Eds.), *Trust in Organizations: Frontiers of Theory and Research.* Thousand Oaks, CA: Sage.

Dhillon, G. (2006). *Principles of information systems security: Texts and Cases*. Hoboken, NJ: Wiley.

Drennan, J., & McColl-Kennedy, J. (2003). The relationship between internet use and perceived performance in retail and professional service firms. *Journal of Services Marketing, 17*(3), 295–311. doi:10.1108/08876040310474837

Evans, P., & Wurster, T. (1997). Strategy and the new economics of information. *Harvard Business Review, 9*(10), 71–82.

Forcht, K., & Richard, E. (1995). Security issues and concern with the internet. *Internet Research: Electronic Networking Applications and Policy of MCB, 5*(3), 23–31. doi:10.1108/10662249510104621

Fornell, C., & Larcker, D. (1981). Evaluating Structural Equation Models with Unobservable Variables and Measurement Error. *Management Science, 40*(4), 440–465.

Garfinkel, S., & Spafford, G. (1997). *Web security & commerce*. Sebastopol, CA: O'Reilly & Associates.

Gefen, D., Straub, D., & Boudreau, M. (2000). Structural Equation Modeling and Regression: Guidelines for Research Practice. *Communications of the Association for Information Systems, 4*(7), 1–70.

Green, D., Barclay, D., & Ryans, A. (1995). Entry strategy and long-term performance: conceptualization and empirical examination. *Journal of Marketing, 59*(4), 1–16. doi:10.2307/1252324

Hair, T., Anderson, R., Tatham, R., & Black, W. (1998). *Multivariate Data Analysis* (5th ed.). Upper Saddle River, NJ: Prentice Hall.

Hart, P., & Saunders, C. (1997). Power and Trust: Critical Factors in the Adoption and Use of Electronic Data Interchange. *Organization Science, 8*(1), 23–41. doi:10.1287/orsc.8.1.23

Higgins, C., Duxbury, L., & Irving, R. (1992). Work-family conflict in the dual-career family. *Organizational Behavior and Human Decision Processes, 51*(1), 51–75. doi:10.1016/0749-5978(92)90004-Q

Hulland, J. (1999). Use of partial least squares in strategic management research: a review of four recent studies. *Strategic Management Journal, 20*(2), 195–204. doi:10.1002/(SICI)1097-0266(199902)20:2<195::AID-SMJ13>3.0.CO;2-7

Jessup, L., & Valacich, J. (2008). *Information Systems Today: Managing in the Digital World*. Upper Saddle River, NJ: Pearson Education.

Kumar, R., Park, S., & Subramaniam, C. (2008). Understanding the value of countermeasures portfolios in information systems security. *Journal of Management Information Systems, 25*(1), 241–279. doi:10.2753/MIS0742-1222250210

Lane, C. (1998). Five essential steps to privacy. *PC World, 16*(9), 116–117.

Laudon, K., & Traver, C. (2008). *E-commerce: Business, Technology, and Society*. Upper Saddle River, NJ: Pearson Education.

Messmer, E. (2000). Security needs spawn services. *New World (New Orleans, La.), 17*(14), 81–100.

Nelson, M. (2000). *Hacker school teaches security*. Information Week.

Nunnally, J., & Bernstein, I. (1994). *Psychometric Theory*. New York: McGraw-Hill.

Oyegoke, A. (1999). Surfing Europe. *The Banker, 1*(2), 72–73.

Parker, C. (1999). E-mail use and abuse. *Work Study, 48*(7), 257–260. doi:10.1108/00438029910294135

Saeed, K., Grover, V., & Hwang, Y. (2005). The Relationship of E-Commerce Competence to Customer Value and Firm Performance: An Empirical Investigation. *Journal of Management Information Systems, 22*(1), 223–256.

Saiedian, M., & Naeem, M. (2001). Understanding, and reducing web delays. *IEEE Computer Journal, 34*(12), 30–37.

Savage, M. (2000). *Attacks bring new security solutions.* Computer Reseller News.

Schou, C., & Shoemaker, D. (2006). *Information assurance for the enterprise: A roadmap to information security.* New York: McGraw-Hill Irwin.

Segars, A. (1997). Assessing the Unidimensionality of Measurement: a Paradigm and Illustration within the Context of Information Systems Research. *Omega, 25*(1), 107–121. doi:10.1016/S0305-0483(96)00051-5

Sheshunoff, A. (2000). Internet banking, an update from the frontlines. *ABA Banking Journal, 92*(1), 51–55.

Totty, P. (2001). Staying One Step Ahead of the Hacker. *Credit Union Magazine, 67*(6), 39–41.

TRC. (2010).*Telecommunication Regularly Commission.* Retrieved January 5, 2010, from http://www.TRC.Jo

Verton, D. (2000). Co-op to certify tools to measure level of security. *Computerworld, 34*(49), 16.

Wold, H. (1985). Systems analysis by partial least squares . In Nijkamp, P., Leitner, L., & Wrigley, N. (Eds.), *Measuring the Unmeasurable* (pp. 221–251). Dordrecht, The Netherlands: Marinus Nijhoff.

Zoliat, A., Ibrahim, A., & Farooq, A. (2009). A Study on the Internet Security and its Implication for e-Commerce in Yemen. In *Proceedings of the Conference on Knowledge Management and Innovation in Advancing Economies* (pp. 911-922).

This work was previously published in International Journal of Business Data Communications and Networking, Volume 7, Issue 1, edited by Varadharajan Sridhar and Debashis Saha, p.p 36-51, copyright 2011 by IGI Publishing (an imprint of IGI Global)

Chapter 3
A Novel Dynamic Noise-Dependent Probabilistic Algorithm for Route Discovery in MANETs

Hussein Al-Bahadili
Petra University, Jordan

Alia Sabri
Applied Sciences Private University, Jordan

ABSTRACT

In mobile ad hoc networks (MANETs), broadcasting is widely used in route discovery and other network services. The most widely used broadcasting algorithm is simple flooding, which aggravates a high number of redundant packet retransmissions, causing contention and collisions. Proper use of dynamic probabilistic algorithm significantly reduces the number of retransmissions, which reduces the chance of contention and collisions. In current dynamic probabilistic algorithm, the retransmission probability (p_t) is formulated as a linear/non-linear function of a single variable, the number of first-hop neighbors (k). However, such algorithm is suffers in the presence of noise due to increasing packet-loss. In this paper, the authors propose a new dynamic probabilistic algorithm in which p_t is determined locally by the retransmitting nodes considering both k and the noise-level. This algorithm is referred to as the dynamic noise-dependent probabilistic (DNDP) algorithm. The performance of the DNDP algorithm is evaluated through simulations using the MANET simulator (MANSim). The simulation results show that the DNDP algorithm presents higher network reachability than the dynamic probabilistic algorithm at a reasonable increase in the number of retransmissions for a wide range of noise-level. The effects of nodes densities and nodes speeds on the performance of the DNDP algorithm are also investigated.

DOI: 10.4018/978-1-4666-2026-1.ch003

INTRODUCTION

A MANET is defined as a collection of low-power wireless mobile nodes forming a temporary network without the aid of any established infrastructure or centralized administration (Bani-Yassin et al., 2006; Scott & Yasinsac, 2004). A data packet in a MANET is forwarded to other mobile nodes within the network through a reliable and efficient route established by routing protocols. The most widely used routing protocols in MANETs are known as dynamic routing protocols (DRPs), such as the ad hoc on-demand distance vector routing (AODV) (Perkins & Royer, 2000), the dynamic source routing (DSR) (Johnson & Maltz, 1995), and the location-aided routing (LAR) (Ko & Vaidya, 2000). DRPs consist of two major phases: (i) route discovery in which a route between source and destination nodes is established for the first time, and (ii) route maintenance in which the route is maintained; and if it is broken for any reason, then the source node either finds other known route on its routing table or initiates new route discovery procedure (Royer & Toh, 1999). The cost of information exchange during route discovery is higher than the cost of point-to-point data forwarding after the route is established (Rahman et al., 2004).

Broadcasting is a fundamental communication primitive for route discovery in DRPs in MANETs. One of the earliest broadcast mechanisms proposed in the literature is simple flooding, which is also called pure or blind flooding. Although it is simple and reliable, simple flooding is costly where it costs n retransmissions in a network of n reachable nodes. Simple flooding in wireless networks results in serious redundancy, contention, and collisions; such a scenario has often been referred to as the broadcast storm problem (BSP) (Tseng et al., 2002).

To eliminate the effects of the BSP during route discovery in MANETs, a variety of flooding optimization techniques have been developed to reduce the number of retransmission for the route request (RREQ) messages. As the number of retransmissions required for broadcasting is decreased, the bandwidth is saved and contention and node power consumption are reduced, and this will improve the overall network performance. Examples of flooding optimization techniques algorithms: probabilistic (Bani-Yassin et al., 2006), LAR (Ko & Vaidya, 2000), multipoint relaying (Al-Bahadili & Jaradat, 2010; Qayyum et al., 2002), counter-based and distance-based (Tseng et al., 2002), cluster-based (Bettstetter, 2004).

In this paper, our main concern is the probabilistic flooding algorithm. In this algorithm, each intermediate node (any node on the network except the source and the destination) is assigned a certain p_t. There are two approaches that can be used to set a satisfactory p_t for intermediate nodes on the network: static and dynamic. In the former, a pre-determined p_t is set for each node on the networks, while for the later, each node locally and dynamically calculates its p_t according to k and it can be expressed as: $p_t = f(k)$, where $f(k)$ is a linear/non-linear function of k.

In reality, communication channels in MANETs are unreliable due to many types of impairments, such as: signal attenuation, free space loss, noise, atmospheric absorption, etc. In addition, in MANETs, error in reception may occur due to rapidly changing topologies that are caused by nodes movement. All of these impairments and changing topologies may cause an error in reception and are represented by a generic name, noise. The effect of noise in MANET can be simulated through introducing a probability factor that is the probability of reception (p_c), and then the effect of noise can be determined randomly by generating a random number ξ (Al-Bahadili & Jaradat, 2007). If $\xi \leq p_c$, then the packets is successfully delivered to the receiving node, otherwise, it is undelivered.

It has been demonstrated that the performance of probabilistic algorithm is severely suffered in presence of noise (Al-Bahadili & Kaabned, 2010). Due to the fact that presence of noise increases packet-loss rate in the network or in other words it decreases p_c of a RREQ packet by neighboring nodes and consequently the destination node.

In order to enhance the performance of the probabilistic algorithm in noisy MANETs, we believe it is necessary to accommodate the inevitable presence of noise in a MANET environment. In this paper, we developed a new dynamic probabilistic route discovery algorithm in which p_t is calculated locally considering both k and p_c, i.e., $p_t=f(k, p_c)$; and the new algorithm is referred to as the dynamic noise-dependent probabilistic (DNDP) algorithm. In this algorithm, the nodes dynamically adjust their p_t for probabilistic flooding based on local network topology information and noise-level. In particular, we developed an efficient and effective linear relation for calculating $p_t(k,p_c)$ by adding a noise-dependent term ($p_t(p_c)$) to the dynamic p_t term ($p_t(k)$). The algorithm is implemented on the MANET simulator (MANSim) (Al-Bahadili, 2009). The performance of the DNDP algorithm was evaluated through a number of simulations. The outcomes of these simulations demonstrated that the DNDP algorithm presents higher network reachability than the current probabilistic algorithm at a reasonable increase in the number of retransmissions for a wide range of p_c's or noise-levels.

PREVIOUS WORK

In this section we present a review of some of the most recent and related work on probabilistic flooding in both noiseless and noisy MANETs. Probabilistic algorithm was used for ad hoc route discovery by Haas et. al. (2002), and they called it a gossip-based route discovery (GOSSIP1) approach. They used a predefined p_t to decide whether or not an intermediate node forwards the RREQ packets. GOSSIP1 has a slight problem with initial conditions. If the source has relatively few neighbors, there is a chance that none of them will gossip, and the gossip will die. To make sure this does not happen, Haas et al. proposed a modified

protocol, in which they gossip with $p_t=1$ for the first h hops before continuing to gossip with $p_t<1$. Their results showed that they can save up to 35% message overhead compared to simple flooding.

S. Tseng et al. (2002) investigated the performance of the probabilistic flooding for various network densities in noise-free environment. They presented results for three network parameters, namely, reachability, saved rebroadcast, and average latency, as a function of p_t and network density. Sasson et al. (2003) explored the phase transition phenomenon observed in percolation theory and random graphs as a basis for defining probabilistic flooding algorithms. They also suggested exploring algorithms in which nodes would dynamically adjust their p_t based on local topology information. Because in their work they made the assumption that all nodes possess the same transmission range, they suggested another potential area for study which is to modify p_t of the transmitting according to its radio transmission range.

Kim et al. (2004) introduced a dynamic probabilistic broadcasting approach with coverage area and neighbors confirmation for MANETs. Their scheme combines probabilistic approach with the area-based approach. A mobile host can dynamically adjust p_t according to its additional coverage in its neighborhood. The additional coverage is estimated by the distance from the sender. The simulation results showed this approach generates fewer rebroadcasts than pure flooding approach. It also incurs lower broadcast collision without sacrificing high reachability.

Scott and Yasinsac (2004) presented a dynamic probabilistic solution that is appropriate to solving broadcast storm problems in dense mobile networks, also referred to as gossip protocol. The approach can prevent broadcast storms during flooding in dense networks and can enhance comprehensive delivery in sparse networks.

Barret et al. (2005) introduced a probabilistic routing protocol for sensor networks, in which an intermediate sensor decides to forward a message with p_t that depends on various parameters, such as the distance of the sensor to the destination, the distance of the source sensor to the destination, or the number of hops a packet has already traveled. They proposed two protocol variants and compared the new methods to other probabilistic and deterministic protocols. The results showed that the multi-path protocols are less sensitive to misinformation, and suggest that in the presence of noisy data, a limited flooding strategy will actually perform better and use fewer resources than an attempted single-path routing strategy, with the parametric probabilistic sensor network routing protocols outperforming other protocols. The results also suggested that protocols using network information perform better than protocols that do not, even in the presence of strong noise.

Viswanath and Obraczka (2005) developed an analytical model to study the performance of plain and probabilistic flooding in terms of its reliability and reachability in delivering packets. Their results indicated that probabilistic flooding can provide similar reliability and reachability guarantees as plain flooding at a lower overhead.

Zhang and Agrawal (2005) proposed a probabilistic approach that dynamically adjusts p_t as per the node distribution and node movement. The approach combines between probabilistic and counter-based approaches. They evaluated the performance of their approach by comparing it with simple flooding and fixed probabilistic algorithms. Simulation results showed that the new approach performs better than the two algorithms.

Abdulai et al. (2006) analyzed the performance of AODV protocol over a range of possible p_t. Their studies focused on the route discovery part of the routing algorithm, they modified the AODV routing protocol implementation to incorporate p_t; the RREQ packets are forwarded in accordance with a predetermined p_t. Results obtained showed that setting efficient p_t has a significant effect on the general performance of the protocol. The results also revealed that the optimal p_t for efficient performance is affected by the prevailing network conditions such as traffic load, node density, and

node mobility. During their study they observed that the optimal p_t is around 0.5 in the presence of dense network conditions and around 0.6 for sparse network conditions.

Bani-Yassein et al. (2006) proposed a dynamic probabilistic flooding algorithm in MANETs to improve network reachability and saved rebroadcast. The algorithm determines p_t by considering the network density and node movement. This is done based on locally available information and without requiring any assistance of distance measurements or exact location determination devices. The algorithm controls the frequency of rebroadcasts and thus might save network resources without affecting delivery ratios.

Abdulai et al. (2007) proposed two probabilistic methods for on-demand route discovery, that is simple to implement and can significantly reduce the overhead involved in the dissemination of RREQs. The two probabilistic methods are: the adjusted probabilistic (AP) and the enhanced adjusted probabilistic (EAP) which address the broadcast storm problem in the existing OADV routing protocols.

Al-Bahadili and Kaabned (2010) and Al-Bahadili and Jaradat (2007) investigated the effect of noise-level on the performance of the probabilistic algorithm in MANETs. They investigated the effect of node density, node average speed, radio transmission range, p_t, and p_c on number of retransmissions, duplicate reception, average hop count, and reachability. Their results showed that the performance of the network is severely suffered as p_c increases, i.e. the noise-level increases.

Bani Yassein et al. (2007) combined probabilistic and knowledge based approaches on the AODV protocol to enhance the performance of existing protocol by reducing the communication overhead incurred during the route discovery process. The simulation results revealed that equipping AODV with fixed and adjusted probabilistic flooding helps to reduce the overhead of the route discovery process whilst maintaining comparable performance levels in terms of saved rebroadcasts and reachability as achieved by conventional

AODV. Moreover, the results indicated that the adjusted technique results in better performance compared to the fixed one.

Khan et al. (2008) proposed a coverage-based dynamically adjusted probabilistic forwarding scheme and compared its performance with simple and fixed probabilistic schemes. The proposed scheme keeps up the reachability of simple flooding while maintaining the simplicity of probability based schemes. Hanash et al. (2009) proposed a dynamic probabilistic broadcast approach that can efficiently reduce broadcast redundancy in MANETs. The algorithm dynamically calculates p_t according to k. They compared their approach against simple flooding approach, fixed probabilistic approach, and adjusted probabilistic flooding by implementing them in a modified version of the AODV protocol using the GloMoSim network simulator. The simulation results showed that broadcast redundancy can be significantly reduced through their approach while keeping the reachability high. It also demonstrates lower broadcast latency than all the existing approaches presented.

PROBABILISTIC FLOODING ALGORITHM

Probabilistic algorithm is widely-used for flooding optimization during route discovery in MANETs. It aims at reducing number of retransmissions, in an attempt to alleviate the broadcast storm problem in MANETs (Tseng et al. 2002). In this scheme, when receiving a RREQ packet, a node retransmits the packet with a certain p_t and with probability $(1-p_t)$ it discards the packet. A node is allowed to retransmit a given RREQ packet only once, i.e., if a node receives a packet, it checks to see if it has retransmitted it before, if so then it just discards it, otherwise it performs its probabilistic retransmission check. Nodes usually can identify the RREQ packet through its sequence number. The source node p_t is always set to 1, to enable the source node to initialize the RREQ. While, p_t for

intermediate nodes (all nodes except the source) is determined using a static or dynamic approach.

Determination of p_t in Noiseless Environment

There are two approaches that can be used to set a satisfactory p_t for intermediate nodes within a noiseless wireless environment. These are:

1. Static approach in which a pre-determined p_t is set for each node on the networks and it can be expressed as: $p_t=P_t$, where P_t is a constant value ($0<P_t\leq1$). $P_t=1$ for pure flooding.
2. Dynamic approach in which each node on the network locally calculates its p_t according to k and it can be expressed as: $p_t=f(k)$, where $f(k)$ is a linear or a non-linear function of k.

Determination of Dynamic p_t in Noiseless Environment

Many functions have been developed for dynamically calculating p_t (Bani-Yassin et al., 2006; Hass et al., 2002; Kim et al., 2004; Sasson et al., 2003; Scott & Yasinsac, 2004; Zhang & Agrawal, 2005). However, in this work, the function presented in Sabri (2009) is considered. Because it demonstrates better performance than other distribution functions in various network conditions, where the dynamic p_t in noiseless environment is calculated as:

$$p_t = \begin{cases} p_{max} & for\ k \leq N_1 \\ p_{max} - \dfrac{k-N_1}{N_2-N_1}(p_{max}-p_{min}) & for\ N_1 < k < N_2 \\ p_{min} & for\ k \geq N_2 \end{cases}$$

(1)

Where p_t the node dynamic retransmission probability.

- p_{min} the minimum retransmission probability that could be assigned for a node.
- p_{max} the maximum retransmission probability that could be assigned for a node.
- k the number of first-hop neighbor for the transmitting node.
- N_1 the number of nodes at or below which $p_t = p_{max}$.
- N_2 the number of nodes at or above which $p_t = p_{min}$.

In this formula, the value of k is divided into three distinct groups:

1. Low ($k \leq N_1$). In this case, p_t is set to p_{max} to increase the probability of forwarding RREQ packets to next-hop neighbors.
2. Medium ($N_1 < k < N_2$). In this case, p_t is calculated as a function of k. The variation of p_t with k between N_1 and N_2 can be chosen as a linear, exponential, parabolic relation or any other distribution. In a linear relation, for example, p_t decreases linearly from p_{max} to p_{min} with increasing k. This looks very acceptable, because as k is relatively high, then despite the fact that some of the intermediate nodes will not retransmit RREQ

packets, but still some will do, so that a chance of forwarding RREQ packets remains high incorporating insignificant reduction in network reachability.

3. Large ($k \geq N_2$). In this case, p_t is set to p_{min} to reduce the probability of forwarding RREQ packets to next-hop neighbors.

Figure 1 shows the variation of p_t with k. In general, selection of satisfactory distribution in the interval $N_1 < k < N_2$ and the values for p_{min}, p_{max}, N_1, and N_2 depend mainly on the number of nodes on the network.

THE PROPOSED DYNAMIC NOISE-DEPENDENT PROBABILISTIC ALGORITHM

Effect of Noise

Before we proceed with the description of the proposed algorithm, let us discuss how noise affects the performance of the network. This can be explained with the help of Figure 2 as follows: Assume that nodes A and G are the source and destination nodes, and nodes B and C are inter-

Figure 1. Retransmission probability as a function of k

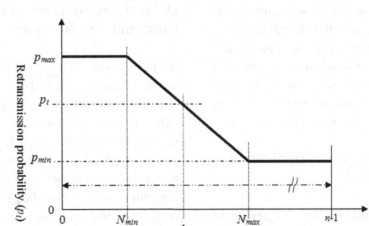

Number of first-hop neighbors (k)

Figure 2. (a) Pure flooding in noiseless environment, (b) Probabilistic flooding in noiseless environment, and (c) Probabilistic flooding in noisy environment

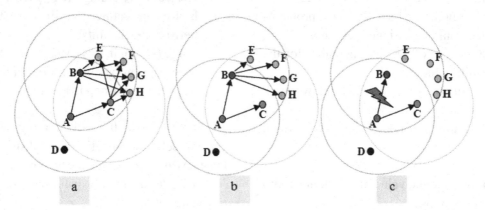

mediate nodes. Node G can be reached through nodes B and C. Figure 2a shows the RREQ packet dissemination from node A to G using pure flooding in noiseless environment, in which node G receives the RREQ twice through nodes B and C. However, it will send only one RREP through node B or C depending on which one forward the RREQ first. On the other hand for the same network topology, if probabilistic flooding is used, there are three possibilities, these are: (i) both B and C, (ii) either B or C, and (iii) neither B nor C will retransmit the RREQ. Assume that only node B succeeds to retransmit the RREQ (Figure 2b). For the same topology in noisy environment, assume that node A be unsuccessful in delivering the RREQ packet to node B (due to presence of noise) and be successful in delivering the RREQ packet to node C (Figure 2c). Thus, the RREQ packet will not be delivered to node G, and node G appears as unreachable. This is because node B has no packet to retransmit and node C prohibits from retransmission by the probabilistic algorithm.

Dynamic Probabilistic Algorithm in Noisy Environment

The probabilistic route discovery algorithm in noisy MANETs can be implemented as follows: When the distance between the transmitting and receiving nodes is less than the radio transmission range of the transmitting node, a random test is

performed to find out whether the RREQ is successfully delivered to the receiving node or being lost due to error. The random test is performed by generating a random number ξ ($0 \leq \xi < 1$) and compared it with p_c, if $\xi \leq p_c$, then the RREQ is successfully delivered to the receiving node; otherwise, the RREQ is not delivered or being lost. The value of p_c is either predetermined or instantly computed using a certain probability distribution function (PDF). If the RREQ packet is successfully delivered to the node, then the receiving node performs its probabilistic algorithm to find out whether it should retransmit the RREQ packet or not.

Determination of Retransmission Probability in Noisy Environment

In this section, we present the derivation of a mathematical formula that can be used locally by each transmitting node on the network to dynamically calculate its retransmission probability in a noisy environment ($p_t(k, p_c)$). In order to calculate $p_t(k, p_c)$, we assume it consists of two terms, one represents p_t as in noiseless environment, which is determined as a function of k ($p_t(k)$), and the second represents p_t due to noise, which is determined as a function of p_c ($p_t(p_c)$). The second term is added as a compensation for the effect of noise. Thus, $p_t(k, p_c)$ can be mathematically expressed as:

$$p_t(k, p_c) = p_t(k) + p_t(p_c) \tag{2}$$

The value of $p_t(k)$) can be calculated using Equation 1. Now the question is how we can formulate a general to calculate $p_t(p_c)$. In order to derive equation for calculating $p_t(p_c)$, the following main constraints must be considered:

1. The value of $p_t(p_c)$ should be ≥ 0 and $\leq 1 - p_t(k)$, so that $p_t(k, p_c)$ will always be ≤ 1.
2. The value of $p_t(k, p_c)$ lies between $p_t(k)$ and pre-adjusted maximum allowable p_t at a certain minimum value of p_c ($p_{c,min}$), namely, $p_{t,pcmin}$.
3. The value of $p_{t,pcmin}$ should be ≤ 1 and $\geq p_t(k)$ (i.e. $p_t(k) \leq p_{t,pcmin} \leq 1$).

According to the above discussion, $p_t(p_c)$ can be calculated as:

$$p_t(p_c) = \alpha \ (p_{t,pcmin} - p_t(k)) \tag{3}$$

Where α is a newly introduced factor and it is referred to as the noise-correction factor. It is a function of p_c and has a value that lies between 0 and 1 ($0 \leq \alpha \leq 1$). It can be expressed mathematically as:

$$\alpha = f(p_c) \tag{4}$$

In this paper, the value of α is calculated using the following simple linear equation:

$$\alpha = \frac{1 - p_c}{1 - p_{c,min}} \tag{5}$$

Now, substituting Equation 5 into Equation 3 and then substituting them into Equation 2 yields the following equation for calculating $p_t(k, p_c)$:

$$p_t(k, p_c) = p_t(k) + \frac{1 - p_c}{1 - p_{c,min}} (p_{t,pc\,min} - p_t(k)) \tag{6}$$

Where $p_t(k, p_c)$ is the dynamic noise-dependent retransmission probability.

* $p_t(k)$ is the noise-independent dynamic retransmission probability.
* $p_{t,pcmin}$ is the maximum allowable retransmission probability in presence of noise.
* p_c is the probability of reception,
* $p_{c,min}$ is the minimum probability of reception.

In a noiseless environment $p_c=1$, $\alpha=0$, and consequently $p_t(k, p_c)=p_t(k)$, i.e. p_t is a function of k only. In a noisy environment, when $p_c=p_{c,min}$, then $\alpha=1$ and $p_t(k, p_c)=p_{t,pcmin}$. If p_c is any value between $p_{c,min}$ and 1, then $p_t(k, p_c)$ varies between $p_t(k)$ and $p_{t,pcmin}$ depending on p_c. According to the above discussion, the variation of $p_t(k, p_c)$ always lies between the dynamic probability curve $p_t(k)$ and the line along which $p_c=p_{c,min}$ as shown in Figure 3.

The Proposed DNDP Algorithm

The description of the DNDP algorithm is straightforward. It is simply similar to the dynamic probabilistic algorithm except p_t is determined using Equation 6 instead of Equation 1. This proposed algorithm will increase the network reachability since p_t will be increased if the noise-level increased. As a result of increasing p_t, the number of retransmission and node average duplicate reception may also increase. Figure 4 outlines the DNDP algorithm.

SIMULATIONS AND RESULTS

The network simulator used in this work is MANSim (Al-Bahadili, 2009), which is developed to simulate and evaluate the performance of a number of flooding optimization algorithms for MANETs. It is written in C++ language, and it consists of four major modules: (1) Network module, (2) Mobility module, (3) Computational module, and (4) Algorithm module. MANSim

Figure 3. Variation of $p_t(k, p_c)$ with $p_{t,pcmin}(k)$

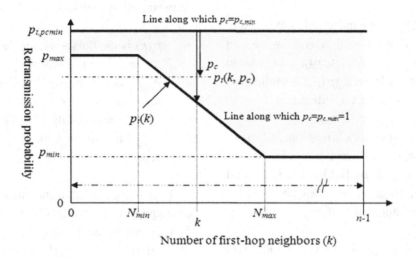

calculates a number of network performance measures, such as: network reachability (RCH), number of retransmission (RET), average duplicate reception (ADR), average hop count (AHP), saved rebroadcast (SRB), and disconnectivity (DIS). These parameters are recommended by the Internet Engineering Task Force (IETF) group to judge the performance of the flooding optimization algorithms. Definition of these parameters

can be found in (Al-Bahadili & Jaradat, 2010). However, in this work, we present results for two parameters only, these are: RCH and RET. RCH is defined as the average number of reachable nodes by any node on the network normalized n. RCH can also be defined as the probability by which a RREQ packet delivered from source to destination node. RET is defined as the average number of retransmissions normalized to n.

Figure 4. The Proposed DNDP algorithm

```
Probabilistic_Algorithm_in_Noisy_Environment
  If (IRange=1) Then {The receiving node is within the transmission range of the sender, in a noiseless
                      environment this guarantees request reception by the receiver, while in a noisy
                      environment a random test must be performed to find out whether a successful
                      delivery occurs or not. IRange=0 means the receiver is not within the transmission
                      range of the sender}
    ξ₁=rnd()  {ξ₁ some random number between 0 and 1}
    If (ξ₁<=p_c) Then {Reception random test}
      IRec(i)++ {Update the node reception index IRec(i)}
      If (IRet(i)=0) Then {The node has not retransmitted the request before (IRet(i) = 0)}
        ξ₂=rnd() { ξ₂ some random number between 0 and 1}
        p_t=function_p_t()
        If (ξ₂<=p_t) Then
          Retransmit RREQ
          IRet(i)=1 {Update the node retransmission index IRet(i) by equating it to 1}
        End if
      End if
    End if
  End if
Function_p_t() {Determining p_t}
  If (IProb="Static") Then {IProb is an integer indicates the approach to be used for determining p_t whether it
                           is static or dynamic}
    p_t=constant value
  Else (IProb="Dynamic")
    p_t=f(k,p_c)
  End If
```

Comparing the Performance of the DNDP Algorithm

In order to evaluate and compare the performance of the proposed DNDP algorithm in noisy MANETs, a number of simulations were performed using MANSim. These simulations investigate the variation of RCH and RET with p_c. The simulation results obtained using the DNDP algorithm are compared with those obtained by using the following flooding optimization algorithms: (i) Pure (simple) flooding (p_t=1), and (ii) dynamic probabilistic algorithm. In which the values of p_{min}, p_{max}, N_1, and N_2 in Equation 3 are taken to be 0.5, 0.8, 4, and 20. For this simulation, the average p_c is 0.744. For the DNDP algorithm, the value of $p_{t,pcmin}$ was taken as a constant value of unity. The input parameters for these simulations are listed in Table 1. The simulations results are plotted in Figure 5 and Figure 6.

It can be clearly seen in Figures 5 and 6 that the DNDP algorithm maintains the same RCH despite the presence of noise at some increase in RET, while for the other two algorithms, RCH decreases with increasing noise-level. This is as a consequence of: (1) High packet-loss introduced by the high noise-level, and (2) No measure is taken by the pure and probabilistic algorithms to accommodate the negative effect of noise. The DNDP algorithm maintains the same RCH because each intermediate node adjusts (increases/decreases) its p_t based on both k and p_c to ensure a successful delivery of RREQ packets to neighboring nodes. The results obtained demonstrated that the DNDP algorithm provides the highest RCH for various network noise-level, when compared with noise-independent dynamic probabilistic algorithm.

Investigating the Effect of n on the Performance of the DNDP Algorithm

In order to investigate the effect of n on the performance of the DNDP algorithm, the variation of RCH and RET against p_c for various n (n=75, 100, 125) is shown in Figures 7 and 8. All other input parameters are remained unchanged from those in Table 1. Figure 7 illustrates that the DNDP algorithm overwhelmed the performance of the dynamic noise-independent probabilistic algorithm in noisy MANETs. This is because the intermediate nodes always adjust (increase) their p_t to ensure RREQ packet delivery to the neighboring node despite the presence of noise (high packet-loss rate). Increasing nodes' p_t leads to increasing RET as shown in Figure 8.

Now, let us define the percentage increases in RET as: A_{RET}=(100x(RET_{DNDP}-RET_D)/RET_D), where A_{RET} is the percentage variation in RET. RET_{DNDP} and RET_D are values of RET achieved by the DNDP and the dynamic probabilistic algorithms, respectively. Then, it can be deduced from Figure 8 that A_{RET} is decreasing with increasing n. For example, for p_c=0.7, the calculated values are 66% (RET increases from 0.230 to 0.382), 58% (RET increases from 0.458 to 0.722), and 50% (RET increases from 0.541 to 0.811) for n= 75, 100, and 125.

Table 1. Input parameters

Parameters	Values
Geometrical model	Random distribution
Network area	600x600 m
Number of nodes (n)	100 nodes.
Transmission radius (R)	100 m
Average node speed (u)	5 m/sec
Probability of reception (p_c)	From 0.5 to 1.0 in step of 0.1
Simulation time (T_{sim})	1200 sec
Pause time (τ)	τ=0.75*(R/u)=15 sec
Size of mobility loop ($nIntv$)	80
Maximum allowable p_t in presence of noise ($p_{t,pcmin}$)	1

Figure 5. Variation of RCH with p_c for various algorithms

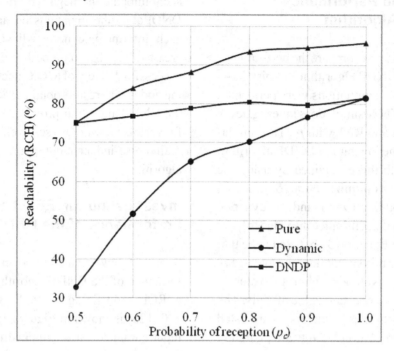

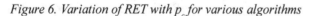

Figure 6. Variation of RET with p_c for various algorithms

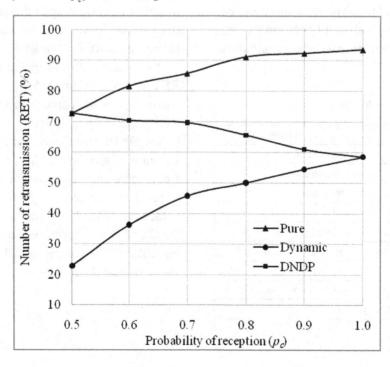

Figure 7. Variation of RCH with p_c for various n

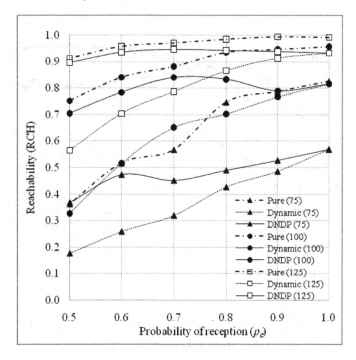

Figure 8. Variation of RET with p_c for various n

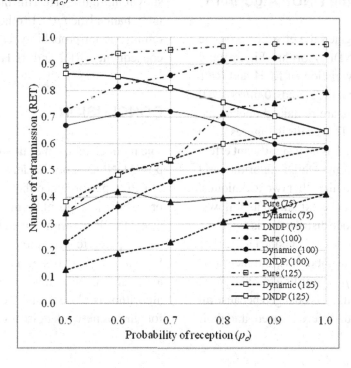

Figure 9. Variation of RCH with p_c for various u

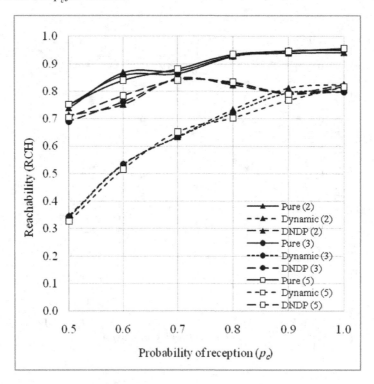

Investigating the Effect of u on the Performance of the DNDP Algorithm

This scenario investigated the effect of u on the performance of the DNDP algorithm. Figure 9 and Figure 10 show the variation of RCH and RET against p_c for various u (2, 5, and 10 m/sec). All other input parameters are remained unchanged from those in Table 1. The results in Figures 9 and 10 demonstrated that u has an insignificant effect on the performance of the DNDP algorithm and also the performance of the other two techniques. The reason for that can be explained as follows: suppose at $u=u_1$, the node distribution is as shown in Figure 11a, where nodes A, B, C, and D, each has 8, 7, 9, and 4 first-hop neighbors (k), and each node will calculate its $p_t(k, p_c)$ according to k and p_c. At $u=u_2$, the node distribution is changed because all nodes are moving with different speed, and their

first-hop neighbors changed to 7, 8, 4, and 9 as shown in Figure 11b. This means the nodes only interchanged their p_t's. In other words, the average retransmission probability remains unchanged and consequently RET and RCH.

CONCLUSION

The main conclusion of this work is that the proposed DNDP algorithm demonstrated better cost-effective performance than the current dynamic probabilistic algorithm in noisy environment. The DNDP algorithm provides a higher RCH as compared to dynamic probabilistic algorithm for various network noise-levels. The results also demonstrated that the RCH of the DNDP algorithm is close to the RCH of pure flooding for various network noise levels at less number of

Figure 10. Variation of RET with p_c for various u

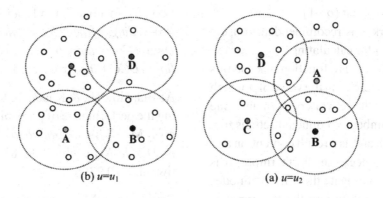

(b) $u=u_1$ (a) $u=u_2$

Figure 11. Nodes distribution at $u=u_1$ and $u=u_2$

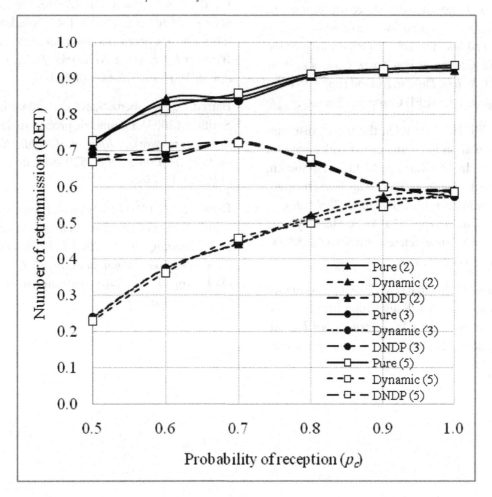

retransmission. The DNDP algorithm provides the same RCH and RET as the dynamic p_t algorithm in noiseless environment ($p_c=1$).

For future work it is recommended to use a certain distribution for calculating $p_{t,pcmin}$, for example, $p_{t,pcmin}$ can be set as a function of k and this is for a purpose of decreasing the value of p_t which in turn will increase the network performance due to decrease the number of redundant retransmission in the network and as a result contention and collisions will also decrease. Furthermore, it is recommended to investigate the effects of nodes density and nodes mobility on the performance of the DNDP algorithm.

REFERENCES

Abdulai, J., Ould-Khaoua, M., & Mackenzie, L. (2007). Improving probabilistic route discovery in mobile ad hoc networks. In *Proceeding of the 32nd IEEE Conference on Local Computer Networks (LCN '07),* Dublin, Ireland (pp. 739-746). Washington, DC: IEEE Computer Society.

Al-Bahadili, H. (2009). On the use of discrete-event simulation in computer networks analysis and design . In Abu-Taieh, E. M. O., & El-Sheikh, A. A. (Eds.), *Handbook of Research on Discrete-Event Simulation Environments: Technologies and Applications* (pp. 414–442). Hershey, PA: Information Science Reference. doi:10.4018/978-1-60566-774-4.ch019

Al-Bahadili, H., & Jaradat, R. (2010). Performance evaluation of an OMPR algorithm for route discovery in noisy MANETs. *International Journal of Computer Networks and Communications, 2*(1), 85–96.

Al-Bahadili, H., & Jaradat, Y. (2007). Development and performance analysis of a probabilistic flooding in noisy mobile ad hoc networks. In *Proceedings of the 1st International Conference on Digital Communications and Computer Applications (DCCA '07),* Irbid, Jordan (pp. 1306-1316).

Al-Bahadili, H., & Kaabneh, K. (2010). Analyzing the performance of probabilistic algorithm in noisy MANETs. *International Journal of Wireless & Mobile Networks, 2*(3), 83–95. doi:10.5121/ijwmn.2010.2306

Bani-Yassein, M., & Ould-Khaoua, M. (2007). Applications of probabilistic flooding in MANETs. *International Journal of Ubiquitous Computing and Communication, 1*(1), 1–5.

Bani-Yassein, M., Ould-Khaoua, M., Mackenzie, L., & Papanastasiou, S. (2006). Performance analysis of adjusted probabilistic broadcasting in mobile ad hoc networks. *International Journal of Wireless Information Networks, 13*(2), 127–140. doi:10.1007/s10776-006-0027-0

Barrett, C., Eidenbenz, S., Kroc, L., Marathe, M., & Smith, J. (2005). Parametric probabilistic routing in sensor networks. *Journal of Mobile Networks and Applications, 10*(4), 529–544. doi:10.1007/s11036-005-1565-x

Bettstetter, C. (2004). The cluster density of a distributed clustering algorithm in ad hoc networks. In *Proceedings of the 2004 IEEE International Conference on Communications (ICC '04),* Paris (Vol. 7, pp. 4336-4340). Washington, DC: IEEE Computer Society.

Haas, Z. J., Halpern, J. Y., & Li, L. (2006). Gossip-based ad hoc routing. *IEEE/ACM Transactions on Networking, 14*(3), 479–491. doi:10.1109/TNET.2006.876186

Hanash, A., Siddique, A., Awan, I., & Woodward, M. (2009). Performance evaluation of dynamic probabilistic broadcasting for flooding in mobile ad hoc networks. *Journal of Simulation Modeling Practice and Theory, 17*(2), 364–375. doi:10.1016/j.simpat.2008.09.012

Johnson, D., & Maltz, D. (1996). Dynamic source routing in ad hoc wireless networks. In Imielinski, T., & Korth, H. (Eds.), *Mobile Computing* (pp. 153–181). Dordrecht, The Netherlands: Kluwer Academic Publishers. doi:10.1007/978-0-585-29603-6_5

Khan, I., Javaid, A., & Qian, H. (2008). Coverage-based dynamically adjusted probabilistic forwarding for wireless mobile ad hoc networks. In S. Giordano, W. Jia, P. M. Ruiz, S. Olariu, & G. Xing (Eds.), *Proceedings of the 1st ACM International Workshop on Heterogeneous Sensor and Actor Networks (HeterSanet '08),* Hong Kong, China (pp. 81-88).

Kim, J. S., Zhang, Q., & Agrawal, D. P. (2004). Probabilistic broadcasting based on coverage area and neighbor confirmation in mobile ad hoc networks. In *Proceedings of the IEEE Global Telecommunications Conference Workshops (GlobeCom '04),* Dallas, TX (pp. 96-101). Washington, DC: IEEE Computer Society.

Ko, Y., & Vaidya, N. (2000). Location-aided routing (LAR) in mobile ad hoc networks. *Journal of Wireless Networks, 6*(4), 307–321. doi:10.1023/A:1019106118419

Ni, S., Tseng, Y., Chen, Y., & Sheu, J. (1999). The broadcast storm problem in a mobile ad hoc network. *Journal of Wireless Networks, 8*(2), 153–167.

Perkins, C., & Royer, E. (2000). *Ad hoc on-demand distance vector (AODV) routing. MANET Working Group.* IETF.

Qayyum, A., Viennot, L., & Laouiti, A. (2002). Multipoint relaying for flooding broadcast messages in mobile wireless networks. In *Proceedings of the 35th Hawaii International Conference on System Sciences (HICSS'02)* (pp. 3866- 3875).

Rahman, A., Olesinski, W., & Gburzynski, P. (2004). Controlled flooding in wireless ad hoc networks. In *Proceedings of the IEEE International Workshop on Wireless Ad Hoc Networks (IWWAN'04),* Oulu, Finland.

Royer, E., & Toh, C. (1999). A review of current routing protocols for ad hoc mobile wireless networks. *IEEE Personal Communication Magazine, 6*(2), 46-55.

Sabri, A. (2009). *Development of a dynamic noise-dependent probabilistic route discovery algorithm in MANETs.* Unpublished PhD thesis, The Arab Academy for Banking & Financial Sciences, Amman, Jordan.

Sasson, Y., Cavin, D., & Schiper, A. (2003). Probabilistic broadcast for flooding in wireless mobile ad hoc networks. In *Proceedings of IEEE Wireless Communications and Networking (WCNC'03),* New Orleans, LA (Vol. 2, pp. 1124-1130).

Scott, D., & Yasinsac, A. (2004). Dynamic probabilistic retransmission in ad hoc networks. In H. R. Arabnia, L. T. Yang, & C. H. Yeh (Eds.), *Proceedings of the International Conference on Wireless Networks (ICWN'04),* Las Vegas, NV (Vol. 1, pp. 158-164). CSREA Press.

Tseng, T., Ni, S., Chen, Y., & Sheu, J. (2002). The broadcast storm problem in a mobile ad hoc network. *Journal of Wireless Networks, 8*(2), 153–167. doi:10.1023/A:1013763825347

Viswanath, K., & Obraczka, K. (2005). Modeling the performance of flooding in wireless multi-hop ad hoc networks. *Journal of Computer Communications, 29*(8), 949–956. doi:10.1016/j.comcom.2005.06.015

Zhang, Q., & Agrawal, D. P. (2005). Dynamic probabilistic broadcasting in MANETs. *Journal of Parallel and Distributed Computing, 65*(2), 220–233. doi:10.1016/j.jpdc.2004.09.006

This work was previously published in International Journal of Business Data Communications and Networking, Volume 7, Issue 1, edited by Varadharajan Sridhar and Debashis Saha, p.p 52-67, copyright 2011 by IGI Publishing (an imprint of IGI Global).

Chapter 4
Semantic Mobile Applications for Service Process Improvement

Markus Aleksy
ABB AG, Germany

Bernd Stieger
ABB AG, Germany

Thomas Janke
SAP Research Dresden, Germany

ABSTRACT

The ongoing evolution of industrial field service is mainly driven by demographical changes, increasing complexity of products, and tremendous amounts of product information from enterprise information systems as well as from the emerging Internet of Things. To cope with these challenges, a combined approach utilizing semantic and mobile technologies fosters the provision of the right information, at the right time, in the right place, and to the right people. This paper investigates the exploitation potential of semantic mobile applications to support industrial service processes. Based on identified application scenarios, the authors developed concepts for process improvement and, thus, derived requirements. The necessary semantic data federations are considered in the presented architecture, which enables an integrated approach for tailored information retrieval from heterogeneous information sources.

1. INTRODUCTION

Instant availability of up-to-date information is a vital prerequisite in today business for decision making and the execution of any job task. Especially in service business, which is to a high degree human-based, knowledge is the key factor to deliver services efficiently and with high quality. It's knowledge about customers, products, application domains, the history of installed equipments and service procedures and processes. In global operating enterprises, this knowledge is

DOI: 10.4018/978-1-4666-2026-1.ch004

in peoples' heads, but also stored as electronic information in many databases of the enterprise information technology infrastructure. Because of the exponential growth of the data volume it's getting more and more difficult to find the right information to the right time with low effort.

Additionally, the preservation of the existing knowledge is reasonable due to the aging structure of the employees in many industrial countries such as Germany. According to ABB AG (2009), 21.1% of the employees of ABB Germany will retire within the next 10 years and 53.7% within the next 20 years, respectively (cf. Figure 1).

The Aletheia project (see http://www.aletheia-projekt.de for details) is investigating in new approaches to retrieve information from various heterogeneous data sources. The obtained information pieces are aggregated to a consistent and meaningful conclusion, and presented with regard to the actual working context to the user.

2. SERVICE PROCESS SUPPORT

The entire service process and involved information systems are depicted in Figure 2. It starts by handling customer's request in a call or customer center. Here, a Customer Relationship Management (CRM) system and a telephony system are utilized to provide the required information to the call agent. Afterwards, the customer request

is forwarded to the corresponding service unit. The dispatching of service engineers, required spare parts, and information is done by the service planner using the CRM system and a dispatching board. Afterwards, the service engineer executes the field service job and records his activities utilizing a reporting software and sometimes still using paper. Finally, a clerk enters the invoicing data in an Enterprise Resource Planning (ERP) system.

Unfortunately, the aforementioned information systems provide only a limited information support to the corresponding users. Some of the required information is split across various information systems, thus requiring additional time-consuming investigations. Here, utilization of installed base information and Internet of Things (IoT) (International Telecommunication Union, 2005) could provide meaningful information. Access to installed base information allows keeping track of all products and systems information at a customer site, including technical and project details that might be very valuable to call center agents, service planners, and service engineers. Moreover, utilizing Internet-of-Things technologies to access the equipment condition information on-site, supplies service engineers with recent information about it and, thus provides a more detailed view on the problem. Figure 3 depicts an improved information supply scenario.

However, there are many other databases, information systems, Wikis, and data sources

Figure 1. Aging structure of ABB in Germany (ABB AG, 2009)

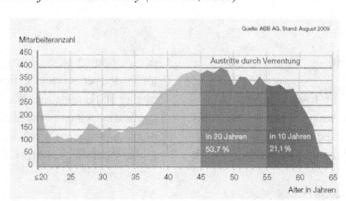

Figure 2. Service process and traditionally utilized information system

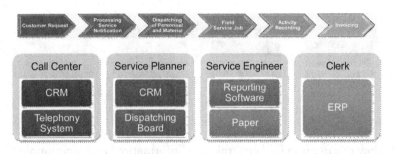

providing valuable information besides the above-named information sources. The Aletheia project aims to close this gap by the means of Semantic Web technologies (Benjamins et al., 2008; Shadbolt et al., 2006). The project scope is the development of Aletheia, an information system that provides federated and semantically structured product knowledge from heterogeneous and often unstructured information sources throughout the product and service lifecycle and corresponding value chains. Such a knowledge base is crucial for a variety of business processes, and hence important for manufacturers, distributors, service providers, and consumers.

Based on the service process and some variants (cf. Stieger et al., 2008) for further details with regard to the service process description), we were able to identify some use cases for knowledge-based support (cf. Figure 4):

- Contact Center Support,
- Service Knowledge Portal, and
- Field service support.

The identification of the customer, the involved equipment, and the problem are common challenges to contact center agents. Nowadays, many of the telephony systems provide the capability to recognize the caller if she is already known by the system. However, many of the callers are using their – maybe frequently changed – mobile phones in case of emergencies. Therefore, in many cases the telephony system cannot recognize the caller appropriately. Additionally, the name of the company can be stored in the CRM system differently, e.g., as ABB, ABB AG, Asea Brown Boveri, etc. Furthermore, it is sometimes hard to identify the equipment due to missing or unreadable identification plates. For these reasons, a semantic-based approach that helps identifying the customer as well as the involved equipment would also help improving the corresponding call center processes.

The service knowledge portal can be used by several actors, such as the service planner or experts providing problem-solving solutions remotely at the same time. Furthermore, it can be used by customer center agents and service

Figure 3. Improved information supply

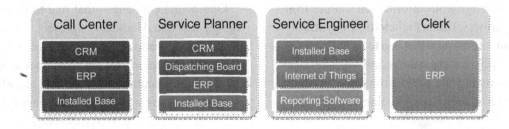

Figure 4. Aletheia-based information supply

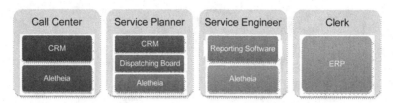

engineers as well. They can use it to find general information about a suitable solution for a customer problem providing some information about the cause and describing the problem.

Complex industrial equipments may lead to unsupported behaviors that are hard to investigate. In that case, the utilization of Internet of Things technologies, like Radio Frequency Identification (RFID) or wireless sensor networks (WSNs) can be applied to identify the cause of the unexpected behavior. However, the gathered data must be also combined together with the data from installed base as well as with other enterprise information systems to provide a holistic view of the problem and suggesting reasonable solutions.

3. SYSTEM REQUIREMENTS FOR ALETHEIA

Based on the presented use cases, we collected 59 requirements regarding required functionality, usability issues, user interfaces, security aspects, maintainability, and boundary conditions. Overall, i.e., including further application scenarios, 250 different requirements for the future Aletheia architecture were identified yet. As already mentioned, the system should enable the federation, semantic integration, and targeted presentation of very heterogeneous information sources from various partners. Due to the heterogeneity and dispersion of information that had to be federated by Aletheia, a distributed architecture with interfaces to many existing and future information systems must be provided. Here, existing and emerging

information and communication technologies, especially local files, file servers, databases, ERP systems, internal and external blogs and wikis, third party Web services, the public Web, as well as data from Internet of Things including wireless sensor networks and RFID had to be integrated and the extracted data and information federated utilizing Semantic Web technologies. These technologies enable the inference of further relevant information by automatic reasoning. Furthermore, it should be possible to rank and tag the federated information according to the user's preferences. Finally, aspects like the capability to work online as well as offline, user- / context-specific information presentation, advanced search capabilities, various user interface and security requirements must also be fulfilled (Aleksy et al., 2009).

In-between a myriad of mobile devices as well as alternative input- and output technologies and techniques exists. In Aleksy and Stieger (2009), we evaluated the suitability of some new kind of hardware devices, such as one-handed keyboards or wrist-mounted devices and alternative input- and output technologies, respectively. According to the results of our case study, a laptop / tablet PC are the most preferred devices in industrial field service since they provide the best mix of performance, required input/output capabilities, software tools and connectivity support nowadays.

One of the challenges that had to be solved was the fact that Aletheia is a project that covers various aspects and different stakeholders at the same time. Therefore, we developed some mockups to provide common understanding of the future user interfaces as well as required functionality.

According to our study (Aleksy et al., 2010), the presented mock-ups were very suitable to elucidate application functions, the requirements for the GUI, as well as the requirements for the dialog windows. Furthermore, they were also helpful to exemplify the underlying business processes and use cases. The major drawback of the developed mock-ups was the coverage of non-functional requirements since these cannot be described mostly that way.

4. SERVICE ONTOLOGY

In order to provide equivalent knowledge support to the mobile workers as well as other service staff, we developed a service ontology focusing on the support of industrial service processes. In literature, there are some ontologies that had been developed in the past but only partially affect the industrial service domain. Hongwei et al. (2003) propose a formal ontology model describing the customer management domain and providing a unified view to customers. The GoodRelations ontology (Hepp, 2008) describes products and services offers on the Web. Fritas et al. (2008) propose an ontology for IT services that covers aspects from services implementation to their management. Finally, Jarrar et al. (2003) propose the construction of an ontology that captures the core knowledge of the customer complaint domain. However, none of the above mentioned ontologies aims on support of industrial service processes, like customer interaction center support or field service support.

The ontology is the building block for various semantic technologies like semantic search. Semantic search (Guha et al., 2003) is a technique utilized to improve searching by using data from semantic networks to disambiguate queries in order to generate more relevant results.

The ontology development has been conducted by service domain professionals and ontology experts in a workshop in order to identify the most relevant concepts describing the service business domain. These concepts are characterized by attributes and complemented by corresponding relations. Thus, the ontology provides a common understanding and vocabulary among different people of a certain domain (Gruber, 1993, 1995). Furthermore, ontologies are formal and explicit, thus, they are machine-readable and -interpretable. Standardized ontology languages such as RDFS or OWL can be used for the modeling (Hebeler et al., 2009; Stuckenschmidt & van Harmelen, 2004; W3C, 2004). Examples for concepts of a service ontology are Branch, Component, Error Code, Installation, Person, Product, Offering, Service Job, Skill, Symptom, and Technology.

For the creation of an ontology it is an advantage, next to the manual ontology modeling process, if existing taxonomies, subject indexes, data dictionaries, or metadata concepts can be used. Challenges in this phase were related to ontology engineering. Especially, the creation of an ontology is very labor intensive, since it can be hardly done automatically, unless the underlying data sources are fully structured and possess similar database field structures. Furthermore, it is possible to add certain rules to the ontology concepts and their relations.

This can be done with rule languages such as Semantic Web Rule Language (SWRL) (Horrocks et al., 2004) or F-Logic (Kifer & Lausen, 1989). Figure 5 depicts one rule example created with F-Logic. It shows certain concepts and their relations as well as one conditional relation *hasExpert*. In this example the relation '*ProductType hasExpert Person*' is an implicit inference. According to the rule, the relation *hasExpert* becomes true under the condition that the other three relations *hasType*, *hasServiceJob*, and *hasServiceEngineer* are fulfilled. As a result, this rule will expose the relation '*ProductType hasExpert Person*'. This rule has a strong impact since this implicit inference is always true but it cannot be derived from the individuals or the real values of the concepts, respectively. As an example, if the contact center agent is searching with the KM system for a service engineer who has skills with a certain generic product type, he will find now all relevant engineers whereas before he would have found only engineers when he included the special single instance of a product into his search.

The ontology and rules are applied to the data sources and an algorithm is constructing an index. In order to have a better performance, the search is performed directly on the index, since it comprises the most necessary information about the data sources and the relevant information in which data sources the corresponding results of a search query are located. During the search the ontology is again applied on the data sources. In the case of searching structured data, e.g., which are stored in database-driven system, the ontology concepts and relations can be partly derived directly from the underlying system structure whereas searching in unstructured data sources is more difficult.

5. ARCHITECTURE

The general architecture of the Aletheia system is based on Service Oriented Architecture (SOA) principles. It consists of various components and services, namely:

- Aletheia Service Hubs,
- Information Providers,
- Registries,
- Repositories,
- Application Servers, and
- Client Applications.

The Aletheia Service Hub (ASH) is the central component of the entire system architecture. It is responsible for inter-domain communication with other Service Hubs. Data and information provider components provide access to dedicated data sources, such as databases, local files, the Web, and Internet of Things. They are used by

Figure 5. F-Logic rule for conditional relation has-Expert in a textual and graphical representation

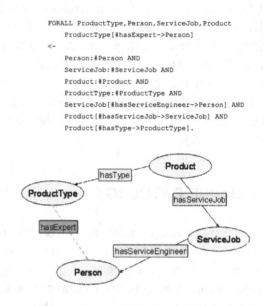

```
FORALL ProductType,Person,ServiceJob,Product
    ProductType[#hasExpert->Person]
  <-
    Person:#Person AND
    ServiceJob:#ServiceJob AND
    Product:#Product AND
    ProductType:#ProductType AND
    ServiceJob[#hasServiceEngineer->Person] AND
    Product[#hasServiceJob->ServiceJob] AND
    Product[#hasType->ProductType].
```

Aletheia Service Hubs to access these data sources and managed by registries. Aletheia Service Hubs can utilize such a registry to obtain access to an information provider component. Registries can be interconnected facilitating the exchange of information provider components. However, there is no central registry provider. Each Service Hub is complemented by a repository that is responsible for storing the semantic model, metadata, and some local data. The overall functionality managed and provided by the repository consists of various subcomponents such as a repository authorization control service, syntactic repository, uncertain information repository, semantic repository, and context repository.

The syntactic repository manages a document index, which can be used to perform Google-like search. Uncertain information extracted from semi-structured data sources is stored in the uncertain information repository. The semantic repository stores the semantic model and corresponding facts. Finally, context-specific facts are recorded in the context repository.

Application Servers provide user access to the information hosted by a Service Hub, while client applications utilize the functionality offered by application servers and Aletheia Service Hubs. Figure 6 gives an overview of the Aletheia architecture and shows the main subsystems.

6. MOBILE ACCESS TO KNOWLEDGE

Mobile access to knowledge is an important success factor in the context of maintenance and field services. It allows service engineers to review manuals, technical specifications, service reports and other information directly at the customer site and herewith helps to optimize and enhance service tasks.

In general, two scenarios for mobile access to information provided by Aletheia can be identified. On the one hand, there are use cases that rely on instant online data access and on the other hand, there are scenarios that demand selective offline

data provisioning. The former use case assumes that the device can establish online connections, either wireless or wired. Furthermore, it assumes that an online connection is available whenever data need to be obtained. Given that, complex and resource intensive tasks can be executed on the server whereas the client merely renders the corresponding results. In contrast to this approach, relevant parts of the server application logic as well as subsets of the server data can be swapped out to the client. As a result, the latter is able to access and process data without any online data connection making the client more independent from the server. Both usage scenarios are valid in the context of executing service jobs by field engineers and therefore need to be supported by Aletheia clients.

However, both approaches pose very different requirements on the architecture and the implementation of the provided client applications as well as on the client hardware specification. In order to reflect this, two types of clients, namely a thin and a fat client, have been considered in the

Figure 6. Overview of the Aletheia architecture

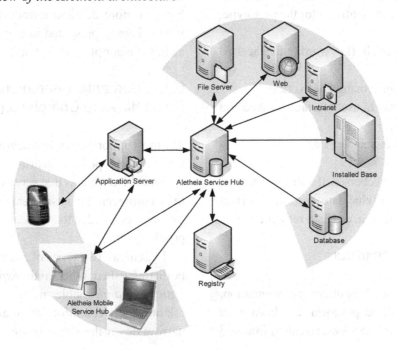

context of Aletheia. Both approaches are described and discussed in more detail in the subsequent sections. Moreover, respective advantages and disadvantages are elaborated.

6.1. Thin Client Approach

The thin client approach implemented in Aletheia addresses scenarios that are based on the usage of mobile devices which rely on a constant online connection in order to remotely access information processed by the server. As a result, the main task of the application is to visualize data in a reasonable and user friendly way. Due to the fact that resource intensive computations are executed on the server side, this approach is especially suitable for mobile devices with a very restricted hardware configuration. Examples for that are smart phones, netbooks or tablet PCs which are in many cases restricted with regard to the display size, to available input and output modules as well as to their processing power. The former constraints have to be reflected in the design of a mobile application in general and in the implementation of semantic mobile applications in particular. The following list of functional as well as non-functional requirements has been identified for the prototype.

- Semantic search (keyword and facetted search)
- Navigation in semantic network
- Clear and easy to use interface for Android smart phones
- Use of SOAP web services

The subsequent sections will elaborate on those requirements and will elucidate the most important design decision taken in order to reflect them.

6.1.1. Client Architecture

As depicted in Figure 7, the client implementation, based on the Android platform, has been built on top of SOAP web services, so called frontend

services, provided by the Aletheia Service Hub. The latter expose functionality to add, edit as well as to query data stored in the various kinds of repositories introduced in section 5. With respect to the requirements listed above, the most important service used by the client is the *facetted keyword search service* which, as the name suggests, provides an interface for explorative as well as selective search. Furthermore, it provides methods to disambiguate keywords by means of semantic auto completion. More details on that can be found in the respective subsection.

The communication and data exchange between the client and the Service Hub is managed by a SOAP client component. Due to lack of SOAP support by the Android platform, we had to develop a custom SOAP client component which is explained in more detail in section 6.1.4. On top of that, we implemented a three-tier application architecture. The business logic layer contains methods to retrieve and send application data with the help of the SOAP client component. Furthermore, it is responsible for data transformation and caching. The presentation logic layer on top of that reacts on and validates user input and triggers the several views, contained in the user interface layer. A more detailed introduction of the provided views is presented in section 6.1.3 as well as in the example screenshots.

6.1.2. Semantic Search and Semantic Auto Completion

The most important requirement a mobile application in the scope of industrial field has to fulfill is search. This means that service engineers need to be empowered to easily search and find all the information needed to efficiently solve customer problems.

In general, two types of search processes can be distinguished. Whereas the *explorative* or *navigational search* enables users to search by using relations between information and/or iteratively narrow down the result space, *selective search*

Figure 7. Overview of the client architecture

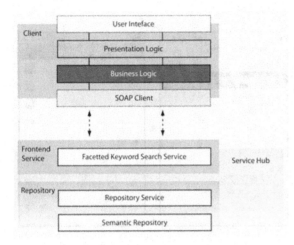

aims at defining a concrete question in forms of a query which then should be answered by the application. Examples of the latter are simple keywords as well as SQL or SPARQL queries. Both approaches have advantages and should therefore be combined in the developed mobile application. In addition to that, semantic queries should be allowed. However, the complexity of using a special purpose query language, like F-Logic or SPARQL, needs to be encapsulated by adequate user interface components.

Explorative search first and foremost is provided by the concept of *faceted search*. The idea behind that is to provide a classification of properties instances in the result set contain. Based on that, the user can iteratively refine the result set by filtering results with regard to their properties resp. facet values. Thereby, every time an additional filter is set, the set of valid facets and their values is reevaluated. An example of the use of facets in the client is illustrated in Figure 8.

The left screenshot depicts the facets view. In order to provide a decent entry point for the explorative search, the user can filter results according to a main category. Categories are derived from the concepts described in the underlying ontology and therefore describe the type of an instance or result. In the example above, the cat-

egory "Company" has been chosen which means only companies are displayed as results. In order to drill down this set, users can apply additional filters which are presented in the second screenshot. Here, the three facets *Category*, *Address* and *City* are presented. Furthermore, filter values for the "City" facet are shown. In addition, the number of results the filter application would yield is depicted. Apart from that, a simple keyword query can be applied on the result set. As a consequence, only results that contain the given term in any of its properties are presented.

By means of building the application on top of the developed domain ontology, the faceted search service as well as the Android application itself could be designed in a very generic way. If, for example, new facets are introduced by inserting facts with new properties into the semantic repository, this is immediately reflected in the application without adopting the internal data model. Therefore, the application can easily be adapted to arbitrary domains just by exchanging the underlying domain ontology.

The second type of search supported by the client is *selective search* by means of keywords. However, in addition to plain syntactic keyword search, semantic auto completion is provided. The latter is illustrated in Figure 9.

Service engineers can enter search terms into the corresponding search text box. This triggers a search request in the Aletheia Service Hub which then generates auto completion proposals and sends them back to the client. In contrast to pure syntactic search, the received terms are typed based on information derived from the underlying domain ontology. With respect to that, every proposal either reflects a concept, an instance or a relation. For keywords that do not match a label of any of the former types and therefore cannot be mapped to any element in the ontology, a fourth type is introduced which describes a simple string. In the example above this is the case for the term *Per*. The second proposal is an example for a matched instance which is labeled as *Peripherals* and which is of type *Cause Code*. In addition to that, there is also a category resp. concept called *Peripherals*. Based on those typing information provided for every auto complete proposal, the user is enabled to identify and even more important to resolve ambiguity. In the given example this is the case for the homonym *Peripherals*. Synonyms are also resolved, because different labels can be mapped to single instance based on its unique uniform resource identifier (URI). This knowledge can then be used by the client to create more concrete semantic queries.

Another form of semantic auto completion is provided by means of concept or category hierarchies. If a proposal is typed as a category, all sub concepts are additionally provided. This is shown in the second screenshot of Figure 9. The user searches for *Person* and retrieves the corresponding category proposal. In addition, he is able to browse through the list of sub types in order to render his search request even more precisely. This is especially helpful if the user does not know the vocabulary of the domain, meaning he for example does not know that a category called *Service Engineer* exists.

After the user has selected one of the proposals, the latter is stored by the application and additional terms can be entered. Finally, the user can start the search by pressing the *go* button. Example queries and their results are illustrated in Figure 10.

If the search has been started, the client sends the list of typed search terms to the Aletheia Service Hub. Based on the given terms, the server creates a number of structured F-Logic queries which are sent to the semantic repository. If, for example, the category *Person* was transmitted by the client, the Service Hub returns all instances of the corresponding concept and its sub concepts as the query result. Whenever more than one search term is specified, reasonable permutations of terms and respective queries are generated. In the second example, the user searches for *Person* and *Mannheim* whereat the former is a category

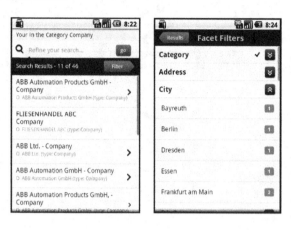

Figure 8. Explorative search through facets the thin client

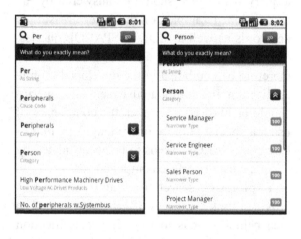

Figure 9. Semantic auto completion

Figure 10. Semantic keyword search

and the latter is a string. As a result, all instances containing the string *Mannheim* that are related to instances of type *Person* are returned. In order to explain the result to the user, in addition to the type of the result, an explanation is presented. As an example, the second *Site* has been selected as a result because one of its attributes contains the term *Mannheim* and it has a *Service Engineer* which is of type *Person*. The explanation component as well as the query generation component are still in an early phase and therefore need to be further evaluated and optimized.

6.1.3. User Interface

The major challenges for the design of user interfaces and user interaction patterns for mobile application are limited display sizes and restricted input capabilities of the corresponding target devices. As a result, applications need to be designed to be as simple as possible avoiding unnecessary navigation paths as well as complex views or hidden functionality.

In order to reflect this, the developed client application only consists of three different views: the search view, the filter view, and the result details view. All of them are implemented by means of separate Screens, which define the basic layout of the view, and their corresponding Activities, which are responsible for handling user input and to control the underlying layout. In addition, various manager classes are used to modularize the business logic layer. The full client architecture is depicted in Figure 11.

Examples of the search as well as the filter view are illustrated in the Figures 9 and 10. They are responsible for the semantic keyword search and for applying facet values as search filter.

The results details view is used to present all information of one single result entry. With respect to the underlying ontology, the latter corresponds to the set of all properties, attributes as well as relations, contained by one single instance. This is illustrated in Figure 12 using information about the instance *ABB Ltd.*

Apart from browsing the attributes of a result entry, it is also possible to navigate to related instances. In the example above, the user can navigate to the instances *Zürich* and *CH* following the respective relations defined in the ontology. Based on this simple interface, it is possible to navigate through and explore the whole semantic net stored in the semantic repository and herewith to make use of the explicit semantics of relations.

6.1.4. SOAP Support

One of the key requirements with regard to the existing Aletheia platform was to design the client in a way that it is able to consume the SOAP web services provided by the Service Hub. Unfortunately, SOAP is not supported by the Google Android platform API. According to Google, this is due to the fact that handling SOAP messages, which basically means serializing and deserializing XML data, can lead to performance issues on mobile devices. Therefore, in contrast to SOAP they propose REST-based services. Nevertheless, the advantage of SOAP is that service interfaces in general are well defined using the Web Service Description Language (WSDL). Based on that, stub generators for various programming languages can be applied which automatically create all data transfer and model classes specified in the service interface. In addition, glue code is generated which encapsulates the serialization and deserilization of data objects as well as the invocation of the actual service and reception of the corresponding results. Apart from that, additional standards are defined around SOAP, for example WS-Security and WS-Notification, which are used by other Aletheia client implementations. The wide adoption of SOAP as an industry standard for web services leads to the reasonable assumption that a similar setting can also be found in many other industry use cases. Porting those systems to support REST-based data access is often either not possible due to existing legacy clients or simply too expensive.

Figure 11. Client architecture

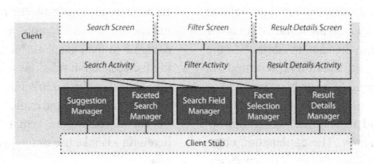

Figure 12. Result details view

With respect to this problem, a SOAP component has been developed as part of the client implementation. As depicted in the architecture illustrated in Figure 13, the client component is based on kSOAP2 (kSOAP, 2011) and the WSDL stub generator provided as part of the Java ME platform (Oracle Corp., 2011).

KSOAP2 is a lightweight client library for SOAP web services designed for constrained Java environments. Its main purpose is to provide a simple API to encapsulate the generation and parsing of XML SOAP messages. In addition, it handles connections to the SOAP server endpoint as well as the serialization and deserialization of messages. Unfortunately, it does not support the generation of client stubs based on the WSDL of the respective service. Moreover, in order to enable serialization of custom object types the respective types have to implement a specific interface. In addition, a mapping has to be defined between the elements of the SOAP message and the target data model. Both tasks require relevant manual implementation and maintenance efforts, especially in environments that are subject of frequent service description changes.

In order to mitigate this issue, the kSOAP2 serializer has been extended to automatically serialize and deserialize the data objects defined in the SOAP service based on Java reflection. In order to derive the underlying data model automatically from the WSDL, a stub generator shipped with the Java ME platform is used. The latter generates Java code which consists of simple data transfer objects which are used as the service parameters as well as request/response objects which reflect the exposed service methods. Java reflection is then used to automatically match and instantiate those model classes with their respective SOAP XML elements. As a result, fully functional SOAP stubs can be automatically generated for Android clients.

Whereas the use of reflection allows for a very generic implementation of the client stub, it poses performance issues for real world enterprise application with huge data volumes. Due to that, further development iterations will replace the use of reflection at runtime in favor of generating

Figure 13. Architecture of the SOAP client component

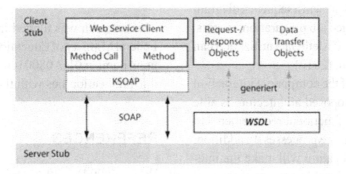

static serialize and deserialize methods for the various data objects at design time.

6.2. Fat Client Approach

We use the service job preparation process to demonstrate Aletheia's component interactions. The interaction starts with a user query that is sent to the application server. The application server transforms the query in a format that is suitable for the Aletheia Service Hub and forwards it to the latter. The Aletheia Service Hub requests information that is related to the query from its internal subcomponents, namely from the semantic repository, the uncertain information repository, and the syntactic repository. Additionally, the registry is contacted, which forwards the request to the corresponding information provider components. Afterwards, the collected information is returned to the application server. The application server prepares the results received to be presented by the client applications. Based on the results received, the service engineer can select which of the returned information and documents should be

Figure 14. Simplified service job preparation sequence diagram

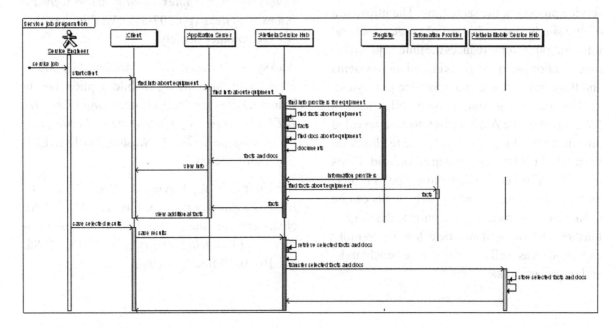

stored in the Aletheia Mobile Service Hub for offline access. Figure 14 present a sequence diagram of the simplified service job preparation process. Additional examples of Aletheia's utilization can be found in Kunz et al. (2010).

This description of the component interaction motivates how the proposed architecture is able to fulfill many of the functional requirements to improve industrial service processes. In addition, Aletheia's distributed nature will make the integration of many additional service partners possible, and will facilitate the coverage of further use cases from other application areas across the whole product and service lifecycle.

7. CONCLUSION

In this paper, we discussed in how far semantic mobile applications can provide support to industrial service processes. We outlined the improvement areas of existing approaches and discussed the role of Aletheia closing the identified gaps. The presented architecture for semantic data federations provides an integrated approach to deliver tailored information from very heterogeneous information sources supporting various user roles in the service process at the same time. The utilization of one single system instead of usage of several information systems reduces the time required for investigations across various information systems and thus, improving existing service processes.

The implementation of the mobile client in the context of the Aletheia architecture revealed promising results. It gives valuable feedback on the feasibility of the integration of Android clients in a SOAP-based service landscape. Furthermore, it shows that mobile search clients can be enhanced by introducing semantic technologies. Further activities will include extensive usability experiments as well as performance benchmarks and improvements.

ACKNOWLEDGMENT

This research was funded in part by the German Federal Ministry of Education and Research under grant number 01IA08001G. The responsibility for this publication lies with the authors.

REFERENCES

W3C. (2004): *OWL web ontology language semantics and abstract syntax*. Retrieved from http://www.w3.org/TR/owl-semantics/

ABB AG. (2009). Ganzheitlich gut: Generations. *Kontakt, 5*, 21.

Aleksy, M., & Stieger, B. (2009). Challenges in the development of mobile applications in industrial field service. In *Proceedings of the 12th International Conference on Network-Based Information Systems* (pp. 586-591). Washington, DC: IEEE Computer Society.

Aleksy, M., Stieger, B., & Fantana, N. (2010). Utilizing mock-ups in the development of distributed information systems for semantic data federations. In *Proceedings of the 4th International Conference on Complex, Intelligent and Software Intensive Systems* (pp. 307-312). Washington, DC: IEEE Computer Society.

Aleksy, M., Stieger, B., & Vollmar, G. (2009). Case study on utilizing mobile applications in industrial field service. In *Proceedings of the 11th IEEE Conference on Commerce and Enterprise Computing* (pp. 333-336). Washington, DC: IEEE Computer Society.

Benjamins, V. R., Davies, J., Baeza-Yates, R., Mika, P., Zaragoza, H., & Greaves, M. (2008). Near-term prospects for semantic technologies. *IEEE Intelligent Systems, 23*(1), 76–88. doi:10.1109/MIS.2008.10

Freitas, J., Correia, A., & Brito e Abreu, F. (2008). An ontology for IT services. In *Proceedings of the 13th Conference on Software Engineering and Databases.*

Gruber, T. (1993). Model formulation as a problem-solving task: Computer-assisted engineering modeling. *International Journal of Intelligent Systems, 8*(1), 105–127. doi:10.1002/int.4550080108

Gruber, T. (1995). Towards principles for the design of ontologies used for knowledge sharing. *International Journal of Human-Computer Studies, 43*, 907–928. doi:10.1006/ijhc.1995.1081

Guha, R. V., McCool, R., & Miller, E. (2003). Semantic search. In *Proceedings of the Twelfth International World Wide Web Conference* (pp. 700-709). New York, NY: ACM Press.

Hebeler, J., Fisher, M., Blace, R., & Perez-Lopez, A. (2009). *Semantic web programming.* Indianapolis, IN: John Wiley & Sons.

Hepp, M. (2008). GoodRelations: An ontology for describing products and services offers on the web. In A. Gangemi & J. Euzenat (Eds.), *Proceedings of the 16th International Conference on Knowledge Engineering and Knowledge Management* (LNCS 5268, pp. 329-346).

Hongwei, W., Fu, J., & Wu, J. (2003). A study on a formal ontology model: Constructing a customer ontology in a CRM context. In *Proceedings of the Americas Conference on Information Systems* (pp. 1201-1212).

Horrocks, I., Patel-Schneider, P. F., Boley, H., Tabet, S., Grosof, B., & Dean, M. (2004). *SWRL: A semantic web rule language combining OWL and RuleML.* Retrieved from http://www.w3.org/Submission/SWRL/

International Telecommunication Union. (2005). *ITU Internet reports 2005: The Internet of things –Executive summary.* Geneva, Switzerland: ITU.

Jarrar, M., Verlinden, R., & Meersman, R. (2003). Ontology-based consumer complaint management. In R. Meersman & Z. Tari (Eds.), *Proceedings of the Workshop on Regulatory Ontologies and the Modeling of Complaint Regulations* (LNCS 2889, pp. 594-606).

Kifer, M., & Lausen, G. (1989). F-logic: A higher-order language for reasoning about objects, inheritance, and scheme. *SIGMOD, 18*(2), 134–146. doi:10.1145/66926.66939

kSOAP2. (2011). *A lightweight and efficient SOAP engine suitable for J2ME or constrained java devices.* Retrieved from http://ksoap2.sourceforge.net/

Kunz, S., Aleksy, M., Brecht, F., Fabian, B., & Wauer, M. (2010). ALETHEIA – Improving industrial service-lifecycle management by semantic data federations. In *Proceedings of the IEEE 24th International Conference on Advanced Information Networking and Applications* (pp. 1308-1313). Washington, DC: IEEE Computer Society.

Oracle Corp. (2011). *Java ME: Java platform micro edition.* Retrieved from http://www.oracle.com/technetwork/java/javame/overview/index.html

Shadbolt, N., Berners-Lee, T., & Hall, W. (2006). The semantic web revisited. *IEEE Intelligent Systems, 21*(3), 96–101. doi:10.1109/MIS.2006.62

Stieger, B., Aleksy, M., & Vollmar, G. (2008). A method to identify mobile optimization opportunities in field service processes. In *Proceedings of the IADIS International Conference on e-Commerce* (pp. 255-259).

Stuckenschmidt, H., & van Harmelen, F. (2004). *Information sharing on the semantic web*. Berlin, Germany: Springer Verlag.

Chapter 5
Acquiring the Gist of Social Network Service Threads via Comparison with Wikipedia

Akiyo Nadamoto
Konan University, Japan

Eiji Aramaki
The University of Tokyo, Japan

Takeshi Abekawa
National Institute Informatics, Japan

Yohei Murakami
National Institute of Information and Communications Technology, Japan

ABSTRACT

Internet-based social network services (SNSs) have grown increasingly popular and are producing a great amount of content. Multiple users freely post their comments in SNS threads, and extracting the gist of these comments can be difficult due to their complicated dialog. In this paper, the authors propose a system that explores this concept of the gist of an SNS thread by comparing it with Wikipedia. The granularity of information in an SNS thread differs from that in Wikipedia articles, which implies that the information in a thread may be related to different articles on Wikipedia. The authors extract target articles on Wikipedia based on its link graph. When an SNS thread is compared with Wikipedia, the focus is on the table of contents (TOC) of the relevant Wikipedia articles. The system uses a proposed coverage degree to compare the comments in a thread with the information in the TOC. If the coverage degree is higher, the Wikipedia paragraph becomes the gist of the thread.

INTRODUCTION

As Internet-based social network services (SNS's) have grown increasingly popular they are producing a great amount of content. An SNS consists of an Internet community, containing multiple threads, with each thread containing comments posted by multiple users. It is difficult to obtain a gist of a thread because these comments are complicated. There are two types of SNS users. The first type becomes a member of the community and discusses the theme of the thread. We call this

DOI: 10.4018/978-1-4666-2026-1.ch005

user an "inside user." The second type, an "outside user," is a casual browser who simply views the SNS to acquire information from it.

Inside users can sometimes enter into heated discussion, which prompts them to concentrate on only one issue and lose track of the actual theme. When this happens, inside users may want to know how relevant their points are to the discussion. We therefore believe it would be beneficial to present these users with information to help them understand the gist of the discussion at a glance.

Outside users can theoretically obtain detailed information on the theme of a thread from the SNS, since community members who are inside users have good knowledge about the theme. Inside users, however, often do not explicitly provide basic information, because this is considered to be tacit knowledge, making it difficult for outside users to obtain. Moreover, a thread might contain many comments from outside users, making it difficult again to grasp the gist. It would be convenient for outside users to obtain the gist of a thread at a glance, while at the same time acquiring basic information about it.

In this paper, we propose a system that presents the gist of an SNS thread's information by comparing the comments in the thread with Wikipedia article content. Wikipedia articles are posted by different users on the basis that a "neutral point of view is the fundamental principle of Wikipedia" (Wikipedia, 2011). We therefore consider a Wikipedia article on a given theme to be based on a general viewpoint. In the present study, we extract articles from Wikipedia and compare each comment in a thread in the community content with the smallest structure in the article's table of contents (TOC). We consider the table of contents in the articles of Wikipedia to be the gist and the content of a paragraph on Wikipedia as basic information.

In this paper, we define a "target thread" as one from which the gist is to be extracted, and a "target article" as an article on Wikipedia that is to be compared with the target thread. The process of extracting a gist and basic information is as follows (Figure 1 and Figure 2):

- Extract noisy comments from a target thread.
- Identify target articles on Wikipedia.
- Compare the target thread and target articles on the basis of the table of contents based on our coverage degree.
- Extract the gist of information about the target thread.

RELATED WORK

In the field of natural language processing (NLP), there is a great deal of research about content summarization. Mani (2001) wrote about automatic summarization. Most research summarizes the content by calculating the importance of the sentences and structure of the text. Tombros et al. (1998) describe the summarization of the results of information retrieval by using a query. Li et al. (2009) proposed a method for enhancing diversity, coverage, and balance in the summarization of content. Their viewpoints were similar to that of our approach. Some research has been done on creating summary sentences from Web pages (Sun et al., 2007; Wang et al., 2007; Delort et al., 2003) using NLP. It is however difficult to use the technique for extracting the gist of SNS threads because almost all comments are short and their conversation is confusing. It would be convenient if inside and outside users could extract this gist at a glance. This paper proposes a system that shows this gist of a thread's information by comparing its comments with Wikipedia article content. To determine the differences between two Web pages, Lim and Ng (2001) proposed a semantic change-detection (SCD) algorithm for detecting semantic changes between two bodies of HTML data. Their approach was based on the transformation of HTML data from the two sources into trees and the removal of common edges between

Figure 1. Illustration of comparison of an SNS thread with Wikipedia article

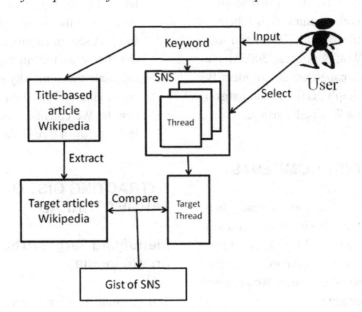

the two trees. This algorithm was mainly intended for detecting important updates made to a Web page. Nadamoto et al. (2005) proposed CWB and B-CWB. In this study, we have focused on examining how the similarities (or differences) between two Web sites can be effectively presented page by page. In order to extract gist of an SNS thread, we compare the thread with a Wikipedia article.

Significant studies on Wikipedia have been carried out. Nakayama et al. (2008), Suchanek et al. (2007), Wu and Weld (2008), and Gabrilovich and Markovitch (2007) obtained information (semantic) from Wikipedia, and analyses were carried out by using category structures and link structures. Our study, in contrast, does not focus on knowledge that can be gained from Wikipedia; rather, we use the structure of an article's table of contents to extract the gist of an SNS thread.

Dialog has mainly been studied using carefully annotated transcription data such as dialog act markup in several layers (DAMSL) (Core & Allen, 1997) and graph-based dialog annotation

Figure 2. Comparison between a target thread and a target article in our system

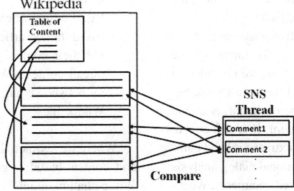

(Bird & Liberman, 1999). This is true of discourse studies as well, and various annotation schemes such as RST-DT (Carlson et al., 2002) and discourse graph-bank (Wolf & Gibson, 2005) have been proposed. In this paper, we do not identify dialog in a thread, but simply perform a comparison between a thread and a Wikipedia article.

EXTRACTING NOISY COMMENTS

Unnecessary comments found in a thread when we determine its gist and basic information are called "noisy comments," and we extract them. These are meaningless comments unrelated to the target thread and question sentence. We propose three types of noisy comments.

- **Meaningless comment:** A meaningless comment is a comment with many confused sentences. We consider a comment to be meaningless when a sentence in it has just one or no nouns. We also consider comments with sentences containing only multiple nouns, multiple verbs, or multiple adjectives to be meaningless.
- **Question comment:** Question comments are usually important in a thread. A question comment gives clues to the present topic, but the comment itself is not important as a semantic element in a thread. Therefore, we remove question comments as noisy comments. We consider questions to be comments that include "?" within the end of sentence five characters.
- **Unrelated comment:** Sometimes a comment is not related to the theme of the target thread. In this case, we consider an isolated comment that has no response but is related to the theme of the target thread to be a related comment. It is difficult to identify the dialog to extract a related comment because conventional dialog analysis method extracts isolated comments. We at-

tempt to identify unrelated comments by comparing the comments of a thread with Internet search results conducted by using the theme as the query. In particular, we calculate the similarity between individual comments and the first 50 Yahoo! Search results. We consider comments with similarity below a threshold to be unrelated.

EXTRACTING GIST OF TARGET THREAD

Identifying Target Articles on Wikipedia

The granularity of information in a thread is occasionally different from that in a Wikipedia article, which implies that information in a thread may sometimes be related to different Wikipedia articles. We consider three types of target articles. We use all types of these target articles when we extract the gist and basic information.

- **Title-based target article:** We first identify a target article with a theme matching a community's keyword. We refer to the target article as a title-based target article, and when we extract other target articles, we use this article as a standard.
- **Link-based target articles:** Link-based target articles are close to title-based target articles on the Wikipedia link graph.
- **Content-based target articles:** Content-based target articles are not close to title-based target articles on the link graph, but their content is similar to the target thread content. We calculate the similarity between a target thread and articles on Wikipedia.

When we extract link-based target articles and content-based target articles, we create a Wikipedia link graph.

1. **Title-based target articles:** We extract articles whose titles match the community's keyword. When there are multiple articles with the same title, the user selects the article from our system.

2. **Link-based target articles:** We first identify articles whose distance from title-similar articles is one path on the link graph. The selected articles become candidates for link-based target articles, and we identify a link-based target by three types of links.

   ○ **Interactive linked article:** An interactive linked article has an inlink and outlink to the title-based target article. We consider that it is important to the theme of the thread, and we regard an interactive linked article as a link-based target article.

   ○ **Outlink article:** An outlink article is linked from the title-based target article. If its title appears in a target thread many times (greater than the threshold), the article is considered a link-based target article (Figure 3).

   ○ **Inlink article:** An inlink article links to a title-based target article. We consider that it is not important to the title-based article, and we ignore it.

3. **Content-based target articles:** Even if the articles are not close to a title-similar article on the link graph, they may have similarities with the thread. We call these content-similar target articles. For these, we first extract a candidate of content-similar target articles from the link graph. If the title of an article appears many times (greater than threshold) in the thread but is not an immediate neighbor, it is considered a candidate for a content-similar target article. We extract content-similar target articles from all candidates for articles on the basis of the page-similar degree. To calculate this, we calculate the similarity between all paragraphs in a candidate content-similar target article and all comments in a target thread in a round-robin manner (Figure 2). The page-similar degree is the ratio of similar paragraphs to all paragraphs. We calculate similarity by using a cosine vector function. Our page-similar degree of a surrounding article Psd (SA_i) is as follows:

$$\text{Psd}\left(\text{SA}_i\right) = \frac{\text{SCA}_i}{\text{PCA}_i}$$

Figure 3. Wikipedia link graph

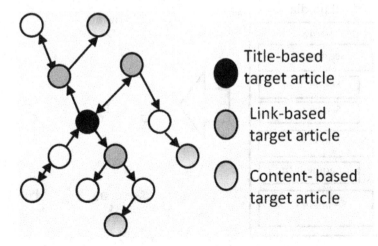

Title-based target article

Link-based target article

Content-based target article

where SA_i is a candidate for a content-similar target article and SCA_i is the total number of similar paragraphs in that article. PCA_i is a combinatorial number between the number of comments in the target thread and the number of paragraphs in the content-similar target article. If $Psd(SA_i)$ is greater than the threshold, the article is considered a content-similar target article.

Comparison Between Target Threads and Target Articles

After identifying the target article, we compare the comments in the thread with small passages in the target article and extract the gist of a thread by using our proposed coverage degree. Here, we focus on the Wikipedia table of contents (TOC). Small passages, called segments, are divided on the basis of the article's TOC. The steps for calculating the important degree are as follows (Figure 4):

1. Divide target articles of Wikipedia based on TOC. We designate the divided minimum units of article as segments.
2. Create a tree structure from the structure of the TOC. A tree node is a segment.
3. Extract all nouns from each segment.

4. Calculate the coverage degree using nouns extracted in step 3.

In the tree structure, the child node is a subsection of the parent node. We consider that the parent node summarizes information of its child nodes, and the presents detailed information on the parent node. We then propose two types of coverage degree based on the node type.

*   Coverage degree of leaf node

When the node is a leaf node, we calculate the coverage degree $cov(N_i)_j$, which is the coverage of comment j in an SNN to a node (Wikipedia segment) N_i as

$$cov(N_i)_j = \frac{|j|}{|N_i|}$$

where N_i is a leaf node, num(j) signifies the number of SNS co-occurrence pairs in j, and $|N_i|$ represents the total number of basic co-occurrence pairs in N_i.

*   Coverage degree of a non-leaf node

Figure 4. Divide Wikipedia articles

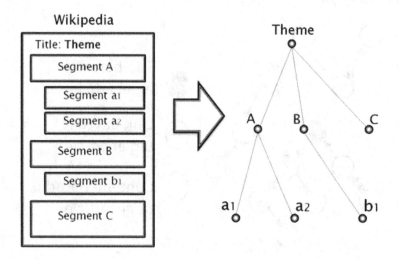

When the node has a child node, it is summarized information of the child nodes; these have an inclusion relation. We consider that the coverage degree of the non-leaf node includes its child nodes. In this case, we calculate coverage degree $cov(N_i)_j$ which is coverage of j to N_i as follows:

$$cov(N_i)_j = \frac{|j|}{|N_i \bigcup n_1 \bigcup \cdots \bigcup n_m|} +$$
$$\frac{|N_i \bigcap n_1 \bigcap \cdots \bigcap n_m \bigcap j|}{|N_i \bigcap n_1 \bigcap \cdots \bigcap n_m|} +$$
$$\sum_{k=1}^{m} \frac{|N_i \bigcap n_1 \bigcap \cdots \bigcap n_m \bigcap j \bigcap \bar{n}_k|}{|N_i \bigcap n_k - N_i \bigcap n_1 \bigcap \cdots \bigcap n_m|}$$

In these equations, N_i signifies a non-leaf node, n_1, n_m are child nodes of N_i, m denotes a total number of comments in the N thread.

PROTOTYPE SYSTEM

We developed a prototype system called Gist of SNS System (GSS). Figure 5 and Figure 6 shows the prototype's user interface. Microsoft C# is used to implement the prototype. The left-hand window in Figure 5 shows the Wikipedia article containing the keywords input by the user and the left-hand window in Figure 6 shows the results obtained with the prototype. We used the topic of the content structure list to identify an accurate gist of the thread. An overview of our system is as follows:

1. A user inputs the theme of the thread he/she wants to use as a keyword for comparison.
2. GSS displays the target Wikipedia article in the left window. The list of candidates in the SNS thread whose theme matches the user's input is displayed on the right window (Figure5).

3. The user selects the SNS thread he/she wants to compare, and this becomes target thread.
4. If there is more than one candidate Wikipedia article, the user selects the target article from the left window.
5. GSS deletes noisy comments from the target thread.
6. GSS extracts the title-based, link-based, and content-based target articles.
7. GSS then compares the target comment with each segment in the target articles by using a coverage degree. When the coverage degree of the segment is higher than the threshold, its TOC title becomes a similar title.
8. In step 7, the system calculates the number of comments in the target thread.
9. The GSS presents a similar title as that on Wikipedia as the gist of the thread (Figure 6). It also it presents multiple articles in each tab in the left window.
10. In the left window, the user selects his/her desired tab in order to get the gist of the information.
11. When the user clicks a heading in the TOC in the left window, the system displays the Wikipedia article.

EXPERIMENTS

We conducted three experiments; for examining the extraction noisy comments, studying the extraction of the gist of an SNS thread content, and testing the usability of our proposed system.

Experiment 1: Extraction of Noisy Comments

Our experiments used data from an SNS on the topic of movies. Results are shown in Table 1. The average recall ratio was 72.2% and average precision ratio was 86.2%. The results are satisfactory and show that our proposed method is effective in extracting noisy comments.

Figure 5. First Display of GSS

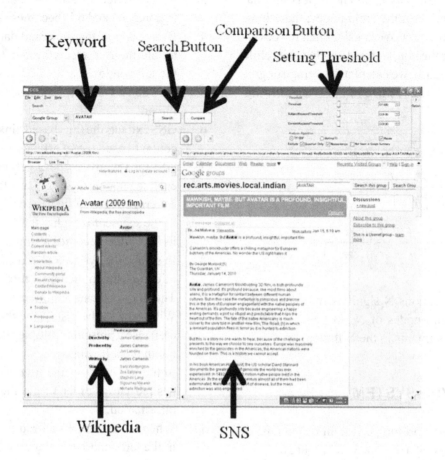

Experiment 2: Extraction of Gist of an SNS Thread

We use the most popular Japanese SNS site, called mixi as the representative SNS. We select two types of topics. One is a popular topic the other is a specialistic topic. We use movie topic as a popular topic and medical topic as a specialistic topic. Six threads were in mixi about movies and the other six were about medical topics. We measured the precision, recall, and F-measure in our system based on the threshold of the importance degree. Experiment steps are as follows:

1. We selected datasets (threads) from 12 threads.

2. Subjects compared comments in each thread with each target thread.
3. A Wikipedia segment is specified by more than half of the subjects being inferred as correct data.

Table 1. Recall and precision ratios

Theme	Number of comments	Recall ratio (%)	Precision ratio (%)
The Da Vinci Code	38	61.3	87.0
I Am Legend	48	64.7	73.0
Avatar	10	100	100
Tales from Earthsea	89	65.6	85.7
20th Century Boys	115	69.5	85.2

Figure 6. Result Display of GSS

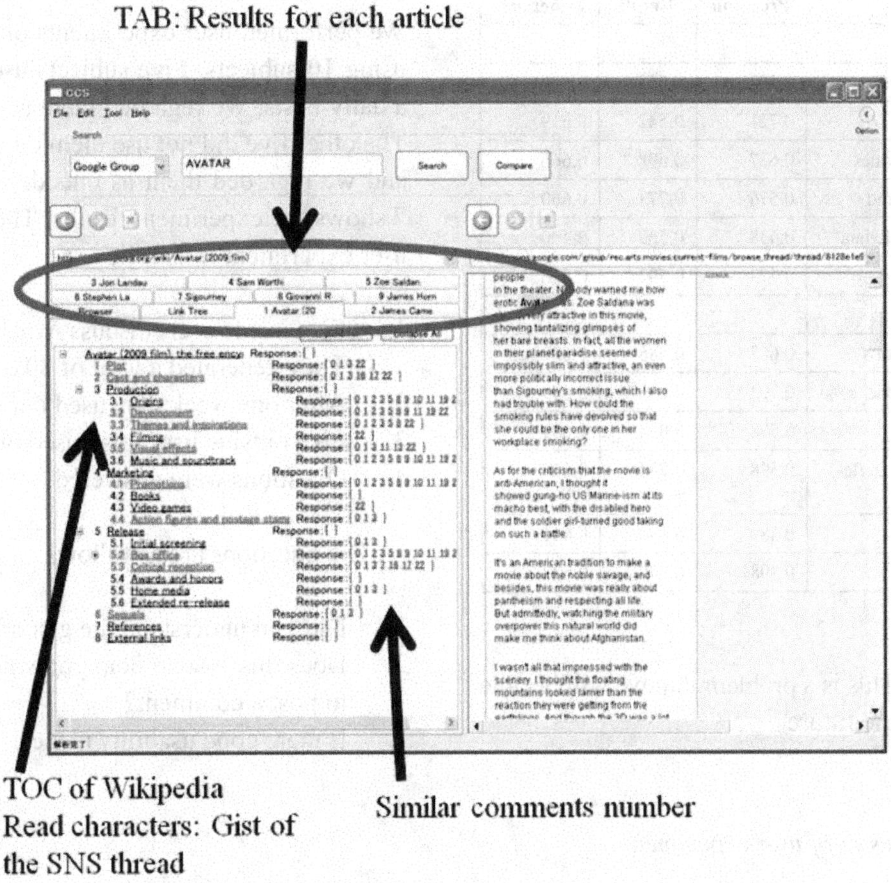

TAB: Results for each article

TOC of Wikipedia
Read characters: Gist of
the SNS thread

Similar comments number

4. Subjects run the system.
5. Subjects checked the result of (4) to determine whether it captured the gist of the content.
6. The precision, recall, and F-measure are calculated by using results of (3) and (5).

(1) Results

Table 2 shows the results of the experiment.

(2) Discussion

The F-measures of all datasets are greater than 0.5, as shown in Table 2. These results show that our proposed method is good for extraction of

the gist of an SNS thread. However, the precision for "Alice in Wonderland" and "Up" is not good, which is because their threads discussed technical terms related to 3D movies, and the respective Wikipedia articles on these movies are not about 3D technical terms. Our technique regards title-based article as seed articles, and we extract target articles based on the title-based article. Our system cannot extract the gist of content that is not written in a title-based article. We expect to be able to solve this problem in the near future.

The precision for "pile" and "ingrown nail" is also poor. In this case, the thread topics are very narrow. The recall is a high score, but our system extracts other topics in Wikipedia as the gist of

Table 2. Results of Experiment 2

Title	Precision	Recall	F-measure
Movie Data			
The Borrowers	0.582	0.663	0.620
District 9	0.721	0.542	0.619
The Lovely Bones	0.637	0.698	0.666
The Fourth Kind	0.576	0.773	0.660
Alice in Wonderland	0.438	0.569	0.490
UP	0.473	0.592	0.526
Medical Data			
Atopic dermatitis	0.687	0.586	0.632
Migraine headache	0.703	0.645	0.673
Hives	0.508	0.834	0.631
Hernia of interverte-bral disk	0.598	0.744	0.663
Pile	0.489	0.890	0.631
Ingrown nail	0.398	0.780	0.527

the thread. This is a problem that we will be able to solve in the future.

Experiment 3: User Experiment

We performed user experiments on our system, using 10 subjects. Five subjects used SNS's on a daily basis. We regarded them as inside users. The other five did not use them on a daily basis, and we regarded them as outside users. Figure 7 shows the experiment results. The flow of the user experiment is as follows:

1. Five inside users discuss Avatar on an SNS. They generated a total of 80 comments.
2. After one week they used our system
3. Five outside users also used our system.
4. Questions were answered.

The questions are as follows:

1. Did you understand the gist of the thread?
2. Does this system help you when you want to post a comment?
3. Is there good usability in the user interface?

Figure 7. Result of user experiment

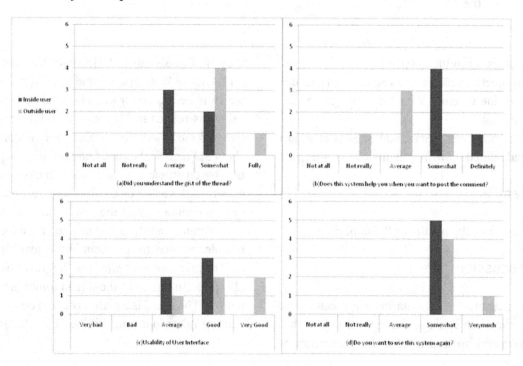

4. Do you want to use this system again?

Most of the users said that our system was useful for obtaining the gist of the thread. The five outside users were more enthusiastic about the system that the five inside users. The users noted the following advantages and drawbacks:
Inside user

1. Advantages
   ○ This system is useful when I want to make new comments because I can get information about the old comments at a glance.
   ○ I can get information that was not discussed.
   ○ The user interface helps me to get the gist of an SNS thread at a glance.
2. Drawbacks
   ○ The calculation time is too slow.
   ○ There are so many target pages that it's difficult to show them all.
   ○ The window is too small, so I can't view all the information.
   ○ It missed some information that we didn't discuss.

Outside user

1. Advantages
   ○ The system lets me understand the gist of the thread.
   ○ The thread is too long, and I can't read and understand it, but the system is very convenient for getting the gist of a thread.
   ○ This is good for getting basic information from Wikipedia, which lets me get the gist of the thread.
2. Drawbacks
   ○ I want to get not only the gist of the thread but also the specific comments.
   ○ The calculation time is too slow.

The feedback indicates that we need to study calculation time in the near future. This experiment only evaluation one type of content. In the future, we will do the same experiment based on other target titles and analyze the results.

CONCLUSION

We proposed a system that presents the gist of and basic information on SNS thread content by using Wikipedia. We focused on Wikipedia article tables of contents; comparing the comments in a thread with the information in the TOC and identifying similar content.

In the near future, we will consider calculation time, extract specific comments in SNSs, and we intend to expand our system to include new words and special community words.

ACKNOWLEDGMENT

Part of this research was supported by a Grant-in-Aid for the Information Explosion Project (Number: 21013044 (A01-39)).

REFERENCES

Bird, S., & Liberman, M. (1999, June). Annotation graphs as a framework for multidimensional linguistic data analysis. In *Proceedings of the Association for Computational Linguistics Workshop on Towards Standards and Tools for Discourse Tagging* (pp.1-10).

Carlson, L., Marcu, D., & Okurowski, M. E. (2002). *RST discourse Treebank*. Retrieved from http://www.ldc.upenn.edu/Catalog/CatalogEntry.jsp?catalogId=LDC2002T07

Core, M. G., & Allen, J. F. (1997). Coding dialogues with the DAMSL annotation scheme. In *Proceedings of the Working Notes of the AAAI Fall Symposium on Communicative Action in Humans and Machines* (pp. 28-35).

Delort, J.-Y., Bouchon-Meunier, B., & Rifqi, M. (2003, August). Enhanced web document summarization using hyperlinks. In *Proceedings of the Fourteenth ACM Conference on Hypertext and Hypermedia*, Nottingham, UK (pp. 208-215).

Gabrilovich, E., & Markovitch, S. (2007, January). Computing semantic relatedness using Wikipedia-based explicit semantic analysis. In *Proceedings of the International Joint Conference on Artificial Intelligence*, Hyderabad, India (pp.1606-1611).

Li, L., Zhou, K., Xue, G.-R., Zha, H., & Yu, Y. (2009, April). Enhancing diversity, coverage and balance for summarization through structure learning. In *Proceedings of the 18th International World Wide Web Conference*, Madrid, Spain (pp. 71-80).

Lim, S.-J., & Ng, Y.-K. (2001, April). An automated change-detection algorithm for HYML documents based on semantic hierarchies. In *Proceedings of the 17th International Conference on Data Engineering* (pp. 303-312).

Mani, I. (2001). *Automatic summarization*. Amsterdam, The Netherlands: John Benjamins Publishing.

Nadamoto, A., Ma, Q., & Tanaka, K. (2005). B-CWB: Bilingual comparative web browser based on content-synchronization and viewpoint retrieval. *World Wide Web (Bussum)*, *8*(3), 347–367. doi:10.1007/s11280-005-1316-8

Nakayama, K., Pei, M., Erdmann, M., Ito, M., Shirakawa, M., Hara, T., & Nishio, S. (2008, July). Wikipedia mining - Wikipedia as a corpus for knowledge extraction. In *Proceedings of the Annual Wikipedia Conference*, Alexandria, Egypt.

Suchanek, F. M., Kasneci, G., & Weikum, G. (2007, May). YAGO: A core of semantic knowledge unifying WordNet and Wikipedia. In *Proceedings of the 16th International World Wide Web Conference*, Banff, AB, Canada (pp. 697-706).

Sun, J.-T., Shen, D., Zeng, H.-J., Yang, Q., Lu, Y., & Chen, Z. (2005, August). Web-page summarization using clickthrough data. In *Proceedings of the 28th Annual International ACM SIGIR conference on Research and development in information retrieval*, Salvador, Brazil (pp.194-201).

Tombros, A., & Sanderson, M. (1998). Advantages of query biased summaries in information retrieval. In *Proceedings of the 21st Annual International ACM SIGIR Conference on Research and Development in Information Retrieval*, Melbourne, Australia (pp. 2-10).

Wang, C., Jing, F., Zhang, L., & Zhang, H.-J. (2007, November). Learning query-biased web page summarization. In *Proceedings of the 16th Conference on Information and Knowledge Management*, Lisbon, Portugal (pp. 555-562).

Wikipedia. (2011). *Neutral point of view*. Retrieved from http://en.wikipedia.org/wiki/Wikipedia:Neutral_point_of_view

Wolf, F., & Gibson, E. (2005). Representing discourse coherence: A corpus-based study. *Computational Linguistics, 31*(2), 249–287. doi:10.1162/0891201054223977

Wu, F., & Weld, D. S. (2008, April). Automatically refining the Wikipedia Infobox ontology. In *Proceedings of the 17th International World Wide Web Conference*, Beijing, China (pp. 365-644).

This work was previously published in International Journal of Business Data Communications and Networking, Volume 7, Issue 2, edited by Varadharajan Sridhar and Debashis Saha, p.p 17-28, copyright 2011 by IGI Publishing (an imprint of IGI Global)

Chapter 6
Query Processing in a Mediator Based Framework for Linked Data Integration

Vânia M. P. Vidal
Federal University of Ceará, Brazil

José A. F. de Macêdo
Federal University of Ceará, Brazil

Marco A. Casanova
Pontifícia Universidade Católica do Rio de Janeiro, Brazil

Fábio Porto
Laboratório Nacional de Computação Científica, Brazil

João C. Pinheiro
Federal University of Ceará, Brazil

ABSTRACT

In this paper, the authors present a three-level mediator based framework for linked data integration. In the approach, the mediated schema is represented by a domain ontology, which provides a conceptual representation of the application. Each relevant data source is described by a source ontology, published on the Web according to the Linked Data principles. Each source ontology is rewritten as an application ontology, whose vocabulary is restricted to be a subset of the vocabulary of the domain ontology. The main contribution of the paper is an algorithm for reformulating a user query into sub-queries over the data sources. The reformulation algorithm exploits inter-ontology links to return more complete query results. The approach is illustrated by an example of a virtual store mediating access to online booksellers.

1. INTRODUCTION

The Semantic Web is attempting to provide technologies for effectively publishing, retrieving and integrating RDF data distributed over the web. We agree with (Langegger, Woss, & Blochl, 2008) that large-scale data integration is probably one of the best use cases for the Semantic Web technology. There are several aspects of the Semantic Web that make it appropriate for the integration of data from distributed and heterogeneous data sources (Wache et al., 2001). Briefly, these are: RDF, the Resource Description Framework, a simple, but powerful and extensible data model; URIs (or IRIs) used for global naming; and the possibility of reasoning based on Description Logic (Calvanese et al., 2008).

DOI: 10.4018/978-1-4666-2026-1.ch006

In this paper, we consider the problem of designing data integration systems (Lenzerini, 2002) when the data sources are published on the Web according to the Linked Data principles (Bizer, Heath, & Berners-Lee, 2009), which require the identification of entities with URI references that can be resolved over the HTTP protocol into RDF data that describes the identified entity. These descriptions may include RDF links pointing to other data sources. RDF links take the form of RDF triples, where the subject of the triple is an URI reference in the namespace of one data source, while the object is a URI reference in the namespace of the other. The notion of identity is an important issue in the Semantic Web. URIs guarantee that resources are uniquely identifiable resources on the Web, but they do not guarantee the uniqueness of the entities the resources refer to (Halpin, 2006). Thus, there is a need for a service that is able to find different URIs that refer to the same real-world entity.

In this paper, we propose a mediator-based framework for implementing data integration over linked data. We provide a sound and complete algorithm for reformulating a SPARQL query into a query over the (linked) data sources. The reformulation algorithm exploits inter-ontology links to return more complete query results.

This paper is organized as follows. Section 2 describes the framework proposed for linked data integration. Section 3 summarizes some basic concepts required in the paper. Section 4 presents an example that will be used throughout the paper. Section 5 discusses the query answering method adopted. Section 6 introduces a strategy for query reformulation, which is the central contribution of the paper. Section 7 lists related work. Finally, Section 8 presents the conclusions and directions for future research.

2. A FRAMEWORK FOR LINKED DATA INTEGRATION

In this section, we discuss the three-level architecture for linked data integration, which is depicted in Figure 1.

The mediated schema is represented by a domain ontology (DO), which provides a conceptual representation of the domain (a globally shared vocabulary and a set of constraints). Each relevant data source is described by a source ontology, published on the Web according to the Linked Data principles, thereby becoming part of the Web of linked data. These source ontologies are depicted in the Web of Linked Data layer in Figure 1.

The local source schemas are accessed via wrappers, like those introduced in Berners-Lee et al. (2006) which export the local data into

Figure 1. Three-level architecture for linked data integration

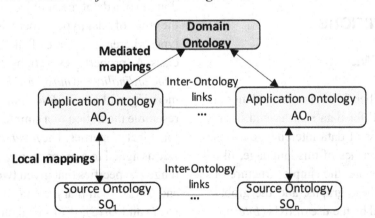

OWL. Each source ontology is rewritten as an application ontology (AO), whose vocabulary is restricted to be a subset of the vocabulary of the domain ontology. In Sacramento et al. (2010) we present a strategy to automatically generate such application ontologies, considering a set of local ontologies, a domain ontology and the result of the matching between each local ontology and the domain ontology. We adopt OWL Lite (Bechhofer et al., 2004) as the ontology language to represent the domain ontology, the source ontologies and the application ontologies.

In our framework, the application ontologies help breaking the query answering problem. They are also a notational convenience to divide the definition of the mappings into two stages: the definition of the *mediated mappings* and the definition of the *local mappings*, thereby facilitating the query rewriting process (Vidal, Sacramento, Macedo, & Casanova, 2009). The mediated mappings specify the concepts of the domain ontology in terms of the application ontologies; whereas the local mappings define the concepts of the application ontologies in terms of the elements of their corresponding local source ontology. Application ontologies enable the identification and the association of semantically corresponding concepts, so they are useful for enhancing tasks such as information discovery and retrieval, and also data integration. We remark that Lutz (2006) also adopts this architecture.

3. BASIC DEFINITIONS

3.1. RDF and OWL

RDF (Manola & Miller, 2004) is a general model language, optimized for data sharing and interchange. The easiness of data interchange arises from some characteristics of this language, like the RDF graph structure, the simple structure of the basic units of these graphs, and the global namespace provided by the use of IRIs (*Internationalized Resource Identifiers*).

In RDF, a data item is represented as *RDF statement* (or simply a *statement*), which is a triple *(s,p,o)*, where *s* is a IRI, called the *subject* of the statement, *p* is a IRI, called the *property* of the statement, and *o* is either a IRI or a literal, called the *object* of the statement; if *o* is a literal, then *o* is also called the *value* of property *p*. Each IRI and literal has a global scope. The use of global names is critically important, because it means that the triples can always be merged without name translations. Since each part of the statement in a graph can be used without translation, entire graphs can be transported and combined without any translation, which is a great advantage when exchanging data.

The *Web Ontology Language* (OWL) (Bechhofer et al., 2004) describes classes and properties in a way that facilitates machine interpretation of Web content. An *OWL schema* is an ontological description that may be serialized into a collection of RDF triples. A concept of an OWL schema is a class, datatype property or object property. The vocabulary of the schema is the set of concepts defined in the schema (a set of IRIs). The scope of a property name is global to the OWL schema, and not local to the class indicated as its domain. The OWL language family is organized as three dialects: OWL Lite, OWL DL and OWL Full.

In this work, we use OWL Lite. Briefly, this dialect supports named classes, datatype and object properties, subclasses, and individuals. The domain of a datatype or object property is a class; the range of a datatype property is an XML schema type, whereas the range of an object property is a class. As property restrictions, the dialect admits *minCardinality* and *maxCardinality*, with the usual meaning; and *InverseFunctionalProperty*, which resemble the notion of a simple key in databases, for object properties. The *InverseFunctionalProperty* assigned to a property *p*, with domain *C* and range *D*, specifies that given two instances *C(x1)* and *C(x2)*, such that *p(x1,y1)* and *p(x2,y2)*, with *D(y1)* and *D(y2)*, if *y1=y2* then *x1=x2*.

Finally, we say that: a property *p* is an *inter-ontology property* or an *inter-ontology link* iff the domain and range of *p* belong to different ontology; *p* is an *inter-ontology* link between *V* and *U* iff *V* is the vocabulary of the domain and *U* is the vocabulary of the range of *p*; *p* is *an inter-ontology link to W* iff *W* is the vocabulary of the domain or of the range of *p*; *p* is *an inter-ontology property* between *V* and *U* iff *p* is a *InverseFunctionalProperty* in *V* and in *U*.

We define two sets, namely *uri-link* and *same-as*, containing information about inter-ontology property and inter-ontology link, respectively. *URI_link* is a set of triples (*oi,oj, p*), where each *oi* and *oj* are distinct application ontology and *p* is a ontology property such that *dom(p)* ∈ *oi* and *range(p)* ∈ *oj*. Similarly, *same-as* is a set of triples *(oi,oj, p)*, where *oi* and *oj* are distinct application ontology and *p* is a common property in both ontologies *oi* and *oj*, such that *p* ∈ *oi, oj*.

3.2. SPARQL Query Language

SPARQL (*SPARQL Protocol and RDF Query Language*) (Prud'hommeaux & Seaborne, 2007) is a W3C standard recommendation. It is a declarative query language that allows extracting data from RDF graphs based on a graph pattern matching, whose basic constructs are *triple patterns*. An example of a triple pattern is *(?book s:title, ?t)*.

As an example, consider the following SPARQL query (applied over the Publishers application ontology presented in Figure 6):

In Figure 2, *?name* and *?phone* are variables, and the prefix '*pub*' identifies the dataset against which the query will be executed. The operator *AND* (denoted as ".") is equivalent to the relational *JOIN* operator, while the operator *OPTIONAL* is very similar to the relational *LEFT-OUTER-JOIN* operator (Pérez, Arenas, & Gutierrez, 2009). More precisely, the OPTIONAL operator joins its inner expression with the outer one; thereby holding outer result mappings for which no join partner exists. Note that the keyword *FILTER* is a restriction for a specified condition, and that the keyword *regex* defines an operation to test strings that is based on regular expressions. Finally, the keyword *ORDER BY* specifies a sorted result list. Thus, this query retrieves the names and phones of all publishers, whose country is *USA*.

3.3. Rule-Based Mapping Formalism

Let F be a set of function symbols and V be a set of variables. A *constant* is a 0-ary function symbol. The set of *terms* over F and V is recursively defined as follows: (1) each variable *v* in V is a term; (2) each constant *c* in F is a term; (3) if $t_1,...,t_n$ are terms, and *f* is an n-ary function symbol in F, then $f(t_1,...,t_n)$ is a term. An *atom* over F, P and V is an expression of the form *c(t)*,

Figure 2. Simple SPARQL query

```
PREFIX pub: <http://publishers/>
SELECT ?name, ?phone
FROM <publishers.owl>
WHERE {
  ?p pub:name ?name .
  OPTIONAL {?p pub:phone ?phone } .
  ?p pub:country ?country .
  FILTER regex(?country, "USA") .
} ORDER BY ?name ?phone
```

where c is a atomic concept and t is a term, or of the form $p(t,u)$, where p is an atomic role and t and u are terms.

Let O_S and O_T be two ontologies. A *class mapping* is specified through a set of *mapping rules*, each one of the form

$$\beta_1(w_1) \Leftarrow \alpha_1(v_1),\dots,\alpha_m(v_m)$$

where, $\alpha_i(v_i)$ is an atom whose atomic concept or atomic role occurs in the source ontology O_S, for $i=1,\dots,m$, and $\beta_1(w_1)$ is an atom whose atomic concept or atomic role occurs in the target ontology O_T. We say that $\alpha_1(v_1),\dots,\alpha_m(v_m)$ is the *body* of the mapping rule, understood as a conjunction, and $\beta_1(w_1)$ is the *head* of the mapping.

A property mapping is likewise specified, except that the head of the rule is a term of the form $p(t,u)$, where p is an atomic role and t and u are terms.

A *virtual class* (or *virtual property*) is a class (or property) that occurs in the head or a rule.

This rule-based formalism supports *Skolem functions* (Hull & Yoshikawa, 1990) for the creation of *new object identifiers* of classes in O_T from one or more properties of O_S. In this paper, the Skolem functions are simply used as URIref generators. So, these mapping rules allow the construction of URIrefs for new objects in O_T as terms of the form $f(t_1, \dots, t_n)$, where f is an n-ary function symbol and $t_1, \dots, t_n$ is a sequence of terms of O_S. Indeed, heterogeneous mappings (Ghidini & Serafini, 2006), that use Skolem functions, are necessary to express the semantic relationships between two ontologies, when, for example, the information represented as a class in one ontology is represented as an object property in the other.

Finally, to simplify the notation, when two or more rules have the same head, we combine their bodies into a single expression with the help of semi-colons. For example,

s:title(t)$\Leftarrow$ ap:title (t); ep:title(t)

denotes the two rules

s:title(t)$\Leftarrow$ ap:title(t)

s:title(t)$\Leftarrow$ ep:title(t)

4. RUNNING EXAMPLE

This section presents an example, adapted from (Casanova et al., 2009), of a virtual store mediating access to online booksellers.

- **Domain Ontology**: We assume that the user provides a domain ontology. Figure 3 shows a conceptual representation of the Sales domain ontology. We use the namespace prefix "*s:*" to refer to the vocabulary of this domain ontology. For example, *s:title* is defined as a datatype property with domain *s:Product* and range *string*, *s:Book* is declared as a subclass of *s:Product*, and *s:hasPub* is defined as an object property with domain *s:Book* and range *s:Publ*. Figure 4 shows the *inverse functional axioms* of the Sales domain ontology.
- **Source Ontologies**: We assume that we have two source ontologies describing data about Amazon and eBay virtual stores, and a third application ontology describing book Publishers. Figure 5 shows a conceptual representation of the source ontologies. We use the namespace prefixes "*am:*", "*eb:*" and "*pub:*" to refer to the vocabularies of *Amazon*, *eBay* and *Publishers* source ontologies, respectively.

Notice that the property *eb:publisher* with domain *eb:Product* and range *pub:Publ* is an inter-ontology property because it connects resources from different ontologies. The instances of the property *eb:publisher* are RDF links that

Figure 3. Domain Ontology

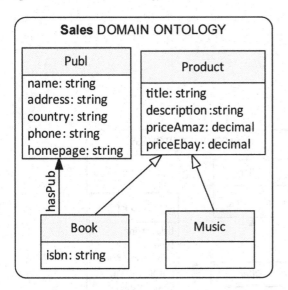

connects an instance of *eb:product* with an instance of *pub:publ*.

- **Application Ontologies:** Figure 6 shows the applications ontologies which are obtained based on the result of the matching between each local ontology and the domain ontology. The vocabulary of an application ontology consists of the classes and properties which are, intuitively, the subset of the domain ontology that matches the source ontology. We use the namespace prefixes "*ap:*", "*ep:*" and "*pp:*" to refer to the vocabularies of *Amazon*, *eBay* and *Publishers* application ontologies, respectively.

The inverse functional axiom *A1* specifies a virtual *same-as* property relating instances of *ap:Publ* and *pp:Publ*, defined as follows:

owl:same-as(X,Y) ⇐ ap:Publ(X), ap:name(X,n), pp:Publ(Y), pp:name(Y,n))

Likewise, the inverse functional axiom *A2* specifies a virtual *same-as* property relating instances of ap:Product and eb:Product, defined as follows:

owl:same-as(X,Y)⇐ap:Product(X),ap:title(X,t), ep:Product(Y),ep:title(Y,t)

- **Local Mappings**: Figure 7(a) and 7(b) show the local mappings.
- **Mediated Mappings:** Figure 8 shows the mediated mappings (note the use of ";" to denote disjunctive rules).

5. QUERY ANSWERING METHOD

The ultimate goal of a data integration system is to answer queries posed by the user in terms of the mediated schema (or Domain Ontology). We adopt the SPARQL query language (Prud'hommeaux & Seaborne, 2007) for posing queries on the domain ontology.

The proposed query processing strategy consists of four steps, summarized as follows:

1. **Translation:** The user starts by posing a SPARQL query Q, expressed in terms of a domain ontology, which is transformed into a parse tree representing the structure of the query in a useful way.
2. **Reformulation:** The query reformulation step is broken into two sub-steps:

Figure 4. Inverse Functional Axioms

```
A1: (s:name rdf:type owl:InverseFunctionalProperty)
A2: (s:title rdf:type owl:InverseFunctionalProperty)
```

Figure 5. Source Ontologies

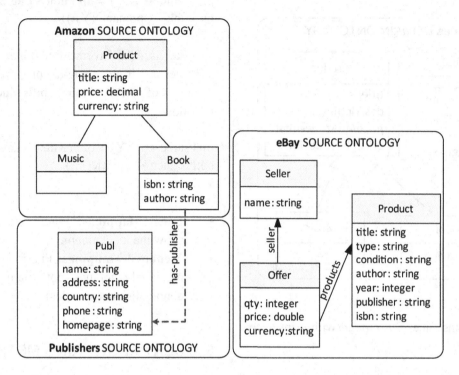

Figure 6. Application ontologies

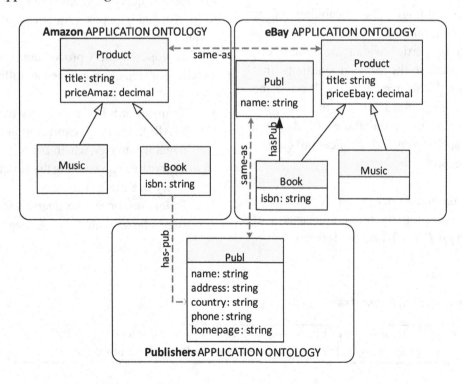

Figure 7(a). Mapping rules from the Amazon source ontology to the Sales domain ontology (b). Mapping rules from the eBay source ontology to the Sales domain ontology

```
#1:  s:Book(b)   ⇐ am:Book(b)
#2:  s:Product(b) ⇐ am:Book(b)
#3:  s:Music(m)  ⇐ am:Music(m)
#4:  s:Product(m) ⇐ am:Music(m)
#6:  s:title(b,t) ⇐ am:title(b,t), am:Book(b)
#7:  s:hasPub(b,p) ⇐ am:has-publisher(b,p), am:Book(b)
#8:  s:title(m,t)⇐ am:title(m,t), am:Music(m)
#9:  s:name(p,n)  ⇐ am:name(p,n), am:Publ(p)
#10: s:address(p,a) ⇐ am:address(p,a), am:Publ(p)
```

A

```
#1:  s:Book(p)   ⇐ eb:Product(p), eb:type(p)= ´book´
#2:  s:Product(p)⇐ eb:Product(p), eb:type(p)= ´book´
#3:  s:Music(p)⇐ eb:Product(p), eb:type(p)= ´music´
#4:  s:Product(p)⇐ eb:Product(p), eb:type(p)= ´music´
#5:  s:title(p,t)⇐ eb:title(p,t), eb:Product(p), eb:type(p)= ´book´
#6:  s:title(p,t) ⇐ eb:title(p,t), eb:Product(p), eb:type(p)= ´music´
#7:  s:Publ(fpubl(n))⇐ eb:publisher(b,n), eb:Product(b), eb:type(b)= ´book´
#8:  s:name(fpubl(n),n)⇐ eb:publisher(b,n), eb:Product(b), eb:type(b)= ´book´
#9:  s:hasPub(b, fpubl(n))⇐ eb:publisher(b,n), eb:Product(b), eb:type(b)= ´book´
```

B

a. Query Q is reformulated, based on the mediated mappings, into a set of sub-queries over the application ontologies. Each sub-query aims at extracting data from a single Application Ontology. All concepts that are relevant for answering the query is discovered in this step.

b. Each sub-query is then reformulated, based on the local mappings, in terms of a query over the source ontology.

3. **Optimization:** This step attempts to find the most desirable execution plan, according to the following objectives:

a. The potential cost reduction obtained by parallelizing sub-query processing. We provide a parallel query execution strategy based on *symmetric hash joins* (Wilschut & Apers, 1993) to deal with the fluctuations on data sources access in the Linked Data environment.

b. The potential cost reduction obtained by moving data from one node to another, using a strategy similar to relational *semi-joins* (Kossmann, 2000). We provide a *set bind join* operator based on the *bind-join* (Haas, Kossmann, Wimmers, & Yang, 1997) operator.

4. **Evaluation:** Each sub-query over a source ontology is evaluated at the local data source. The data source is accessed via a Linked Data wrapper, such as the D2R Server (Bizer & Cyganiak, 2006). The results of the sub-query are returned to the mediator, where the final result is built according to the optimized execution plan.

We now give an example of how a SPARQL query is processed.

Figure 8. Some of the mediated mappings

Class Mappings:	Property Mappings:
s:Product(p) ⇐ ap:Product(p); ep:Product(p)	s:title(t) ⇐ ap:title(t); ep:title(t)
s:Book(b) ⇐ ap:Book(b); ep:Book(b)	s:name(n) ⇐ ap:name(n); ep:name(n)
...	

Example 5.1: Consider a query *Q* over the *Sales* domain ontology that asks for titles and names of their publishers for all books whose publishers' country is "USA". Figure 9 shows this query in SPARQL syntax:

Each processing step of the SPARQL query *Q* is illustrated as follows:

1. **Translation:** The query is parsed, that is, transformed into a query tree representing the structure of the query, as illustrated in Figure 10. Each node of this tree is labeled with a datatype or object variable. Each edge is labeled with a property. Each object variable node has an annotation with respective type. The root node of the tree is called the *primary concept*.

2. **Reformulation:**
    a. First, the query *Q* is reformulated in terms of queries over the application ontologies (Figure 11).

    b. The query tree in Figure 11 consists of four sub-queries *Q1, Q2, Q3* and *Q4*, which aim at extracting data from single application ontology. The generated query tree represents the SPARQL query illustrated in Figure 12.

    c. Then the sub-queries are reformulated, based on the local mappings in Figure 7, in terms of a query over the data source schema (Figure 13). The reformulation is unambiguous and therefore straightforward.

3. **Optimization:** Figure 14(a) shows a graphical and intuitive representation of the execution plan for the queries shown in Figure 13.

First, equivalents queries are identified to avoid fetching the same data more than once. Note that queries *Q2'* and *Q4'* are similar. Hence, the execution plan is rearranged, as shown in Figure 14(b).

In this example, the join operator is implemented as a *set bind join*. The latter adapts the *bind join* operator to the data integration context. Considering that each data source is capable of

Figure 9. Query Q in SPARQL syntax

```
PREFIX s:<http:// sales/>
PREFIX rdf:<...>
SELECT ?t
WHERE {
 ?p rdf:type s:Book.
 ?p s:title ?t .
 ?p s:hasPub ?pub .
 ?pub s:country ?c
 FILTER regex(?c, "USA") .
}
```

Figure 10. Parse tree for query Q

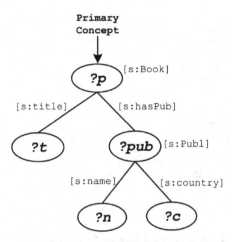

answering SPARQL queries, the *set bind join* corresponds to rewritting the data source subquery adding bind values to join predicates and submitting to the data source.

Our algorithm essentially consists of the following three phases:

1. *Scan phase*, which performs bind pattern projections on join properties, with duplicate elimination. In our example, Q_2'(Figure 15) projects the name (*?n*) and publisher URI-link (*?pub*) of publishers located in '*USA*'.

2. Set bind processing phase.

2.1 The bind/invoke phase, which executes several bind joins in parallel to decrease the size of intermediate results and speed up query evaluation. A constraint (SPARQL FILTER expression) is used to specify which data must be joined. Note that sub-queries Q_1' and Q_2' are rewritten adding the bind patterns as filter into sub-queries Q_1'' and Q_2'' (Figure 16).

2.2 The transmission phase, which sends to the mediator data previously obtained, in a parallel asynchronous fashion. In our example, the results returned to mediator from queries *Q1''* and *Q3''* are: "*Fundamentals of Database Systems*" and "*A Semantic Web Primer*".

3. *Final Processing*, which transmits to the mediator all data needed to compute the query answer. In our example, the final result is the union of the results of *Q1''* and *Q3''*, computed in pipeline by reading the HTTP response stream. The final result would be: "*Fundamentals of Database Systems, A Semantic Web Primer*".

4. *Evaluation*, which transforms the plan that the optimizer produces by into a *query executable plan*. Currently, we support two

Figure 11. Query Plan

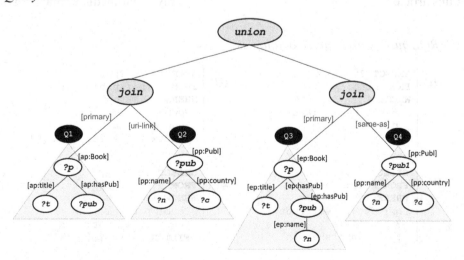

Figure 12. SPARQL queries over application ontologies

```
Q1    SELECT ?t, ?pub            Q2    SELECT ?n, ?pub
      FROM http://amazon               FROM http://publ
      WHERE {                          WHERE {
        ?p rdf:type ap:Book .            ?pup pp:name ?n .
        ?p ap:title ?t .                 ?pup pp:country ?c
        ?p ap:hasPub ?pub }              FILTER regex(?c,"USA").}


Q3    SELECT ?t, ?n             Q4    SELECT ?n
      FROM http://eBay                FROM http://publ
      WHERE {                         WHERE {
        ?p rdf:type ep:Book .           ?pup1 pp:name ?n .
        ?p ep:title ?t .                ?pup1 pp:country ?c
        ?p ep:hasPub ?pub .             FILTER regex(?c,"USA").}
        ?pub ep:name ?n .}
```

join implementations: *symmetric hash join* and *set bind join*.

6. QUERY REFORMULATION

In this section, we first discuss the idea of using inter-ontology property links during query answering to overcome incompleteness. Then, we present our query reformulation algorithm that takes into account inter-ontology links for rewriting queries over the application ontologies. The subsequent step to the query reformulation algorithm is the mapping of rewritten queries over ontology sources. This local mapping can be applied through a simple unfolding mechanism. Despite its importance, the algorithm to accomplish this simple unfolding is not part of the scope of this article.

6.1. The Role of Inter-Ontology Links in Query Answering

An important issue related to linked data integration is that, in the presence of *same-as* inter-ontology properties, the mediated mapping does not completely specifies the domain ontology data. Therefore, a simple unfolding strategy is in general not sufficient for providing all correct answers, as illustrated in the following example.

Example 6.1: Referring to our case study, consider the source ontology instances in Figure 17. Figure 18 shows the application ontologies instances obtained by applying the mappings in Figure 7. Figure 19 shows the instance of the domain ontology Sales obtained by applying the mediated mappings in Figure 8.

Figure 13. SPARQL queries over source ontologies

```
Q1'    SELECT ?t, ?pub           Q2'    SELECT ?n, ?pub
       FROM http://amazon               FROM http://publisher
       WHERE {                          WHERE {
         ?p rdf:type am:Book .            ?pub pub:name ?n .
         ?p am:title ?t .                 ?pub pub:country ?c
         ?p am:hasPub ?pub }              FILTER regex(?c, "USA").}


Q3'    SELECT ?t, ?n            Q4'    SELECT ?n
       FROM http://eBay               FROM http://publisher
       WHERE {                        WHERE {
         ?p rdf:type eb:Product .       ?pub1 pub:name ?n .
         ?p eb:title ?t .               ?pub1 pub:country ?c
         ?p eb:publisher ?n .}          FILTER regex(?c, "USA").}
```

Figure 14. (a) query plan tree; (b) equivalent plan tree without duplicate queries

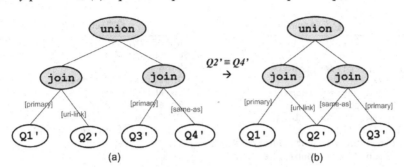

Consider the query in Figure 9. Referring to the instance of the domain ontology in Figure 19, the query returns only one title *"Fundamentals of Database Systems"*. But the correct answer for the query is *"Fundamentals of Database Systems, A Semantic Web Primer"* because, based on the virtual same-as property, we can infer that that *P1* and *P2* are the same entity (recall that we say that the same-as property is virtual because it is derived by applying a rule, as discussed in Section 3).

Figure 12 shows the query obtained from unfolding the query *Q* over the application ontologies on the basis of the mediated mappings in Figure 8. Referring to the data graph in Figure 18, the query returns only one title *"Fundamentals of Database Systems"*. Note that the query in Figure 19 provides all correct answers *"Fundamentals of Database Systems, A Semantic Web Primer"*.

Figure 15. SPARQL queries over Publisher Source ontologies

```
SELECT distinct ?n, ?pub
FROM http://publisher
WHERE {
  ?pub pub:name ?n .
  ?pub pub:country ?c
  FILTER regex(?c, "USA").

}
```

6.2. The Query Reformulation Algorithm

Figure 20 shows the query reformulation algorithm. Briefly, the main steps of the algorithm are:

1. First, select the application ontologies whose vocabularies contain the *primary concept* of the query tree (QT). We say that these are the *primary ontologies*.
2. Then, for each primary ontology vocabulary *V*, generate the *reformulated query tree* (RQT), using the recursive REWRITE_ NODE procedure in Figure 20. This procedure rewrites each property of a node N of a query tree (QT) in terms of *V*, or uses inter-ontology properties to discover other vocabularies for rewriting the properties which are not in *V*.
3. The final query plan (FQP) consists of the union of the reformulated query plans of the primary ontologies.

The following example illustrates how the algorithm reformulates a query tree.

Example 6.2. Consider the query tree (QT) in Figure 10. The primary concept is *s:Book*, which occurs in the vocabularies of the Amazon and the eBay application ontologies. To generate the RQT for a primary ontology, the algorithm calls the REWRITE_NODE

Figure 16. Variable bindings in SPARQL with FILTER expression

Q_1" (Amazon)	Q_3" (eBay)

SELECT ?t, ?pub
 	
FROM http://amazon
WHERE {
 ?p rdf:type am:Book .
 ?p am:title ?t .
 ?p am:hasPub ?pub
 FILTER (
 (?pub='http://publisher/p1#')||
 (?pub='http://publisher/p2#'))
}
	SELECT ?t, ?n
	FROM http://eBay
	WHERE {
	 ?p rdf:type eb:Product .
	 ?p eb:title ?t .
	 ?p eb:publisher ?n .
	 FILTER (
	 (?n = 'Addison-Wesley')||
	 (?n = 'Mit-press'))
	}

procedure with two parameters: the QT with root node r and the vocabulary of the primary ontology. The procedure recursively transverse each node N of QT and rewrites each property p of N. The procedure considers three different types of properties:

1. When *p* is in the vocabulary *V* and *p* is not an inter-ontology property (line 5), then replace the namespace of *p* by *V*. For example, in Figure 21, property "*s:name*" is replaced by "*am:name*".
2. When *p* is in the vocabulary *V* and *p* is an inter-ontology property with range of *p* in

vocabulary *Vt* (line 7-10), then a secondary query tree SQT is created with root node r_{new}, which is a copy of the node r_{next}, incident to p; the children of r_{new} are all the descendents of r_{next}. Next, the query tree SQT is rewritten using *Vt* namespace. In our example, property "*s:hasPub*" is an inter-ontology link (*ap:book, pp:publ, ap:hasPub*).

Figure 21 summarizes the main steps for rewriting property "*s:hasPub*": (1) create the SQT shown in Figure 22; delete all descents of node *?pub* from primary query tree; (3) rewrite SQT with the publisher's (*pub*) namespace. In Figure 21, the join variable *?pub* of the *ap:hasPub* property

Figure 17. Example RDF data located at three different linked data sources, namely Amazon, eBay and Publishers

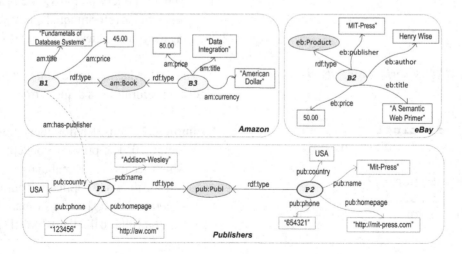

Figure 18. Example RDF data for Application Ontologies: Amazon, eBay and Publishers

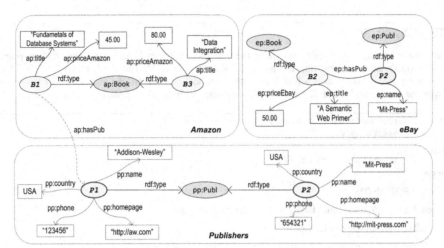

is used in the SQT tree to implement the URI join between both queries.

3. If p is not in the Vocabulary *V* (lines 16-20), then for each virtual *same-as* inter-ontology link *(V:cr, Vi:cr, PJ) in V*, create a secondary query tree SQT which is a copy of the subgraph containing node *N* and all the descendents of the properties not in *V*. Next, rewrite SQT with *Vi*.

In our example, the property *country* is not in the Amazon vocabulary. Using the virtual *same-as* link (*am:Publ, pub:publ, pub:name*) we are able

to join instances of *am:publ* with instances of *pub:publ* to get the country that is in publisher's vocabulary.

Figure 22 summarizes the main steps for rewriting the property s:*country:* (1) create the SQT show in Figure 22 delete the edge *country* from primary query tree; (3) rewrite the SQT with the Publisher's namespace (*pub*).

Figure 22 shows the secondary query graph for the virtual *same-as* link (*am:Publ; pub:publ, pub:name*).

The result of REWRITE_NODE (N, V) is a reformulated query tree (RQT) whose root is a join node with the following children: the primary

Figure 19. Example RDF data for Sales domain ontology

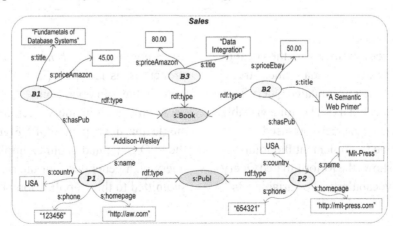

Figure 20. The query reformulation algorithm

REWRITE_NODE (r , V)

Rewrites the properties (edges) of a node r in a query tree with the vocabulary V, and uses inter-ontology properties to discover other vocabularies for rewriting the properties that are not in V. The result of REWRITE_NODE is a reformulated query tree, whose root is a join node with the following children: the primary query tree (Query tree rewritten with the vocabulary V) and all the query trees rewritten with other vocabularies for the properties which are not in V.

---

input:	root node r of a query tree QT
	vocabulary V
output:	
	reformulated query tree RQT

```
1    Begin
2    SS ← ∅; RQT ← QT;
4    for each edge e(r, rnext) with label pe whose range is in V do
5        replace the label pe of e by V:pe
6        if pe is an inter-ontology link whose range is in Vt such that Vt ≠ V
7            createUriLinkSQT(r)
9            rewrite_Node (rnew ,Vt)
10           add rnew to SS
11       Else
12           rewrite_Node (rnext ,O)
13       end-if
14   end-for
15   let E ={ label(e) /e is an edge that leaves node r and label (e)∉ V}
16   for each Vocabulary Vi such that there exists a virtual same-as link (V:cr, Vi:cr, PJ ) such that E ∩ Vi ≠∅
17       createSameasLinkSQT (r)
18        rewrite_query(rnew, Vi)
19       add rnew to SS
20   end-for
21   if SS≠ ∅
22       add r to SS
23       RQT ← SS
24   end-if
25   End
```

---

query tree (Query tree rewritten with the vocabulary V) and all generated secondary query trees.

Figure 21 shows the reformulated Query Tree for the Amazon vocabulary. The join variable "*?pub*" of *am:hasPub* property is used in the secondary query tree to implement the joint operation. Figure 22 shows the Reformulated Query Tree for the eBay vocabulary. The variable "*?n*",

corresponding to "*eb:name*" and "*pub:name*" properties, is required (in both query trees) to process the join operation.

Finally, all join query trees are grouped into a single final query plan (FQP). Figure 23 illustrates the FPQ generated in our example. Note that this query plan generates four queries that should be submitted to three application ontologies.

Figure 21. Property link processing

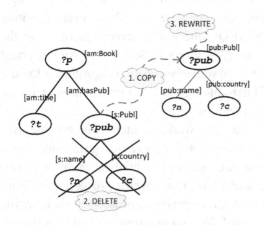

Figure 22. Same-as property processing

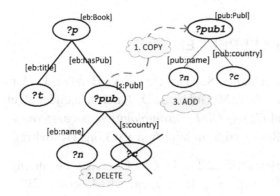

Figure 23. Final Query Plan

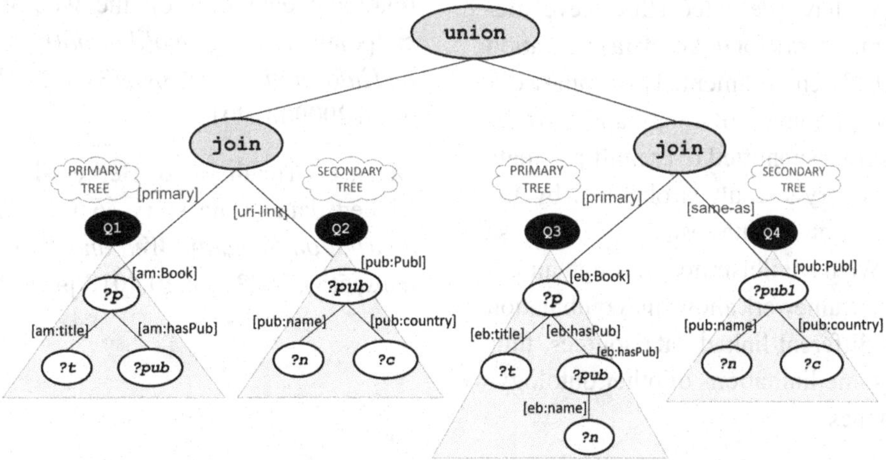

7. RELATED WORK

Data integration has been a topic of research in the database field for a long time (Ziegler & Dittrich, 2004).

In Cruz, Xiao, and Hsu (2004) it is provided an ontology-based approach to the integration of heterogeneous XML documents that transforms heterogeneous XML sources into local RDF ontologies, which are then merged into a RDF global ontology. Note that this work does not define an approach for the unification of the results that are returned from different data sources.

Some proposals have been provided recently for the integration of data from distributed RDF data sources. In Quilitz and Leser (2008) the DARQ engine for federated SPARQL queries is presented. DARQ decomposes a SPARQL query in sub-queries, sends the sub-queries to distributed data sources, and integrates the results of the sub-queries.

The SemWIQ system, proposed in (Langegger, Woss, & Blochl, 2008), is a mediator-based system (Wiederhold, 1992), which provides transparent access to distributed RDF data sources. In Sem-WIQ, the data can be retrieved using SPARQL queries, while RDF schema or OWL ontologies can be used to describe the data sources. Makris et al. (2009) presents a mediator framework based on OWL and SPARQL. In the proposed framework, query reformulation is based on a set of mapping types.

In the above systems, all relevant data sources that provide queried data are discovered before the query execution. Since inter-ontology links are not considered during query reformulation, the result of the query may be incomplete.

Hartig et al. (2009) presents an approach to query the Web of Linked Data where the queried data is discovered and retrieved at query execution time. This approach is based on the idea of looking up URIs during query execution time proposed by Berners-Lee et al. (2006) According to Hartig, Bizer, and Freytag (2009) basically, a SPARQL query is executed by iteratively dereferencing URIs in order to fetch their RDF descriptions from the web, and building solutions from the retrieved data. Although, this centralized approach would return more complete query results, only URI links are considered. Another limitation of that approach is that the query must have a seed URI as the subject of the first query pattern. Besides, optimization techniques for this centralized approach is still a challenge.

8. CONCLUSION AND FUTURE WORK

In this paper, we have presented a three-level mediator based framework for linked data integration over Linked Data environment. This framework takes a query on domain ontology and rewrites it into sub-queries submitted over multiples data sources. The query's result is obtained by the proper combination of data resulting from these sub-queries. We have illustrated, through an example, how our framework allows the combination of data from different linked data sources, thus overcoming some limitations of other ontology-based approaches.

We have focused in this paper on describing a sound and complete algorithm for reformulating a SPARQL query into several queries over the linked data sources (Section 6). An important feature of the reformulation algorithm is the use of inter-ontology links to return more complete query results.

As a future work, we intend to investigate post-processing of instances resulting from query processing and query plan optimization mechanisms. Particularly in instances post-processing, we want to analyze the data fusion problem, which consists in identifying and merging equivalent instances provided by multiples RDF datasets. Concerning query plan optimization, we will define heuristics for generating cost-effective query plan.

REFERENCES

Bechhofer, S., Harmelen, F. v., Hendler, J., Horrocks, I., McGuinness, D., Patel-Schneijder, P., et al. (2004). *OWL web ontology language reference.* Retrieved from http://www.w3.org/TR/owl-ref/

Berners-Lee, T., Chen, Y., Chilton, L., Connolly, D., Dhanaraj, R., Hollenbach, J., et al. (2006, November). Tabulator: Exploring and analyzing linked data on the semantic web. In *Proceedings of the 3rd Semantic Web User Interaction Workshop.*

Bizer, C., & Cyganiak, R. (2006). Publishing relational databases on the web as SPARQL-endpoints. *International Journal on Semantic Web and Information Systems*, 5(3), 1–22. doi:10.4018/jswis.2009081901

Bizer, C., Heath, T., & Berners-Lee, T. (2009). Linked data - The story so far. *International Journal on Semantic Web and Information Systems*, 5(3), 1–22. doi:10.4018/jswis.2009081901

Calvanese, D., Giacomo, G. D., Lembo, D., Lenzerini, M., Poggi, A., Rosati, R., et al. (2008). Data integration through DL-LiteA ontologies. In *Proceedings of the 3rd International Workshop on Semantics in Data and Knowledge Bases* (pp. 26-47).

Casanova, M. A., Lauschner, T., Andre, L. L., Breitman, K. K., Furtado, A. L., & Vidal, V. M. (2009). A strategy to revise the constraints of the mediated schema. In *Proceedings of the 28th Conference on Conceptual Modeling*, Gramado, Brazil (pp. 265-279).

Cruz, I. F., Xiao, H., & Hsu, F. (2004, July). An ontology-based framework for XML semantic integration. In *Proceedings of the International Database Engineering and Applications Symposium* (pp. 217-226).

Ghidini, C., & Serafini, L. (2006). Reconciling concepts and relations in heterogeneous ontologies. In Y. Sure & J. Domingue (Eds.), *Proceedings of the 3rd European Semantic Web Conference on the Semantic Web: Research and Applications* (LNCS 4011, pp. 50-64).

Haas, L. M., Kossmann, D., Wimmers, E. L., & Yang, J. (1997, August 25-29). Optimizing queries across diverse data sources. In *Proceedings of the 23rd International Conference on Very Large Data Bases*, Athens, Greece (pp. 276-285).

Halpin, H. (2006). Identity, reference, and meaning on the web. In *Proceedings of the Workshop on Identity Meaning and the Web*.

Hartig, O., Bizer, C., & Freytag, J.-C. (2009). Executing SPARQL queries over the web of linked data. In A. Bernstein, D. R. Karger, T. Heath, L. Feigenbaum, D. Maynard, E. Motta et al. (Eds.), *Proceedings of the 8th International Semantic Web Conference on the Semantic Web* (LNCS 5823, pp. 293-309).

Hull, R., & Yoshikawa, M. (1990). *ILOG: Declarative creation and manipulation of object identifiers* (pp. 455–468). San Francisco, CA: Morgan Kaufmann.

Kossmann, D. (2000). The state of the art in distributed query processing. *ACM Computing Surveys, 32*, 422–469. doi:10.1145/371578.371598

Langegger, A., Woss, W., & Blochl, M. (2008). A semantic web middleware for virtual data integration on the web. In S. Bechhofer, M. Hauswirth, J. Hoffmann, & M. Koubarakis (Eds.), *Proceedings of the 5th European Semantic Web Conference* (LNCS 5021, pp. 493-507).

Lenzerini, M. (2002, June 3-5). Data integration: A theoretical perspective. In *Proceedings of the Twenty-First ACM SIGMOD-SIGACT-SIGART Symposium on Principles of Database Systems*, Madison, WI (pp. 233-246).

Lutz, M. (2005). *Ontology-based discovery and composition of geographic information services.* Unpublished doctoral dissertation, Institute for Geoinformatics, University of Munster, Munster, Germany.

Makris, K., Bikakis, N., Gioldasis, N., Tsinaraki, C., & Christodoulakis, S. (2009). Towards a mediator based on OWL and SPARQL. In M. D. Lytras, E. Damiani, J. M. Carroll, R. D. Tennyson, D. Avison, A. Naeve et al. (Eds.), *Proceedings of the Second World Summit on Visioning and Engineering the Knowledge Society: A Web Science Perspective* (LNCS 5736, pp. 326-335).

Manola, F., & Miller, E. (2004). *RDF primer.* Retrieved from http://www.w3.org/TR/rdf-primer

Pérez, J., Arenas, M., & Gutierrez, C. (2009). Semantics and complexity of SPARQL. *ACM Transactions on Database Systems, 34*(16), 1–45. doi:10.1145/1567274.1567278

Prud'hommeaux, E., & Seaborne, A. (2007). *SPARQL query language for RDF (working draft)*. Retrieved from http://www.w3.org/TR/rdf-sparql-query/

Quilitz, B., & Leser, U. (2008). Querying distributed RDF data sources with SPARQL. In S. Bechhofer, M. Hauswirth, J. Hoffmann, & M. Koubarakis (Eds.), *Proceedings of the 5th European Semantic Web Conference* (LNCS 5021, pp. 524-538).

Sacramento, E. R., Ponte, V. M., Fernandes, J. A., Lóscio, B. F. R. F. L., & Casanova, M. A. (2010). Towards automatic generation of application ontologies. In *Proceedings of the 25st Brazilian Symposium on Databases*, Belo Horizonte, Brazil (pp. 535-550).

Vidal, V. M., Sacramento, E. R., Macêdo, J. A., & Casanova, M. A. (2009). An ontology-based framework for geographic data integration. In C. A. Heuser & G. Pernul (Eds.), *Proceedings of the 3rd International Workshop on Semantic and Conceptual Issues in GIS in conjunction with the 28th International Conference on Conceptual Modeling* (LNCS 5833, pp. 337-346).

Wache, H., Vögele, T., Visser, U., Stuckenschmidt, H., Schuster, G., Neumann, H., et al. (2001). Ontology-based integration of information - A survey of existing approaches. In *Proceedings of the Workshop on Ontologies and Information Sharing* (pp. 108-117).

Wiederhold, G. (1992). Mediators in the architecture of future information systems. *Computer, 25*, 38–49. doi:10.1109/2.121508

Wilschut, A. N., & Apers, P. M. G. (1993). Dataflow query execution in a parallel main-memory environment. *Distributed and Parallel Databases, 1*, 103–128. doi:10.1007/BF01277522

Ziegler, P., & Dittrich, K. R. (2004). Three decades of data integration - All problems solved? In *Proceedings of the 18th IFIP World Computer Congress* (Vol. 12, pp. 3-12).

This work was previously published in International Journal of Business Data Communications and Networking, Volume 7, Issue 2, edited by Varadharajan Sridhar and Debashis Saha, p.p 29-47, copyright 2011 by IGI Publishing (an imprint of IGI Global)

Chapter 7
Micro Context–Awareness for Autonomic Pervasive Computing

Bessam Abdulrazak
University of Sherbrooke, Canada

Yacine Belala
SAP Labs, Canada

Patrice Roy
University of Sherbrooke, Canada

Sylvain Giroux
University of Sherbrooke, Canada

Charles Gouin-Vallerand
University of Sherbrooke, Canada

ABSTRACT

Context-aware software provides adapted services to users or other software components. On the other hand, Autonomic Pervasive Computing uses context to reduce the complexity of pervasive system utilization, management and maintenance. This paper describes two context-awareness models, the macro and micro approaches, that define and integrate contextual views of individual pervasive components (micro level) and global knowledge of the system (macro level), and provides a more detailed overview of a micro Context-aware programming model for open smart space problems. These models are presented and compared with respect to their ability to meet the requirements of the Autonomic Pervasive Computing concept of the four selves.

INTRODUCTION

Pervasive computing offers ubiquitous access to information at any time. It relies on "environments of devices with computing and communication capabilities for integrating directly with the human (sic.)" (Campiolo, 2007). Autonomic Pervasive Computing (Gouin-Vallerand et al., 2008, Kephart & Chess, 2003) transforms a space into a smart space that is easy to use; it integrates distributed applications and mobile devices, allows dynamic interaction of components with the environment, offers personalized services and interfaces, etc. Furthermore, the "four selves" of Autonomic Pervasive Computing (Kephart & Chess, 2003) (self-configuration, self-optimization, self-healing

DOI: 10.4018/978-1-4666-2026-1.ch007

and self-protection) hint towards the implementation of pervasive systems that will make it easier to use, manage and maintain pervasive technologies such as devices and software applications.

The implementation of autonomic functionalities results from the selves of individual components performing reasoning on the systems, analyzing the environment, noticing events and responding to them. Therefore, such systems need to be Context-aware, i.e., "aware of the state of the computing environment and requirements and current state of computing applications" (Indulska & Sutton, 2003). This makes Context and its corollary, Context-awareness, the key terms to define. In a general sense, we will define Context-aware components and systems as those components and systems that use and rely on Context to perform their tasks.

Context-aware systems and components host Agents that infer additional, synthetic Context from the raw Context provided by sensors and from synthetic Context provided by other Agents. Context-awareness enables such systems and such components, among other things, to assist users in performing daily life activities or warn specialized personnel should human intervention be required. Agents can consume Context, produce Context for others to consume, or use Context to decide upon an application domain-dependent course of action.

Numerous efforts have been made in the development of platforms to support Context-awareness for pervasive computing. Most applications and studies today rely on smart spaces, most of which are controlled smart spaces i.e. known locations equipped with a stable set of sensors and actuators where the basic physical layout is known beforehand. These spaces include any controlled environment where Context-awareness could play a role such as assisting people with disabilities (e.g. hospitals, hotel rooms, apartments, houses, classrooms etc.).

Controlled smart spaces are necessary but not sufficient. A limitation of controlled spaces is that they can only assist people within their confines. When an individual leaves such an environment, the ability of a given Context-aware system to provide assistance is sorely affected or disappears completely. Open smart spaces take away this limitation and let Context follow users wherever they go, although with varying degrees of support and assistance capabilities due to strong variations in support from the environment and from neighboring nodes.

In this paper, we present two models of Context-awareness that operate at distinct levels, namely macro-level and micro-level Context-awareness. These models help program systems and components for both controlled and open space environments. Micro Context-awareness revolves around the subjective perception and the understanding an Agent has of its environment, while macro Context-awareness is the global, emergent picture that Agents help build of entities in their environment. Both have different implications when studied under autonomic computing paradigms.

We first present both models in general terms; then, we describe and compare the impact of each one on the four selves of Autonomic computing. Then, we describe implementations that rely on each model and show how they interact. Finally, we provide a more detailed overview of a micro-level Context-aware components programming model and show how this approach fills the needs of autonomic pervasive computing.

RELATED WORK

A popular concept nowadays, Context-awareness, is needed in situations where software and hardware must collaborate in order to cope with complex data. Many definitions exist for this concept which often involve semantic data and semantic Web technology (Feki & Mokhtari, 2006) as well as devices that take into account external data in order to build a workable, usable model (i.e. an awareness) of their surroundings, their relationships with other devices (McCann *et al.*, 2004) or their subject of interest (Miaou *et al.*, 2007). Context-awareness also applies to software that can both assist users and take into account some of the complex and subtle relationships between them and their (usually immediate) environment.

Context involves no small amount of richness and complexity, and can refer to the situation of a device or of a human being, depending on the selected angle. Neovius *et al.* (2006) defines context as "a setting in which an event occurs", a very broad definition that ties context to a (physical) location. According to Abowd *et al.* (1999), "context is any information that can be used to characterize the situation of an entity. An entity is a person, place, or object that is considered relevant to the interaction between a user and an application, including the user and applications themselves". Gessler *et al.* (2005) distinguishes between situation-awareness, which is related to the user's location, and context-awareness, which is related to the conditions (temperature, weather, lighting …) that prevail in that location.

Context-awareness is hard to achieve due to the complexity and richness of Context. It involves dealing with a rich set of real world data, sometimes while respecting real-time constraints. It may also involve statistical inferences (Katsiri, 2002) to build synthetic information from raw data or from other synthetic information, information filtering (Gessler *et al.* 2005) to cope with the possibility of information overload, agent specification (Zaslavsky, 2004) to distribute subsets of the required processing over many processing nodes, service publishing and discovery mechanisms (Gouin-Vallerand & Giroux, 2007), distributed data sources (Kiani *et al.*, 2005), conflicting data management (Agostini *et al.*, 2005) to address malfunctioning sensors or multiple sensors not agreeing as well as differing results from distinct analytic processes and extensive versioning (Abowd *et al.*, 1999), especially when dealing with distributed data, as well as various networking issues.

The word Awareness suggests many additional questions: who (or what) is aware? Who (or what) is it aware of? What actions can be taken given said awareness? For how long does this awareness remain valid and in what context is it valid? (Kernchen, 2006). Awareness goes hand in hand with Context since the former can be perceived, in a way, as an emergent property of a complex (contextualized) system made of a number of software Agents. These Agents are software components on distributed nodes that perform processing on Context and that can be either Context consumers (some say Utilizers) or (synthetic) Context providers (Neovius *et al.*, 2006). When Context consumers require what is produced by Context providers, the resulting relationship is named a Context-dependency (Neovius *et al.*, 2006).

Context-awareness usually serves a functional purpose. Most Context-aware systems known today are built with specific goals in mind such as assisting people with disabilities performing activities of daily life, or ADL, ensuring maximal comfort of tourists during their stay in a hotel resort by adapting their environment to their needs and preferences, controlling the way people move to and from given areas (Sun & Song Dong, 2006) or automatically adapting car seat temperature depending on the individual seated (Yaiz et al., 2006).

On the other hand, several works on Autonomic pervasive computing propose different applications of Context-awareness approaches. The initial Autonomic Computing proposition (Kephart & Chess, 2003), for example, suggests the utilization of system knowledge over itself and its components to automate some of the management actions. Moreover, it emphasizes the independence of each device in its Context reasoning. Trumler *et al.* (2006) uses inner devices' knowledge and orchestration to dispatch process in pervasive environments. Ranganathan *et al.* (2005) and Ghorbel *et al.* (2006) use global environment knowledge of Context to provide applications to users' devices within controlled smart spaces. From these works, we can infer that Autonomic pervasive computing is tied to and dependent on Context-awareness. However, no specific Context-awareness model can be extracted from these works; some focus more on device context independence while others coordinate or orchestrate Context utilization between components.

Distributed Context-aware systems based on Web services (Truong & Dustdar, 2009) for are a related research area, and share some characteristics with both the macro and micro approaches discussed below. Web services are useful for interoperability of Context-aware systems with each other and with other types of software systems, and the distributed nature of such systems leads them to tackle issues similar to those discussed here, although with different methods.

MACRO AND MICRO CONTEXT-AWARENESS

Macro Context-Awareness

A macro Context-aware system can be defined as a system that obtains information from numerous sensors arranged in spaces (the home, workplace, cities...) where people engage in everyday activities. It is used to determine the details of the user's actions and the constantly-changing conditions of the controlled environment, both of which are part of the Context.

Under the macro approach, Context is presented as something directly tied to a systemic model of the user and the conditions around this individual; the human is the center of attention. The system's main goal is to try to keep an up-to-date representation of a human being and of its environment, and to ensure that all nodes that need partial or total access to this representation can get it efficiently. The human, given its central role in the world, becomes not only the main mutator of Context, but is also the focus of Agent activity. A typical macro Context-aware system will focus on

a single human being. The logical representation of a human being within a Context-aware system (the Profile) is also Context. Since they typically try to build an accurate Profile of a human being, macro Context-aware systems lend themselves well to applications made to assist a given user in a controlled environment, and are the dominant model in controlled spaces.

Macro Context-aware systems are essentially coherent, organized systems, and can be considered as such. They can be observed as a whole and can be built of specialized, key nodes or key components that provide specialized services on which other nodes depend.

Micro Context-Awareness

A micro Context-aware system can be defined as "Context-awareness for devices that can be split up into three components: activity, environment and self. The activity describes the task the user is performing at the moment or more generally what his or her behavior is. The environment describes the status of the physical and social surroundings of the user. Finally, the self component contains the status of the device itself." (Van Laerhoven, 2000). Micro Context-aware systems are distributed, self-organizing systems with varying, ad hoc topologies. The hallmark constituents of controlled spaces, for example key nodes, can be used in micro Context-aware systems but cannot be depended upon by individual components. Micro Context-awareness is not only awareness of micro Context, sometimes named raw Context, but rather a model of Context-awareness that focuses on information available to the acting components and that maintains no dependence on system-wide knowledge or tools.

Whereas components in the macro model described in the Macro Context-Awareness section operate at a systemic level on globally available Context, those in the micro Context-awareness model take a subjective view based on locally accessible Context, including Context related to the components themselves.

Micro Context-aware systems motivate the development of systems and devices considered as active entities. Each entity can see itself as the center of a local pocket of Context-awareness, or of awareness of the Context it possesses at a given time. Context local to a component is built from what has been available to that component through its lifetime, and is located in that component's Context space; thus, micro Context-aware systems have many Context spaces, and the Context spaces of individual components can differ from one another.

The user is a source of Context among others and is interesting in a Context-related sense mostly because it is an active agent of change. Building Profiles in micro Context-awareness is a synthetic task, and can be the task of individual Agents, but is not the main objective of the approach: some Agents can work continuously towards that end, while other Agents can infer information from this state (to predict future actions, to prevent harmful situations, to suggest a potential mistake somewhere along a sequence of actions, and so on), and other Agents still can perform Context-based tasks unrelated to any specific Profile. Still, the system exists and functions with or without humans: micro Context-awareness is independent of the presence of users at a given location. Micro Context-awareness does not need the user in order to stay useful; it produces and consumes Context independently of the presence of a user. Each user in an environment appears like an (interesting) object from which modifications to existing Context tend to stem, and is particularly interesting because it is an active agent of change (Pakucs, 2003).

The micro approach supposes that it is difficult, sometimes impossible, to obtain snapshots of a global system. In contrast, the macro approach leads to an architecturally coherent whole where such a snapshot could be taken but where systems can find themselves unable to perform their usual tasks outside of controlled spaces and into open space. On the other hand, systems based on a micro approach remain operational under such constraints and conditions.

Micro and Macro Awareness Models for Autonomic Systems

Autonomic computing usually refers to the four selves: self-configuration, self-protection, self-healing and self-optimization. Some distributed component capabilities, such as upgrading one's own software, can involve several selves. Autonomic components can offer strong support in terms of continuity of service: being self-protecting and self-healing, they tend to remain active even under hostile conditions and can be made to maintain services throughout.

We examine the impacts of both the macro and micro Context-awareness models on each of these principles.

- **Self-Configuration:** Self-configuration is defined as "the automatic configuration of the applications and devices" (Gouin-Vallerand *et al.*, 2008). It is seen as an important characteristic of autonomous components once they are deployed. A self-configuring component can learn enough about its environment to adapt itself in order to better integrate with it.

Self-configuration suggests adaptability; as such, it influences the other three selves. Configuration is based on information about the component's tasks, its surroundings and the requirements of the other selves.

- **Macro Context-Awareness vs. Micro Context-Awareness:** Self-configuration involves knowledge specific to environment nodes and their neighborhood. When it is limited to device resources and location, or when it implies negotiation without resorting to specialized mediator nodes, self-configuration can be done with micro Context-awareness. When self-configuration involves directed organization between nodes, for example when configuring software for a given environment or when the configuration information has to be gather from a specific repository, or when self-configuration involves negotiation using key nodes, it can be achieved through macro Context-awareness. There is nothing preventing a micro Context-aware component from applying the macro approach to self-configuration when circumstances allow it, but micro components have to remain able to self-configure in the absence of such support tools as key nodes.

Macro Context-aware self-configuration can be achieved through a higher-level analysis of the environment and its components, which can be performed by a central coordinating agent such as an orchestrator node (orchestration). By contrast, self-configuration performed using micro Context-awareness avoids relying on key nodes, relying instead on decentralized negotiation processes (choreography).

In controlled spaces, knowledge of global states can be achieved (Chandy & Lamport, 1985). A macro Context-awareness approach allows offering stable, global state-providing services to Context-aware components. With such an approach, readily available repositories of configuration information can be integrated in the environment and exposed to self-configuring agents.

The advantages of a macro approach to self-configuration include the possibility to rely on available key nodes, such as a repository for configuration information or configuration assistants. Access to global states makes it possible for a component to understand the overall structure of the environment. Such components can know what

Context to expect, where and whom to expect it from, and can self-configure in an optimal way.

However, when addressing open space issues, a macro approach is not really possible, since there is no guarantee of globally known system states. Open space self-configuring components that pass through controlled spaces can use assistants and repositories made available to them, but in general, micro approach self-configuring components cannot depend on the availability of such key nodes. A micro approach to self-configuration has to be self-relying, based on both a priori knowledge (what was known upon deployment, for example configuration files data) and acquired knowledge (Context obtained during the component's active lifetime through learning, reasoning and interaction with other components).

In summary, a micro approach is more tolerant of systemic failure, due to a lower reliance on nodes other than the self-configuring one, and the additional complexity resulting from a design that can both use fixed nodes' services (and do without it if needed) is a worthwhile investment when addressing problems related to open space. A macro approach provides a more stable set of services, leads to simpler components that can safely rely on specialized nodes; in controlled environments, where the architecture can be modeled as a whole, macro Context-aware systems can do more with less effort.

- **Self-Protection:** Self-protection is defined as "the automatic identification and resolution of the security threats" (Gouin-Vallerand *et al.*, 2008). A self-protecting component is less likely to be compromised by outside forces and can thus be useful longer, even in environments that could be perceived as hostile. In the case of user-centered pervasive computing systems, self-protection is also related to user safety, i.e. the protection of both the physical environment and users facing physical threats.

Such protection can be achieved by identifying or anticipating possible threats through Context reasoning followed by taking appropriate actions. One such action could be the isolation of a compromised device and re-deploying its software and services on other devices in the environment, which can be implemented as an Agent migration mechanism. Another potential action could be hiding private data on a screen when non-authorized people (visitor, maintenance staff, etc.) approach it. Yet another potential action, or set of actions, involves collaborating components that work together to face hostile situations, such as detecting and relaying information to one another about a dangerous element in the environment. Such reactions depend on Context-awareness.

Self-protection in its mechanisms, concepts and reactions is highly related to self-healing. In protection cases, security threats are the sparks that start protective processes; in healing cases, detection of failures or faults provoke system healing. Self-healing can be a consequence of a complete or partial self-protection failure. Context awareness needs for these two selves are similar.

- **Macro Context-Awareness vs. Micro Context-Awareness:** Controlled spaces offer a known, bounded environment for components to exist and operate in. By virtue of these boundaries, self-protecting components that apply a macro approach can be designed in a way that lets them rely on other nodes to provide part of the protection services.

For example, in a room with doorways serving as physical entry points, where sensors that can detect a subset of all possible threats can be installed, self-protecting components can be designed to count on such a first line of defense, reducing the attack surface they consider for self-protection accordingly. Under the macro approach, as systemic knowledge of the environment is a given or is at least theoretically achievable, reliance on

known environment factor for self-protection is acceptable. Since autonomic components tend to have limited resources, the resources saved by relying in part on the environment can be invested in other tasks.

When applying a micro approach, a self-protecting component cannot assume that other components will be available to participate in its protection. Components that follow this approach can use such nodes as security policy repositories or protection assistants when they are accessible, but have to be self-sufficient in their absence. Micro Context-aware components can share Context about potential threats and can collaborate to solve potentially harmful situations, for example by delegating to a neighboring component the task of informing an actuator that specific actions have to be taken in the environment to ensure the safety of individuals when the delegator cannot reach said actuator on its own.

Self-protecting components in a micro approach to Context-awareness have to comply with more stringent constraints than those following a macro approach. Under the macro model, assumptions about assistance provided by the environment can be made, and a holistic strategy to self-protection can be defined; components can ask for help and enquire about local threat history. Under the micro model, components can enlist the help of others for mutual protection as long as a protocol is put in place to ensure a form of mutual trust, mitigated by the limited a priori knowledge components have on one another; components can discuss potential threats and cooperate to face them while remaining careful and (literally) self-protective.

- **Self-Healing:** Self-healing is defined as "the automatic detection and correction of the (sic) faults" (Gouin-Vallerand *et al.*, 2008). A self-healing component has a longer useful life, being less likely to fail once deployed.

- **Macro Context-Awareness vs. Micro Context-Awareness:** Where self-protecting components seek to prevent harm, self-healing components seek to repair harm; both types of components ultimately target their efforts toward a longer useful life and better fault tolerance. Self-healing components and self-optimizing components are also related as both perform introspective analysis as to their current state, the former doing so in order to detect risks of failure or performance degradation while the latter do so in order to enhance performance given current environment conditions.

Self-healing can be divided into two sub-categories: self-diagnosis and self-modification. A given Context-aware and autonomic component can fall into either or both of these categories. Self-healing components can benefit from the assistance of other components when available: in the advent of self-failure, the assistance of other components for diagnosis and healing processes can be invaluable.

A macro Context-aware self-healing approach paves the way for a systemic approach to self-healing, where components that detect a risky or harmful condition contact key doctor components to assist them in their repair tasks. Each component can reduce its personal load to the level where only problem detection and reporting become available, while well-known nodes provide advanced diagnostic and repair (or replacement) services.

As with the other selves, systematic collaboration with key nodes is made possible by systemic knowledge of the environment by the self-healing component, and by the well-known availability of said key nodes, which are characteristics of macro Context-aware systems; individual components are never really isolated, and have access to those specialized services as needed.

When applying a micro Context-aware approach, components have to be able to perform self-healing within the limits of what self-knowl-

edge they can gather and infer. This is a direct consequence of micro approach components not being able to depend on systemic knowledge of the environment or on the availability of any specific node other than their own.

Self-healing micro approach components know enough to perform the most critical self-repairs in order to remain operational, and can use specialized help when it becomes available. If there is an adequate diversity of talents in a general area, such components can share their strengths and mutually diagnose one another. The micro approach both suggests an autarkical attitude (one has to be able to fulfill its duties even when no other component is available to help) and a societal attitude (components discover their mutual strengths and cooperate to achieve their respective goals).

The amount and complexity of first-line repairs that micro Context-aware components have to be able to perform by themselves is more important than what macro Context-aware components have to do, but applying the micro approach makes components ready to face the challenges of open space. Not being able to perform self-healing in isolation hampers the capacity of a given micro Context-aware component to ensure its own continuity of service.

There are some specific self-healing characteristics that micro Context-aware components need to offer, including strict resource management, coupled with mechanisms for the detection and resolution (or at least reporting) of potentially harmful situations such as resource leaks or accumulation of Context that might not be needed. A micro Context-aware component has to consider resource management as signs of good or bad health. Since the extent of resources made available to individual nodes varies with the underlying technologies, self-healing involves a capability for self-description and the capacity for a component to compare resource consumption with overall resource availability.

Self-healing for micro Context-aware components can be considered as a special case of self-modification or of self-update. Given that component-local Context changes over time, obsolete Context can be replaced by newer Context, less precise Context about specific states can be replaced by Context that is more precise on the same topic, and faulty Context that leads to incorrect assumptions on the part of individual components can be corrected over time.

In both micro and macro approaches, Context-aware self-healing strongly depends on the quality of the fault and failure detection mechanisms (Chetan *et al.*, 2005). Such detection quality can be achieved by aggregating several detection events from difference sources, something made easier by the macro approach.

- **Self-Optimization:** Self-optimization is defined as "a proactive mechanism (sic.) that continually enhances [performance]" (Gouin-Vallerand *et al.*, 2008) A self-optimizing component adapts itself to changing conditions, and seeks to maintain satisfactory performance levels or ensure it gets better with time. Where self-configuration involves components that adapt to the environment, self-optimization involves components that try to get better at achieving their tasks.
- **Macro Context-Awareness vs. Micro Context-Awareness:** The initial configuration of a component is based on a priori knowledge of the environment and the situations that component will face when deployed. Like current-day JVMs that self-optimize compiled code according to live profiling that looks at actual usage (Sun Microsystems, 2001), components can realize that they are being used in ways that differ from the initial expectations and reorganize themselves in order to better meet the needs of their actual reality.

Self-optimization can be a local or a systemic process, in both the micro and macro approaches. Local self-optimization can be performed within both micro and macro models. Macro Context-aware components can rely on readily available, specialized analysts to assist them and suggest potential optimization paths; self-optimization can be as simple as reporting local history and gathered states, then acting upon the results of specialized analyses performed on that data by fixed nodes. Macro Context-aware components can also optimize group behavior by acting under the guidance of an orchestrator node that supervises and orients coordinated actions by a network of components.

Local optimizations under a micro Context-aware approach have to be performed under the assumption that there might be no other component to collaborate. Self-analysis is performed on locally gathered Context (the only Context that is necessarily available), which can be limited in scope due to scarce resources (at worst, there is none and the component reacts to the most recent Context available), and adjustments are made when a richer (and trusted) source becomes accessible. Coordinated group action is realized through ad hoc negotiation between neighboring components in a choreographed fashion; no orchestrator is assumed, which does not preclude using one if it becomes available.

There are a number of tasks that micro Context-aware components have to perform and that require optimization over time, due to the need for continuous Context discovery and update of locally-known Context. Some of these tasks are covered in the future works of this article, as they impact the long-term behavior and responsiveness of autonomic components.

- **Summary:** Macro Context-awareness can be achieved when it is possible to obtain locally a snapshot of the global environment at a given time, thus making locally known global system states possible, and ensuring the relative stability of specialized node availability.

Rich smart space systems can be built under this assumption; the macro approach for Context-aware systems opens up the possibility of detailed analysis of user behavior and sophisticated assistance. Macro Context-aware systems allow for reliable distributed architectures that can be thought of as integrated entities, and designed according to tried and true techniques.

Micro Context-aware systems accept weaker support from the environment and neighboring components. The support they offer is not as rich as what their macro counterparts can offer, but the fact that micro approach-based systems require less support than macro approach-based systems means that they are more suited to general smart spaces such as open space, and lend themselves better to the supervision and assistance of mobile users.

Micro Context-aware systems encompass more than macro Context-aware systems since they demand less from the environment, and since they are built to function even when no other component is available, including in the absence of key nodes. Where macro systems are extremely useful in controlled environments such as scientific laboratories, micro systems are required if continuity of service is required no matter where individuals go.

MICRO AND MACRO CONTEXT-AWARENESS IMPLEMENTATIONS

Core Architecture

We designed a distributed multi-level architecture ($L_0..L_n$) that integrates the micro and macro Context-awareness models by providing structures, Context descriptions, ontologies and services to the embedded middleware and software. Figure 1 presents this multi-level architecture from the macro perspective.

The architecture is instrumented with customized nodes. Each L_i node (mobile or fixed) offers L_i-level services. L_1 nodes are hardware abstraction gateways that enable the system to interact with L_0 real world data (sensors and actuators). $L_i, i > 1$ nodes are concentrators that aggregate the services offered by $L_j, j < i$ nodes in a zone (location of influence). The hierarchy can be based on actor needs: location (e.g. L_1 is for devices, L_2 for a room, L_3 for a floor...), processing requirements (e.g. a $L_i, i > 1$ node concentrates instances of L_{i-1} nodes, to perform load balancing), or to address security, confidentiality and ethical concerns.

In this architecture, the ideas of micro and macro Context-awareness are applied to the different layers. In hierarchical scenarios such as those that can be built using a macro approach, L_0 devices gather information from sensors to build Context. This Context is retrieved by L_1 devices and is used to create the first Context-aware functionalities related to a component and its neighborhood, i.e. raw Context. L_2 devices aggregate micro Context information from L_1 devices, building a larger vision of Context for a given zone; this produces macro Context-awareness. In layers L_3 and up, devices aggregate Context from lower layers and construct a global vision of the known environment.

To support micro and macro Context-awareness, the different layers of the architecture use an extensible meta-ontology description (Abdulrazak *et al.*, 2010) to describe Context. This meta-ontology description defines three high-level concepts: Being, Environment and Dynamic, to describe the Smart Space universe. It also includes a classification of sub-concepts based on international classifications and standards (World Health Organization, 2001; Sonmg & Lee, 2008;

Figure 1. Overview of the overall architecture used for open smart space development

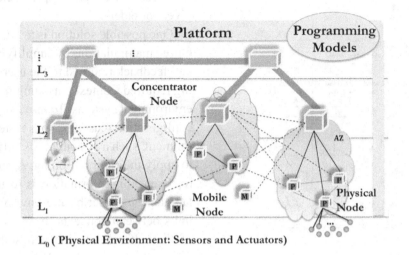

WIPO, 2008), and introduces the concepts of location and time referentiality. In the specific case of micro Context-awareness, individual Agents limit themselves to locally-known subsets of the meta-ontology.

Furthermore, we have developed a service-oriented, OSGi-based middleware on top of the architecture, in which all components (nodes, sensors and actuators) are represented as services. This core middleware provides services to manipulate Context concepts in ontologies; these services are accessible to the different software applications built on top of the architecture.

To meet the needs of components following the micro approach, Agents on individual fixed or mobile nodes $L_i i \geq 0$ are managed as smaller systems in special components we name Hosts. Hosts appear as nodes that can occupy various levels in the architecture described in Figure 1 and are themselves described by Figure 2.

Our Host components are similar to OSGi bundles (OSGi Alliance, 2009) and OpenCom (Coulson *et al.*, 2008) in the sense that they manage deployment and execution of Agents, but are specialized in the sense that they exclusively trade in Context, ensuring that Agents work strictly on local knowledge which we name Context space.

Individual hosted Agents consume and expose services and Context through their Host. Hosts are part of the developed middleware; they interact with one another and with OSGi-based nodes on behalf of their hosted Agents. Hosts implement such facilities as network isolation, neighborhood discovery and overall management of the Agents' life cycle. Agents are either standard, performing some of the Host's functions, or domain-specific, performing Context-awareness related tasks. Agents trade Context through their respective Hosts and typically express themselves through a Context variant of the Belief-Desire-Intention model (Plesa & Logrippo, 2007).

Hosts can be deployed on both fixed and mobile nodes; for that reason, mobile Hosts perform continuous network discovery, and find themselves interacting with various other nodes. Consequently, the level of a given Host component in the hierarchy described by Figure 1 varies over time and so does the contribution of Hosts to the overall system.

The following sections present individual Context-awareness implementations that use the macro and micro Context-awareness models for smart environments, both supported by the presented architecture. We also provide a detailed overview of the main components of our micro

Figure 2. Overview of micro approach host component architecture

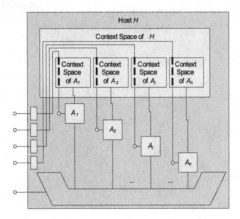

Context-aware programming model, including the Context representation model, the Context identification model, and the model we use to operate on Context while providing a short discussion on practical self-organization for micro Context-aware components.

A Macro Context-Awareness Implementation: Software Self-Organization/Configuration Middleware for Smart Spaces

Smart spaces are made from several devices (computers, sensors, actuators, communication devices, etc.) and software applications (GUI, services, embedded processes, etc.). The heterogeneity and the quantity of components complicate the task of understanding the environment's systems. In addition, implementation and maintenance costs of pervasive technologies may slow the democratization of smart environments.

Device and application heterogeneity, along with usability deficiencies, complicate utilization and make it resource- and time-consuming by non-experts (Talwar *et al.*, 2005; Weiser, 1993). To organize the environment's software in a suitable configuration, one must have good knowledge of the pervasive environment, which is not the case

for most non-expert people such as healthcare givers or elders.

One possible solution is to eliminate most required manipulations by simplifying information and feedback returned to the users, and by moving required Context reasoning from the users to environment systems. To move organization and configuration reasoning to a system in the environment, such a system needs sufficient Context to apply the right reasoning. A powerful way to represent this information is to use a semantic language to describe the environment and the links between concepts. In our implementation of the self-organization and self-configuration middleware, we used the Web Ontology Language (OWL), and implemented the resulting description using the JENA framework. The environment description approach used is described in (Abdulrazak *et al.*, 2010).

The contextual information of a pervasive environment includes a large variety of data types, ranging from quantitative information such as the room's temperature to qualitative information such as the user state. Our fuzzy logic approach, based on fuzzy set theory (Ross, 2010), lets us compare quantitative and qualitative information through a common set of reasoning rules. Moreover, a reasoning algorithm based on fuzzy logic does not require accurate knowledge of the model and can work with a high level of imprecision such as what occurs in pervasive environments, where it can be difficult to describe precisely the model and get accurate data.

We implemented a middleware using macro contextual information to reason about software provision and organization in smart spaces. This middleware is built on top of the OSGi framework, which provides service-oriented functionalities to deploy, manage, update and use services in a dynamic way. As presented above, we integrated the JENA Semantic Framework to our middleware by embedding it in middleware modules and by providing middleware services to query and manipulate Context. A series of Context gatherers use these middleware query and manipulation services to provide contextual information to the middleware's ontology. These gatherers can be user software, event sources, location systems, etc. Context related to device description is provided by the device discovery mechanisms, which extract device descriptions from the devices during the discovery process. Figure 3 presents the middleware architecture with its organization, management, ontology and discovery modules.

The contextual information is used by the Fuzzy Logic Organization Reasoner Engine (FLORE) to match the needs of applications deployed in a pervasive environment (hardware resources, contextual location, peripherals, etc.) with Context and resources provided by devices in the environment. As some of the data is qualitative and some of it is quantitative, we use fuzzy logic to work with it in a fuzzy (qualitative) perspective. Through fuzzy reasoning rules and membership functions, FLORE qualifies the capacity and viability of environment devices by assigning them a Device Capability Quotient (DCQ). The DCQ is used during software deployment to find the more suitable devices for the actual software used; the device with highest DCQ is the more suitable one.

This Context-aware middleware implementation is using a mainly macro Context-awareness approach. By giving universal access to Context and to the tools to manage Context, the implementation of such middleware and its utilization by the environment components is made easier and faster. Moreover, JENA's query and manipulation services provided by the middleware implementation gives authorized third-party applications access to the global environment contextual information.

A Micro Context-Awareness Implementation: Self-Organizing Evolving Smart Spaces

Controlled smart spaces can be organized into an architecture where components are planned by domain experts, managed through specialized tools, and where key components offer important services such as Context aggregation or automated reasoning. Such smart spaces are planned, complex entities that can be examined as a whole.

Planned architectures are organized, but not necessarily self-organizing. For components to rely on key nodes, these nodes have to be made available, efficiently localized to ensure their availability and published as such. This can make smart space management tedious, requiring a number of deployment and monitoring tools. Moreover,

Figure 3. Self-organization middleware architecture with its two main components: the environment manager coordinator and the device nodes

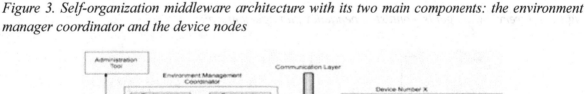

with mobile users in open space, such features as constant availability of key nodes cannot be guaranteed at all times (Roy *et al.*, 2008). Unless the smart space is small enough for each device to have continuous access to all others, or unless key component availability can be ensured at all times, reorganizing such spaces involves significant planning and tests.

Efforts have been invested in dynamic service publishing and discovery, but the physical layout of smart spaces is limited by the requirement that systems that rely on the availability of key nodes have to ensure this availability for all requesting components. The micro Context-aware approach we apply solves this problem.

The overall architecture we use follows the one presented above in Figure 1 using the Host middleware presented in Figure 2. Since Agents are Context-dependent components, they are involved in a continuous Context-dependency management cycle as described by Figure 4.

The way we are addressing the design of micro Context-aware components is by representing as Context the usual (Abowd *et al.*, 1999) categories of Context (Activity, Identify, Location, Time), but also the representation of such operations and entities as the act of requesting Context and the criteria for filtering Context in order to obtain an ontologically meaningful subset for a given Agent, and self-descriptive data such as individual node status and Agent services. Thus, in our model, an Agent publishing Context also expresses the private or public results from its own reasoning and submits requests for Context to neighboring Agents.

- **Overview of the Context Representation Model:** To be able to represent as Context the wide range of entities described above, we have designed a simple but flexible and open Context representation model.

Using this model, Context C is represented as $C = \{N, V\}$ where N stands for *name* and is a globally non-ambiguous name while V stands for *value* and is a set of Context. Thus, Context is recursively defined and can be used to construct descriptions of arbitrary complexity which can be trivially expressed in many structured formats such as XML (W3C, 2011) or JSON (Crockford, 2006) for interoperability purposes.

We accept $C = \{N, V\} : V = \varnothing$ as describing a *terminal Context* whose name is also its value, which we write $C = \{N\}$ for simplicity. We also accept terminal Context where name N is empty as being the special case of *empty Context*, often written $C = \{\ \}$, technically equivalent to $\varnothing$, which is often encountered when operating on Context, for example when searching for a Con-

Figure 4. Overview of agents' context-dependency management cycle

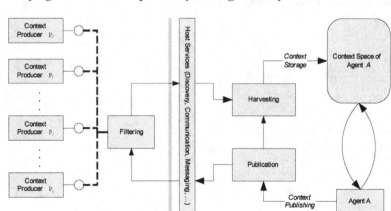

text having specific properties or when filtering from a given Context all Context for which some predicate holds.

An expression such as $C = \{N, V\} : N = "" \wedge V \neq \varnothing$, or C with values but no name, is not considered to be well-formed.

Depending on the needs of individual Agents, operations on Context can be shallow (based on the N component only) or deep (recursively applied on $\forall c (c \in V)$). Building Context C' such that C' contains other Contexts $C_i, 0 \leq i \leq n$ is as trivial as adding a name to a set containing each C_i.

- **Overview of Context Naming:** We rely on globally identifiable Context names for many operations on Context; Context identity is based on names, such that two Contexts are distinct from one another only if they have distinct names. Thus, ensuring the global uniqueness of Context names is important for our model.

The responsibility for ensuring the global uniqueness of a given Context's name is ensured by the Context's producer Agent. We use a naming hierarchy to ensure non-ambiguous identifiers for individual Agents and Contexts: Hosts have globally unique identifiers by design; Agents have locally unique identifiers on a given Host, which becomes globally unambiguous when paired with its Hosts' identifier; all Context produced by an Agent has to bear a distinct identifier from that of all other Contexts produced by the same Agent.

This hierarchical naming scheme allows us to use lightweight names where possible and more fully qualified names when necessary. One interesting effect of this structure is that it reduces resource consumption on individual nodes where the Host name can be considered implicit.

Using locally unique Agent names instead of globally unique ones ensures individual Hosts' standard Agents can have locally recognizable names while remaining distinct from their equivalent counterpart on other Hosts. References made by an Agent to any standard Agent are thus transferrable to any Host as long as they do not involve state in said standard Agent's Context space.

Unambiguous Context naming through a scheme that associates the identifier of the Context's producer with the identifier of the Context itself has applications for autonomic computing since it can help recognizing defective Hosts or Agents given recurrent production of Context judged unsatisfying by Context-consuming Agents. When necessary, the producer of synthetic Context C can integrate information about Contexts $C_i, C_j, .., C_n$ on which the generation of C was based. This can be used by consumer Agents in order to evaluate the validity of C.

- **Overview of the Context Operation Model:** As stated in Winograd (2001), "Context is an operational term: Something is context (sic) because of the way it is used in interpretation, not due to its inherent properties". Even though the model we use represents Context as data, our Agents treat Context as dynamic entities. A Host's Context space is a continuously changing repository, and the same is valid for individual Agents' Context spaces. A given Context space can be represented as a Context that contains all Context therein.

To manage and process Context, we use a generic combination of *algorithm* and *operation*, inspired by Stepanov and Jones (2009). We define algorithms as formal problem resolution strategies that operate on Context. Our algorithms are generic based on operations, or *criteria*, that help customize them for specific tasks. The combination of algorithm and criteria lets us build a great number of complex Context-processing operations.

A simple example of algorithm is $contains(\varphi, c)$, described in Figure 5.

Figure 5. Example of a simple generic algorithm on context

$$contains : Crit \rightarrow C \rightarrow bool$$

$$contains(C : Type)(\varphi : Crit, c : C) \triangleq \varphi(c) \vee \exists x(x \in c \Rightarrow contains(C)(\varphi, x))$$

Algorithm $contains(\varphi, c)$ uses φ as a generic predicate on Context c, and evaluates is true only if $\varphi(c)$ is true. Note that the definition of $contains(\varphi, c)$ is applied on c, which stands here as shorthand for the Context implicitly identified by the name of c, and then recursively applied on every element x in the set of values found in c (which, in this definition, are also Context) through $contains(\varphi, x)$.

In the definition of $contains(\varphi, c)$ above, criterion φ can be any arity 1 operation, function or functor, which operates on Context. The specific case of algorithm $contains(\varphi, c)$ expects φ to be a predicate, but other algorithms can accept other types of criteria.

The prime example of non-predicate criterion is an accumulator, used for harvesting algorithms such as $accept(\varphi, c)$ as found in $find\_all(\varphi, c)$ illustrated in Figure 6. Here, we use the formal φ as a predicate and $accept(\varphi, c)$ as a functor internal to $find\_all(\varphi, c)$ for the purpose of formal expression, but a stateful accumulator φ could be used to perform $accept(\varphi, c)$ in practice.

In this case, criterion φ is an arity 1 predicate and the result of $accept(\varphi, c)$ is either c or $\varnothing$.

Algorithm $find\_all(\varphi, c)$ is a standard Context harvesting algorithm on our Hosts: given a suitable φ to express the needs of Agent A, φ it can be used to gather all Context of interest for A.

We use criteria combinations to build more complex criteria from simpler ones. Expressions such as $\neg f(x), f(g(x)), f(x) \wedge g(x)$ or $f(x) \vee g(x)$ for some Context x and criteria f and g are built from such combinations.

The potential for criteria combination enhances the potential of our approach. An example would be $accept(\varphi, c)$, above, that performs an $f(g(x))$ combination. Another example would be $negate(\varphi, c)$ as described in Figure 7.

We express $filter(\varphi, c)$ as an algorithm that returns a set of Context that does not meet criterion φ as shown in Figure 8.

$$filter 7 \quad Crit \rightarrow C \rightarrow C$$

$$filter(C : Type)(\varphi : Crit, c : C) \triangleq find\_all(negate(\varphi), c)$$

As can be seen from the combination of algorithms and criteria, by the capability to combine criteria in many ways to create new criteria, and

Figure 6. Algorithm **find_all** $(Æc)$

$$accept :: Crit \rightarrow C \rightarrow C$$

$$accept(C : Type)(\varphi : Crit, c : C) \triangleq if \varphi(c) then c else \varnothing$$

$$find\_all :: Crit \rightarrow C \rightarrow C$$

$$find\_all(C : Type)(\varphi : Crit, c : C) \triangleq accept(\varphi, c) \bigcup_{x \in c} find\_all(C)(\varphi, x)$$

Figure 7. Example of a criterion that uses another criterion

$$negate\,7 \quad Crit \to Crit \to bool \to bool$$
$$negate\big(\varphi:Crit\big) \triangleq \omega\big(C:Type\big)\big(\varphi,c\big) \triangleq \neg\varphi\big(c\big)$$

by the fact that some algorithms can be expressed in terms of others, this model shows significant promise.

- **Context Model Operationalization:** To make the Context model into an operational entity, we transform some Context descriptions into combinations of algorithms and criteria.

$$C = \Big\{?\big\{value\{?\}\big\{unit\{Celsius\}\big\}\big\}\Big\}$$

For example, given C in Figure 9, we produce a request that searches the Context space of the receiving Agent or Host for all Context that has a *value* expressed in *Celsius* units. Such an operation can be expressed in many ways, for example the one displayed in Figure 10:

$$C' = \bigcap \left| \begin{array}{l} find\_all\big(match\_name\big(value\big),C\big), \\ contains\big(exact\_match\big(unit\{Celsius\}\big),C\big) \end{array} \right|$$

Transforming Context into operations is a promising but complex ongoing process at this moment. As can be deduced from the expression in Figure 10, automatically optimizing the expressions generated from Context requests will at some point be required to ensure the complexity

of these expressions remains manageable in time and space.

While individual Contexts are distinct by design, it is common that two competing Contexts appear in the same Context space. This can be due to the normal passage of time (a previous Context and a more recent Context from a given producer arrive in the same Context space), for example, to mobility (a given Context consumer encountering more than one producer for Context about the same topic) or for any other reason.

Naming ensures Context identity but identifying whether two Contexts describe the same entity or situation can be more complex. In light of autonomic computing concerns such as self-configuration and self-optimization, our model uses a limited standard vocabulary and puts emphasis on automating the discovery of equivalent forms for similar Contexts. Among the standard Agents found on Hosts are equivalence providers, specialized in the task of transforming the Context as expressed by an Agent into an equivalent form that fits the needs of another.

Our current implementation uses equivalence providers to automate direct translation for individual words and to perform linear transformations between values expressed in different measurement units, and we are working on more general pattern matching to integrate Context and Context-formatted ontology, such as what is performed by Erlang (Armstrong, 2007) or in C++ template instantiation and specialization (International Organization for Standardization, 2011).

Consumer Agents have to perform local assessment as to the respective worth of individual Contexts with respect to their own requirements. Some filtering criteria can be seen as self-evident,

Figure 8. Algorithm **filter** $\big(\textit{Æc}\big)$

$$filter\,7 \quad Crit \to C \to C$$
$$filter\big(C:Type\big)\big(\varphi:Crit,c:C\big) \triangleq find\_all\big(negate\big(\varphi\big),c\big)$$

Figure 9. Sample context request

$$C = \left\{ ? \left\{ value \left\{ ? \right\} \left\{ unit \left\{ Celsius \right\} \right\} \right\} \right\}$$

Figure 10. Sample context request

$$C' = \bigcap \left(\begin{array}{l} find\_all \left(match\_name \left(value \right), C \right), \\ contains \left(exact\_match \left(unit \left\{ Celsius \right\} \right), C \right) \end{array} \right)$$

for example keeping only the most recent version of a given Context from a given producer, while others can be as complex as determining the most appropriate version of two Contexts describing variants of information on a given topic but in different ways. In our model, each Agent can perform this assessment in its own way and using its own criteria. This keeps individual Agents both able to collaborate yet essentially independent from each other in their decision-making processes.

CONCLUSION AND FUTURE WORK

When building Context-aware systems, one can apply a macro or a micro approach. The macro approach to Context-awareness views smart spaces as coherent systems that can be analyzed as a whole. Specialized components can interact with confidence; node deployment can be planned and controlled; snapshots of the global system state can be taken when needed. This approach is the dominant one within controlled smart spaces, in part due to the bounded nature of these locations.

The micro approach to Context-awareness does away with some premises of the macro approach: users and components can move in and out of controlled smart spaces, yet Agents have to ensure continuity of service; key components can be accessible at one time and be unreachable at another; there are moments in an agent's existence when the agent has to keep on performing its tasks alone or with nearby nodes, without guarantee of specialized functionality availability. To assist in the development of micro Context-aware components, we use a flexible recursive Context model and a programming model that

involves middleware (Host components) which in turn supports the management and execution of Context-aware Agents.

The four "selves" of autonomic computing can be addressed under both approaches, albeit with different assumptions and different results. Autonomic systems do not depend on either approach for their existence, but the choice of approach impacts the ways and means through which these systems are designed. Components in macro systems can rely on other elements in their environment, and the environment can be designed as a coherent, reliable system; this approach is a natural fit for controlled smart spaces. In micro systems, components are designed to collaborate when possible and act in strict autonomy when required, using key components when they are available only; this approach is tailor-made for the challenges of open space.

Pushing further the micro Context-awareness model in to address open space problems, while providing better integration with macro Context-awareness services wherever they are available, we have developed autonomous Hosts that dynamically recognize one another and trade Context as needed. Work ahead includes addressing the following, non-exhaustive list of issues.

- As has been mentioned in the section describing self-organizing evolving smart spaces, automatically transforming Context requests into operations is a promising but ongoing process. The development of a more complete grammar for Context-formatted patterns will lead us to better describe complex requirements on the part of Context consumers, and will be required to fully integrate Agent-local ontology with the overall Context model.

- Some Agent-local requests are focused on Context space management, for example determining what constitutes stale Context, or Context that automatically recognizes as having been replaced by more appropriate Context. Establishing standard practices and formats for such management Context will help avoiding that Context spaces grow to fill available memory over time.

- As mentioned in the Micro and Macro Awareness Models for Autonomic Systems section, an Agent migration mechanism can help in maintaining continuity of service even under hostile conditions, such as device failure or when device resources become dangerously low. While Context can be serialized as simply as it can be persisted, Agent names are only required to be locally unique. There are some solutions to this problem, including using globally unique names for domain-specific Agents, though not necessarily for standard Agents, or using automatic renaming of Agents when migrating an Agent from one Host to another. Which of these approaches should be preferred is a currently open question.

- The individual algorithms that operate on Context combine well-known practices with recursive structures. Their algorithmic complexity needs to be studied, and the actual data structures used to represent Context in practice might need to be refined in order to get better performance out of individual algorithms and criteria. Dynamic adaptation of the Context operations over time and circumstances is part of the self-optimizing characteristics of autonomic micro Context-aware components.

- Likewise, automatically generated requests based on Context-format descriptions of requirements will benefit greatly from the addition of optimizer components, which also directly ties into the self-optimization concerns of autonomic computing.

We believe the integration of macro and micro Context-aware systems will provide better continuity of service for mobile individuals, as it will allow building more robust Context-aware components, easier to deploy smart spaces, and offer a richer set of services to human users. We also believe in the importance of facing the open smart space problem and ensuring continuity of service for fully mobile users, which motivates our work on the micro Context-awareness programming model.

With the strong support of macro systems in controlled space and the robust implementation of micro systems in Open space, we hope to be able to provide continuity of service to those individuals and systems that need it.

ACKNOWLEDGMENT

Special thanks to DOMUS Laboratory for its support

REFERENCES

W3C. (2011). *Extensible markup language*. Retrieved from http://www.w3.org/XML/

Abdulrazak, B., Chikhaoui, B., Gouin-Vallerand, C., & Fraikin, B. (2010). A standard ontology for smart spaces. *International Journal of Web and Grid Services*, *6*(3), 244–268. doi:10.1504/IJWGS.2010.035091

Abowd, G. D., Dey, A. K., Brown, P. J., Davies, N., Smith, M., & Steggles, P. (1999). Towards a better understanding of context and context-awareness. In *Proceedings of the 1st international Symposium on Handheld and Ubiquitous Computing*, Karlsruhe, Germany.

Agostini, A., Bettini, C., & Riboni, D. (2005). Loosely coupling ontological reasoning with an efficient middleware for context-awareness. In *Proceedings of the Second Annual International Conference on Mobile and Ubiquitous Systems: Networking and Services*.

Armstrong, J. (2007). *Programming Erlang, software for a concurrent world*. Raleigh, NC: Pragmatic Bookshelf.

Campiolo, R. (2007). On modeling for pervasive computing environments. In *Proceedings of the 10th ACM International Workshop on Modeling Analysis and Simulation of Wireless and Mobile Systems* (pp. 240-243).

Chandy, K. M., & Lamport, L. (1985). Distributed snapshots: Determining global states of distributed systems. *ACM Transactions on Computer Systems, 3*(1), 63–75. doi:10.1145/214451.214456

Chetan, S., Ranganathan, A., & Campbell, R. (2005). Towards fault tolerance pervasive computing. *IEEE Technology and Society Magazine, 24*(1), 38–44. doi:10.1109/MTAS.2005.1407746

Coulson, G., Blair, G., Grace, P., Taiani, F., Joolia, A., & Lee, K. (2008). A generic component model for building systems software. *ACM Transactions on Computer Systems, 26*(1), 1–42. doi:10.1145/1328671.1328672

Crockford, D. (2006). *The application/JSON media type for JavaScript object notation (JSON)*. Retrieved from http://www.ietf.org/rfc/rfc4627.txt

Feki, M. A., & Mokhtari, M. (2006). Context aware and ontology specification for assistive environment. *International Journal of Human-friendly Welfare Robotic Systems, 4*(2), 29–32.

Gessler, S., Martin, M., & Weiss, S. (2005). Context awareness in future life scenarios: Impact on service provisioning platforms. *Applications and the Internet Workshops*, 144-147.

Ghorbel, M., Mokhtari, M., & Renouard, S. (2006). A distributed approach for assistive service provision in pervasive environment. In *Proceedings of the 4th International Workshop on Wireless Mobile Applications and Services on WLAN Hotspots* (pp. 91-100).

Gouin-Vallerand, C., & Giroux, S. (2007). Managing and deployment of applications with OSGi in the context of smart home. In *Proceedings of the Third IEEE International Conference on Wireless and Mobile Computing, Networking and Communications* (p. 70).

Gouin-Vallerand, C., Giroux, S., Abdulrazak, B., & Mokhtari, M. (2008). Toward the autonomous pervasive computing. In *Proceedings of the International Conference on Information Integration and Web-Based Applications & Services*.

Indulska, J., & Sutton, P. (2003). Location management in pervasive systems. In *Proceedings of the ACSW Frontiers Workshop on Wearable, Invisible, Context-aware, Ambient, Pervasive and Ubiquitous Computing* (pp. 143-151).

International Organization for Standardization. (2011). *ISO WG21: Programming Language C++, Document Number: N3290*. Retrieved from http://www.open-std.org/jtc1/sc22/wg21/

Katsiri, E. (2002). Principles of context inferences. In *Proceedings of the International Conference on Ubiquitous Computing*, Gotenborg, Sweden.

Kephart, J. O., & Chess, D. M. (2003). The vision of autonomic computing. *IEEE Computer, 36*, 41–50. doi:10.1109/MC.2003.1160055

Kernchen, R., Bonnefoy, D., Battestini, A., Mrohs, B., Wagner, M., & Klemettinen, M. (2006). Context-awareness in MobiLife. In *Proceedings of the 15th IST Mobile Summit*, Mykonos, Greece.

Kiani, S. L., Riaz, M., Zhung, Y., Lee, S., & Lee, Y.-K. (2005). A distributed middleware solution for context awareness in ubiquitous systems. In *Proceedings of the 11th IEEE International Conference on Embedded and Real-Time Computing Systems and Applications* (pp. 451-454).

McCann, J. A., Kristofferson, P., & Alonso, E. (2004). Building ambient intelligence into a ubiquitous computing management system. In *Proceedings of the International Symposium on Challenges in the Internet and Interdisciplinary Research*, Amalfi, Italy.

Miaou, S.-G., Shih, F.-C., & Huang, C.-Y. (2007). A smart vision-based human fall detection system for telehealth applications. In *Proceedings of the IASTED Telehealth Conference*, Montreal, QC, Canada.

Neovius, M., Sere, K., Yan, L., & Satpathy, M. (2006). A formal model of context-awareness and context-dependency. *Software Engineering and Formal Methods*, 177-185.

OSGi Alliance. (2009). *OSGi technology*. Retrieved from http://www.osgi.org/About/Technology

Pakucs, B. (2003). SesaME: A framework for personalized and adaptive speech interfaces. In *Proceedings of the EACL Workshop on Dialogue Systems: Interaction, Adaptation and Styles of Management* (pp. 95-102).

Plesa, R., & Logrippo, L. (2007). An agent-based architecture for context-aware communication. In *Proceedings of the 21st IEEE Conference on Advanced Information Networking and Applications*, Niagara Falls, ON, Canada (pp. 133-138).

Ranganathan, A., Shankar, C., & Campbell, R. (2005). Application polymorphism for autonomic ubiquitous computing. *Multiagent Grid Systems, 1*, 109–129.

Ross, T. J. (2010). *Fuzzy logic with engineering applications*. Chichester, UK: John Wiley & Sons. doi:10.1002/9781119994374

Roy, P., Abdulrazak, B., & Belala, Y. (2008). Approaching context-awareness for open intelligent space. In *Proceedings of the 6th International Conference on Advances in Mobile Computing and Multimedia* (pp. 422-426).

Song, E. Y., & Lee, K. (2008). Understanding IEEE 1451-networked smart transducer interface standard. *IEEE Instrumentation & Measurement Magazine, 11*(2), 11–17. doi:10.1109/MIM.2008.4483728

Stepanov, A., & McJones, P. (2009). *Elements of programming*. Reading, MA: Addison-Wesley.

Sun, J., & Song Dong, J. (2006). Design synthesis from interaction and state-based specifications. *IEEE Transactions on Software Engineering, 32*(6), 349–364. doi:10.1109/TSE.2006.55

Sun. (2001). *The Java HotSpot™ Virtual Machine*. Retrieved from http://java.sun.com/products/hotspot/docs/whitepaper/Java_HotSpot_WP_Final_4_30_01.pdf

Talwar, V., Milojicic, D., Wu, Q., Pu, C., Yan, W., & Jung, G. (2005). Approaches for service deployment. *IEEE Internet Computing, 9*(2), 70–80. doi:10.1109/MIC.2005.32

Trumler, W., Klaus, R., & Ungerer, T. (2006). Self-configuration via cooperative social behavior. In L. T. Yang, H. Jin, J. Ma, & T. Ungerer (Eds.), *Proceedings of the Third International Conference on Autonomic and Trusted Computing* (LNCS 4158, pp. 90-99).

Truong, H.-L., & Dustdar, S. (2009). A survey on context-aware web service systems. *International Journal of Web Information Systems, 5*(1), 5–31. doi:10.1108/17440080910947295

Van Laerhoven, K. (2000). *Characteristics of context awareness.* Retrieved from http://www.teco.edu/tea/tea_vis.html

Weiser, M. (1993). Some computer science problems in ubiquitous computing. *Communications of the ACM,* 74–84.

Winograd, T. (2001). Architectures for context. *Human-Computer Interaction, 16*(2), 401–419. doi:10.1207/S15327051HCI16234_18

WIPO. (2008). *International classification of the figurative elements of marks under the Vienna agreement.* Retrieved from http://www.wipo.int/classifications/vienna/en/

World Health Organization. (2001). *International classification of functioning, disability and health.* Retrieved from http://www.who.int/classifications/icf/en/

Yaiz, R. A., Selgert, F., & den Hartog, F. (2006). On the definition and relevance of context-awareness in personal networks. In *Proceedings of the 3rd Annual International Conference on Mobile and Ubiquitous Systems* (pp. 1-6).

Zaslavsky, A. (2004). Mobile agents: Can they assist with context awareness? In *Proceedings of the IEEE International Conference on Mobile Data Management* (pp. 304-305).

This work was previously published in International Journal of Business Data Communications and Networking, Volume 7, Issue 2, edited by Varadharajan Sridhar and Debashis Saha, p.p 47-68, copyright 2011 by IGI Publishing (an imprint of IGI Global)

Chapter 8
Semantic Federation of Product Information from Structured and Unstructured Sources

Matthias Wauer
Technische Universität Dresden, Germany

Andreas Konzag
BMW Group, Germany

Johannes Meinecke
SAP Research Dresden, Germany

Markus Aleksy
ABB Corporate Research, Germany

Daniel Schuster
Technische Universität Dresden, Germany

Till Riedel
Karlsruhe Institute of Technology, Germany

ABSTRACT

Product-related information can be found in various data sources and formats across the product life-cycle. Effectively exploiting this information requires the federation of these sources, the extraction of implicit information, and the efficient access to this comprehensive knowledge base. Existing solutions for product information management (PIM) are usually restricted to structured information, but most of the business-critical information resides in unstructured documents. We present a generic architecture for federating heterogeneous information from various sources, including the Internet of Things, and argue how this process benefits from using semantic representations. A reference implementation tailor-made to business users is explained and evaluated. We also discuss several issues we experienced that we believe to be valuable for researchers and implementers of semantic information systems, as well as the information retrieval community.

INTRODUCTION

Product-related information is generated, accessed and manipulated along the product lifecycle in heterogeneous formats. Only part of this information can be accessed using state-of-the-art

product information systems as large parts of this information are only available in unstructured sources or distributed along different databases and legacy systems. The challenge to create an all-embracing view on products is huge. Such a comprehensive product information system has to

DOI: 10.4018/978-1-4666-2026-1.ch008

integrate and harmonize data from all phases of the product lifecycle, all different source formats like unstructured documents, sensor information or product databases. Furthermore, it must even cross organization boundaries as different stakeholders may be responsible for the design, production, delivery, and service of a product.

The Aletheia project (Aletheia, 2009) is a unique attempt to bring together industry partners (ABB, BMW, Deutsche Post DHL, Otto, SAP) with five innovative application scenarios from different phases of the product lifecycle and five different landscapes of current state-of-the-art product information management. All these partners have a keen interest in improving the information flow internally as well as with their customers and partners and to open up new sources of product-related information like Web 2.0 pages.

In this paper we try to answer the research question if it is possible to federate structured as well as unstructured sources of product information along the product lifecycle. We use semantic technologies for this purpose and deploy and advance information extraction techniques. The scenarios describe two of the use cases of the Aletheia project clarifying the opportunities of federated product information systems (FPIS). We further discuss requirements derived from these and other scenarios. A discussion of existing architectures for semantic information management and federation shows the need for a new architecture matching the requirements mentioned. The contributions of this paper consist of

1. A discussion of *design decisions for FPIS*,
2. A high-level *component architecture for FPIS*, including a concept for data sharing between organizations,
3. A detailed *concept of the Aletheia Service Hub*, our central component for information federation within organizations,
4. *A reference implementation* of a semantic FPIS.

We conclude with a discussion of the results achieved so far.

SCENARIOS AND REQUIREMENTS

In order to motivate our research, we discuss two scenarios in the industrial sector. They are derived from two case studies conducted in the Aletheia project, focusing on

1. Product lifecycle management (PLM) at ABB, a large company providing power and automation products, technology, and service[1], and
2. Knowledge management in automotive engineering at the BMW company.

Use Case ABB

The customer has installed several products of the company at their local site. A service team of the customer notices that one of the devices is defective. Even though they have the knowledge which devices are applied at this installation, they lack the capability of identifying the actual cause and repairing the device. Hence, they contact the company's call center that records the service request. However, neither the customer's service team nor the call center associate has expert knowledge about the defective device. The service report therefore is frequently inaccurate, and preparing the service operation is laborious for an assigned service technician on the basis of this report.

On site, most of the suitable unstructured information is not consulted by the service technician because finding it based on the available information is cumbersome. If additional spare parts are required to repair the device, the service technician has to manually coordinate the order of a spare part and its delivery with the company's call center, the logistics provider, and the customer's service team. This causes several phone calls and requires much effort because the service technician's available information is not integrated with those of the other parties.

This use case can be optimized by three means. First, the customer should be able to solve well known problems with defined solutions without the need to consult a company's service technician.

Aletheia can support this by providing such information related to the customer's actual installed base and corresponding historical information. On top of that, the different vocabulary of customers and service documents can be translated with semantic search. Second, this previously collected information is useful to more accurately define detailed problem descriptions for identifying the most appropriate service engineer, who can find related information from unstructured documents easier if they are extracted and semantically related to the respective device and problem symptoms. Third, the federation of RFID and sensor data correlated to the defective device can improve failure analysis by providing all relevant information, while the connected information helps assisting processes like ordering spare parts between the involved parties.

Use Case BMW

The development of vehicles is characterized by high complexity, a strong network of development issues, and many participants who work in a matrix organization. The product development process can be divided into the phases of concept and series development. In the concept phase, technical requirements are derived by customer requirements. It is characterized by dynamic processes and few formalisms. In addition, a large amount of unstructured data is needed for the main part, called the concept phase.

The use case identifies relevant requirements of the technology and methods development. For this purpose, the research group has examined key elements of the product development applied in a business process with its data, actors, and interaction patterns (Figure 1).

This process describes the derivation of functional requirements of customer-related product goals by the feature managers and provision of design solutions by the function managers. The concept engineer is responsible for ensuring consistency and plausibility, which are ranked above all relevant development issues in the project. As illustrated in Figure 2, a major part of the relevant data for the concept phase is unstructured. Structured data are created during the concept phase of the development process.

Conventional methods and tools for data management, as they are productively employed in the series development of automobiles, are limited in their applicability due to the characteristics of the vehicle concept development.

The challenges which have to be mastered for the Aletheia use case can be roughly divided into two classes:

1. **Federation of Different Sources:** The data and information required for early product development are stored in different information silos. Not only structured data have to be considered. Especially during concept development, mostly unstructured data is produced, with office documents being common examples. Furthermore, these data are not accessible corresponding to its content or context, and the relations to structured data are not covered or described inadequately.

2. **User Access to the Federated Information:** From a user perspective, the physical location of data and information is secondary. The information itself is more important. Between the various development issues there are several dependencies which are not well-known by all parties. It is not just about finding individual documents or facts. In addition, the dependencies between different information fragments from different sources should be useable and visible for users.

Figure 1. Development of vehicle concepts

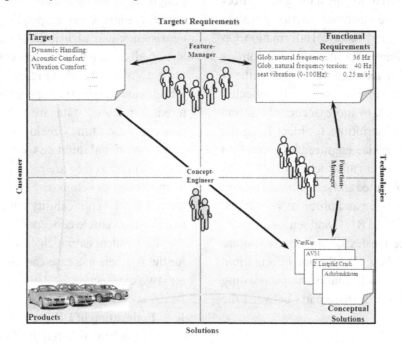

Conventional systems focus either on the search for structured data (like database knowledge discovery systems), or on the search of unstructured data (such as desktop search). Therefore, at the technical level, mechanisms must be provided to enable uniform access to data and documents from different physical sources. From a user perspective, methods and suitable surfaces are necessary to allow an integrated view of the federated information and the dependencies between them.

Figure 2. Relevance of managing unstructured data in the concept phase of vehicle development

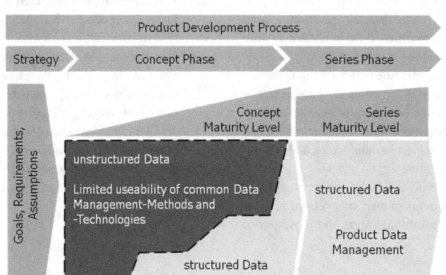

Requirements

Out of these and other scenarios from the use case partners we identified a large number of requirements. The requirements were acquired on-site in 2-day workshops at each industrial partner. The resulting large set of requirements then has been further analysed and condensed to the following main categories:

Requirement 1: Federated Information Retrieval

The central functionality users want to use an FPIS for is federated information retrieval, i.e., formulating an information need and retrieving relevant results from the FPIS. There are many features similar to classical search engines like natural language queries, auto-complete, clustering of results, personalization, and faceted search that users expect from an FPIS. Beyond that, we also identified FPIS specific requirements: search results that mix up document links and ontology facts relevant to the search query. A sort of federated ranking method is needed to bring order to this result list. Furthermore, one should be able to restrict the sources to search for by a query, or some kind of intelligent source selection method should identify the best sources for each query.

Requirement 2: Information Exploration

Besides the retrieval part, users should also be able to navigate through the information space created by an FPIS and to explore connections between different information entities, documents, and related concepts. Information exploration and information retrieval can also be mixed up as exploration may be refined by a query and vice versa.

Requirement 3: Information Integration

Federation of product information means integrating existing sources of information that were formerly used separately to create an all-embracing view on all product-related information. Thus a large number of requirements targets on using existing databases and make them searchable within the FPIS. Other types of information sources include file shares with formatted documents such as Word, PowerPoint or PDF and information from the Internet of Things, i.e., RFID and sensor data. Information integration includes appropriate mapping schemas, the management of access policies for the different sources as well as the actual access technologies like Web service interfaces or the like.

Requirement 4: Information Extraction

Full-text indexing of unstructured information (i.e., documents on file shares as well as websites) is not enough to reach the goal of semantic federation of product information along the product lifecycle. Information extraction techniques are needed to obtain information from unstructured documents. This mainly means (but is not restricted to) Named Entity Recognition (NER) to recognize entities with different keywords but belonging to the same semantic concept. Meta information should also be extracted from the documents to improve the relevance assessment.

Requirement 5: Information and Ontology Management

Once an FPIS gets deployed we also need means to directly manipulate the information presented to the user. It might be incorrect or important information may be missing. This may optionally require update mechanisms to populate changes made in the FPIS back to the information sources. Another important point is the ability to easily manipulate the ontologies used to realize the information integration and information extraction.

Requirement 6: Information Sharing

Interestingly, the aspect of information sharing between organizations did not play an important role in the interviews. Only in the ABB case we actually found a use case where we need sharing of information as partner companies do part of the service for machines on behalf of ABB. But if FPIS will get used in organizations, the need for information sharing will soon arise and will be the next step in the evolution of FPIS. If we really want to create an all-embracing view covering all phases of a product's lifecycle, we need to share at least part of the information between a product's designer, producer, retailer, logistics provider, and service provider.

RELATED WORK

Since the suggested federated product information system incorporates a multitude of functionality, related research spans a number of areas. Thus, this section will discuss federated information systems in general before moving on to systems that introduce semantic processing. After a survey of frameworks for information extraction the application of the extracted information for semantic search will be discussed. Finally, we present related work with a focus on product information.

Federated Information Systems

An early approach to federated search was presented as the Information Manifold (Kirk, Levy, Sagiv, & Srivastava, 1995). The system uses source descriptions, describing contents and capabilities of different structured information sources, in order to determine appropriate execution plans

for a query. In contrast to Aletheia, unstructured information is only integrated by applying manually defined "topics" to such information sources. Furthermore, the approach assumes a global schema, referred to as world view, to federate the information. Aletheia should instead provide the means to integrate information based on different models, as stated in requirement 3. Nevertheless, Information Manifold is an important guideline as it applies description logic based knowledge representations for its federation algorithms.

Semantic Federation Systems

The complex nature of the presented requirements led to the investigation of Semantic Web technologies in order to handle the complex task of relating the federated information. In this context, the NeOn project provides a generic architecture (Tran et al., 2007) for ontology-driven applications. It separates the required services for ontology engineering and ontology usage with a clear focus on the engineering part. The aspects that are most important regarding Aletheia, such as the interaction of the core services and the extraction of information from the data sources, is not covered in detail. Instead, the creation and maintenance of semantic information is the key aspect of NeOn. With its focus on the usage of federated information, Aletheia instead needs to define components and interfaces that not only handle semantic information, but also integrate them with uncertain information that has been extracted from unstructured sources. This also requires the definition of appropriate services that enable access to this comprehensive knowledge base.

Considering distributed semantic information, projects like SemaPlorer (Schenk et al., 2009) have shown the benefits of federating such data sources. It proposes the use of NetworkedGraphs, providing distributed views over RDF datasets that can be queried using SPARQL. It presents scalable reasoning by preprocessing a transitive closure of the SKOS hierarchies of configured datasets.

Again, it only partly supports the requirements of Aletheia, as it neither connects arbitrary sources, nor is there any distinction between public and confidential information.

Related to that, but based on a different motivation of the social semantic desktop, the NEPO-MUK project (Reif, Groza, Scerri, & Handschuh, 2008) developed a semantic personal information search system and different ontologies suitable for ordinary desktop entities. As such, it also addresses the extraction of semantics from documents and how they can be indexed and stored, but apparently there are no means to handle databases. It proposes a P2P architecture for distributed storage of documents, but this overlay network does not ensure that all documents are accessible. Thus, it does not address the issue of actually connecting truly heterogeneous information in our context, but the document extraction components are highly valuable for Aletheia.

Several other architectures have been proposed that deal with semantics. The Knowledge Content Carrier Architecture KCCA (Behrendt, Gangemi, Maass, & Westenthaler, 2005) focuses on semantically describing documents, in this case paid content, and leveraging them using a proposed architecture. However, most of the work is about the definition of a schema, and the upper ontologies that provide its foundation, for describing facets such as content, presentation, a usage context called community, and business descriptions like negotiation protocol and pricing scheme. The only hints on the actual federation is given by a high-level overview of components like Registry and Manager, and a stateful protocol which is said to be based on serialized RDF graphs.

Information Extraction Related Research

Regarding unstructured information, Schütz (2008) presented SMILA (Semantic Information Logistics Architecture), a simple data extraction model for different unstructured sources and an architecture based on OSGi, SCA, and BPEL. This allows for dynamically switching extraction components and flexible management of the execution depending on specific use cases. Compared to the Aletheia requirements, it does not connect this data with structured information, and any semantic processing is designed to be executed on a higher level. Indeed, the ontology store proposed by the architecture is rather a wildcard for further extensions.

With regards to the extraction of information, Ferrucci and Lally (2004) developed the Unstructured Information Management Architecture (UIMA) which can act as a blueprint for the extraction components of Aletheia, separating the information access, analysis, and acquisition aspects. Some design decisions of UIMA, such as the annotation of metadata as simple sets of key-value pairs, may have to be revisited in order to gain major benefit of this data for the integration process, as explained in requirement 3.

Gaining precise knowledge from different sources is the objective of YAGO (Kasneci, Ramanath, Suchanek, & Weikum, 2008), which relies on few core sources that are assumed to provide correct information and semantically connects this information. Core extractors use rules to derive the knowledge base. The extracted facts are further restricted to those validated using the WordNet taxonomy. In a second two-step process, additional information is gathered from Web resources that are then judged with regards to the existing knowledge base. Although we generally follow a similar approach, the presented Aletheia use case would not benefit from publicly available but irrelevant core sources like Wikipedia, as intended by YAGO.

Semantic Information Retrieval

One major motivation of federating heterogeneous data sources can be found in the potential increase of relevance of the found documents, given that at the moment, no information extraction process can faithfully extract completely reasonable knowledge from unstructured data. Providing humans with more accurate search results that they can utilize to gain that knowledge therefore is more promising. The matching of a semantic representation of documents with a query model based on the same semantic representation is likely to achieve that.

An early study showing that potential was performed by Paralic and Kostial (2003) who compared traditional full-text TF-IDF information retrieval and latent semantic indexing (LSI) with a similarity metric that compares the respective sets of concepts for query and documents:

$$sim_{onto}\left(\vec{Q},\vec{D}_i\right) = \begin{cases} \dfrac{\left|Q_{con} \bigcup D_{i,con}\right| if \left|Q_{con} \bigcup D_{i,con}\right| \neq 0}{k} \end{cases}$$

where Q_{con} and D_{con} are sets of concepts assigned to query Q and document D_i, respectively.

According to the authors, results can be improved when this similarity metric is multiplied with the TF-IDF similarity. On a MEDLINE related corpus with manually assigned query concepts, this knowledge based approach showed a significantly improved performance.

In reality, users prefer to use free text input methods to formulate a query for their information need, in contrast to ontology terms that would be required for the above method. Hence, user input needs to be translated into such semantic concepts. Tran, Cimiano, Rudolph, and Studer (2007) studied how such an interpretation can be executed using a graph-based approach. Users can provide keywords that are matched with a set of concepts. Assuming that a subgraph of the concepts for the set of keywords is more relevant if the concepts are closely related, the system ranks each subgraph accordingly, based on the number of edges in that graph.

This approach struggles with mapping terms to concepts when the terms aren't defined in the ontology. As a result, the average recall is rela-

tively low (43-52%), whereas the F-measure in their evaluation averages between 64% for the generated query selected by hand, and 53% for the automatically selected highest-ranked query. If appropriate lexical knowledge is available, this could be utilized to improve the performance.

In order to circumvent the problem of vocabulary coverage, the K-search system (Bhaghdev, Chapman, Ciravegna, & Lanfranchi, 2008) proposes an improved *hybrid search* method that applies semantic search for query parts where metadata is available, and traditional keyword-based search for parts that are not covered. Originally conceived by Rocha, Schwabe, and Aragao (2004), which basically re-ranks the original search results returned by a syntactic search, K-search extends this combined approach with a method for directly addressing concepts and relations in the semantic model. Thus, a query is parsed into different parts for keyword, semantic, and keyword-in-context queries that are each processed by the respective search engines. Finally, the individual results are merged and ranked using the *provenance* information of each semantic assertion, i.e. the document each triple has been extracted from. Note that this provenance requires all semantic information (metadata) to arise from documents, which is not a valid assumption within Aletheia.

Evaluation of this hybrid search system showed that the accuracy is much better and combines high recall measures better than keyword search with the improved precision of semantic search, without the drawbacks of either method. In fact, the F-measure improved by 49% and 55% with regards to keyword and ontology based search, respectively. Additionally, a user-based evaluation was carried out with service engineers and designers. Here, the service engineers favored hybrid search by 61%, whereas designers did not have a clear preference. For Aletheia, this is of interest with regards to one of the use cases with a similar user group. As a detail, the user interface of K-search is form based, because the intended audience is familiar with it.

Product Information Related Research

Focusing on product information, Brunner et al. (2007) examine the use of semantic technologies in the context of Master Data Management (MDM). For their system named SOR, they argue that a subset of OWL DL is sufficient for most product information management scenarios. Furthermore, they present a generic meta-model for defining scenario-specific product information as well as a basic architecture for processing such product information. Although it shows how product information can be management semantically, it does not explain how to keep the complexity of the ontology from the user. The integration of existing data sets is not discussed either.

The Product Semantic Representation Language PSRL (Patil, Dutta, & Sriram, 2005) instead focuses on the exchangeability of product information, and how they can be formalized in order to be interpreted by the involved parties. Similar to the paper mentioned above, they use W3C standards and a description logics representation. However the work mainly consists of a semantic mapping methodology between assumed ontologies for collaborating parties, for which the paper notes "no application has an explicit ontology". Thus, they simply suppose that the involved applications already use the proposed model for their terminologies.

Other product information management architectures appear to ignore Semantic Web standards, e.g. OpenPDM (Srinivasan, Lämmer, & Vettermann, 2008). They implement a product data sharing architecture on top of the ISO STEP standard data model and existing SOA middleware. Although this approach helps to reduce the cost of developing and maintaining connectors and data formats, we believe that the underlying data model enables an MDA-based code generation, but fails to support a more thorough processing and integration of product information, such as extensible reasoning.

All of these approaches do not seem to incorporate any mechanisms for extracting information from unstructured documents.

CONCLUSION

All of the presented research only solves part of the requirements. Hence, the architecture proposed subsequently aims to provide an integrated approach for a FPIS. Table 1 compares the discussed related work with regards to fulfilling the requirements towards a federated product information system.

DESIGN DECISIONS

Based on the requirements mentioned above, there are several design alternatives that are not straightforward to decide when designing an FPIS. We discuss the main design decisions we faced in the Aletheia project in the following.

Data Sources and Processing

The nature of federated information retrieval, as described in *requirement 1*, implies a range of data sources that may provide relevant information for a user. In most cases these data sources are beyond the control of the Aletheia system. We therefore decided to design a layer of data providers, components which are physically separated from the actual data processing and management. Furthermore, the flexibility of implementing the data-providing components using the technology of choice is valuable. That way, data sources can be made available that would otherwise not be accessible, or would require an extensive re-implementation of access logic.

These data-providing components can be further distinguished by their access characteristics. The content of some data sources often changes. Ideally these data sources should be queried on

Table 1. Comparison of Related Work w.r.t. Aletheia requirements

Related Work	Federated	Exploration	Requirements Data Integration	Extraction	Management	Sharing
IM	x	o	structured, unstructured	-	-	-
NeOn	o	x	semantic	-	x	o
SemaPlorer	x	x	semantic	-	-	o
NEPOMUK	o (P2P)	x	semantic, unstructured	x	x	x
KCCA	o	-	unstructured	-	o	o
SMILA	-	-	unstructured	o	-	-
UIMA	-	-	unstructured	x	-	-
YAGO	-	o	semantic, structured, unstructured	x	x	-
PaKo, Tran, K-Search	-	-	semantic, unstructured	-	-	-
SOR	o	-	semantic	-	o	-
PSRL	-	-	semantic	-	o	x
OpenPDM	o	-	structured	-	o	x

x *supported* o *partially supported* - *not supported*

demand in order to ensure current data, such as the status of a system or the current location of a parcel. However, response times can be longer due to the increased communication overhead and the performance of the slowest data source. In some cases, it is not practical to *pull* all information because it may be required for, e.g., input suggestions (auto-complete).

On the other hand, much of the content in data sources can be considered static, and translating the source format into a processable form is costly. For such data sources, *push* access, i.e. loading the data into a logically centralized storage, is more appriopriate. However, modifications of the original data sources need to be propagated, and updated pushed information may be inconsistent with previously stored information from this or a different source. We therefore explicitly decided to support both access paradigms and let FPIS system architects decide which method is most appropriate for each data source.

Push access frequently occurs for data sources like Web and file share documents. This access paradigm also makes for a more thorough processing of the source documents, such as semantic annotation, which would take too much time during query processing. It is possible to use a *pipes and filters* architectural style to connect the individual processing steps.

However, we found that separating document discovery, extraction, and storage from the semantic annotation tasks yield two major advantages. The implementation of the document preprocessing, such as crawling and full text extraction can evolve independently from annotation processing like named entity recognition, given a defined data model. Additionally, documents that have already been crawled do not have to be crawled again if the annotation process is modified or restarted on a different knowledge base. The negligible drawback of this approach is a potential scalability limitation if the intermediate document storage is too slow or too small.

Storage of Structured and Unstructured Information

During the requirement analysis, we found the need for a strict separation of facts, such as data extracted from a curated database, and possibly erroneous information resulting from, e.g., automated document annotation. The latter kind of information always contains a level of uncertainty which, in some cases, can be quantified by the respective algorithm, and is linked to mostly unstructured data.

Furthermore, we noticed that semantic middleware is not equally appropriate for these two kinds of information that must be clearly distinguished. Some systems provide semantic views on a large number of instances and reasoning on assertions. Others are more suitable for document storage and attaching probabilities to annotations, which is necessary for reasonable ranking algorithms. In most cases, algorithms differ for fact and data search, e.g. in terms of navigation facets and ranking methods.

As a result, we decided to separate the management and processing of structured information from managing unstructured information, similar to Tran, Wang, and Haase (2008). This repository split increases the flexibility of modeling the ontologies, e.g., regarding the definition of certain concepts as instances or classes. Information can still be semantically connected between the two repository components by using the same URI. Reasoning about both repositories, however, is not possible, but it would not be sensible with regards to the nature of stored information. As a side effect, certain functionality that requires data from both repositories requires additional programming.

With this decision in mind, the implementation of core services accessing the repository is tightly coupled with the underlying semantic technology. An abstraction on that layer would require unnecessary effort and hinder performance optimizations, which regularly require direct access to the platform. As a drawback, switching the semantic middleware to another API would result in re-implementing most of these basic services.

Although the federation of structured data sources is a core aspect of the federated product information system, we found that our semantic middleware of choice already supports extension points for most of this functionality. The use of another semantic middleware may require additional design and implementation effort.

Front-End Interactions

In general, front-ends including additional back-end support are separated from the core services. Thus, any required technology can be applied, e.g. Google Web Toolkit (GWT) or Adobe Flex. Initial tests showed that communication overhead that may lead to a perceived increased response time is only marginal.

Additionally, the interfaces between the front-end and core services are independent of specific semantic technologies. Here, we favored reusability and additional control over extended functionalities that may result in, e.g., directly exposing a SPARQL interface.

Finally, benchmarks (Liang, Fodor, Wan, & Kifer, 2009) and tests showed that certain expansive semantic queries may result in increased response times. Even though we selected a semantic middleware that performs very well, we decided to employ asynchronous communication between the front-end and Aletheia services, typically based on AJAX (Garrett, 2005) Web interfaces, in order to improve the system's user-perceived responsiveness. As a result, the implementation of the front-end tends to be more complex, depending on the applied technology.

REFERENCE ARCHITECTURE

Based on the design decisions described above, we developed a service-oriented reference architecture consisting of distributed components for information access and extraction, information federation and information presentation. All these components communicate via Web service interfaces thus separating these different concerns and ensuring a maximum flexibility and extensibility. Our reference architecture consists of five major entities that are described in the following. The central component connecting each of these entities is then explained in detail previously.

Components and Information Flow

Figure 3 illustrates the architecture of an Aletheia system. With regards to requirement 6 (information sharing), it includes the connection of instances across different organizations and departments. It is comprised of the following major components:

- *Application Servers* enable clients to access the Aletheia system and map domain-specific functionality to the generic interfaces. This includes a user-centered preparation of the available information. Both stand-alone and Web applications are supported as front ends.
- *Aletheia Service Hubs* (ASH) are the key component for managing the semantic model, indexed documents, and stored facts and metadata that are stored inside the repository component. They offer Web Service interfaces for application servers and access information sources using Web Service interfaces again. They can be connected to each other across organizational boundaries.

Figure 3. Aletheia reference architecture

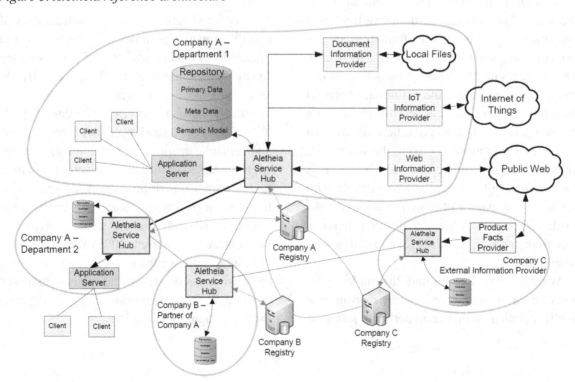

- *Repositories* are attached to each ASH to store or cache the primary data retrieved from the information sources, additional meta data about this information and a semantic model to harmonize all the information from the different sources.
- *Information Providers* act as wrappers to existing data and information sources that should be leveraged by the Aletheia system, and facilitate both push and pull access depending in the type of source. They are the components that actually access the data sources.
- *Registries* store information about each ASH (external registry interface) and the connected information sources and services (internal registry interface), enabling discovery for more or less close cooperations between different departments and organisations.

With regard to distribution, each of the Aletheia Service Hubs is the central node of a generally closed system that can be connected to external parties due to defined terms and conditions. This decision was an implication to the data sovereignty required by all the industry partners. Nevertheless, the platform may be configured to provide publicly available information via various channels, particularly with regards to linked data (Bizer, Heath, & Berners-Lee, 2009).

As the ASH and its connected repository are the central entities of our architecture, their specific composition is explained in detail subsequently.

Aletheia Service Hub

A more detailed view on the Aletheia Service Hub's components, corresponding to the architecture, can be seen in Figure 4, a fundamental modeling concepts (FMC) block diagram. Here, the client components are shown at the top, whereas the data sources appear at the bottom of the architecture. This detailed architecture can be separated into different layers.

A few vertical services such as generic configuration and monitoring features can be used by all components. Please note that many connections have been left out in order to improve readability.

Front End Services

These Web services are supposed to abstract the user queries from the technical implementation of the repository, hence reducing the complexity of the system from the client's point of view. The major task of finding federated semantic information is supported by the Semantic Search and Navigation Service providing faceted search for extracted and stored knowledge as well as documents corresponding to this knowledge. The semantic integration of these different types of information into one condensed result list is one of the major achievements of Aletheia. Besides the search functionality, a user can also browse the virtual catalog of product information using this service.

The result lists can be downloaded for offline processing using the Export Service if needed. The Update Service provides the ability to modify the information presented in the result lists thus enabling a feedback channel for the users of the system.

User customization is realized by the Login Service, setting up user sessions and assigning roles to these users as well as managing the user profile (context, preferences, history) to improve the quality of search results by personalization. The Configuration Service complements the frontend services by providing a tool for administrators to manage and configure the components of the Aletheia Service Hub.

Figure 4. Architecture of the Aletheia service hub

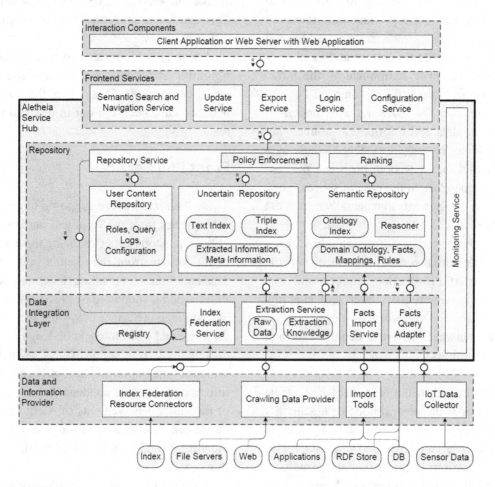

Repository

Due to the different types of stored information, we conceived a combination of different repository components. The general and domain ontologies, stored facts, mappings and rules as well as the reasoner component are considered part of the semantic repository. An additional text index enables search of ontology concepts and facts. This part of the repository is capable of managing different modules, which can be exploited for storing the individual ontologies of the participants for a certain use case.

In addition to that, the uncertain information repository manages knowledge that has been automatically extracted using approaches such

as natural language processing (NLP), i.e., it has a certain probability and cannot be safely trusted like facts. The uncertain repository stores the extracted information and assigned meta information (source, time of extraction, trust value, ...) as RDF triples. A triple index enables search on this information. Additionally, the documents are also indexed in a classic text index so information can be searched in two ways either syntactically or semantically.

The third sub-repository stores the user context, i.e., the roles, query logs, preferences and other configuration information. This information is exploited by the policy enforcement point as well as the ranking component to improve ranking by personalization.

The three different repositories are tied together to a virtual repository by the Repository Service providing a single query interface. Queries are then transmitted to the different repositories to fetch information already inside the repository as well as to federation components like the Index Federation Service and the Facts Query Adapter relaying the queries to external information providers.

Data Integration Layer

The actual federation of information is done in the Data Integration Layer supporting both push and pull semantics. Facts from structured information sources can be integrated in the semantic repository using the Facts Import Service. Unstructured documents can be delivered to the Extraction Service which executes information extraction processes and pushes the extracted information as well as the raw text of the document to the Uncertain Repository.

Pull semantics for structured information is supported by the Facts Query Adapter, a plugin in the Semantic Repository which forwards structured queries to external sources. It provides a mapping of Aletheia queries to SPARQL and SQL thus enabling any SPARQL endpoint or SQL database to be integrated in the Aletheia system. Nevertheless, a schema mapping to the respective domain ontology has to be created for each structured data source regardless if it is integrated on push or pull basis.

Pull integration of unstructured information is done by the Index Federation Service. It uses a registry of external indexes to be queried at runtime. Such indexes could be existing search engines or special Aletheia information providers capable to do Named Entity Recognition. We are currently investigating resource selection methods for this data integration path to be able to selectively query external indexes depending on query topics.

Data and Information Provider

The last layer of our architecture comprises the Data and Information Providers which are residing at the information source to pre-process information for the Aletheia system. The Crawling Data Provider is a Web and file share crawler delivering raw document data to the Extraction Service in a unified format. Several Import Tools are necessary to get product information out of existing enterprise applications or RDF stores and databases. These tools export the information to XML which is then further processed and semantically lifted by the Facts Import Service. Thus, RDF stores and databases can be accessed in both modes - push and pull.

Internet of Things Integration

A special challenge for a future FPIS is the integration of the so called Internet of Things (IoT). Wireless Sensor Network (WSN) technology and Radio Frequency Identification extends information systems towards real world objects enabling fine granular updates of the product state. RFID technology in particular can play an important role for product life cycle management (Soga, Hiroshige, Dobashi, Okumura, & Kusuzaki, 1999). WSNs can provide important maintenance critical information, especially for products and parts that otherwise could not be accurately captured by information technology (Tiwari, Lewis, & Ge, 2005).

Technology like WSNs and RFID can both link information to the physical reality and provide fine-granular and up-to date information about the state of physical entities and make this information accessible towards an FPIS. Especially, as Figure 5 illustrates, the Aletheia architecture can integrate Internet of Things technologies in two different ways: at the frontend and at the backend.

Figure 5. Integration of the Internet of Things via gateways, and interaction components towards Frontend and Data and Information Provider

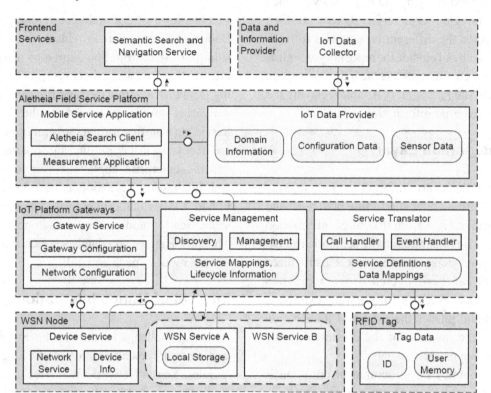

We use RFID technology as frontend extension for Information discovery. E.g., in the ABB use case we focus on identifying machinery and parts by linking physical items to named entities via a machine readable nameplate. This enables physical interaction with both real world systems and the FPIS connecting physical products and their digital counterpart. Therefore, the physical objects play in important role in practical product information management and retrieval. In the architecture depicted in Figure 4 this is reflected by the fact that the mobile application queries both the real world via the IoT Platform Gateways as well as its virtual representation via the Semantic Search and Navigation Services.

The second aspect of Internet of Things integration comprises the federation aspect of our FPIS architecture. As already highlighted in Figure 4, the Internet of Things is a distinguished federation source for the Aletheia system. However, at the

lowest layer of the architecture we have to deal with (structured, non-human readable) binary data that is stored or communicated via an arbitrary radio interface. The IoT platform gateways technically abstract a very heterogeneous IoT hardware landscape that can be found practically in the field.

Building upon the standard Devices Profile for Web Services (DPWS), we can technically and semantically uniquely identify measurement devices as named entities via an URI. This URI can be resolved locally via an infrastructure-less discovery mechanism to a Web Service communication endpoint. We use automatic translation mechanisms to generate platform specific (Web) Service Translators (Riedel et al., 2010) towards the devices that dynamically translate any communication to schema-based XML messages. At the level of the IoT Platform Gateways we can thus provide structured, well-typed and self-descriptive Web Services interfaces towards the Measurement Application.

The WSDL interfaces already contain important syntactical information like data types, minimum and maximum, or numerical precision of a value but are also used to semantically enrich the information by adding, e.g., information about quality of the sensor. Such annotation information can be provided as unstructured text or as Semantic Annotations for WSDL and XML Schema, or RDFa. The important aspect of this gateway architecture is that beyond we can provide technology independent, homogeneous access to heterogeneous IoT sources for identification and measurement.

The major challenge when federating real world sensor information is including necessary context information necessary for an interpretation of such data. Typically, this interpretation is strongly dependent and interlinked with the real world processes. In the ABB use case this is the service and diagnosis tasks performed by a field service engineer on site. One example is the mapping of sensor readings to locations and products, which may change over the temporal domain. The measurement application informs the IoT Data Provider of such changes. E.g., when an engineer places a sensor or tracking device on a part for diagnosis or monitoring the part on site or during transportation, the semantic association between the named product entity and the IoT device has to be made explicit. Further, when a node is reconfigured or calibrated, the configuration data are also associated with the consecutive sensor readings, together with additional annotations and data such as images provided by the service worker on site. All data relations are captured in the underlying work flow of the ABB measurement application and are serialized as XML, based on a domain specific schema.

IoT Data Provider interfaces the Data Integration Layer of the architecture as a structured document-based (XML) data source. For the ABB use case we have decided not to embed raw sensor data into the semantic repositories. The actual raw sensor data is not embedded, but linked via additional serialized documents. We chose this interface separation at the current point, because the sensors make up a significant amount of data that can rarely be stored efficiently or semantically queried in the proposed repository. Instead, they are transferred to file servers.

The platform still obtains all the necessary metadata available that contains part associations, placement, calibration and configuration information, but can also feature statistical information about the readings such minima, maxima, or median values aggregated over time or discrete critical events detected by the IoT devices. By connecting the individual measurements with machine product information they can be discovered and accessed later on, e.g., in specific analyzing applications via the FPIS.

PROTOTYPICAL REALIZATION

The presented architecture has been implemented with the most important components as a fully-working prototype within the Aletheia project and applied to real application partner data. In this section, we give an overview of the technical realization and used components, present the different semantic-aware user interface modes for accessing information, explain the activities that stand behind the information integration in the Service Hub, briefly describe the realization of data source lifting mechanisms and give an end-to-end example that shows the interaction of the technical components.

Overview of Technical Realization

Figure 6 gives an overview of the realized components and the technologies used for them. This implementation architecture can be seen as one possible instance of the reference architecture presented.

The front end of the Aletheia prototype has been realized as an AJAX Web application based

Figure 6. Overview of implemented components

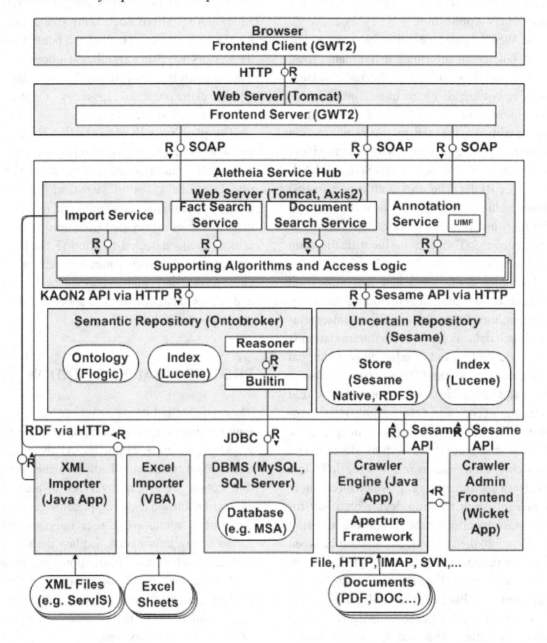

on Google Web Toolkit (GWT2). This asynchronous user interface technology was chosen to account for the need for sending multiple complex semantic queries to the Service Hub. Hence, partial results can be presented to the user before all queries complete, greatly improving the user experience.

The Aletheia Service Hub currently encompasses 4 major services for importing facts into the repository, searching for structured informa-

tion, searching semantically indexed documents and annotating text. As syntactic and uncertain repositories, we have integrated an Ontobroker (Angele & Gesmann, 2006) and a Sesame store (Broekstra, Kampan, & Van Harmelen, 2002). With these choices, we take advantage of the Ontobroker support for querying large numbers of instances over live data sources (e.g. relational databases over JDBC) and of the interoperability of Sesame with the Aperture extraction framework

(Aperture, 2010) applied inside the Web crawling data provider (crawler engine). The semantic document annotation service is implemented based on the UIMA framework. Other facts providers have been integrated via the import service's very lightweight interface that can easily be accessed from many different platforms, including from Microsoft Excel macros.

In order to support the different domain models of individual use case participants, we utilize the Ontobroker capability of managing several ontologies in terms of multiple modules and respective namespaces. For example, the prototype can be switched from an ABB centric ontology to one that has been developed at BMW, simply by an appropriate selection in the front end, as shown in Figure 7.

User Interaction Paradigms

The Aletheia Frontend supports user to find the product-related information they need with appropriate user interfaces. Depending on the situation of the user, different interaction paradigms are suitable. We implemented several paradigms

that leverage the knowledge of how the objects of interest are related to each other (via the links in the Semantic and Uncertain Repository). The focus was on realizing generic mechanisms that can generate the user interface completely from the domain models, without any domain-specific programming. Furthermore, the goal was to support complex structured queries (to take advantage of the semantic relationships), while not forcing the user to think in terms of complex queries (to account for the analyzed non-IT user needs in the PLM domain).

Search

Search in this context (Figure 8) means that users enter text in a search box which is interpreted as a structured query, using the ontology of the Semantic Repository as background knowledge. The user is supported to disambiguate the query so that he can find precisely what he meant. In the prototype, this takes the form of auto-complete suggestions. The system can support homonyms (disambiguating different things with the same name) and synonyms (finding the same thing via

Figure 7. Selection of different ontology configurations by users in the prototype

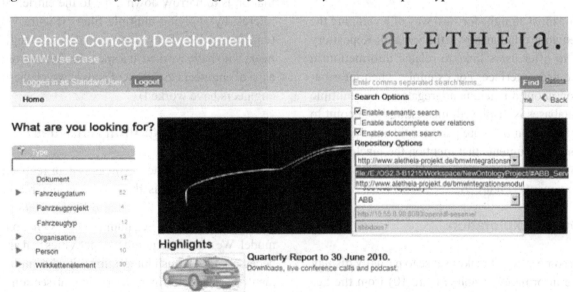

Figure 8. Search example

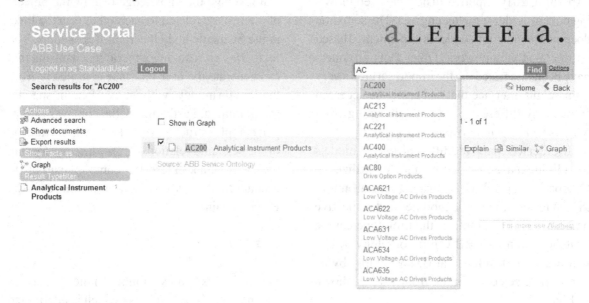

different names). The search text can be interpreted as a structured query by taking into account semantic relationships (e.g. "Mueller service job reports": finding all reports on jobs performed by a service engineer Mueller). The system can explain to the user why a result was found with natural text or graphically.

Navigation

The most straight-forward way of leveraging the semantic relationships in the Semantic Repository is to offer users links to related information in the user interface. For example, when information about a machine aggregated from multiple databases is displayed, interesting links point to information on spare parts for the machine, to a list of documents that mention the machine and to other machines that are also mentioned in the documents (Figure 9).

Graph Exploration

In some cases, it makes sense to partially display the information graph (Figure 10) from the Semantic Repository itself to the user and let him navigate and explore the nodes by expanding neighboring nodes and links. This allows the user to understand complex dependencies that are otherwise hard to see (e.g. "Who worked together in which service jobs?").

Filtering

Another paradigm we realized for finding information is to narrow down a list to the entries of interest by applying multiple filters (Figure 11) (e.g. from a list of engineers to only those engineers who have worked at a specific site; or from a list of engineers to the list of sites at which these engineers have worked).

Information Integration Activities

A core function of the Aletheia system realized in the Service Hub is the semantic integration that makes the data from the different sources correspond to one unified human-understandable model. We describe a number of activities that are necessary to establish integration with the implemented Service Hub in the following sub sections.

Figure 9. Navigation example

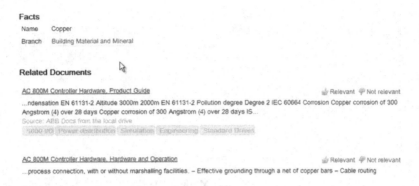

Domain Modeling

The first and foremost pre-requisite for setting up the Service Hub is that someone has modeled the domain of interest by creating an ontology. The ontology defines, among other things, classes (e.g. "company", "product"), relationships (e.g. "sells") and attributes (e.g. "company name"). The modeling is performed by domain experts that have been trained or are supported by ontology engineering experts. It is created based on a formal language (in our case: F-Logic) with the help of an ontology tool (in our case Ontostudio) (Figure 12).

The modeling task must necessarily be manual and cannot be automated, because the model is supposed to reflect how humans understand the domain and how they want to view and search for the data. In practice, the ontology often already exists partially in other forms (e.g. an Excel sheet with product categories) that can be imported into the ontology.

Source Mapping

Structured data residing in different data sources have different schemas (e.g. different database schemas and XML schemas). When the data sources are lifted to graph representations, they usually adhere to different technical ontologies that have been automatically generated from the data source schemas. In order to resolve the

Figure 10. Graph exploration example

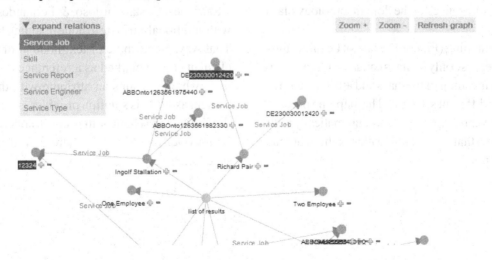

Figure 11. Filtering Example

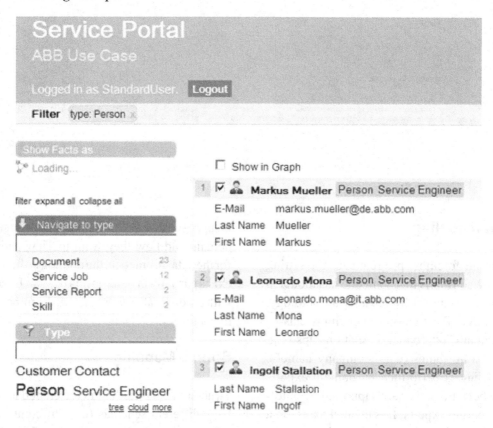

semantic gap between the different ontologies and make the data sources queryable according to the central domain ontology, we defined mappings. We created mapping rules with the help of tools, which were then executed by the semantic middleware automatically (e.g. when a query is posted for instances of the domain ontology class "Company").

The mapping (Figure 13) cannot be fully automated, because only humans can say with certainty what the meaning of the class and attribute names are in the different schemas. The mapping process can however be supported semi-automatically with algorithms that detect similarities in the schemas to be mapped.

Furthermore, we were faced with XML schemas that contain implicit references. These kind of internal links between nodes are important in order to model relationships, but current tools do not recognize them. Thus, we provided a semi-automatic mapping tool that extends JXML2OWL (Rodrigues, Costa, Cardoso, & Fernandes, 2006) with additional attribute to node mapping features. That way, an attribute or text node *id* of a XML element can be marked as a reference to another node which contains an attribute with the same content as *id*. This solution provides an increased flexibility for schemas that don't adhere to the XLink (DeRose, Maler, Orchard, & Walsh, 2010) specification.

Figure 12. A domain ontology modeled in a tool

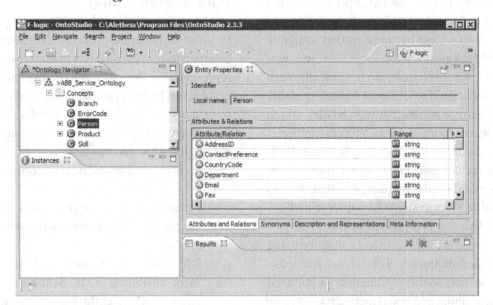

Link Generation

One important aspect of the semantic integration is the computation of the semantic links that capture how the objects of interest are related to each other. In some cases, we derived these with certainty from the data sources, e.g. from foreign-key-relationships in a database schema or the respective technical ontology. Here, we manually defined rules for detecting these relationships and making them explicit.

In other cases, if there was no certain rule, the links had to be computed by comparing individual instances and their attribute values. Here, we developed a tool that proposes links based on similarity measures and having a human confirm or alter these links.

Text Analysis

In order to fill the Uncertain Repository with information on unstructured data, text has to be analyzed so that explicit links can be drawn between terms occurring in the text and the objects in structured sources (e.g. linking the mentioning of a company name in a bill to the customer entry in a CRM

Figure 13. Example of mapping between technical data source ontology (left) and central domain ontology (right)

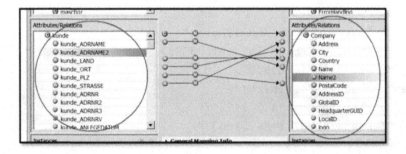

system). In the project, named entity recognition was used to identify entities (i.e. concepts and instance data) in text by transforming available structured background knowledge into dictionaries valuable for text based search. Typically, each entity is associated to different human readable natural language representations (labels), which occur in text corpora. Each such representation is treated as a cue for the according instance. Each cue has a certain associated information content which is based on the frequency of that term in structured data. An example for a created dictionary looks like that is presented in Box 1:

Documents are tokenized and annotated using the cue-based dictionary. Tokens and entity annotations are persisted in separate query-optimized indices containing additional meta-data about the annotation process. In addition global document corpora statistics (mean document length, document count) needed for ranking are calculated. Having this information, different ranking schemes based are applied on the information content, TF-IDF and the distance of terms and entities to each other within one document.

The creation of dictionaries from the structured data and the text analysis are fully automated processes. Human manual effort might have to be necessary when a new document corpus has to be integrated that uses language that is not well covered by the ontology / the structured data. In this case, the ontology might have to be extended with new labels.

Data Source Lifting

In order to integrate different data sources, the heterogeneity of the different media types and data representation formats has to be overcome. This is achieved by data providers that make the data from the sources available as graphs in an RDF format that corresponds to source-specific F-Logic ontologies. This step can be done fully automatically, as it is just a syntactic transformation.

- Database tables are transformed into classes, rows into instances and columns into attributes.
- XML nodes are transformed into instances or attributes, XML Schema types into classes, XML child nodes are linked to their parent nodes with relationships.
- Spreadsheets are transformed in a very similar way as databases. The transformation can be done.
- For unstructured documents, the metadata attributes (e.g. title, author, date of creation etc.) are transformed into RDF statements. The text itself is left as analyzed later by the annotation service.

Example

The screenshot in Figure 9 shows an example where a user searches for configurations of devices used in the Chemical industry branch with AC it their name. The search terms are entered in a

Box 1.

```
<token canonical="http://.../a1/bmw#Thorax">
<variant base="beifahrerairbag" i="4.515037"/>
<variant base="Thorax" i="5.767800"/>
<variant base="thorax" i="4.615120"/>
<variant base="gurtsystem" i="4.301462"/>
<variant base="fahrerairbag" i="4.515037"/>
</token>
```

similarly simple way as users know from public Web search engines. However, to leverage the semantic model underneath, auto-complete suggestions with terms from the domain are offered to the user. This is supported by the fact search service that uses the ontology index of the semantic repository. When entered, the keyword query is than interpreted by the fact search service as a structured query, depending on disambiguated instance names, class names, role names and free-text terms. This is then executed by the semantic repository over the ontology designed collaboratively by domain and ontology experts. An excerpt of the ontology, modeled in FLogic, is shown in Figure 14.

The reasoner executes the query and, based on mapping rules, decides, for which sub queries to perform database SQL queries via the JDBC builtin, similar as in Angele and Gesmann (2006). Other facts necessary for the query may be permanently stored in the semantic repository, e.g. imported from an XML dump of a legacy application via the XML importer before query time. After query execution, graphs are generated that explain to the user, why each particular found instance is considered to be a match for the entered keywords. The same search box can also return documents from the uncertain repository. In this case, the query is interpreted by the document search service, not as a structured query, but as a vector of free text terms (via the document full-text index in Lucene) and disambiguated URIs (via the semantic annotations in the RDFS store).

EVALUATION AND DISCUSSION

Although the work on the reference implementation of Aletheia is still in progress, we already evaluated the initial results with regards to aspects such as usability, search functionality, data sources, interfaces, and added value due to the semantic technologies.

Internal Evaluation

The evaluation involved all Aletheia project members and has been conducted using a survey on the prototype variants built for all of the five scenarios. With ten responses and a total of 59 rated criteria, this initial feedback was mixed:

- In summary, an earlier version of the implementation received 26 positive, 15 negative and 15 "partially fulfilled" ratings, with regards to the collected use cases

Figure 14. FLogic code sample of the ontology

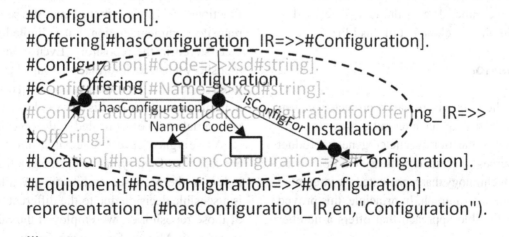

```
#Configuration[].
#Offering[#hasConfiguration_IR=>>#Configuration].
#Configuration[#Code=>>xsd#string].
#Configuration[#Name=>>xsd#string].
(#Configuration[#isStandardConfigurationforOffering_IR=>>
#Offering].
#Location[#hasLocationConfiguration=>>#Configuration].
#Equipment[#hasConfiguration=>>#Configuration].
representation_(#hasConfiguration_IR,en,"Configuration").
...
```

and requirements. Here, partially fulfilled means that the evaluator did see some of the capabilities implemented w.r.t. a certain requirement, but not in its entirety that is expected for a final prototype.

- Several of the individual solutions that have been implemented for scenario-specific use cases, such as the recognition of product terms in full-text requests and graph visualizations, received very positive feedback, both for highlighting the benefits of semantics and usability of the search function. Hence, we currently integrate them as components to the reference implementation.

- As expected, some evaluators criticised that not all potential information sources are integrated already. They evaluated a comparatively early version of the prototype. Since then, the available data providers have been extended considerably.

- The benefit of semantics is not obvious for a few use cases related to the Internet of things. The implementation did not utilize this information in conjunction with the stored knowledge, and the higher-level integration is clearly necessary to show the advantage.

We will present the results of a more comprehensive evaluation to be executed later this year. Hence, we rather discuss the lessons learned to date with the development of this FPIS.

Discussion

Within the Aletheia research project, we prototypically set up an integrated browsing and searching application over heterogeneous product data sources in realistic industry environments, using a technology that represented the integrated information as a graph. In principle, this proved to be a feasible approach that offers a number

of advantages acknowledged by the application partners.

The most important advantage is that users can intuitively enter search queries whose answers require knowledge of how objects are related to each other (independently from where the objects are stored). The relationships can also be leveraged for graph visualizations to provide end users with advanced insight into complex dependencies in the underlying data. Moreover, the graph model makes it easier to let users access all relevant pieces of information together, including documents related to objects described in a database. Such features can be supported in a generic way for all relationships, without the need to hard-code special cases. It is generally not necessary to result to heavy-weight semantic technology with advanced reasoning capabilities. Instead, it is sufficient to be able to view and query data according to a graph model.

As shown above, the current reference implementation exhibits most of the benefits of the intended Aletheia system. Although the architecture proposes the federation of at least structured information at the time a client actually poses a query, we noticed that this is difficult to accomplish. For the auto-complete functionality presented in Figure 9, an index of the name and other properties a semantic entity can be referred to *must* be available in the system in order to meet response time constraints (latency). This functionality is present in the employed semantic repository implementation, but is limited to the facts stored in the repository. Even though the repository federates information from other structured sources like relational databases, it does not make them available on this index unless this data is materialized, i.e. replicated to the repository.

As we argued, uncertain semantic information are separated from syntactic data, e.g. a full-text index, in the proposed architecture. While this is a sensible decision due to the different nature of those repositories, we employed the Sesame LuceneSail (Minack, Sauermann, Grimnes, Fluit,

& Broekstra, 2008) component which combines both aspects. Hence, the management of extracted facts like <Document1> <isAbout> <DriveComponentA> is accomplished by the same component that stores the full-text index of that document.

We further noticed that the traceability of federated information is difficult. This is due to the overhead of storing provenance information for every fact in the repository, and gets even more complicated if the information should be annotated with confidence or trust ratings. While initially considering RDF reification, we also studied whether named graphs can be used appropriately for such annotations. The requirement of federated ranking would benefit from such reliable confidence assertions. We found, however, that this poses a high processing load on the system that can't be handled using current technology for the required amount of information.

The authentication and, to a greater degree, the authorization of users to access certain information remains an issue. Considering the federation during a client's request, existing single-sign-on (SSO) solutions can be applied. As the autocomplete issues have shown, the ad-hoc federation is an approach that causes several difficulties. However, federating the information prior to actual requests and, hence, not requesting the original information sources requires the repository to keep track of access rights to individual information. Additionally, this causes the data providers to determine and relay this authorization information in the first place. This is a critical aspect for all studied scenarios, and is subject to current work on integrating an authentication and authorization component.

Collectively, the current implementation provides a complete "vertical cut" through the architecture, integrating different heterogeneous data sources. It also proved to be applicable to different domains by means of switching the semantic model, i.e. the ontology, and connected data sources.

CONCLUSION

In this paper, we have presented an architecture that supports the federation of heterogeneous information, originating from various data sources and arising throughout the product lifecycle. We propose this solution with regards to the limitations of current product information management products. These are less flexible than this semantic approach and usually only cover few aspects of the product lifecycle.

Prior to that, we generalized a number of requirements derived from multiple real-life scenarios. The proposed architecture and associated reference implementation enables the exploration of information, both using semantic search and exploring related information. Most of the required data sources have already been integrated, based on generic solutions like XML to RDF transforms, in order to provide the desired all-embracing view. Internet of Things devices, such as wireless sensor networks and RFID tags, can be integrated using the proposed gateway architecture. Existing frameworks for information extraction are attached that integrate unstructured information, using the respective domain ontology and existing knowledge.

The presented information can also be modified by the users of the system, thereby keeping the product information up to date, even though these modifications are not performed at the information's origin. Finally, we presented our vision of enabling collaboration of such federated product information systems between different organisations, which is a requirement for exploiting the full potential of such a solution.

Compared to an earlier publication (Wauer, Schuster, & Meinecke, 2010), this paper presents our approach and related work in much more detail. It also discusses the Internet of Things integration and more thorough results regarding the reference implementation.

ACKNOWLEDGMENT

This work was partly funded by the German Ministry of Education and Research under the research grant number 01IA08001. We would like to thank many Aletheia project members contributing to this architecture and reference implementation, including but not limited to Bernd Stieger, Nic Fantana, Thomas Janke, Tobias Münch, Robert Rieger, Sandro Reichert, and Maximilian Walther, as well as project partners for fruitful discussions on use cases and requirements.

REFERENCES

Aletheia. (2009). *Semantische Föderation umfassender Produktinformationen*. Retrieved from http://www.aletheia-projekt.de/

Angele, J., & Gesmann, M. (2006). Data integration using semantic technology: A use case. In *Proceedings of the* Second International Conference on Rules and Rule Markup Languages for the Semantic Web (pp. 58-66). Washington, DC: IEEE Computer Society.

Aperture. (2010). *A java framework for getting data and metadata*. Retrieved from http://aperture.sourceforge.net/

Behrendt, W., Gangemi, A., Maass, W., & Westenthaler, R. (2005). Towards an ontology-based distributed architecture for paid content. In Proceedings of the Second European Semantic Web Conference (pp. 257-271).

Bhagdev, R., Chapman, S., Ciravegna, F., & Lanfranchi, V. (2008, June). Hybrid search: Effectively combining keywords and ontology-based searches. In Proceedings of the 5th European Semantic Web Conference (pp. 554-568).

Bizer, C., Heath, T., & Berners-Lee, T. (2009). Linked data–The story so far. *International Journal on Semantic Web and Information Systems*, 5(3), 1–22. doi:10.4018/jswis.2009081901

Broekstra, J., Kampman, A., & Van Harmelen, F. (2002). A generic architecture for storing and querying RDF and RDF schema. In I. Horrocks & J. Hendler (Eds.), *Proceedings of the First International Conference on* the Semantic Web *(LNCS 2342, pp. 54-68)*.

Brunner, J.-S., Ma, L., Wang, C., Zhang, L., Wolfson, D. C., Pan, Y., et al. (2007). Explorations in the use of semantic web technologies for product information management. In Proceedings of the 16th International Conference on World Wide Web (pp. 747-756). New York, NY: ACM Press.

DeRose, S. J., Maler, E., Orchard, D., & Walsh, N. (2010, 3 6). XML linking language (XLink) Version 1.1. Retrieved from http://www.w3.org/TR/2010/REC-xlink11-20100506/

Ferrucci, D., & Lally, A. (2004). UIMA: An architectural approach to unstructured information processing in the corporate research environment. *Natural Language Engineering*, 10(3-4), 327–348. doi:10.1017/S1351324904003523

Garrett, J. J. (2005). AJAX: A new approach to Web applications. Retrieved from http://www.adaptivepath.com/ideas/essays/archives/000385.php

Kasneci, G., Ramanath, M., Suchanek, F., & Weikum, G. (2008). The YAGO-NAGA approach to knowledge discovery. *SIGMOD Record*, 37(4), 41–47. doi:10.1145/1519103.1519110

Kirk, T., Levy, A. Y., Sagiv, Y., & Srivastava, D. (1995). The information manifold. In Proceedings of the AAAI Spring Symposium on Information Gathering from Heterogeneous, Distributed Environments (pp. 85-91).

Kunz, S., Brecht, F., Fabian, B., Aleksy, M., & Wauer, M. (2010). Aletheia–Improving industrial service lifecycle management by semantic data federations. In Proceedings of the 24th International Conference on Advanced Information Networking and Applications (pp. 1308-1314). Washington, DC: IEEE Computer Society.

Liang, S., Fodor, P., Wan, H., & Kifer, M. (2009). OpenRuleBench: An analysis of the performance of rule engines. In Proceedings of the 18th International Conference on World Wide Web (pp. 601-610). New York, NY: ACM Press.

Minack, E., Sauermann, L., Grimnes, G., Fluit, C., & Broekstra, J. (2008). *The Sesame Lucene-Sail: RDF queries with full-text search.* Retrieved from http://citeseerx.ist.psu.edu/viewdoc/summary?doi=10.1.1.125.9864

Paralic, J., & Kostial, I. (2003). Ontology-based information retrieval. In Proceedings of the 14th International Conference on Information and Intelligent Systems, Varaždin, *Croatia* (pp. 23-28).

Patil, L., Dutta, D., & Sriram, R. (2005). Ontology-based exchange of product data semantics. *IEEE Transactions on Automation Science and Engineering, 2*(3), 213–225. doi:10.1109/TASE.2005.849087

Reif, G., Groza, T., Scerri, S., & Handschuh, S. (2008). Final NEPOMUK architecture – Deliverable D6.2.B. Retrieved from http://nepomuk.semanticdesktop.org/xwiki/bin/view/Main1/D6-2-B

Riedel, T., Fantana, N., Genaid, A., Yordanov, D., Schmidtke, H., & Beigl, M. (2010). Using web service gateways and code generation for sustainable IoT system development. In *Proceedings of the Conference on the* Internet of Things (pp. 1-8).

Rocha, C., Schwabe, D., & Aragao, M. P. (2004). A hybrid approach for searching in the semantic web. In Proceedings of the 13th International Conference on World Wide Web (pp. 374-383). New York, NY: ACM Press.

Rodrigues, T., Costa, P., Cardoso, J., & Fernandes, J. (2006). JXML2OWL. Retrieved from http://jxml2owl.projects.semwebcentral.org

Schenk, S., Saathoff, C., Baumesberger, A., Jochum, F., Kleinen, A., & Staab, S. (2009). Semaplorer–Interactive semantic exploration of data and media based on a federated cloud infrastructure. *Web Semantics, 7*(4), 298–304. doi:10.1016/j.websem.2009.09.006

Schütz, T. (2008, Sep). D11.1.1.B concept and design of the integration framework. Retrieved from http://www.eclipse.org/smila/docs/ORDO_D.11.1.1.b_ConceptIntegrationFramework_V1.0.pdf

Soga, S., Hiroshige, Y., Dobashi, A., Okumura, M., & Kusuzaki, T. (1999). Products lifecycle management system using radio frequency identification. In Proceedings of the IEEE International Conference on Emergent Technologies and Factory Automation (pp. 1459-1467). Washington, DC: IEEE Computer Society.

Srinivasan, V., Lämmer, L., & Vettermann, S. (2008). On architecting and implementing a product information sharing service. *Journal of Computing and Information Science in Engineering, 8*(1), 011006. doi:10.1115/1.2840775

Tiwari, A., Lewis, F. L., & Ge, S. S. (2005). Wireless sensor network for machine condition based maintenance. In *Proceedings of the 8th IEEE* Control, Automation, Robotics and Vision Conference (Vol. 1, pp. 461-467). Washington, DC: IEEE Computer Society.

Tran, D. T., Cimiano, P., Rudolph, S., & Studer, R. (2007). Ontology-based interpretation of keywords for semantic search. In K. Aberer, P. Cudré-Mauroux, K.-S. Choi, N. Noy, D. Allegmang, K.-I. Lee et al. (Eds.), Proceedings of the 6th International Semantic Web Conference and the 2nd Asian Semantic Web Conference Proceedings of the 6th International Semantic Web Conference (LNCS 4825, pp. 523-536).

Tran, T., Haase, P., Lewen, H., Garcia, O. M., Gomez-Perez, A., & Studer, R. (2007). Lifecycle-support in architectures for ontology-based information systems. In K. Aberer, P. Cudré-Mauroux, K.-S. Choi, N. Noy, D. Allegmang, K.-I. Lee et al. (Eds.), Proceedings of the 6th International Semantic Web Conference and the 2nd Asian Semantic Web Conference *(LNCS 4825, pp.508-522).*

Tran, T., Wang, H., & Haase, P. (2008). Search-WebDB: Data web search on a pay-as-you-go integration infrastructure. Retrieved from http://academic.research.microsoft.com/Publication/5647448/searchwebdb-data-web-search-on-a-pay-as-you-go-integration-infrastructure

Wauer, M., Schuster, D., & Meinecke, J. (2010). Aletheia - An architecture for semantic federation of product information from structured and unstructured sources. In Proceedings of the 12th International Conference on Information Integration and Web-based Applications & Services (pp. 325-332). New York, NY: ACM Press.

ENDNOTES

[1] In addition to this company, the scenario includes a customer from the chemical sector that uses the company's products and services, and a logistics provider that stores and ships the company's spare parts. A similar use case is studied in more detail in Kunz, Brecht, Fabian, Aleksy, and Wauer (2010).

This work was previously published in International Journal of Business Data Communications and Networking, Volume 7, Issue 2, edited by Varadharajan Sridhar and Debashis Saha, p.p 69-97, copyright 2011 by IGI Publishing (an imprint of IGI Global)

Chapter 9
The Role of Twitter in the World of Business

Kevin Curran
University of Ulster, UK

Kevin O'Hara
University of Ulster, UK

Sean O'Brien
University of Ulster, UK

ABSTRACT

This paper examines the services people seek out on Twitter and the integration of Twitter into businesses. Twitter has experienced tremendous growth in users over the past few years, from users sharing to the world what they had for lunch to their opinions on world events. As a social media website, Twitter has become the third most popular behind only Facebook and YouTube. Its user base statistics ensure a wide audience for business to engage with. However, many find this a daunting prospect as there are no set guidelines as to how business might use the service. The ability to post quick short messages for the whole of the social network to see has encouraged people to use this microblogging platform to comment and share attitudes on company brands and products. The authors present how the business world is using the social network site as a new communication channel to reach customers and examine other possible uses for Twitter in a business context. This paper also discusses how Twitter plans to move forward and evolve with its service, ensuring that personal, business and third party developers' best interests are catered to.

INTRODUCTION

Twitter is a microblogging service that allows users to follow each other and to post or 'tweet' a message with a strict 140 character limit. Twitter differs from other social networking sites in that relationships can be completely one sided. For example, one user can follow another user and there is no obligation for the latter to follow the original. Twitter exploded onto the scene in March 2006 driven by its minimal user interface, which was in stark contrast to its competitors

DOI: 10.4018/978-1-4666-2026-1.ch009

where the trend at the time was to allow users full customisation of their personal page, often resulting in a cluttered, garish design (Experian, 2009). Twitter also embraced third party developers from the beginning, offering a versatile application programming interface (API) and it also enjoys an unprecedented popularity with celebrities (Twitter Counter, 2010).

However interestingly, even with its popularity and substantial mainstream media coverage, Twitter has failed to match the growth of both Google and Facebook after their respective first three years. Google has 18,000,000 users, Facebook 27,000.000 and Twitter 8,000,000 (Battelle, 2009). As Twitter enters its fifth year in operation, it can no longer be labeled as the new kid on the block, however there are many who still do not know what its purpose is or if it even has a value for them. Twitter have described it as "... for discovering and sharing what's happening in your life right now". While this is true and unfortunately by its very nature, results in a lot of the information shared being 'pointless babble', it does not highlight the potential Twitter has in business (Java et al., 2007).

The online advertising sector is growing year on year and with technology changing there are now more ways than ever to market products and business. However, it is the 'people' who now want control and they have the 'acute editing skills' to listen to be exposed to whatever messages they want. With consumers having the power to eliminate media messages been shown to them, marketers need to discover a way of reaching their customers without them knowing it is a method of advertising. Media buying is the process of contacting the owner of a website and purchasing advertising space, usually as a banner placement, on their website. High volume websites such as YouTube and Facebook, all offer media buying placements. Businesses rely on the information provided by these websites to estimate how much of their target audience they will reach. When a business buys a placement on a high volume

website, they may have the majority of their demographic seeing it, but they will also be paying a lot of money on users who have next to no interest in what the business has to offer.

Social networking sites such as Facebook now account for one out of every five ads people view online. As the top social media sites can deliver high reach and frequency against target segments at a low cost, it appears that some advertisers are eager to use social networking sites as a new advertising delivery vehicle. A social networking site can be used to gain new customers, keep in touch with current customers and promote new products, sales/offers and events, creating overall high-quality PR that is specific to a company. It was only a matter of time before business associates woke up to the possibilities that lie beneath Social Networking. It seems obvious that they would want to promote their brands to an audience that is continuously growing at such a healthy rate.

There are many different features on each Social Networking website that can be used to promote a business. Users can post links, videos, pictures, fan pages, groups and even ads on some social networking websites. Businesses can create generic pages just like standard user pages. Once the page is, 'friends' can be added in the hope they gather more friends via 'word of mouth' promotion. Once the initial network of friends is exhausted, events can be created and other friends invited.

Twitter offers a different model however to YouTube and Facebook but it still has enormous potential to support a thriving and innovative ecosystem of users, business and media outlets and to enable them to engage in discussion on topics relevant and important to them. Twitter started out with the tagline "What are you doing?" which suited their model in its infancy. They wanted users to discuss things happening in their life, in real time. As the service grew, it began to evolve organically. Users began to share information on a global scale in real time, businesses got involved and encouraged discussion on their brand and news began to break via the platform quicker and more efficiently than the traditional mainstream media services. For these reasons the Twitter tagline now reads something more befitting and relevant to the service it offers: "The best way to discover what's new in your world". The question remains however, just how this potential can be realised and put into practice. Twitters lack of a profitable business model has raised concerns with many, and has perhaps been slightly detrimental in regards to some businesses investing time and financial resources in the service. This lack of a profitable business model also resulted in no clearly defined strategic route for business to embark on, again raising question marks on Twitters relevance and benefit to them (Stutzbach et al., 2006).

Twitter has soared in popularity since its inception in 2006. Two years ago Twitter had 3 million registered users and could boast approximately 1.25 million tweets per day, today that figure has ballooned to 165 million registered users and 90 million tweets per day (Reynolds, 2006). This 5400% growth results in a substantial platform for business to operate within. It is important however that business realise that it is not simply follower numbers that brings success but the influence which they wield. Influence is much more difficult and time consuming to obtain and requires posting quality content and actively taking part in discussions and engaging with users (Kumar et al., 2006)

Edison Research in a report, "*Twitter usage in America 2010*" pulled data obtained from a survey of 2000 Americans carried out in February 2010. The results were combined with similar studies carried out in 2009 and 2008 to provide a comprehensive representation of Twitter related user statistics. One of the noticeable findings was that people are much more aware of Twitters existent as a social network service than in the previous two years. Twitter has now roughly acquired the same awareness amongst the population as Facebook. This massive surge in the percentage of Americans that are aware Twitter has likely been driven by traditional media saturation, with many mainstream television, radio and print media outlets prominently highlighting their Twitter accounts throughout the course of their programming (Webster, 2010).

Despite the awareness between the two social networks practically being equal, Facebook has significantly more amount of users with 41% surveyed use Facebook with only 7% using Twitter. A conclusion can be drawn with sites like Facebook and LinkedIn have well-defined use cases and benefits, Twitter has yet to establish a clear value proposition (even as a purely entertainment service) for a majority of the current users of social networking sites and services (Webster, 2010). Perhaps the most interesting outcome from the survey for a business perspective would be the frequency of twitter users exchanging information about products and services. With 42% of people using Twitter to learn about products and services and 41% using Twitter to give their opinion about products and services this is an area businesses could use to their advantage. People are expressing their opinions here about products and services without being asked by anyone, this data maybe far more prevalent than on other monitored sites and services, which may introduce a bias into the data provided by social media monitoring platforms (Webster, 2010). Companies are receiving honest criticism from their customers on Twitter (Mislove et al., 2007).

Combining these results with the results from asking users if "Twitter were to incorporate targeted advertising into its service, how would this affect your Twitter usage?": here 50% said no effect and 16% saying they would use twitter more. This shows that this might be the base for the future of Twitter. By commercialising these interactions Twitter will gain revenue for opening the communication channel for businesses advertising to their customers and potential customer base (Webster, 2010).

Word of mouth (WOM) is the process of conveying information from person to person and plays a major role in customer buying decisions (Twitter Blog, 2009). In the business environment this involves consumers sharing attitudes and opinions about a company's products or services. A company with a positive WOM is a very powerful marketing asset to have. WOM communication relies on social networks. People use their friends, family and other members of their social network as a dependable source of information. Research also indicates that people appear to trust seemingly disinterested opinions from people outside their immediate social network, such as online reviews (Duana et al., 2008). This form is known as electronic word of mouth (eWOM). This broad reach of eWOM provides consumers tremendous clout to influence brand image and perceptions (Reynolds, 2006).

Twitter opens up a new area of eWOM for businesses as people can describe things of interest and express attitudes that they are willing to share with others in short posts. A research study carried out investigating Twitter as a form of electronic word-of-mouth for sharing consumer opinions concerning brands show that 19% of tweets mentioned a brand name (Jansen & Zhang, 2009). Of the branding tweets, nearly 20% contained some expression of brand sentiment. Of these, more than 50% were positive and 33% were critical of the company or product (Webster, 2010).

Firstly with 19% of tweets mentioning a brand indicates that Twitter is a viable area for organisations for viral marketing campaigns, customer relationship management and to influence their eWOM branding efforts. Secondly with 20% of branded tweets containing an expression of brand sentiment shows that Twitter can affect brand awareness and brand image. Companies can receive brand exposure from Twitter users who tweet about the company and products. This also leaves 80% of tweets that contain a brand but express no sentiment to the brand. This shows people are using Twitter to seek information and asking/ answering questions about companies and their products. Businesses can use Twitter to monitor discussions about their brand and provide informa-

tion to consumers. There is also an opportunity here to advertise products to the people who are seeking information and commenting on products.

Thirdly 50% of branded tweets were said to be of positive wording, it could be argued that this may have been influenced by commercial viral marketing this being companies hiring persons to post positive tweets about companies or products. Positive comments on Twitter are available for the world to see. If a user does a search on Twitter for a brand these positive comments will be a part of the returned results. This is free advertising and marketing for a company. With the 35% of tweets containing negative comments businesses can use this information to identify consumer preferences and finding out product defects and can then correct such issues.

There is much support around for Twitter, many high profile celebrities see it as an opportunity, which they previously did not have, to interact with their fans. Celebrities on Twitter is a new boom in itself as pop stars like Lady Gaga and Britney Spears have followers well in excess of six million. As you might expect, the business and technology sectors have embraced Twitter with many high profile personalities and companies speaking positively of it. Slightly more surprising is the embracement and uptake of the service by news corporations. As it turns out, Twitter, perhaps by chance, has found that it is one of the most effective tools for breaking news stories. Its real time model is perfect to get news out there quick and built in features like retweet, and its trending service enhance the experience and efficiency of this further. The rapid growth of Twitter and its rise in popularity with celebrities and within the business and current affairs sectors is helping to push it further into the main stream and greatly enhances its popularity and the influence that it has (Gill et al., 2007).

This paper looks at how Twitter as a service can add value to a business. We examine how Twitter plans to provide a viable and stable platform for business to operate from and we look at examples of good practice to date in using Twitter in business.

TWITTER AND MARKETING

Until recently, Twitter did not have a defined marketing model in place to directly target its users. As a result of this, a new environment has evolved. As the traditional methods of reaching an audience did not exist, businesses instead had to be as creative and innovative as possible in order to attract an audience. This approach though puts many companies off allocating resources to a dedicated marketing campaign via Twitter, and while it may work for some, it is not suited to every business type. However with careful planning and allocation of resources there have been companies who have reaped the benefits from this unconventional approach. One such company is Old Spice, who ran a hugely successful social media marketing campaign which started in the more traditional format of television but evolved when they decided to engage with their audience and have the star of the campaign 'the Old Spice Guy' film personalised videos to users who requested them via Twitter, Facebook, Reddit or Digg (Halliday, 2010). It was a huge success resulting in Old Spice increasing their followers on Twitter by 2700% and Facebook followers by 800%. The campaign increased sales by 107% over one month, 55% over a three month period and 27% after six months (Creativity-online, 2010). The campaign generated media coverage on a global scale with the star, Isaiah Mustafa, even winning an Emmy. Without question this was a genius campaign and is seen as the bench mark for social media advertising.

For every successful campaign there are of course many failures. Creating a buzz around a campaign is difficult to achieve and many approach the realm of social media marketing unprepared or with a certain naivety, none more so than the Mars confectionary company who would become one of the most high profile casualties of social media marketing with its brand Skittles. Skittles transformed its homepage into a social media experiment; it prominently displayed a feed from Twitter, scraping tweets which mentioned the Skittles brand name. While this started positively enough after a day or two the tweets turned nasty, filling the feed with profanity and abuse. The company quickly had to u-turn on this campaign and pull the feed from its homepage. This campaign was poorly planned and the agency was clearly there are in their assumption of how users would react to and indeed use it. Skittles received a lot of negative publicity over this, and while some say 'no publicity is bad publicity', this was a disaster for them. Not all businesses have been using Twitter to facilitate marketing campaigns. Some high profile corporations have begun using it, successfully, to interact with and engage with their customers. The PC manufacturer Dell have a number of Twitter profiles, one of the most popular being the Dell Outlet (Dell, 2010), where users can follow Dell to be updated with the latest offers and competitions. Dell Outlet will often engage with its followers by answering questions directly.

One of the most innovative approaches to using Twitter, and one which many companies are now employing and gaining benefit from is having a dedicated customer relations profile. The profile will usually be named with a more personal approach, for example user@company. Jetblue (2010) are an excellent example of doing this well, answering customer questions, providing flight information and actually daring to have a 'personality' by engaging in a social manner with its customers and posting interesting links. Twitter is redefining the concept of breaking news and has arguably become the best suited vehicle for it. Its real-time 140 character messages are perfect to put out a headline or synopsis of what is happening right now. A perfect example of this was the January 19th 2009 New York plane crash. Twitter users broke the news a full fifteen minutes before the mainstream media. Jim Hanrahan, four minutes after the plane went down tweeted: "I just watched a plane crash into the abell riv[sic] in Manhattan" (Twitter Blog, 2010). Twitter users continued to tweet throughout the course of the event, posting their experiences, what was happening and pictures they had taken on their camera phones. These posts and pictures were picked up by news corporations, blogs and websites as the day and events progressed. This event highlighted the power Twitter can have as the source of a wealth of information for a breaking news story, and as such many news corporations now have their own Twitter profiles.

As yet Twitter has not implemented a native analytics service, however their flexible application programming interface (API) has allowed third party developers to create sophisticated tools to analyse data and provide comprehensive feedback on accounts. Two of the most prominent analytic services are Klout and Twitalyzer. Klout specifically focus on influence on the social web. Each user is allocated their individual graph which tracks the content they create, how others interact with it and the composition of the users network. To measure influence, Klout use what they call 'The Klout Score' which scores overall influence using 25 variables broken down into three categories; 'True Reach', 'Amplification Score' and 'Network Score'. Twitalyzer is another comprehensive analytics tool available to users of Twitter. Like Klout it provides a dashboard which allows the user to analyse and track their impact and influence by measuring certain statistics such as followers, engagement in conversation, success of links provided and retweet numbers. Using these services, business or personal users can get an excellent visual representation of their influence and use this information to plan and improve how they engage with Twitter going forward. There are many other third party tools available to analyse the influence of an account, most of which provide extremely detailed and thorough analysis. Twitter does have plans to roll out their own set of analytic tools and has acquired analytics company 'Small Thoughts', in order to do so.

Prior to the emergence of social media websites and the marketing opportunities which they present, advertising and promoting a brand or service

was an expensive undertaking. Television, radio, newspapers and magazines offer a successful, established direct targeting line of communication to the consumer, but they come with a high financial commitment. Reaching a large audience at a national or international scale has until now been beyond the resources of many. Twitter presents the opportunity for anyone to reach an audience of potentially millions for almost zero financial commitment. This of course is difficult, and requires an innovative approach which will engage users, but the fact that the opportunity exists in the first place cannot be ignored. While technically, Twitter is free, it would be incorrect to label it so from a business aspect. Often companies will employ an agency to take care of their marketing campaign, which still comes at a high cost. More recently however, Twitter has introduced a paid model for 'Promoted Tweets' (Twitter Blog, 2010) where companies pay to have their product or service promoted to users of Twitter. This is a return to the more traditional approach of marketing and it is much too early to evaluate the success of this new venture. There is no denying that to run a successful marketing campaign or customer service portal, requires a lot of dedication and time. Employing staff to deal with customers will incur a financial commitment and the cost of the time which must be dedicated to running a successful marketing campaign should not be underestimated.

Twitter has been labelled by some as the 'Wild West' of marketing; the opportunity to prosper is there for those daring enough to seize it. This is not without risk however. Success is not guaranteed and as demonstrated the incorrect approach can have a detrimental effect. It is unfair though to label Twitter as more risky than a traditional method of advertising, which of course comes with its own problems. It is simply a by-product of the evolution of advertising and its utilisation of technology. Perhaps the most viable way for most businesses to 'dip their toes' in Twitter is to use it initially as a customer relations tool. Business must move with the trends of society and as Twitter and other social networks grow, the public will demand the ability to engage with vendors of any variety of products or services via a social networking platform, and Twitter with its robust infrastructure, user model and real time engagement is perhaps best suited to this.

Twitter's open API has created a goldmine for third party developers to create applications to utilise their service, resulting in a highly distributed, convenience driven ecosystem. It is estimated that ten times the traffic of the Twitter homepage comes via this ecosystem (Benjamin, 2009). Some of the ways to interact and use the Twitter service include a plethora of mobile apps crossing the iOS, Android, Symbian, BlackBerry OS and the soon to be released Windows Phone 7 platforms. These apps mirror the web application in that they allow the user to see their Twitter feed, post updates and follow other users with the user interface (UI) tailored for the mobile device. Twitter also offers a service for those users who do not have access to a smart phone, giving them the functionality to both send and receive updates via SMS. There is also a growing market for desktop clients in the 'Twitterverse'. These desktop clients often provide an enhanced UI and provide the ability to integrate other services like Facebook and LinkedIn. This varied ecosystem empowers the user to choose which ever service they prefer and best suits their needs, Twitter has embraced and encouraged this trend which ultimately facilitates their continued growth.

THE TWITTER ECOSYSTEM

Twitter has created great opportunities for existing companies to take part in its service, whether it be in the guise of interacting with their customers or promoting their brands, products, or services. There is another side to the coin however, as Twitter has given new ventures the opportunity to create and focus their business around Twitter.

StockTwits is a real time platform for stock traders and investors to share information. Users are encouraged to eavesdrop on traders and investors and to contribute to the conversation. StockTwits allows its users to track specific stocks in a personal portfolio and view a stream of ongoing relevant discussions. StockTwits hard sell is their lightweight and simplistic approach which allows users to take in information from various sources at a glance.

As Twitter does not directly support image attachments, this has given rise to many third party services. TwitPic is perhaps the most prominent of these services for uploading and sharing photos via Twitter. Users have the option to upload photos from their computer, phone, through a variety of third party clients and through the website itself.

Characters are valuable in Twitter; the aim is to be as concise as possible within the 140 character limit. Naturally lengthy website URLs are not viable in this environment and as such URL shortening services have become an essential tool for users. Bit.ly offer such a service in that they take URLs and shorten them to a format more suited for Twitter, or just about anywhere else on the web. Bit.ly offer other services in line with their core functionality, notably the ability to manage links by searching a personal history, posting links directly from any page to Twitter via a sidebar, and an analytics service which provides a visual representation of clicks, referrals and location data.

Twestival is a social media fundraising initiative which brings people together for events to raise funds to support local charities and organisations. Twestival uses Twitter to spread the word of their upcoming events and to encourage people to come along and help out. Twestival is the largest global grassroots social media fundraising initiative to date, raising over $1.2 million within 14 months for 137 nonprofits (Twestival, 2010).

Exectweets is the brainchild of Federated Media and operates in partnership with Microsoft. ExecTweets endeavours to make it easier to find and follow 'smart people' on Twitter. ExecTweets collates the 'tweets' from the world's top executives. It allows users to vote on the most interesting tweets and users, search easily with the use of hash tags and recommend new execs to follow. The ExecTweets platform can be accessed from Twitter, their website or via a mobile application.

TwitJobSearch is a venture from search specialist Workdigital. Its goal is to provide a job search engine for Twitter which will scrape tweets for job vacancies and information. Workdigital estimate that 25000 jobs are mentioned on Twitter every hour (Kiss, 2009), they take this information and contextualise it. The service allows a user to search a specific job role which they might be interested in and from the results returned they can drill down through the data using options provided such as location, salary and date 'tweeted'.

THE NEW BUSINESS MODEL

Twitter has been much maligned for not having a stable business model in place, and not providing a clear marketing strategy has put many off using their service. However In April 2010 Twitter announced that it was ready to implement a business model aimed at making a profit, providing a structured way for business to advertise and to incorporate all their third party partners. Twitter have certainly taken their time in developing such a model but it is important to remember that the epicentre of their ethos is the user, and they wanted their model to be as considerate as possible, not only to keep their current user base but to enable their continued growth. Taking this into account Twitter has planned a two pronged approach to its business model: promoted tweets and commercial accounts.

Promoted Tweets are sponsored messages which will be displayed to the user. Twitter is quick to point out that these are not advertisements but rather normal tweets that can be viewed, retweeted, replied to or marked as a favourite. Twitters stance on not deeming these promoted tweets as advertisements is perhaps a ploy to not

agitate their existing user base who have become accustomed to an advertising free service. Twitter have stated that these promoted tweets will take up very little actual screen space appearing under trending topics and within the results of relevant searches performed. It is also planned to include location data in future, so for example an independent book store could target users in their city, this functionality is still in its infancy and more will become clear in the coming months.

Twitter is keen to stress that their model is fair and transparent to both advertisers and third party developers who have aided their popularity and success. In regard to advertising Twitter is initially employing the traditional Cost Per Mile (CPM) model, which involves an advertiser paying for their advertisement on a per view basis, so it would cost X per one thousand views. This model is simplistic and fair to the advertiser but perhaps not so much to the user. It is for this reason that Twitter plans to roll out a more complex model which will empower the user and be more organic to their service; this new service is described as 'resonance'. Resonance is a system which incorporates how many times a tweet is viewed, retweeted, replied to or added as a favourite and in turn assigns it a score. If a user is not interested in a link they simply do what they have always been doing and ignore it. If the resonance score for a tweet is low, it will be dropped from the system and the advertiser will cease to be charged. This in principle seems to be a system which will work well for all parties concerned, the user is not bothered with the ad and the advertiser can rethink their strategy without wasting further money. Only time will tell how successful this will be.

With this new model implemented, Twitter will be under scrutiny as to how they deal with user data and privacy. Twitter is a goldmine of personal data, users tweet a lot of personal information, such as what they are doing, listening to, watching, their location and products they have purchased, all of which is information advertisers would be extremely interested in. It is imperative that Twitter implements this is a way in which users will not fall victim to spam.

The second component of the new model, commercial accounts, are at present still in beta testing with no firm indication of when they will be rolled out for public use. These are paid-for accounts which a business can subscribe to in order to interact with and increase its customer base. Details are somewhat vague at present, Twitter has stated that these accounts will offer statistics and analytic services to gauge how the profile is performing and that a commercial API will be released at some stage during this year. It is thought that these subscription accounts will include a feature similar to the 'verified' tag which is currently applied to celebrity accounts. This is critical as Twitter evolves and as more businesses are using it as a base for customer relations. A 'verified' account will enable the customer to know that they are in a discussion with a reputable source. A commercial account will also facilitate multiple users to contribute to a single account. An example of this would be a tweet from @company tagged with the author responsible for it.

Two-sided markets, also called two-sided networks, are economic platforms having two distinct user groups that provide each other with network benefits (Caillaud & Jullien, 2003; Parker & Van Alstyne, 2005). People and products often have complementary relationships and we can think of them as forming a network. In networks the more subscribers there are then the more a new participant is willing to pay and social networks such as Twitter are powerful tools that allow for complex interaction on a global scale (Economides, 2008; Economides and Joacim, 2009).

STRATEGIES FOR TWITTER

This paper has established that many high profile businesses have begun to invest in Twitter. Some may be tweeting, some simply listening to gauge what the community is discussion while there are some doing both. There are, essentially four strategies available to take part in a service like Twitter: Direct, Indirect, Internal and Inbound Signalling. We look at each in turn.

The direct approach is perhaps the most widespread and most immediately obvious way to become involved with Twitter. This method is centred on marketing and public relations. There are opportunities available to reach a diverse and global audience. Depending of the type of business involved with this strategy there will be differing ways of promoting their brand. Retail companies may run competitions, post their latest offers and announce forthcoming sales. Alternatively a marketing company may take a different route; posts may be concerned with corporate achievements and awards, blogs, white papers, and press releases. While this is a fantastic way to promote a brand or service it is not without its pitfalls. Twitter is a community first and foremost and much like in a traditional social circle of people, those who only speak of themselves are often thought of self serving and not well regarded by others, they can even be perceived as a nuisance. This is a fine line which must be carefully tread. The Twitter users want conversation and the sharing of information and ideas, a brand could easily fall victim to a selfish approach and ultimately find themselves being ignored, so caution is a must.

The indirect approach is where employees engage with the community and build relations. This is in contrast to a corporation being solely responsible for their Twitter 'personality'. This approach is more suited to some and can be effective for businesses of any size, from a large multinational firm with thousands of employees, right down to a small firm with just a few. The immediate benefit that this strategy gives to these large multinational companies is that it helps to put a face and personality to the brand. Employees are encouraged to build relations with a community of interested parties. The employees are given free range to discuss topics that excite or interest them. Perhaps they may discuss and share information on current projects they are working on and how they excite them. The great thing about this method is that as the employees reputation and influence grows, the businesses does as well. Again like all strategies this one is not without problems. For this to work successfully, employees should, in a perfect world, be happy and enthusiastic about their jobs and be motivated enough to want to spread a positive image of the business. Of course this is not always the case and employees tweeting negatively about the company, whether under an approved scheme or not can be extremely damaging. During a difficult period experienced by Internet giant Yahoo! in 2008, they were forced into laying off a considerable number of employees, 1500 on one specific day. Unfortunately for Yahoo! one employee, Emily West, updated her Twitter account throughout the whole event (Carson, 2008). Emily described the emotional state of the office, of colleagues being taking into rooms to be told the bad news, and even an incident where she broke down in tears as her best friend lost her job. While Yahoo! was only doing what any company would do to ensure survival in difficult times, their image was tarnished as a result of an employee's use of Twitter.

The Internal strategy ignores the public aspects of Twitter, instead utilising it as a service for internal communication and knowledge sharing. Knowledge sharing can be an important factor in many fields of business. It breeds a sense of community within an organisation and provides employees with a platform from which they can voice their opinions, ideas and concerns. While this is possible with Twitter, it would involve all employees protecting their tweets from public view, however even with this measure in place, Twitter still does not offer any security guarantees. Perhaps an alternative microblogging service like Yammer, which is purpose built for this type of activity, would be more suitable.

Inbound Signalling is a strategy best suited for the company who does not desire to actively take part in Twitter but acknowledges that there are benefits to be gained from it. Inbound Signalling

is an excellent way to monitor a brand, dedicating resources to track brand mentions, trending topics or issues which consumers may be having. With Twitter brand mentions can be tracked in real time, using a variety of tools. It is possible to track standard brand mentions; however the option is also available to track hash tags, responses to tweets and retweets. There key benefits which a company can take from internal signalling are the ability to see what people's attitude toward their brand is and what they are saying about it and it is also possible to monitor the competition and identify potential problems with a brand and address them before they have the chance to gain large scale media attention. These benefits can help a company improve its products and services and by proxy the consumer also benefits from these improvements.

TWITTER CASE STUDY

We have discussed how Twitter provides publishing quick, frequent 140 character messages for businesses to use as a promotion tool but here we deliberate if Twitter can be used by a company as its main form of communication to its customers. The following example relates to an IT services company call Codero based in the US. Codero experienced a power failure at their headquarters and the firm had to recover hundreds of servers for their clients with many customers experiencing additions problems getting back up and running to normal. Codero kept their customers informed of the situation and the progress being made in rectifying issues by using Twitter. Codero was able to interact with customers on a real time basis and as tweets posted are kept on their profile page by default this enabled Codero to keep a log for each customer that was easy to manage. In this respect during the recovery activities Twitter worked well for Codero as the main method to support and communicate with its customers. From this example we can compile some advantages of companies using Twitter in this way:

1. Customers who want to follow a business just need to set up a Twitter account themselves and then opt to follow the business. Therefore the actual company does not have to remember or maintain contact details for each of their customers.
2. Customers following a company's tweets can also elect to receive updates to an Email address of their choosing or mobile telephone. The company (tweeter) has no need to know where to send the message the receiver chooses the delivery media according to their needs and preference.
3. The direct message facility Twitter offers allows a tweeter and a follower to have a private conversation that's not on the public message log which is displayed on the tweeters Twitter page.
4. Twitter also maintains a complete history of Tweets and follower responses, so when the dust dies down a company has a log of all of the conversations as a record of their customer conversation via Twitter.

So in the event of a similar incident happening, a company can use Twitter as a basic mass communication tool. To implement a company would have to open an account and decide which individuals within the company will create the Tweets during a crisis. They would also have to advise their customer base first about the setup and have them create their own Twitter accounts. In the event of an incident a tweet can be posted onto a company's Twitter page and further updates can be send to customers to inform them of developments as they occur and be received on the device and channel of their choosing. This example shows Twitter can be used as an effective tool in a corporate incident management situation. It has unique features that are provided by the principle of 'following' that support low

maintenance communication and interaction with a large audience which make it suitable for many types of organisations such as local government organizations using it to provide community updates for different types of emergency without the need for specialised applications and devices (Dance, 2010).

Using Twitter as a communication channel during a business communication incident can work and might suit some companies but it is unlikely Twitter will spell the end of the incident notification system, for example Everbridge. Twitter is a good communication tool but lacks certain features to be a full replacement for an incident notification system and big companies will demand trust in a system to deal with the safety of their people and continuing operations during a communication failure. On the flip side, for some enterprises the risk may be low and consequences may not be so serious, therefore the level of trust may not be as important as say the cost of the system and let us not forget that Twitter is free.

ALTERNATIVES TO TWITTER

Twitter is a popular and efficient social messaging service but is not without competition. There are alternative services such as Facebook, Yammer, Foursquare and Tumblr.

While not technically a micro blogging service, Facebook cannot be ignored as it is the undisputed goliath of social media websites. Facebook has well in excess of 500 million registered users and continues to grow (Facebook, 2010). Facebook allows its users to create a personal profile, where they can enter topics and activities that interest them, post their photographs and build a social network of friends, relatives and colleagues. Facebook gives a business the opportunity to create a profile page from which they can operate, building a community and interacting with it. They have a clearly defined and effective marketing structure in place, allowing businesses to directly target specific user demographics. Facebook offers a much more complex service than Twitter in that a profile page can contain a feed of posts, photographs, and they have the ability to create apps, start groups and organise events.

Yammer is a service best suited to the business that would prefer to keep their micro blogging in house and use it as a vehicle to transfer knowledge and ideas. Yammer provides a private and secure network to operate in, and has the option to facilitate the local storage of all data submitted, further enhancing security. Yammer sells itself not only on the basis of sharing knowledge throughout an organisation but also as a service that can improve communication, collaboration; as document sharing is possible, and efficiency by negating the need for so many internal meetings. Some further key features of Yammer are the options for employees to create profiles, create smaller private groups within an organisation, administration features and the versatility of integrating third party applications with use of their API.

Foursquare is a totally new social networking service which builds on the trend of consumer access to smart phones and their location tracking ability. A truly innovative service and one which is perhaps much more engaging to the user, it allows them to 'check-in' into a venue using a mobile application, text message or website. Users are then awarded points based on where they are and how many times they have been there previously. The value to the user is that they are awarded points and badges when they check in and can even become 'mayor' of the venue availing of prizes and special discounts. Foursquare is most suited to, although not restricted to, the retail sector. The benefit for a business is that they can increase traffic to their store by offering prizes and discounts to their most loyal customers and while this has obvious monetary benefits it also creates good feeling and a fun buzz around the business.

Tumblr resembles something akin to a hybrid of Twitter and more traditional blogs. Tumblr allows users to follow other users, sharing information, links, photos, video, and provides a platform to voice their opinions. It supplies an excellent foundation for business to keep cliental informed on products and services, to promote themselves and expand. A major selling point of Tumblr is the versatility available to create a new blog post; users can do so via text message, email or even with a telephone call. Businesses also have the option of being listed in the Tumblr Directory making them more accessible to potential clients. This highlights just a few of the services currently on offer which can be utilised successfully if used correctly by business. It also highlights the diverse opportunities that social networks present to business to increase awareness of their brands and services.

TWITTER RELIABILITY

Twitter is well known for its reliability issues, the popularity of this fast growing network site has often lead to the website unable to handle the amount of traffic created by its users. In the year 2007 on the whole it was estimated that Twitter was offline for 6 days in total (Ryan, 2009). Vast improvements to the architecture of the website have been made over the years and continue on in order to cope with the vast growth of the service but Twitter have also experienced their fair share of security problems. Twice in 2009 Twitter were on the end of two separate hacking attacks causing the website to go offline for several hours. Another recorded issue are old tweets disappearing off of a profile page (Parr, 2010). The availability and reliability of Twitter would be a cause for concern for businesses if used in the way described in the previous section. Companies would not want to rely too heavily on Twitter as an emergency form of communication if they cannot guarantee Twitter being online. A '*fail whale*' appears to some users when the service is unavailable during heavy usage periods. The image notifies the user that Twitter is over capacity, this is most likely seen around a prominent event when Twitter usage is at a peak such as big sporting occasion like a World Cup.

Another security concern companies may have with entering the Twitter network has been the widely reported phishing scams aimed at tricking Twitter users. During the first weekend in January 2009, 33 Twitter accounts had been hacked including some accounts with the largest 'followers' on the network, names such as Barack Obama, Rick Sanchez and Britney Spears. These accounts were compromised by a hacker who posted lewd tweets and links to pornography sites. A Company in this situation would have its brand name tarnished and known and associated for the wrong reasons amongst the world with such tweets being posted through their account. It is clear that Twitter lack security and standards when it comes to the user authentication but are endeavouring to tighten up these issues by releasing OAuth, allowing users to protect their account credentials when using third party applications (Webster, 2010).

Security is a concern for companies who have brands to protect and cannot afford to have sensitive information leaked for all to see. There is a need for companies to have a mass communication platform but the service Twitter offers does not meet strict security and administration standards that can be provided by business-oriented mass communication services such as services like Everbridge (http://www.everbridge.com). However it must be noted that current services like this do not adopt the social networking model like Twitter. Perhaps there is a niche here where a separate 'Twitter for Business' service could be developed combining features from both area. This is something that requires further investigation.

CONCLUSION

Twitter has established itself as a platform for sharing instant update. It is now proving that it is a robust platform for business to deploy. Twitter opens up new opportunities to reach a global audi-

ence for a small cost or even in some scenarios for free. It has also demonstrated loyalty to its users and third party developers in a cautious approach to implementing a self sustaining business model. The early signs are that one half of the business model, promoted tweets, is a success. Time and the implementation of the second part of the business model, commercial accounts, will give a clearer indication of its acceptance by the community. Twitter must ensure that their tactic of promoted tweets remains sympathetic to the user and does not enter the realm of spam. As the majority of Twitter users have a public profile, it is difficult to protect external entities from analysing information posted. It is however within their control to monitor how individual profiles interact with the community. An example of this would be a profile sending out a large set of direct spam messages to users.

Twitter provides an excellent service to promote and sell brands. Twitter enables powerful communities. A loyal community can make a brand. It is important that businesses engage socially with the community and empathise with their needs and concerns. There is also the option for businesses to learn from their competitors and their industry as a whole. Success is not always driven from building the longest list of followers but by learning from others, taking part in discussions and engaging with consumers. It terms of businesses engaging with customers, Twitter is fantastic for real time communication and feedback. If a business does decide however to allow employees to use Twitter, they must ensure that employees are aware that the same guidelines apply as to interaction with any other type of online service, if such guidelines do not exist within a business, it is recommended that they be drafted.

Twitter provides a platform for businesses to see what customers really feel about their own brand and also their competitors and in near real time. In addition to this Twitter allows businesses to connect directly in near real time with customers, which gives them the opportunity to build and enhance customer relationships. More businesses are using Twitter as a research, marketing and customer support tool. Companies can discover more about their customers and receive feedback. Marketing a business on Twitter requires considerable amount of effort and time. Profiles must be kept up to date with interesting content and fresh ideas or followers will quickly lose interest. A balanced Twitter strategy is the key to the success of a brands reputation on Twitter. Striking the right balance with promoting the product and other company news is vital. No follower of a brand will want to be inundated with tweets regarding special offers and discounts every hour or even every day. Twitter allows companies to become friends with their customers; the interaction of short messages gives an informal feel to the relationship. Businesses can show off their character and connect with real people who use or potential might use their products. Most importantly, they can listen and react in real time as Twitter brings the customer and the business closer together. Twitter does have shortcomings with reliability issues and security.

Perhaps the most effective use for Twitter in recent times has been for breaking news. Twitter must continue to ensure its service remains easily accessible and retains its core functionality of short real time messaging. It is easy to get waylaid with unnecessary and bloated feature set. To ensure this ease of access, third party developers will be imperative to the growth and sustained use of Twitter. The immediate signs are good and that the new business model incorporates third party developers fully and offers them a percentage of profits from traffic originating from their application, it would be an unwise move to cut them out of the equation. The future certainly looks prosperous for Twitter, its clean simplistic approach, robust infrastructure and user centric business model will ensure its popularity continues to grow, offering an exciting and vibrate community to share information, promote ideas and meet like mined people for both personal and business users.

REFERENCES

Battelle, J. (2009). *Comparing Twitter's growth to Facebook and Google*. Retrieved from http://www.businessinsider.com/comparing-twitters-growth-to-facebook-and-google-2009-3

Beaumont, C. (2010, January 16). *New York plane crash: Twitter breaks the news, again*. Retrieved from http://www.telegraph.co.uk/technology/twitter/4269765/New-York-plane-crash-Twitter-breaks-the-news-again.html

Benjamin, K. (2009). Battle of the brands. *Revolution (Staten Island, N.Y.)*, 41–43.

Caillaud, B., & Jullien, B. (2003). Chicken & egg: Competing matchmakers. *The Rand Journal of Economics*, *34*(2), 309–328. doi:10.2307/1593720

Carson, N. (2008) *Yahoo employee twitters through layoff*. Retrieved from http://www.businessinsider.com/2008/12/twittering-the-yahoo-layoffs-yhoo

Creativity-online. (2010). *Old Spice: Responses case study*. Retrieved from http://creativity-online.com/work/old-spice-responses-case-study/20896

Dance, S. (2010). *Can Twitter save the day?* Retrieved from http://www.continuitycentral.com/feature0762.html

Dell. (2010). *Dell outlet twitter feed*. Retrieved from http://twitter.com/DELLOUTLETUK

Duana, W., Gub, B., & Whinston, A. (2008). Do online reviews matter? An empirical investigation of panel data. *Decision Support Systems*, *45*(3), 1007–1016. doi:10.1016/j.dss.2008.04.001

Economides, N. (2008). *Net neutrality, non-discrimination and digital distribution of content through the Internet* (pp. 209–233). New York, NY: New York University.

Economides, N., & Joacim, T. (2009). *Net neutrality on the Internet: A ywo-sided market analysis (Research Rep. 2451/26057)*. New York, NY: New York University.

Experian. (2009). *Top websites and search engines*. Retrieved from http://www.hitwise.com/uk/resources/data-centre

Facebook. (2010). *Facebook statistic*. Retrieved from http://www.facebook.com/press/info.php?statistics

Gill, P., Arlitt, M., Li, Z., & Mahanti, A. (2007, October 24-26). Youtube traffic characterization: A view from the edge. In *Proceedings of the 7th ACM SIGCOMM Conference on Internet Measurement*, San Diego, CA.

Halliday, J. (2010) *Old Spice viral campaign a hit*. Retrieved from http://www.guardian.co.uk/technology/blog/2010/jul/14/old-spice-viral-video-campaign

Jansen, B., & Zhang, M. (2009). Twitter power: Tweets as an electronic word of mouth. *Journal of the American Society for Information Science and Technology, 60*(11), 36–48. doi:10.1002/asi.21149

Java, A., Song, X., Finin, T., & Tseng, B. (2007, August 12). Why we twitter: understanding microblogging usage and communities. In *Proceedings of the 9th WebKDD and 1st SNA-KDD Workshop on Web Mining and Social Network Analysis*, San Jose, CA (pp. 56-65).

Jetblue. (2010). *Jetblue Twitter feed*. Retrieved from http://twitter.com/jetblue

Kiss, J. (2009). *Twitter job service launched*. Retrieved from http://www.guardian.co.uk/media/2009/mar/17/digital-media-twitter

Kumar, R., Novak, J., & Tomkins, A. (2006, August 20-23). Structure and evolution of online social networks. In *Proceedings of the 12th ACM SIGKDD International Conference on Knowledge Discovery and Data Mining*, Philadelphia, PA.

Mislove, A., Marcon, M., Gummadi, K., Druschel, P., & Bhattacharjee, B. (2007, October 24-26). Measurement and analysis of online social networks. In *Proceedings of the 7th ACM SIGCOMM Conference on Internet Measurement*, San Diego, CA.

Parker, G., & Van Alstyne, M. (2005). Two-sided network effects: A theory of information product design. *Management Science, 51*(10). doi:10.1287/mnsc.1050.0400

Parr, B. (2010). *Thousands of archived tweets mysteriously disappear*. Retrieved from http://mashable.com/2010/01/13/tweets-vanish/

Reynolds, G. (2006). *An army of Davids: How markets and technology empower ordinary people to beat big media, big government, and other Goliaths*. Nashville, TN: Thomas Nelson.

Richins, M., & Root-Shaffer, T. (1988). The role of involvement and opinion leadership in consumer word-of-mouth: An implicit model made explicit. *Advances in Consumer Research. Association for Consumer Research (U. S.), 15*, 32–36.

Ryan, K. (2009). *Twitter study*. San Antonio, TX: Pear Analytics.

Stutzbach, D., Rejaie, R., Duffield, N., Sen, S., & Willinger, W. (2006, October 25-27). On unbiased sampling for unstructured peer-to-peer networks. In *Proceedings of the 6th ACM SIGCOMM Conference on Internet Measurement*, Rio de Janeriro, Brazil.

Twestival. (2010). *What is twestival?* Retrieved from http://twestival.com/about-twestival-global-2010/

Twitter Blog. (2010). *Hello world*. Retrieved from http://blog.twitter.com/2010/04/hello-world.html

Twitter Counter. (2010). *The 1000 most popular Twitter users*. Retrieved from http://twittercounter.com/pages/100

Webster, T. (2010). *Twitter usage in America: 2010, The Edison Research/Arbitron Internet and multimedia study*. Somerville, NJ: Edison Research.

This work was previously published in International Journal of Business Data Communications and Networking, Volume 7, Issue 3, edited by Varadharajan Sridhar and Debashis Saha, p.p 1-15, copyright 2011 by IGI Publishing (an imprint of IGI Global)

Chapter 10
Performance–Enhanced Caching Scheme for Web Clusters for Dynamic Content

A. Raghunathan
Bharat Heavy Electricals Limited, India

K. Murugesan
National Institute of Technology, Tiruchirappalli, India

ABSTRACT

In order to improve the QoS of applications, clusters of web servers are increasingly used in web services. Caching helps improve performance in web servers, but is largely exploited only for static web content. With more web applications using backend databases today, caching of dynamic content has a crucial role in web performance. This paper presents a set of cache management schemes for handling dynamic data in web clusters by sharing cached contents. These schemes use either automatic or expiry-based cache validation, and work with any type of request distribution. The techniques improve response by utilizing the caches efficiently and reducing redundant database accesses by web servers while ensuring cache consistency. The authors present caching schemes for both horizontal and vertical cluster architectures. Simulations show an appreciable performance rise in response times of queries in clustered web servers.

INTRODUCTION

Web services have become an important component of business and enterprise operations. In order to meet the current need for their improved availability, scalability and performance, clusters of web servers are increasingly being employed in many installations (Hyun et al., 2003; Sharifian et al., 2009, 2010). Caching of data in a web server provides a further improvement in the application's response time (Adams, 2004; Anbazhagan & Nagarajan, 2002) but till recently caching has

DOI: 10.4018/978-1-4666-2026-1.ch010

largely been exploited only for static web content. Today, however, most web applications serve up dynamic content to the clients by acquiring data from backend databases (Challenger et al., 2004). While caching of this dynamic data, wherever possible, does improve the response times of the servers (Holmedahl et al., 1998), the need for maintaining cache currency with the database is a problem that needs to be addressed, and its complexity increases when caching is employed in multiple servers within the cluster.

When requests from clients for web pages are distributed across a cluster, different requests for a given page may be directed to different web servers at different times. Each server uses its own cache to respond to this request, accessing the cache immediately without re-querying the database. In case of static content the data does not change and so the cached result would be valid to answer subsequent requests. But if the content is dynamic, it becomes necessary to maintain data consistency among all the caches in the cluster, since each server's cache is independent, to ensure that the cluster members do not return different results for the same request. In addition, visiting the database by several servers to fetch the same data is inefficient. There is a wide scope for further work on caching of dynamic content in web clusters towards improving QoS of Web services. In this paper we present a set of cache management schemes to improve the overall performance of a web cluster by sharing cached contents with the help of the front-end web switch. Our methods differ from earlier shared caching approaches (Chen et al., 2003; Cuenca-Acuna et al., 2001; Holmedahl et al., 1998). Our schemes utilize the server caches efficiently, reducing redundant database accesses by web servers while also ensuring consistency of cache contents. The proposed techniques could be used with any algorithm used for request distribution within a cluster.

Two principal methods are generally used for cache validation of dynamic data: automatic and expiry-based. The former is preferred for frequently changing data while the latter is em-

ployed when the data does not change frequently or when data does not have to be refreshed to the client whenever it changes. We present our caching algorithms for both these methods.

Clusters are also classified in two ways: horizontal and vertical (Turaga et al., 2006). Constituent servers in a horizontal cluster reside on different physical machines; in a vertical cluster they reside on a single physical machine. We propose our caching schemes for both types of clusters. Our simulations show an appreciable performance increase in all cases.

CACHING OF DYNAMIC DATA IN WEB SERVERS

Cache Revalidation

Since dynamic web content is usually treated as non-cacheable, caching has largely been confined to static web content. However, accessing the backend servers is expensive in terms of time and resources and should be preferred only for frequently changing data. Even on many web sites that display dynamic content, the backend data either does not change often, or when it does, it may not be necessary to display the data on every change; some latency in data refreshes may be tolerable. Examples of such cases include data from product catalogs, vendor information, customer information, archived data, etc. In such cases it would make sense to respond with cached data rather than fetch it from the backend every time.

Web queries that fetch content from a backend data source are fired by the clients usually in the form of URLs with or without parameters either as hyperlinks or through forms. The web (application) server that receives a query re-transmits it to the backend, fetches the query results and stores the results in its cache (Figure 1). It then formats the results as a HTML web page and serves it to the client for display on the browser. When a client invokes the same query again, the (web) application server attempts to verify that the stored result in its cache is current enough to be returned to the client. If it is not, the server executes the query again at the backend, refreshes its cache and returns the new result to the client. This method of ensuring cache consistency is called *revalidation*.

Cache Validation Methods

There are two common methods in cache revalidation, expiry-based revalidation and automatic revalidation (Raghunathan & Murugesan, 2010).

In an expiry or time-based method, a validity period is specified for each query or URL whose results are cached. Upon expiry of this period the cache entry for this query is invalidated. When the query is fired again, the web server checks the data source to see if the data has changed. If the data has not changed, the server returns the existing cached results to the client without re-executing the query. If the data has changed, the server re-executes the query at the backend and reloads the contents into the cache. Expiration settings give more control over and flexibility in presenting data to the web clients since they interact with the data source only when required. This method is suitable for more predictable, less frequently changing data.

In an automatic invalidation method, whenever the data changes the database server sends a message to the application server to invalidate the server's cache segment that contains the changed data. This kind of a messaging scheme is usually implemented through the use of trigger-like mechanisms in the database. While this method ensures cache currency, its implementation is expensive and best reserved only for very frequently changing data.

CACHING IN WEB CLUSTERS

Cluster Architecture

A cluster is a networked group of servers that offers improved performance, availability and scalability over a single server. Web requests that originate from clients and addressed to the cluster are generally routed through a front-end server called the web switch (Andreolini, 2001; Cardellini et al., 2001). The switch, with the use of scheduling and load balancing algorithms, determines a suitable web server in the cluster for executing a query, and dispatches the query to that server. The input requests may come in a single queue (single class) or multi-queue (multi-class) and are classified according to type or priority.

The cluster itself can either be horizontal or vertical (Turaga et al., 2006). In a horizontal cluster (Figure 2), the servers are physically separate but networked machines; in a vertical cluster (Figure 3) the servers are different processes running on the same physical machine.

Request Distribution in a Cluster

Extensive work has been done on classification and scheduling of client requests to web servers.

Figure 1. Web cache architecture

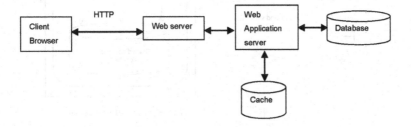

Figure 2. Web query processing in a horizontal cluster with separate servers

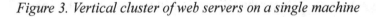

Several algorithms have been proposed for distribution of requests by the switch among the servers (Cardellini et al., 2001). Well-known among these are Weighted Round-Robin (WRR) (Cardellini et al., 2001; Hyun, 2003; Sharifian et al., 2009). Locality-Aware Request Distribution (LARD) (Pai et al., 1998) or Content-Aware Policy (CAP) (Casalicchio & Colajanni, 2001). Our caching techniques proposed in this paper are independent of the method of request distribution.

Cluster Caching Techniques

The caching and cache invalidation techniques discussed previously have been largely used only in single web servers. The caching techniques for a single web server could be easily extended to web clusters - each member server would process each request assigned to it independently as though it were a stand-alone web server and simply save

the results in its own individual cache. However, we find that the overall performance of a web cluster could be significantly improved by sharing the caches wherein the query results that have been fetched and stored by one server could be effectively utilized by the other servers trying to execute the same query. In this paper we formulate cache-sharing and management schemes for various cluster models and show their performance improvement over existing schemes.

RELATED WORK

Web caching as a means of achieving QoS in web services has been the subject of considerable research. Several commercial products such as Oracle Application Server Web Cache 11g (Oracle, 2010) and IBM WebSphere (Turaga et al., 2006) are also available that provide caching features

Figure 3. Vertical cluster of web servers on a single machine

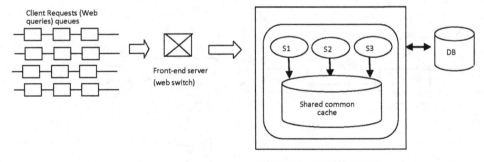

to speed up query processing and enhance overall web performance. Caching of pages is done at various levels – proxy, mid-tier (web server) or database (called backend). Although dynamic data has often been treated as non-cacheable and is so set in HTTP headers, it has been shown that dynamic content is indeed cacheable and a variety of techniques have been proposed for caching dynamic web pages at all these levels (Challenger, 1999, 2004; Iyengar, 1997). A summary of these is given in Mohan (2001). A proxy caching technique is described in Datta et al. (2002) where both content and layout can be dynamic, with significant reductions in bandwidths and response times. DBProxy (Amiri et al., 2002, 2003), an edge semantic data cache for web applications, combines a flexible query answering technique with efficient techniques for storage and cache replacement. Middle-tier database caching has also evolved as an effective approach to improve scalability and performance. A scheme for relational database caching, known as DBCache, has been described in Altinel et al. (2002) and Luo et al. (2002) for web application servers. This caches entire or part of tables or materialized views based on declarative specification, with updates being propagated through asynchronous data replication. In order to reduce delays in caching entire dynamically generated pages, Datta et al. (2001) has proposed identifying and caching fragments of them, so that the static part in those pages can be cached, with the dynamic part alone being replaced. The Weave System (Yagoub et al., 2000) offers customisable caching at different levels using declarative caching rules. A middleware layer that uses hashing techniques to detect similarities with previous cached query results is described by Tolia and Satyanarayanan (2007). It thus seeks to avoid transmissions of redundant fragments, thus improving performance.

In order to maintain consistency of dynamic content between the cache and the backend data source, cache invalidation is often used. These are mainly of two kinds – expiry or time-based and automatic. The former is generally used for more predictable and less frequently changing data, while the latter is used for less predictable and more frequently changing content, where consistency is usually maintained by mapping and data update propagation. A Data Update Propagation algorithm is used by Challenger (2004) to identify changed and obsolete pages in the cache for replacement by maintaining a mapping between cacheable data items and the corresponding cached pages. Database triggers are invoked whenever changes are made to database, which in turn propagate the changes to the cache. Degenaro et al. (2000) improved the techniques to selectively invalidate cache objects in case of database updates. Candan et al. (2001) use sniffer and invalidator modules to invalidate stale cached pages. Sniffer creates a mapping between the web pages identified by URLs and the underlying queries, and invalidator discards the cached pages dependent on queries affected by updates. As triggers used to sense updates introduce a lot of load on the database, the authors use off-line policies in order to select the query types and URLs for invalidation. The DBCache (Luo et al., 2002) also uses triggers on their database to track changes. Database change notifications are also used to invalidate the cache in case of updates, and Galindo-Legaria et al. (2005) describe the mechanism implemented in SQL server 2005 to communicate to the application through subscriptions regarding database changes for taking action for invalidation. Subscriptions are also used by DBProxy (Amiri et al., 2003) for synchronizing cache with database for consistency. Amza et al. (2005) also propose a similar technique for automatic cache invalidation both at table and column levels with a dependency mapping built between database items and cached objects. Of the commercially available web application servers, Lee et al. (2009) propose lease-based consistency-maintaining schemes for proxy caching. Oracle AS Web Cache (Oracle, 2010) features both time-based and automatic invalidation. However, it does not specify a mechanism for automatically invalidating and updating cached pages upon database changes. IBM WebSphere Application Server's Caching Proxy (Turaga et al., 2006) has very similar features. A schema-based cache invalidation scheme has been proposed by Raghunathan and Murugesan (2010). Current time-based web caching solutions use a declarative specification of expiry settings and validation for each web application/URL.

An equal amount of work has been done on web clusters, which are increasingly used to enhance QoS of web servers (Hyun et al., 2003; Sharifian et al., 2009, 2010). A detailed report on various architectures and algorithms used for web clusters is given in Cardellini (2001). Several papers are devoted to improvement of QoS of web services for clusters in various aspects – service differentiation, admission control, request classification, scheduling and distribution, resource scheduling, load balancing, etc (Andreolini et al., 2004; Cardellini et al., 2001; Sharifian et al., 2009; Teo et al., 2001; Xiong et al., 2005). However, caching is also a significant contributor to web QoS, and poor cache performance could reduce benefits of load balance (Bunt et al., 1999).. As mentioned earlier, till now caching of dynamic content has been largely deployed only in stand-alone web servers. In this paper we seek to extend these cache management techniques to web clusters using invalidation and sharing of cache contents among the cluster nodes.

Sharing of cache memories of cluster nodes to achieve higher performance has also been explored earlier through *cooperative caching* (Chen et al., 2003; Cuenca-Acuna et al., 2001; Holmedahl et al., 1998). These techniques involve providing either an in-memory cache layer or a middleware layer forming a global shared pool of the caches of the servers. Using suitable memory management, the techniques seek to locate and share cached results from other cluster nodes in case of a cache miss at a given node to save on disk accesses. However, such methods have not been developed further for dynamic content caching

for clusters. Moreover, in our schemes we have used the front-end switch itself as the mechanism of sharing among the cluster nodes, because the switch is also the distributor of the query and as such is in a better position to coordinate the sharing among the nodes. This also dispenses with the overhead involved in using any additional layer.

Hierarchies of caching servers are often deployed in content distribution/delivery networks to deliver content to users with increased availability, speed and response by reducing server access, bandwidth and latency (Lowery, 2001). Hence the caches of the web application cluster can form part of such networks to distribute the cached results to users to improve the response.

OUTLINE OF EXISTING AND PROPOSED SCHEMES

Existing Scheme

Cache management techniques for dynamic content involving cache invalidation have been implemented in most current commercial web servers such as OracleAS Web Cache and IBM WebSphere. However, these are mostly single web servers executing requests from web clients as illustrated in Figure 1.

Extension of the Existing Scheme for Web Clusters

The existing cache invalidation mechanisms for a single web server could also be extended to a cluster of web servers, as each server will only process requests independently. As such, in the following discussion, we assume that these mechanisms also hold good for a web cluster; all the algorithms presented in this paper describe the action taken by any one server in the cluster. As explained earlier, the web switch distributes each client request to a web server in the cluster. When repeated requests for the same query arrive from the clients, these requests might be queued for execution with more than one server, and a server might execute them, say, on a FIFO basis. In the case of static queries, the server may return the query results from its local cache if available. But dynamic queries, usually treated as non-cacheable by HTTP, are executed on the database each time. We discuss below a typical situation in processing web queries submitted to a cluster (Figure 4). We confine the scope of this paper to dynamic content only.

Drawbacks in the Extended Cluster Caching Scheme

Assume that web requests for three different queries (or URLs) Q_1, Q_2 and Q_3 (Figure 4) are submitted to the switch repeatedly, which then distributes these requests to a cluster comprising three web servers S_1 to S_3. Since the switch could distribute the requests to any of these servers, any server may receive any query, and cache the responding query result QR_1 to QR_3 for future use (In the case of the LARD algorithm, Pai et al., 1998; Zhuang et al., 2008, it could be a group of servers executing a subset of queries rather than the entire cluster). For example, when each of the three servers S_1 to S_3 receives Q_1 for processing, then each would execute Q_1 independently and have QR_1 cached locally. Assume S_1 takes up Q_1 first, while S_2 still has Q_1 waiting in its input queue. S_1, after consulting the database, might

find the result QR_1 in its cache to be valid and so return QR_1 to the client. Later when S_2 dequeues Q_1, it might find its cached QR_1 invalid. Hence it might have the database re-execute Q_1, refresh its cache with a new QR_1 and return this result, which may be different from that returned by S_1. This may be the case even if Q_1 is assigned to S_2 first before it is assigned to S_1, since the sequence of query executions within the cluster cannot be guaranteed. As such, for the same query, the cluster could be returning different results by different constituent web servers due to the inconsistency among their cache contents.

Another performance issue to consider is that after one of the servers, say S_2, visits the database to revalidate or execute Q_1, S_1 and S_3 might follow up with their own visits to the database to process their Q_1 requests, since each server and its cache are independent. These redundant visits result in increased response times.

Algorithms for Extended Caching Schemes in Web Clusters

Expiry-Based Cache Invalidation Scheme

When a query is received by the server, its status is checked in the cache table (Table 1). If it has expired, the server checks the database to see if there is any change in the cached query result. If there is no change, the server revalidates the

Figure 4. Query caching in a web cluster

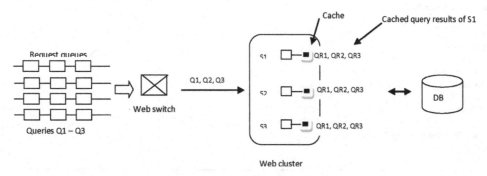

Table 1. Cache structure of a web server in a horizontal cluster for expiry-based invalidation

URL / Query (Q)	Validity Period (VP)	Query Validity Flag (V_Q)	Timestamp of Last Validation (TS_V)	Query Result (QR)
...	...	...	...	...

cached result; otherwise it re-executes the query and refreshes the cache with the new result. A background process traverses the cache entries and, based on the timestamp field TS_V, marks any expired queries as Invalid. (i.e., sets V_Q = False.) Each server in the cluster executes Algorithm A independently for repeated requests for the same query.

Automatic Cache Invalidation

In this scheme, the database system makes use of triggers to send a message to the web servers automatically whenever the data in the tables relevant to a query changes. The web server reads the message and invalidates the query results in its cache (Table 2). When a query request is received from the switch, if its cached result is invalid, it is re-executed at the database and the cache replaced with the new query result. Algorithm B is executed by each server independently for handling the same query. Table 3 shows a mapping maintained by each web server to invalidate the cached results of the queries affected by changed tables in the database. For example, a database change in table T1 will trigger a message to be

Algorithm A. Web server in a horizontal cluster with non-shared caching – Expiry based invalidation. Process client query and return result.

```
Input:    Query Q, Cache Table 1.
Output:   Cache Table 1, Query Result QR.
Method:
if Q ∈ Table 1 then    // query is already cached in Table 1
    if V_Q = True for Q in Table 1 then // if query is valid i.e., not expired
        return existing cached QR
    else
        //perform revalidation
        if Q-related data has changed in the database then
            execute Q
            store new query result into QR
            return QR
        else
            // Q-related data has NOT changed in the database
            return existing cached QR
    end if
    set V_Q = True
    set TS_V = current time
        end if
    else //new query
        add Q to Table 1
        initialize VP, TSv
        set V_Q = True
        execute Q
        store new query result into QR
        return QR
end if
```

Table 2. Structure of a web server cache table for automatic invalidation

URL/ Query (Q)	Query Validity Flag (VQ)	Query Result (QR)
Q1	True	QR 1
Q2	False	QR 2
Q3	False	QR3

sent to all servers, which in turn will invalidate cache results for queries Q1 and Q2.

Proposed Scheme

A better utilization of the cache will minimize visits to the database and go a long way in improving the performance of dynamic queries. Both the current and extended caching schemes have limitations on performance due to redundancy and lack of consistency as discussed above, chiefly because the servers are independent. In order to improve the cluster performance, we propose mechanisms in which cache validation information and cached query results are shared among the sibling servers in the cluster while at the same time maintaining cache consistency.

For the common horizontal cluster model where the web servers are physically separate and independent, we propose a cache sharing scheme through message passing. Since a cluster can be dynamically reconstituted, the servers may not be

acquainted with their siblings and so do not communicate directly among themselves. Therefore we assign to the switch the additional role of a coordinator to enable sharing of cache contents among the web servers. This way, when a server processes a query and either merely revalidates its cache or refreshes it from the database, that information is shared with the sibling servers that might execute the same query subsequently; redundant trips to the database are thus avoided. The messages are assumed to be communicated and acted upon instantly by both the servers and the switch. The switch maintains enough essential data about the status of a request to the web servers for control, communication and sharing purposes.

We also propose similar cache-sharing schemes for a vertical cluster with independent web servers (processes) in a single physical computer. For this cluster configuration, we make use of a common cache held in main memory that is shared by the cluster server processes. For a single location, this scheme would make the vertical model more manageable and economical than the horizontal model while achieving a comparable performance.

Business Implications of Our Work

The objective of enterprise web services is to provide fast access to content with high availability making minimal demands on the network. Caches help to meet this objective in a large way to reduce

Algorithm B. Horizontal cluster Web server Automatic Cache Invalidation - Process client query and return result.

```
Input:    Query Q, Cache Table 2.
Output:   Cache Table 2, Query Result QR.
Method:
if V_Q = True for Q in Table 2 then          // if cached query result is valid i.e., not expired
     return existing cached QR
else if Q ∉ Table 2 or V_Q = False then       // query is new (not cached yet) or cached but expired
     // execute query and replace cached result
     Execute query Q
     return QR
     Set V_Q = True for Q in Table 2
end if
```

Table 3. Structure maintained by the web server for automatic cache invalidation of queries when backend data changes

URL/ Query (Q)	Table (T)
Q1	T1
Q2	T1
Q3	T2

load on origin servers by minimizing access to them and saving bandwidth. Our scheme makes the cluster work more efficiently by effectively exploiting the cached info with the servers and sharing them to deliver content by minimizing database accesses. This improves cache utilization and overall user response of the system to boost performance of business web services.

DESIGN OF THE PROPOSED CACHING SCHEMES

Horizontal Cluster

Expiry-Based Cache Invalidation Scheme

For each of the queries processed by a web application, a validity period is determined based on estimates of how often the underlying data changes occur. If a server receives a query within the query's validity period, it retrieves the query result from its cache, if available. If the server receives the query after the validity period, it needs to revalidate its cache, which may involve one or two trips to the database server depending on whether an actual data change has occurred.

Since a query's validity period is the same for all the servers in the cluster, the validity will expire at the same instant across all the servers. When multiple servers receive requests for the same query at various times, in some of those servers the cached query result may be past its validity

period. Each of these servers may then seek to revalidate its own cache entry by checking with the database. To avoid redundant database accesses by multiple servers, our proposed scheme requires that only the first server that receives the query post-expiration should be allowed to communicate with the database. To enforce this requirement we propose a mechanism by which any server that receives a query and needs to revalidate its cached result has to request a token from the front-end switch. Receipt of this token will grant that server exclusive access to the database for that query.

When the switch receives this token request from a server, say S_X, it checks its cache table structure (Table 4 and Table 5) to see if any other server in the cluster has a valid result for the query in question. If no such server exists, the switch issues the token to S_X, which is then free to access the database. After S_X performs the needed database checks and fetches, it returns the token to the switch. Meanwhile, a token request from any other server is denied by the switch.

If another server, say S_Y, does have a valid cache result, then the switch determines when S_Y itself last fetched the query result from the database. If S_X and S_Y had the same fetch date, it implies that there have been no changes to database since the last fetch by S_X; S_Y had simply revalidated its cache the last time it accessed the database and there was no need to re-execute the query. In this case S_X and S_Y will have identical entries in their caches and S_X just needs to revalidate its cache entry as well. The switch sends a message instructing S_X to perform this revalidation.

If S_Y's data fetch rate was later than S_X however, there has indeed been a change in the database contents and S_Y's cache entry will be newer than S_X's. The switch now instructs S_X to update its cache entry with S_Y's. S_X then communicates with S_Y to perform this action after which both S_X and S_Y will have the latest cache results. In both these cases, the switch denies the token requested by S_X

Table 4. Structure of a web server cache table in a cluster

URL/ Query (Q)	Validity Period (VP)	Query Validity indicator (V_Q)	Timestamp of last validation (TS_V)	Timestamp of last fetch from DB (TS_P)	New expiry date (TS_E)	Query Result (QR)
Q1	30 days	true				QR1
Q2	1 day	false				QR2
Q3	60 days	false				QR3

and a visit to the database by S_X is avoided. The switch updates Table 5 with the status of the latest cache entry location. Note that the switch does not take part in the actual data transfer between S_X and S_Y and acts as a facilitator only. After this process, S_X will transmit its cache result to the requesting web client.

Tables 4 and 5 detail the cache management data structures to be maintained by each web server in the cluster and by the web switch. A background process crawls the server's cache table entries and, based on the validity period *VP* and timestamp field TS_V, marks any expired queries as invalid (set V_Q = false.). A similar background process executes in the switch to invalidate Table 5 entries whose TS_E has expired (V_Q = false). The cache management procedures followed by the server and the switch are detailed in Algorithms A1-1 and A1-2.

Automatic Cache Invalidation Scheme

The design of this scheme is similar to the expiry based invalidation scheme, except that a query's cached result is invalidated by the web server automatically through a database trigger whenever the contents of a database table relevant to the query change. The database change notification messages are sent to all the servers since any one of them may receive the query request. However, unlike Algorithm A1, no database check is necessary to detect changes in the cached query result - an invalidated cache already implies change of data at the backend. Algorithm B1 also uses data structures similar to Tables 4 and 5 that are used by A1, with expiration–related particulars being excluded.

The functionality of the web switch in this case is similar to that of the switch in Algorithm A1-2.

Vertical Cluster

Unlike the horizontal model where a web server is an independent physical machine with its own cache, in a vertical cluster the (web) servers are distinct processes running on a single computer. To our knowledge there are no methods, existing or proposed, for efficient handling of dynamic queries for vertical clusters. Here we propose a set of techniques for the vertical cluster model that rely on a shared common cache among the server processes. This common cache automatically ensures cache consistency. In addition, since

Table 5. Structure of the web switch cache table

URL/ Query (Q)	Validity Period (VP)	Query Validity indicator (V_Q)	Server that most recently validated the result for Q with DB (WS_Q)	Timestamp of last fetch from DB (TS_P)	Expiry date (TS_E)
Q1	30 days	true	S2		
Q2	1 day	false	S1		
Q3	60 days	true	S3		

Algorithm A1-1. Web server in a horizontal cluster, shared caching, expiry based invalidation.

Purpose: Process client query request sent by the switch.
Input: Query Q_i, Cache Table 4.
Output: Cache Table 4, Query Result Q_i
Method:
// *token_requested, token_issued, token_denied* and *query_revalidated*
// are messages transmitted between a web server, S_x, and the web switch.

if V_Q = true for Q_i **in** Table 4 **then** // cached query result is valid
  return existing cached QR_i
else if $Q_i \not\subseteq$ Table 4 **or** V_Q = false **then** // query is new (not cached) or invalid
  // request permission from the switch to access the database
  send_message (S_x, switch, token_requested, params:= (Q_i))
  receive_message (switch, S_x, message_type, params:= (Q_i...)) // reply from switch
  if message_type = token_issued **then** // permission granted
    check_database_status (Q_i)
    if Q_i related data has not changed in the database **then**
      // simply revalidate
      set V_Q = true for Q_i in Table 4
      set TS_V = current time
      set TS_E = current time + VP // new expiry date
      // switch to instruct other web servers to revalidate Q_i
      send_message (S_x, switch, query_revalidated, params:= (Q_i, TS_F, TS_E)) // no database change **else**
      // Q_i related data has changed in the database
      execute Q_i, store result in QR_i
      set V_Q = true
      set TS_V = current time
      set TS_E = current time + VP // new expiry date
      // switch needs to instruct other web servers to revalidate Q_i
      send_message (S_x, switch, query_revalidated, params:= (Q_i, TS_F, TS_E)) // database change
    end if
    return QR_i // to client
  else if message_type = token_denied
    // another server in the cluster, S_y, has a valid cache result for Q_i
    // retrieve data from SY, through a process initiated by the switch
    // new expiry time of Q_i is determined by S_Y
    process_params (S_Y .TS_F, S_Y .TS_E, cache_transfer_indicator)
    if cache_transfer_indicator = 0 then
      //database has not changed, simply revalidate
      In Table 4, set V_Q = true, TS_E= S_Y TS_E
    else
      // database has changed
      // retrieve data from SY, through a process initiated by the switch
      // copy cache contents for Q_i from S_Y and store it into QR_i
      Set QR_i = S_Y.cached_result
      In Table 4, Set V_Q = true, TS_E= S_Y TS_E, TS_F = S_Y.TS_F
    end if
    return QR_i // to client
  end if
end if

---

the cache result for a query is stored only in one place, the cached result fetched by one server is made available to the other servers that receive requests for the same query subsequently, avoiding redundant trips to the database and improving cluster performance.

Expiry-Based Cache Invalidation

When a server in the cluster is assigned a query to execute, it first looks for the query result in the common cache where all query results are stored. If the query result exists and is valid, it

Algorithm A1-2. Web switch in a horizontal cluster, shared caching, expiry based invalidation

```
Purpose:      Process messages from web servers.
Input:        Table 5
Output:       Table 5.
Method:
// Switch helps communication among web servers in the cluster in order to share query results in the servers' caches
// token_requested, token_issued, token_denied, etc. are messages transmitted
// between a web server and the web switch in order to process queries.

receive_message (S_X, switch, message_type, params:= (Q_i, TS_F, TS_E)) // receive message from server S_X
if message_type = token_requested then
    // Check if Q_i is valid in Table 5
    if V_Q = false for Q_i in Table 5 then // no server has a valid cache result for Q_i
        // permit S_X to access the database
        send_message (switch, S_X, token_issued, params:= (Q_i))
    else // query is currently valid with another web server S_Y ; deny token
        // Compare fetch dates of S_Y and S_X
        if S_Y.TS_F = S_X.TS_F then
            // S_X simply needs to revalidate QR_i
            send_message (switch, S_X, token_denied, params:= (Q_i, S_Y.TS_F, S_Y.TS_E, 0))
        else if S_Y.TS_F > S_X.TS_F then
            // S_Y has newer result in cache
            send_message (switch, S_X, token_denied, params:= (Q_i, S_Y.TS_F, S_Y.TS_E, 1))
            //initiate cache transfer from S_Y to S_X
        end if
    end if
else if message_type = query_revalidated then
    // result of a new query or an existing query which is not valid with any other server
    In Table 5, set TS_F = S_X.TS_F, WS_Q = S_X, TS_E = S_X.TS_E, V_Q = true
end if
```

is returned to the client. Otherwise, if the query is new or the result invalid, it is executed at the database, refreshing the cache. Since the cache is common, Table 4 is shared by all the server processes in the cluster and there is no need for any cache coordination by the switch. Therefore the technique used to manage the cache will be a reduced case of Algorithm A1-1 alone; Algorithm A1-2 does not apply. However, to distinguish the vertical cluster cache management technique from that of the horizontal cluster's, we will denote it as Algorithm C1 without relisting.

Automatic Cache Invalidation

The proposed scheme is similar to that given for the horizontal cluster in Algorithm B1, except that Table 2 is shared by all the web servers (processes). We will denote it as Algorithm D1 without relisting.

SIMULATION, ANALYSIS AND RESULTS

Summary of Cache Management Algorithms

For easy reference, the algorithms discussed are summarized.

Simulation Setup and Methodology

The performances of all the algorithms were compared by simulating a web cluster. The server cluster was simulated using processes on a computer with an Intel Xeon 2-way processor and 4GB memory, running Apache under Linux. A computer with a similar configuration was used to simulate the web switch. The database server was run on an IBM Xeon 4-way processor with 8 GB RAM and storage of 1000 GB. Oracle 10g was

Algorithm B1-1. Automatic cache invalidation by a web server in a horizontal cluster

---

Input: Query Q_i, Cache Table similar to Table 5.
Output: Same as input Cache Table, Query Result QR_i.
Method:
// The first server, S_x, to find a cached result invalid upon a query receipt
// re-executes the query and replaces the cache.
// It then shares the result with the other servers on demand.
if V_Q = true for Q_i in Table 5 **then** // if cached query result is valid, i.e., not expired
   return existing QR_i
else if $Q_i \notin$ Table 5 or V_Q = false **then** // query is new (not cached) or expired
   // attempt revalidation
   // get permission from switch to access database
   send_message (S_x, switch, *token_requested*, Q_i)
   receive_message (switch, S_x, Q_i, message_type, params) // reply from switch
   if message_type = *token_issued* **then** // Permission issued to access database
      execute Q_i
      store new result into QR
      set V_Q = true
      // send message to switch to inform other web servers of revalidation of Q
      send_message(S_x, switch, *query_revalidated*, Q_i)
   else if message_type = *token_denied*
      // Token denied, another server in the cluster, S_Y, has a valid cache result for Q
      // Get parameters from switch
      // valid cache contents of Q_i transferred from S_Y with the help of the switch
      // new expiry time of Q_i set by S_Y
      Set QR_i= S_Y.cached_result
      Set V_Q = true
   end if
   return QR_i
end if

---

used as the database engine. The desktop client hardware consisted of a computer with a dual core processor and 2GB memory, running Windows XP. During the simulation, HTTP requests from the desktop client to the server cluster were randomly distributed to the constituent servers by the switch, different web servers receiving requests for the same query at different times during a certain time interval.

The simulation was done using languages Java and Oracle PL/SQL. The web applications were written in Java Server Pages (Mogha et al., 2003).

The time taken by a server in the web cluster to process a dynamic query depends on the following factors:

- The query is already in the server's cache or it is a new query not yet cached.

- If it is already in the server's cache, whether the cached query result is valid.

- If the query-related data has changed in the database. (If there was a change, the cached query result needs to be replaced; otherwise it just needs to be revalidated.)

- If the server shares the query result from another server in the cluster or it has to execute the query at the database (determined by whether it gets a token issued by the switch).

To benchmark the algorithms listed in Table 6, a set of all applicable combinations of the above factors was assembled – i.e., each element of the set specified a cluster state, which included the state of the cache of the server which ultimately received the client request, the availability of cached query result from other servers, the state of the database etc. Repeated requests for a given query were then submitted to the cluster using a random element from the set and the times taken to return the query result to the client were computed. The computation assumed r time units for a database visit to perform a mere check and possible revalidation of a cached query result, s time units for executing a query at the database, fetching its result and replacing the server cache with the new result, and t time units for the web switch to transfer the cache contents from one web server to another if needed.

Representative values for r and s were determined by running a number of queries on several database tables and computing the average time taken for their execution. Average cache transfer time, t, was estimated by performing several FTP transfers between two servers, assuming a local cluster. Values in milliseconds of $r=0.02$, $s=0.04$ and $t=0.00045$ were obtained. The value of t, however, could increase with the network latency and the geographical distribution of the cluster. We have assumed that the time taken for messaging between the switch and the web servers is insignificant when compared to query execution and data transfer times. Simulations were repeated by varying the number of input requests for the same query and also by varying the number of servers in the cluster.

Horizontal Cluster

Expiry-Based Cache Invalidation

Figure 5 shows the percentage improvement of A1 over A in total time taken for n requests to a cluster of m servers. Note that A1's advantage over A increases with m; with just 2 servers it is about 50% more efficient, with 50 servers it is > 90%. However, for a given m, as n increases, A1's gain over A does not increase any further, due to the fact that in both the methods, more and more servers return the query results from their own caches, neutralizing A1's advantage.

Figure 6 shows the results of a single simulation run in terms of instantaneous percentage improvement for each successive request. Note that immediately after each invalidation, which in this run was triggered after every 100 requests, A1 gains over A. This is because in the shared caching scheme the database is accessed just once, after each invalidation, by the server that receives the first request to the query. When another server receives a successive request for the same query from the distribution mechanism, it is prevented from a database access by the switch; the request is answered by copying the cache contents of the first server to this one. In A, as the caches are not shared, it takes a finite time for all the servers in the independent cache cluster to populate their caches with valid results, after which they catch up to the shared caching cluster members. This results in A1 being able to scale well with both the number of servers and the number of requests - from the second request onwards the

Table 6. List of cache management algorithms

Revalidation method	Horizontal cluster		Vertical cluster
	Current (Single server caching extended to a cluster) (Independent Caching)	Proposed (Shared caching)	Proposed (Shared caching)
Expiry-based	A	A1	C1
Automatic	B	B1	D1

Figure 5. Percentage improvement of A1 over A, horizontal cluster, expiry based caching

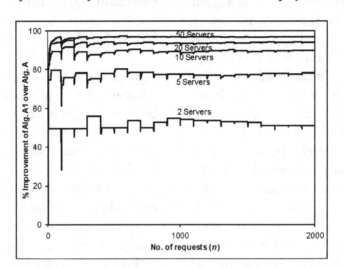

response from any server to the client is almost instantaneous (considering only the server time and ignoring the client to server overhead). A1's improvement over A starts building up almost immediately after an invalidation and persists until the all the servers in A have valid cache results.

Automatic Cache Invalidation

In the query-expiry based method, a server's cache is invalidated at predetermined time intervals based on the data change frequency and the data staleness permissible. In the automatic invalidation scheme the cache is invalidated automatically by the use of trigger mechanisms as soon as the underlying data in the database is modified. This frequency of this data change is expected to be much higher than is presumed in an expiry based mechanism.

Figure 7 shows the results of multiple simulation runs where the data change occurred every 4th, 5th, ... or 1000th request. Percentage improvements in total processing times of up to 97% were observed. Note that as the frequency of invalidations increases, the comparative advantage of the shared caching scheme decreases. This is because even

in shared caching, after each and every invalidation, a new database visit must be undertaken by the first requested server, in effect increasing the total number of visits in any given time period.

Figure 8 shows the percentage improvement of B1 over B in total processing times as a function of the number of requests. The observed results are similar to that of the expiry-based method; Algorithm B1 is able to scale with both number of servers and number of requests.

Vertical Cluster

Expiry-Based Cache Invalidation

As mentioned earlier, currently there are no caching methods specific to vertical clusters; we have therefore proposed a similar caching technique to speed up query processing in the vertical model using a single shared common cache among the server processes. Figure 9 compares the performance gains of Algorithm C1 (vertical cluster with shared caching) and Algorithm A1 (horizontal cluster with shared caching) over Algorithm A (horizontal cluster with independent caching). In C1 the revalidation action, when performed by a server for a given query, also benefits sibling

Figure 6. Instantaneous improvement of A1 over A immediately after cache invalidation

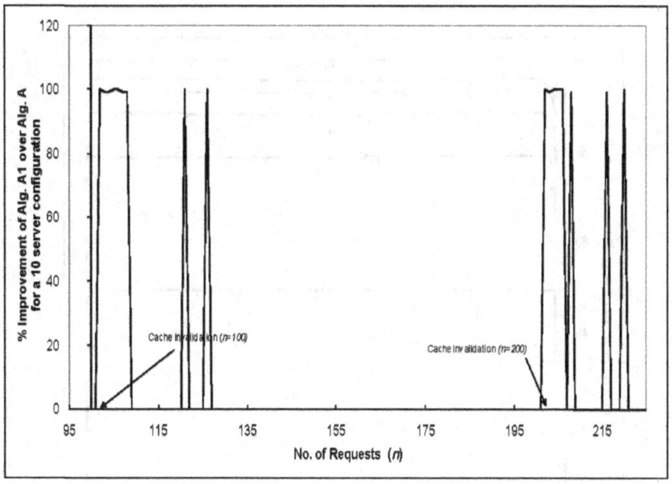

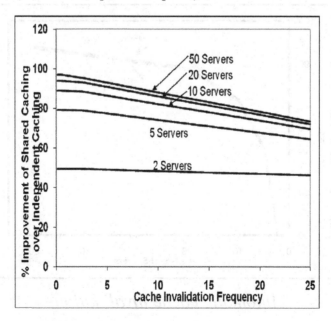

servers by enabling cache hits for their subsequent requests for the same query. This yields C1 a slight advantage over A1, which suffers a penalty of cache transfer time *t* due to separate server caches.

Automatic Cache Invalidation

A similar improvement was also noted in the automatic cache invalidation methods, D1 and B1 over B. For the sake of brevity, the results are not included here.

Figure 7. Percentage improvement of shared caching over independent caching with varying cache invalidation frequencies (Invalidations per 100 requests)

Figure 8. Performance improvement of shared caching over independent caching with increase in number of requests

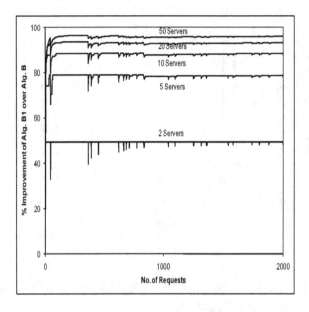

CONCLUSION

In this paper we have proposed improved techniques for processing of dynamic queries in a cluster of web servers through sharing the cached contents with the help of the web switch. We have presented methods for both the horizontal and vertical clusters, using both expiry-based and automatic cache invalidation. Our techniques essentially work on making available the cached

Figure 9. Performance improvement of C1 and A1 over A

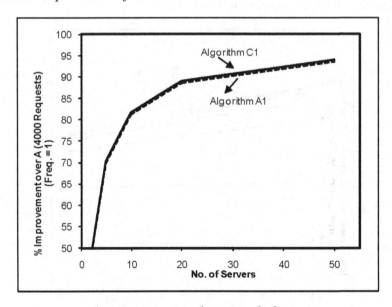

Automatic cache invalidation

query result of one server to subsequent servers processing requests involving the same query, so that duplicate visits to the database for revalidation of the same query are avoided. We provide for sharing in a horizontal cluster by means of messages communicated between the web server and the switch, and in the case of a vertical cluster, by means of a single common cache that is shared by all the web servers. Moreover, by efficiently coordinating and combining caching among multiple web servers, our techniques achieve cache consistency. Our simulation results show that these techniques achieve a significant speedup of query processing times over the existing algorithms. The techniques also demonstrate that efficient cache management is effective in improving the QoS of web clusters in respect of dynamic content as well.

ACKNOWLEDGMENT

The authors are thankful to Dr. Soundar Rajan for his valuable contributions to this paper.

REFERENCES

Adams, H. (2001). *Best practices for web services: Web services performance considerations, Parts 1 & 2*. Retrieved from http://www.ibm.com/developerworks/library/ws-best9/ and http://www.ibm.com/developerworks/library/ws-best10/

Altinel, M., Luo, Q., Krishnamurthy, S., Mohan, C., Pirahesh, H., Lindsay, B. G., et al. (2002). DBCache: Database caching for web application servers. In *Proceedings of the ACM SIGMOD International Conference on Management of Data* (p. 612).

Amiri, K., Park, S., & Tewari, R. (2002). A self-managing data cache for edge-of-network web applications. In *Proceedings of the Eleventh ACM CIKM International Conference on Information and Knowledge Management* (pp. 177-185).

Amiri, K., Park, S., Tewari, R., & Padmanabhan, S. (2003). DBProxy: A dynamic data cache for web applications. In *Proceedings of the 19th IEEE ICDE International Conference on Data Engineering* (pp. 821-831).

Amza, C., Soundararajan, G., & Cecchet, E. (2005). Transparent caching with strong consistency in dynamic content web sites. In *Proceedings of the 19th Annual ACM ICS International Conference on Supercomputing* (pp. 264-273).

Anbazhagan, M., & Nagarajan, A. (2002). *Understanding quality of service for Web services*. Retrieved from http://www.ibm.com/developerworks/webservices/library/ws-quality/index.html

Andreolini, M., Casalicchio, E., Colajanni, M., & Mambelli, M. (2001). *QoS-aware switching policies for a locally distributed web system*. Retrieved from http://www2002.org/CDROM/poster/141.pdf

Andreolini, M., Casalicchio, E., Colajanni, M., & Mambelli, M. (2004). A cluster-based web system providing differentiated and guaranteed services. *Cluster Computing*, 7, 7–19. doi:10.1023/B:CLUS.0000003940.34740.be

Apache HTTP Server. (2011). *Caching guide*. Retrieved from http://httpd.apache.org/docs/2.2/caching.html

Bunt, R. B., Eager, D. L., Oster, G. M., & Williamson, C. L. (1999). Achieving load balance and effective caching in clustered web servers. In *Proceedings of the 4th International Web Caching Workshop*, San Diego, CA (pp. 159-169).

Candan, K. S., Li, W.-S., Luo, Q., Hsiung, W.-P., & Agrawal, D. (2001). Enabling dynamic content caching for database-driven web sites. In *Proceedings of the ACM SIGMOD International Conference on Management of Data* (pp. 532-543).

Cardellini, V., Casalicchio, E., & Colajanni, M. (2001). A performance study of distributed architectures for the quality of web services. In *Proceedings of 34th IEEE Annual Hawaii International Conference on System Sciences*.

Cardellini, V., Casalicchio, E., Colajanni, M., & Mambelli, M. (2001). *Enhancing a web-server cluster with quality of service mechanisms.* Retrieved from http://www.ce.uniroma2.it/publications/ipccc2002.pdf

Cardellini, V., Casalicchio, E., Colajanni, M., & Mambelli, M. (2001). *Web switch support for differentiated services.* Retrieved from http://portal.acm.org/ft_gateway.cfm?id=572320&type=pdf

Cardellini, V., Casalicchio, E., Colajanni, M., & Tucci, S. (2001). Mechanisms for quality of service in web clusters. *Computer Networks, 37*(6), 761–771. doi:10.1016/S1389-1286(01)00252-3

Cardellini, V., Casalicchio, E., Colajanni, M., & Yu, P. S. (2001). The state of the art in locally distributed web-server systems. *ACM Computing Surveys, 34*(2), 263–311. doi:10.1145/508352.508355

Casalicchio, E., & Colajanni, M. (2001, May1-5). A client-aware dispatching algorithm for web clusters providing multiple services. In *Proceedings of the Conference on World Wide Web*, Hong Kong (pp. 535-544).

Challenger, J., Iyengar, A., & Dantzig, P. (1999). A scalable system for consistently caching dynamic web data. In *Proceedings of the Eighteenth IEEE INFOCOMM Annual Joint Conference* (pp. 294-303).

Challenger, J. R., Dantzig, P., & Iyengar, A. (2004). Efficiently serving dynamic data at highly accessed web sites. *IEEE/ACM Transactions on Networking, 12*(2), 233–246. doi:10.1109/TNET.2004.826289

Chen, G., Wang, C.-L., & Lau, F. C. M. (2003). P-Jigsaw: A cluster-based web server with co-operative caching support. *Concurrency and Computation, 15*, 681–705. doi:10.1002/cpe.723

Cuenca-Acuna, F. M., & Nguyen, T. D. (2001). Cooperative caching middleware for cluster-based servers. In *Proceedings of the 10th International Symposium on High Performance Distributed Computing* (pp. 303-314).

Datta, A., Datta, K., Thomas, H. M., VanderMeer Suresha, D. E., & Ramamritham, K. (2002). Proxy-based acceleration of dynamically generated content on the World Wide Web: An approach and implementation. In *Proceedings of the ACM SIGMOD International Conference on Management of Data* (pp. 97-108).

Datta, A., Datta, K., Thomas, H. M., VanderMeer Suresha, D. E., Ramamritham, K., & Fishman, D. (2001). A comparative study of alternative middle tier caching solutions to support dynamic web content acceleration. In *Proceedings of the 27th Conference on Very Large Data Bases*, Rome, Italy.

Degenaro, L., Iyengar, A., Lipkind, I., & Rouvellou, I. (2000). A middleware system which intelligently caches query results. In *Proceedings of the IFIP/ACM International Conference on Distributed Systems Platforms* (pp. 24-44).

Fielding, R., Gettys, J., Mogul, J., Frystyk, H., Masinter, L., Leach, P., & Berners-Lee, T. (1999). *Hypertext transfer protocol--HTTP/1.1.* Retrieved from http://www.w3.org/Protocols/rfc2616/rfc2616.html

Galindo-Legaria, C., Grabs, T., Kleinerman, C., & Waas, F. (2005). Database change notifications: Primitives for efficient database query result caching. In *Proceedings of the 31st International Conference on Very Large Data Bases*, Trondheim, Norway (pp. 1275-1278).

Holmedahl, V., Smith, B., & Yang, T. (1998). Cooperative caching of dynamic content on a distributed web server. In *Proceedings of the Seventh IEEE International Symposium on High Performance Distributed Computing*, Chicago, IL (pp. 243-250).

Hyun, J., Jung, I., & Maeng, S. (2003). Content sniffer based load distribution in a web server cluster. *IEICE Transactions on Information and Systems, 86*(7), 1258–1269.

Iyengar, A., & Challenger, J. R. (1997). Improving web server performance by caching dynamic data. In *Proceedings of the USENIX Symposium on Internet Technologies and Systems* (pp. 49-60).

Lee, B.-H., Lim, S.-H., Kim, J.-H., & Fox, G. C. (2009). Lease-based consistency schemes in the web environment. *Future Generation Computer Systems, 25*(1), 8–19. doi:10.1016/j.future.2008.06.001

Lowery, J. C. (2001). Caching hierarchies: Understanding content distribution/delivery networks. *Dell Power Solutions, 1*, 91–94.

Luo, Q., Krishnamurthy, S., Mohan, C., Pirahesh, H., Woo, H., Lindsay, B. G., & Naughton, J. F. (2002). Middle-tier database caching for e-business. In *Proceedings of the ACM SIGMOD International Conference on Management of Data* (pp. 588-593).

Mogha, R., & Preetham, V. V. (2003). *Java web services programming*. New York, NY: Wiley Dreamtech.

Mohan, C. (2001). Tutorial: Caching technologies for web applications. In *Proceedings of the Conference on Very Large Data Bases*.

Oracle Corporation. (2010). *Oracle application server web cache 11g*. Retrieved from http://www.oracle.com/technetwork/middleware/ias/webcache11goverview- 128137.pdf

Pai, V. S., Aron, M., Banga, G., Svendsen, M., Druschel, P., Zwaenepol, W., & Nahum, E. (1998). *Locality-aware request distribution in cluster-based network services*. Retrieved from http://www.research.ibm.com/people/n/nahum/publications/asplos98-lard.pdf

Raghunathan, A., & Murugesan, K. (2010). Schema-based cache validation of dynamic content to improve query performance of web services. *Journal of Web Engineering, 9*(2), 116–131.

Sharifian, S., Motamedi, S. A., & Akbari, M. K. (2009). Estimation-based load balancing with admission control for cluster web servers. *ETRI Journal, 31*(2).

Sharifian, S., Motamedi, S. A., & Akbari, M. K. (2010). A predictive and probabilistic load balancing algorithm for cluster-based web servers. *Applied Soft Computing, 11*(1), 970–981. doi:10.1016/j.asoc.2010.01.017

Teo, Y. M., & Ayani, R. (2001). Comparison of load balancing strategies on cluster-based web servers. *Transactions of the Society for Modelling and Simulation, 77*(5-6), 185–195. doi:10.1177/003754970107700504

Tolia, N., & Satyanarayanan, M. (2007). Consistency-preserving caching of dynamic database content. In *Proceedings of the ACM Conference on World Wide Web* (pp. 311-320).

Turaga, R., Cline, O., & Van Sickel, P. (2006). *WebSphere application server step by step*. Van Nuys, CA: MC Press.

Xiong, Z., & Yan, P. (2005). A solution for supporting QoS in web server cluster. In *Proceedings of the International Conference on Wireless Communications, Networking and Mobile Computing* (Vol. 2, pp. 834-839).

Yagoub, K., Florescu, D., Issarny, V., & Valduriez, P. (2000). Caching strategies for data-intensive web sites. In *Proceedings of the Conference on Very Large Data Bases* (pp. 188-199).

Zhuang, S.-Y., & Yeh, Y.-C. Chiang, & M.-L. (2008). Locality-aware request distribution with frequency-based replication in web server clusters. In *Proceedings of the International Computer Symposium*, Taipei, Taiwan.

This work was previously published in International Journal of Business Data Communications and Networking, Volume 7, Issue 3, edited by Varadharajan Sridhar and Debashis Saha, p.p 16-36, copyright 2011 by IGI Publishing (an imprint of IGI Global)

Chapter 11
Fuzzy Logic–Based Mobility Metric Clustering Algorithm for MANETs

P. Venkateswaran
Jadavpur University, India

Kanika Orea
Jadavpur University, India

Mousumi Kundu
SAMEER, Kolkata Centre, India

R. Nandi
Jadavpur University India

Srishti Shaw
Jadavpur University, India

ABSTRACT

Mobile ad-hoc network, (MANET) is a collection of wireless mobile nodes dynamically forming a temporary communication network without using any existing infrastructure or centralized administration. To reduce routing overhead, computational complexity and overcome the problem of low bandwidth utilization, MANET is divided into several clusters. The authors propose a fuzzy logic based mobility metric for MANET that had been utilized as the basis of cluster formation in the algorithm viz., FUZZY CLUSTERING. This algorithm leads to more stable cluster formation compared to the existing MOBIC algorithm as evidenced by significant reduction in the number of clusterhead changes. As the frequency of cluster reorganization is a significant attribute, the proposed algorithm is expected to yield improved performance for MANETs.

INTRODUCTION

MANET (Mobile Ad hoc NETwork) is a collection of wireless mobile nodes dynamically forming a temporary communication network without the use of any existing infrastructure or centralized administration (Aggelou, 2005). With the increase in size of the networks, routing table could grow to an immense size resulting in low bandwidth utilization with high load due to longer source routes and thus, large byte overhead (Johansson et al., 1999), which raise scalability issue. Therefore,

DOI: 10.4018/978-1-4666-2026-1.ch011

clustering algorithms are proposed in MANETs to address scalability issue by providing a hierarchical network structure for routing.

The MANET is divided into several clusters. From each cluster certain nodes are elected to be clusterheads. The clusterhead collects information signaling, message, etc. and allocates resources within its cluster and communicates with other clusterheads. By partitioning the network into clusters of nodes and performing hierarchical routing, scalability is improved since a reduced number of mobile nodes participate in the routing algorithm, hence a low routing-related control overhead. Clustering perform reduced amount of routing computation as local movement of member nodes is now handled locally. Clustering overcomes mobility of nodes by adjusting cluster size according to network stability and makes dynamic topology to appear less dynamic by considering cluster stability when they form (McDonald & Znati, 1999). Hence, network state information is less variable (Perkins, 2001). This minimizes link breakage and packet loss.

Clustering algorithm in MANETs should be able to maintain its cluster structure as stable as possible while topology changes. Since mobility is the main cause for the changes in clusterheads and cluster memberships, (i.e., stability of cluster) it is logical to have mobility metric as a basis of cluster formation and clusterhead selection.

In this paper, a mobility metric is presented that is based on fuzzy logic considering the successive measurements of received power at any node from its neighbors (Korotkich & Dimitrov, 2002). This metric neither needs the availability of any absolute location information at a node nor the availability of velocity information at every node. The new mobility metric is therefore used as the basis of cluster formation of our proposed algorithm, FUZZY_CLUSTERING.

Our simulation work show that the proposed algorithm yields certain improved response over the existing MOBIC algorithm (Basu, Khan, & Little, 2001), e.g.,

- 39.27% reduction in average number of clusterhead changes
- 20.84% reduction in time after which probability of reclustering is minimal

LITERATURE SURVEY

A number of clustering algorithms have been proposed in literature such as Linked Cluster Algorithm (LCA) (Baker & Ephremides, 1981), Lowest-ID Algorithm (L-ID) (Ephremides et al., 1987), Maximum Connectivity Clustering (MCC) (Parekh, 1994), Least Clusterhead Change Algorithm (LCC) (Chiang et al., 1997), Distributed Clustering Algorithm (DCA) (Basagni, 1991), MOBIC (Basu, Khan, & Little, 2001) and MobDHop (Er & Seah, 2004). LCA (Baker & Ephremides, 1981; Ephremides et al., 1987) organizes nodes into clusters on the basis of node proximity. Parekh suggested MCC in which the clusterhead election is based on degree of connectivity instead of node id (Parekh, 1994). LCC (Chiang et al., 1997) is designed to minimize clusterhead changes. Lowest ID algorithm (Ephremides et al., 1987)) is generalized to a weight based clustering technique, referred to as DCA (Basagni, 1991).

Location Aided Hierarchical Cluster Routing (LHCR) (Yang & Chou, 2009) divides the nodes of the network are into various hierarchical clusters recursively, based on the amount of electricity amount and ID (Identification). Electricity level consideration prevents lowest ID nodes selected as clusterheads from failing due to electrical overload.

Weight Based Adaptive Cluster Algorithm (WBACA) (Dhurandher & Singh, 2007) based on the transmission rate, mobility, and battery power of nodes chooses the optimized number of clusterheads. But it requires many parameters and large 'frozen time' for calculation.

Weight Based Adaptive Clustering for Large Scale Heterogeneous MANET (WACHM) (Wang et al., 2007) finds the optimal number of cluster-heads, optimal hops and elects clusterhead based on degree-difference, battery power, average link stability and dependency probability.

Fuzzy based clustering is proposed in literature (Zhao & Wang, 2004; Adabi et al., 2008; Xiao & Xing, 2004). Zhao and Wang (2004) proposed a clustering algorithm based on a distributed mobility prediction scheme. A fuzzy membership function was defined to predict a more stable link. A fuzzy-inference rule base generates the fuzzy cost of each link.

Distributed Fuzzy Score-based Clustering Algorithm (DFSCA) (Adabi et al., 2008) considers the remaining battery power, number of neighbors, number of members and stability with a fuzzy inference algorithm in order to select clusterheads. It is weight-based clustering algorithm which performs selection of cluster heads in a distributed manner. It uses the most recent information about current status of neighbor nodes for calculation.

Xiao and Xing (2004) proposed a new time degree definition for the highly dynamic topology and absence of any fixed infrastructure in a MANET. By analyzing the link relationship of the neighboring nodes, a network model based on the link life of two nodes is created. A fuzzy-inference rule base is implemented to generate the fuzzy cost of each link. A clustering algorithm based on a mobility prediction scheme is introduced in a distributed manner.

MOBIC, which is similar to L-ID is proposed by Basu, Khan, and Little (2001). Instead of node ID, MOBIC uses a new mobility metric, Aggregate Local Mobility (ALM), to elect a clusterhead. The ratio between the received power levels of successive transmissions between a pair of nodes is used to compute the relative mobility between neighboring nodes, which determines the ALM of each node. Mobility-based d-hop (MobDHop) (Er & Seah, 2004) clustering algorithm forms variable-diameter clusters based on node mobility patterns in MANETs. Nodes which have similar moving patterns are grouped into one cluster in order to achieve maximum cluster stability. Er and Seah (2004) have proposed an analysis of MobDHop, based on clustering performance metrics; i.e., formation time and traffic congestion due to control message formation and have made a comparison with other clustering algorithms used in MANETs.

A. Gu et al. (2007) have provided a quantitative comparison of the scalability of clustering protocols, modeling a better scalable method for adhoc clustering namely Personal Network Clustering Protocol (PNCP).

Clustering algorithms that generate clusters which may be greater than two hops in diameter have also been proposed in the literature (Ramanathan & Steenstrup, 1998; Krishna et al., 1997).

Table 1 provides the comparative study of various clustering algorithms used in MANETs.

THE PROPOSED CLUSTERING ALGORITHM: FUZZY_CLUSTERING

The main design goals of our clustering algorithm are:

1. The algorithm minimizes the number of times clusterhead changes by considering group mobility pattern.
2. The algorithm must be distributed and executed asynchronously.
3. The algorithm must incur minimal clustering overhead, be it cluster formation or maintenance overhead.
4. Network-wide flooding must be avoided.

Before introducing, FUZZY_CLUSTERING we first make a few assumptions on the network:

1. Two nodes are connected by bi-directional link (symmetric transmission).
2. Each node can measure its received signal strength.

Table 1. Comparison of various clustering algorithms

Name of Clustering Algorithms	Author (Year of publication)	Advantages	Disadvantages
MOBIC	Basu, Khan, and Little (2001)	1) Stable cluster formation 2) Higher throughput 3) Smaller delay 4) Applicable to different mobility scenarios	Relation between the performance of clustering algorithms and the parameters such as area, number of nodes, transmission radius, mobility speeds etc is not reflected in the literature.
Mobility-based d-hop (MobDHop)	Er and Seah (2004)	1) Estimation of the stability of clusters based on relative mobility of cluster members. 2) Unlike other clustering algorithms, the diameter of clusters is not restricted to two hops. Diameter of clusters is flexible and determined by the stability of clusters. 3) MobDHop can be used to provide hierarchical routing structure to address the scalability of routing protocol in large MANETs.	Algorithm implementation is complex
Location Aided Hierarchical Cluster Routing (LHCR)	Yang and Chou (2009)	1) Avoids the nodes that are far away from each other being assigned to the same cluster 2) Considers nodes' power amount to avoid over- transformation. 3) Lesser collision and higher throughput. 4) LHCR is more efficient and effective in data delivery than ZRP and AODV in larger networks.	1)No analysis under different mobility rate patterns 2) Not effective in smaller networks
Weight Based Adaptive Clustering for Large Scale Heterogeneous MANET (WACHM)	Wang et al. (2007)	1) Good scalability 2) Cluster head election and cluster formation algorithm is effective and suitable for large-scale network.	Not suitable for small networks.
Distributed Fuzzy Score-based Clustering Algorithm (DFSCA)	Adabi et al. (2008)	Algorithm performs better than Weighted Clustering Algorithm and Fuzzy Cluster Mean algorithm with smaller number of clusters, longer lifespan of nodes in the system and higher end-to-end throughput.	1) Distance between nodes is not considered 2) Limited analysis of parameters for score calculation
Personal Network Clustering Protocol (PNCP)	Gu et al. (2007)	1) PNCP better scalable than others wrt load, stable cluster structure, energy efficiency, and load balance	1) Scalability study and comparison is limited within the overhead analysis. 2) No analysis of the schemes with respect to performance metrics, such as the average number of clusters, the average cluster formation delay and the average cluster life time.
Clustering overhead and convergence time analysis	Er and Seah (2004)	The overhead incurred by multi-hop clustering has a similar asymptotic bound as 1-hop clustering while also having the benefits of multi-hop clusters	1) limited complexity analysis 2) No competitive analysis as used in online algorithms
Fuzzy-Control-Based Clustering Strategy	Xiao and Xing (2004)	Higher clusterhead survival time compared to LCC and HD clustering scheme	1)Limited analysis of parameters for link cost calculation 2) Clustering depends on parameters other than link cost that are not taken into consideration.

Mobility Metric

Let us first describe the mobility metric which is used in formation of clusters. The basic idea in this paper is that the clustering process should be aware of the mobility of the individual nodes with respect to its neighboring nodes. A node should not be elected as a clusterhead if it is highly mobile relative to its neighbors, since, in that situation, the probability that a cluster will break and that reclustering will happen is high (Basu, Khan, & Little, 2001). Instead, we should attempt to select a node that is less mobile relative to its neighbors for the role of a clusterhead. Several attempts have been made in the recent past to characterize mobility as an inherent phenomenon in a MANET (Gerla & Tsai, 1995; Johansson, 1999), and an attempt has been made to incorporate it into routing schemes (Toh, 1997). The mobility metric proposed here does not assume the availability of any absolute location information or velocity information at every node. Through periodic beaconing or hello messages, a mobile node can estimate its distance to its neighbor based on measured received signal strength from that particular neighbor as given in Friss' free space propagation model.

$$P_r = P_t * G_t * G_r * \frac{\lambda^2}{(4 * \pi * d)^2} \qquad (1)$$

where P_r = received power, P_t = transmitted power, G_t = antenna gain of the transmitter, G_r = antenna gain of the receiver, λ = wavelength (c/f), d = distance.

In practice, an exact calculation of the distance between a transmitter and a receiver may not be possible from the measured signal strengths owing to the complexities involved in accurate channel modeling. However, FUZZY_CLUSTERING does not depend on accurate estimation of distances between two nodes to operate correctly. We use the received signal strength measured at the arrival of every packet to estimate the dis-

tance from one node to its neighbor node. The stronger the received signal strength, the closer the neighbor node. It is important to know that the "closeness" between two nodes is not necessarily measured by their absolute or physical distance. For example, node B may be very close to node A. However, it runs out of energy and transmits packets at lower power. In this case, it behaves like a distanced node from node A. But power received from node C, though situated far away compared to node B, is high and so it behaves as a nearer node. The scenario is shown in Figure 1.

Therefore, absolute distance may not be useful in predicting link stability in this case. The uncertainty of the mobile environment is taken care using the method of

fuzzy logic as fuzzy logic is inherently robust since it does not require precise, noise-free inputs. They can be used to represent an unknown mathematical model.

So the distance (d) between two nodes is defined as

$$d = k / \sqrt{P_r} \qquad (2)$$

Measured signal strength of successive packets is used to estimate the change of distance (cod = Δd). We calculate the difference of estimated distance from a neighboring node at two successive time moments as follows:

$$\Delta d = d_c - d_p \qquad (3)$$

where d_c and d_p are the distances of the two nodes at the current time and previous time respectively.

Here we have used fuzzy logic where d and Δd act as input parameter and output parameter is proximity value.

The term sets of input variable 'dist' have the following fuzzy names: short, med (i.e., medium) and long (Kundu, 2007). The term sets of input variable 'Δd' have the following fuzzy names: neg (i.e., negative), zero, pos (i.e., positive) (Kundu, 2007). The membership functions chosen for the

Figure 1. Proximity determination by received power at node A

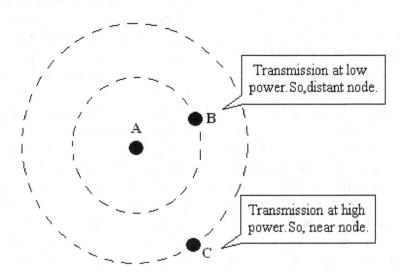

fuzzy sets are shown in Figure 2. In both the cases we have first normalized the inputs with respect to transmission range.

The term sets of output variable 'proximity' has the following fuzzy names: vl (i.e., very low), low, med (i.e., medium), high, vh (i.e., very high) (Kundu, 2007). The membership function of proximity is shown in Figure 3.

We can argue that the shorter the distance is, and more and more negative the (Δd) cod is (i.e., nodes are moving nearer to), the higher the proximity; the longer the distance is, more and more positive the cod is (i.e., nodes are moving farther away), the lower the proximity. This logic is used to generate the rule base of the fuzzy controller. The corresponding Rule matrix (Kundu, 2007) is shown in Figure 4.

Thus using fuzzy logic (Gerla, 2001) every node calculates pair wise proximity value with its neighbor. For a node with m neighbors, there will exist m such proximity values named proximity(Y,X_i), where X_i is the neighbor of Y. We calculate the aggregate local proximity value P(Y) (Kundu, 2007) at any node Y by calculating the variance (with respect to zero) of the entire set of proximity values proximity(Y,X_i), where X_i is a neighbor of Y, as presented in Box 1.

It is the expected value of the squares of the m local proximity samples from Y's neighbors. The main rationale behind calculating the variance of the local proximity values with respect to each neighbor is that a high value of P(Y) indicates that more nodes are moving nearer to Y and it is relatively less mobile with respect to its neighbors. On the contrary, a low value of P(Y) indicates that nodes are moving away from Y and it is highly mobile with respect to its neighboring nodes. So we should favor the nodes that have a high proximity value with respect to its neighbors, for becoming clusterheads.

The calculation of the local proximity value proximity(Y,X_i) needs two successive packet transmissions, we require that the aggregate local proximity value P(Y) is calculated at Y after two successive "hello" message transmissions from all Y's neighbors. Thus, only those nodes which have been in the neighborhood of Y for that particular time interval are considered for the mobility metric calculation. This calculation is performed at every node, and thus, each node will maintain an aggregate local proximity metric. In order to

Figure 2. Membership function for the input variables (a) 'dist' (b) 'cod'

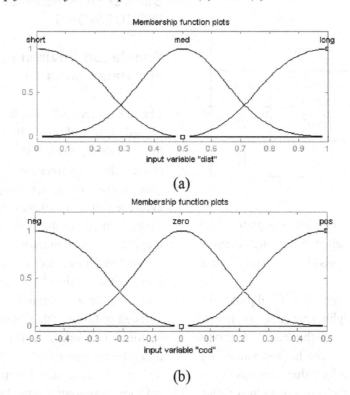

(a)

(b)

Figure 3. Membership function for the output variable

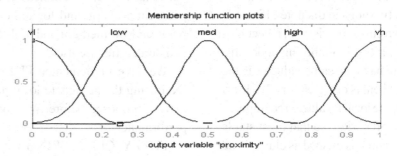

use this mobility metric for clustering, we propose a distributed, fuzzy logic based lowest mobility clustering algorithm, FUZZY_CLUSTERING, where the mobility metric described above is used as a basis of cluster formation.

Clusterhead Selection

This is an initial setup stage when the network is first initialized. All nodes periodically broad-

cast "Hello" messages including their aggregate proximity value P. At the first two time instants when proximity value is not been calculated it is initialized to zero. Each node measures the received power levels of two successive "Hello" message transmissions from every neighbor, and then calculates the pair wise local proximity metrics using fuzzy logic. Then a node computes the aggregate local proximity metric P using (4). And then broadcasts "Hello" message with the

Figure 4. Rule matrix

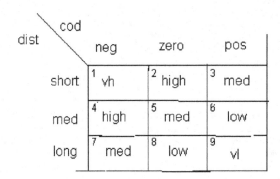

computed local aggregate P value at the next broadcast time. It is then stored in the neighbor table of each neighbor. This algorithm is executed in a distributed manner.

After receiving the aggregate local proximity values from all of its neighboring nodes, each node compares its own value with those of its neighbors (Figure 5). If a node has the highest value of P (aggregate local proximity value) amongst all its neighbors, it assumes the status of a clusterhead; otherwise it declares itself to be a cluster member. This algorithm leads to the formation of clusters which are at most two hops in diameter. If a node is a neighbor of two clusterheads, then it becomes a "gateway" node. If two neighboring nodes in a non-clustered state have the same value of P, the clusterhead assignment is deferred for a back-off period. The aggregate local P value is recomputed at the end of back-off period, so that most stable node among its neighbor is elected as clusterhead (Figure 6).

SIMULATION RESULTS AND DISCUSSIONS

Simulation Environment and Parameters

The movement of mobile nodes is generated according to Reference Region Group Mobility Model (Hong et al., 1999). With this mobility model, the effectiveness and the efficiency of group communication routing protocols could be evaluated under a more realistic environment. We have assumed that the movement of mobile nodes is continuous within the whole simulation period.

The performance of FUZZY_CLUSTERING is evaluated via simulations using MATLAB. The scenarios were generated with input parameters as listed in Table 2 that resemble real life models. Maximum speed of nodes is chosen as 20m/s. It can be anything from 0m/s to 20m/s which is realistic. Membership function can be of different form: gaussian, triangular, rectangular etc. It has been chosen depending on practical scenario. Rule matrix is also designed depending upon the practical scenario and logic. For differentiating between low, medium and high classes fuzzifier and defuzzifier are used.

We have implemented FUZZY_CLUSTERING using the aggregate local proximity metric that we proposed before. We have compared the performance of FUZZY_CLUSTERING with MOBIC, with respect to a cluster stability metric which denotes the average number of clusterhead, changes in a given time period. MOBIC has been chosen for comparison as it also chose its CH depending on its relative mobility metric, but it is in determin-

Box 1.

```
P(Y) = var_0[proximity(Y,X_1), proximity(Y,X_2), .....proximity(Y,X_m)]
     = (1/m)∑(proximity(Y,X_i))² (4)
```

Figure 5.

```
PSEUDO-CODE FOR AGGREGATE PROXIMITY VALUE
Initialisze: Set y= no_of_nodes;
for(j=1 to y)
    begin
    Set m= no_of_neighbors;
    for(i=1 to m)
        begin
            input(distance);
            input(change_of_distance);
            dist=distance;
            cod=change_of_distance;
            if (dist==short) and (cod<0) then
                    proximity(i,j)=very_high ;
            end if;
            if (dist==short) and (cod==0) then
                    proximity(i,j)=high ;
            end if;
            if (dist==short) and (cod>0) then
                    proximity(i,j)=medium ;
            end if;
            if (dist==medium) and (cod<0) then
                    proximity(i,j)=high ;
            end if;
            if (dist==medium) and (cod==0) then
                    proximity(i,j)=medium ;
            end if;
            if (dist==medium) and (cod>0) then
                    proximity(i,j)=low ;
            end if;
            if (dist==large) and (cod<0) then
                    proximity(i,j)=medium ;
            end if;
            if (dist==large) and (cod==0) then
                    proximity(i,j)=low ;
            end if;
            if (dist==large) and (cod>0) then
                    proximity(i,j)=very_low ;
            end if;
        end for;
    sum=0;
    m= no_of_neighbors;
    for (i=1 to m)
        begin
            sum=sum+(proximity(i,j))^2;
        end for;
        aggregate_proximity=sum/m;
end for;
```

istic way whether the proposed scheme is using fuzzy logic.

The aggregate mobility values (P) were stamped onto each "hello" broadcast packet and sent by the sender node to its neighbors. The receiver nodes receive the packets and extract the aggregate mobility information P and received power of the current packet. The proximity value is calculated from two successive power received. Then the P values are calculated by using (1) and stamped onto the next broadcast packet. Once the P values of all neighbors are known, the clustering

215

Figure 6. Pseudo-code for clusterhead selection

```
PSEUDO-CODE FOR CLUSTERHEAD SELECTION
Initialisze: Set y= no_of_nodes;
for(j=1 to y)
     begin
     Set m= no_of_neighbors;
     Declare an array Aggregate_Prox[m] of size m storing
     the aggregate proximity value for each neighbor
     Set :
         Prox[]=0 for all the neighbours
       Aggregate_prox_max_value=0
       Aggregate_prox_max_node=0
     for(i=1 to m)
         Aggregate_Prox(i)= aggregate_proximity(i)
      End for
     Aggregate_prox_max_value= max(Aggregate_Prox(i))
     Aggregate_prox_max_node=i
   Mark node i as the 'clusterhead'
End for
```

process is executed. FUZZY_CLUSTERING does not use additional control packets for information exchange to form or maintain cluster.

Discussion

Figure 7 shows the comparison between the performance of MOBIC and FUZZY_CLUSTERING for a reasonably mobile scenario with MaxSpeed = 20 m/s and PT = 0 sec, i.e., constant mobility.

It is evident from Figure 7 that, FUZZY_CLUSTERING outperforms MOBIC. It gives

Table 2. Simulation Parameters

Parameter	Meaning	Value in our Simulation
N	Number of Nodes	25,50
M x n	Network Size	500^2 m^2
MaxSpeed	Maximum speed of nodes	20 m/sec
Tx	Transmission Range	50-250m
PT	Pause Time	0 sec
BI	Broadcast Interval	1 sec
S	Simulation Time	200 sec

less clusterhead changes over the transmission range of 250m i.e., lesser shifting of cluster controlling responsibility and lesser movement of maintenance information. Hence it results in more stable clusters. In both the cases nodes with the lowest relative mobility in a neighborhood get chosen as clusterheads, but electing the clusterhead using fuzzy logic gives better performance.

This is also clear from Figure 8 that shows duration after which clusters are altered within the range of 250m. So, clusters are almost stable, i.e., possibility of reclustering triggering is minimal. The simulation is done with transmission range varying from 50m to 250m and more improvement is shown with lower transmission range. When transmission range is approaching 250m, both the algorithms are giving the same result as CH in that case may not change at all in that scenario.

The proposed scheme is scalable. The input variables to the fuzzy clustering algorithm in normalized form and output variable is also described in normalized form. Hence the proposed scheme is scalable.

Figure 7. Average number of CH (clusterhead) changes: MOBIC vs. FUZZY_CLUSTERING

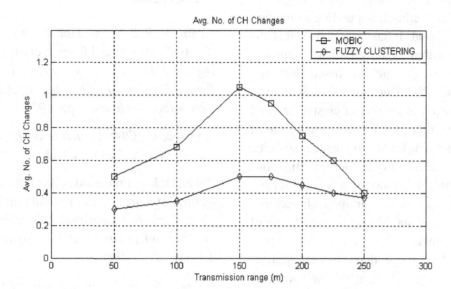

CONCLUSION

We had presented an improved clustering algorithm for MANETs based on the postulation of Fuzzy Logic based mobility metric. Clustering of nodes reduced the routing overhead of network and increased the efficiency of sealing packages to delivery data. Therefore, the possibility of collision is also reduced. The proposed algorithm does not need any absolute position or velocity information for cluster formation. Only measurements of received power at successive intervals are required to determine the distance and change of distance from a node to its neighbor. It establishes the closeness by aggregate local proximity value P computed from pair wise proximity value with

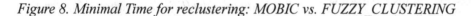

Figure 8. Minimal Time for reclustering: MOBIC vs. FUZZY_CLUSTERING

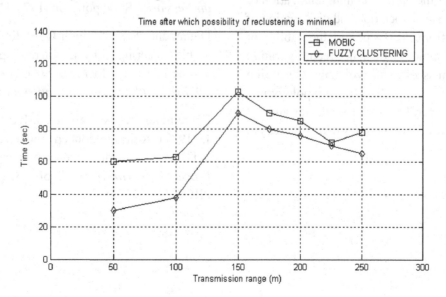

its neighbor using fuzzy rule. Node with highest P is selected as clusterhead. Supporting simulation results are reported. It has been shown that the proposed algorithm yields significant improvement over the existing mobility based clustering algorithm - MOBIC. Our initial studies showed 39.27% reduction in number of clusterhead and a 20.84% time reduction for reaching a state of minimal reclustering leading to enhanced stability.

Presently we are carrying out investigations in our department laboratory to obtain further reduction in clusterhead variation characteristics with enhanced stability for a given frame of transmission range.

MANETs have tremendous business applications. They are the only available and working networks in military and battlefields situations, where terrestrial conditions are extremely unpredictable and unreliable. Also MANETs have potential applications in festivals-fairs, make-shift carnivals, exigencies like natural calamities and security breaches (terrorist activities) etc. In such scenarios, MANETs provide low-cost and effective connectivity.

Success of MANETs in these scenarios, require effective bandwidth utilization which is a scarce and costly natural resource. Also, effective configuration and management of the network is imperative for the optimal commercialization of the network. The association and dissociation of nodes to and from clusters perturb the stability of the network topology, and hence reconfiguration of the system is often unavoidable. Clustering schemes allows us to organize the topology in a structured manner. The present work is an attempt in that direction for optimum use of resources in a MANET.

REFERENCES

Adabi, S., Rezaee, A., Jabbehdari, S., & Adabi, S. (2008). Distributed fuzzy score-based clustering algorithm for mobile ad-hoc networks. In *Proceedings of the IEEE Asia Pacific Services Computing Conference* (pp. 193-198).

Aggelou, G. (2005). *Mobile ad hoc networks*. New York, NY: McGraw-Hill.

Baker, D. J., & Ephremides, A. (1981). The architectural organization of a mobile radio network via a distributed algorithm. *IEEE Transactions on Communications, 29*, 1694–1701. doi:10.1109/TCOM.1981.1094909

Basagni, S. (1991, June). Distributed clustering for ad hoc networks. In *Proceedings of the International Symposium on Parallel Architectures, Algorithms and Networks* (pp. 310-315).

Basu, P., Khan, N., & Little, T. D. C. (2001). Mobility based metric for clustering in mobile ad hoc networks. In *Proceedings of the Workshop on Distributed Computing Systems* (pp. 413-418).

Chiang, C. C., Wu, H. K., Liu, W., & Gerla, M. (1997, April). Routing in clustered multihop, mobile wireless networks with fading channel. In *Proceedings of the IEEE International Conference on Networks*, Singapore (pp. 197-211).

Dhurandher, S. K., & Singh, G. V. (2007, January). Stable clustering with efficient routing in wireless ad-hoc networks. In *Proceedings of the COMSWARE 2nd International Conference* (pp.1-12).

Ephremides, A., Wieselthier, J. E., & Baker, D. J. (1987). A design concept for reliable mobile radio networks with frequency hopping signaling. *Proceedings of the IEEE, 75*, 56–73. doi:10.1109/PROC.1987.13705

Er, I. I., & Seah, W. K. G. (2004). Mobility-based d-hop clustering algorithm for mobile ad hoc networks. In *Proceedings of the IEEE Conference on Wireless Communications and Networking* (pp. 2359-2364).

Gerla, G. (2001). *Fuzzy logic: Mathematical tools*. Boston, MA: Kluwer Academic.

Gerla, M., & Tsai, J. T. C. (1995). Multicluster, mobile multimedia radio networks. In. *Proceedings of the Wireless Networks Conference, 1*, 255–265. doi:10.1007/BF01200845

Gu, Y., Lu, W., Prasad, R. V., & Niemegeers, I. (2007). Clustering in ad hoc personal network formation. In Y. Shi, G. Dick van Albada, J. Dongarra, & P. M. A. Sloot (Eds.), *Proceedings of the 7th International Conference on Computational Science, Part IV* (LNCS 4490, pp. 312-319).

Hong, X., Gerla, M., Pei, G., & Chiang, C. (1999, August). A group mobility model for ad hoc wireless networks. In *Proceedings of the 2nd ACM/IEEE International Workshop on Modeling, Analysis and Simulation of Wireless and Mobile Systems*, Seattle, WA (pp. 53-60).

Johansson, P., Larsson, T., Hedman, N., Mielczarek, B., & Degermark, M. (1999, August). Scenario-based performance analysis of routing protocols for mobile ad hoc networks. In *Proceedings of the 5th ACM/IEEE International Conference on Mobile Computing and Networking*, Seattle, WA (pp. 195-206).

Korotkich, V., & Dimitrov, V. (2002). *Fuzzy logic: A framework for the new millennium*. Berlin, Germany: Physica-Verlag.

Krishna, P., Vaidya, N. H., Chatterjee, M., & Pradhan, D. K. (1997). A cluster based approach for routing in ad hoc networks. In *Proceedings of the Second ACM SIGCOMM Symposium on Mobile and Location-Independent Computing* (pp. 1-10).

Kundu, M. (2007). *An improved clustering algorithm for mobile ad-hoc network using fuzzy logic*. Unpublished master's thesis, Jadavpur University, Kolkata, India.

McDonald, A. B., & Znati, T. F. (1999). A mobility-based framework for adaptive clustering in wireless ad hoc networks. *IEEE Journal on Selected Areas in Communications, 17*, 1466–1486. doi:10.1109/49.780353

Parekh, A. K. (1994). *Selecting routers in ad hoc wireless networks*. Paper presented at the Intelligent Tutoring Systems Conference.

Perkins, C. E. (2001). *Ad hoc networking*. Reading, MA: Addison-Wesley.

Ramanathan, R., & Steenstrup, M. (1998). Hierarchically-organized multihop mobile networks for quality-of-service support. *Mobile Networks and Applications, 3*(1), 101–119. doi:10.1023/A:1019148009641

Toh, C. K. (1997). Associativity-based routing for ad-hoc mobile networks. *International Journal on Wireless Personal Communications, 4*(2).

Wang, Y., Chen, H., Yang, X., & Zhang, D. (2007). WACHM: Weight based adaptive clustering large scale heterogeneous MANET. In *Proceedings of the International Symposium on Communications and Information Technologies*.

Yang, S. J., & Chou, H. C. (2009). Design issues and performance analysis of location-aided hierarchical cluster routing on the MANET. In *Proceedings of the International Conference on Communications and Mobile Computing*.

Zhao, C. X., & Wang, G. X. (2004, June 15-19). Fuzzy-control-based clustering strategy in MANET. In *Proceedings of the 5th World Congress on Intelligent Control and Automation*.

This work was previously published in International Journal of Business Data Communications and Networking, Volume 7, Issue 3, edited by Varadharajan Sridhar and Debashis Saha, p.p 37-50, copyright 2011 by IGI Publishing (an imprint of IGI Global)

Chapter 12

How Evolving Network Access and Network Management Technologies are Redefining the Competitive Wireless Markets

Fernando Beltrán
University of Auckland, New Zealand

Jairo A. Gutiérrez
Universidad Tecnológica de Bolívar, Colombia

José Luis Melús
Universidad Politécnica de Cataluña, Spain

ABSTRACT

This paper examines some of the key problems users encounter when accessing current generation wireless networks. Using a case study of a hypothetical user, the authors explore the emerging services and the new broadband wireless network technologies necessary to carry them out. This paper analyses the issues associated with an observed trend in the industry that exposes potential changes to the long-term, rigid commercial relation between wireless providers and users: as a result of a range of evolved broadband wireless access standards and technologies, autonomic communications and policy-based management, and new pricing schemes, consumers will likely face new opportunities to enter short-term and spot contracts with the new wireless providers. This new landscape also allow multiple competing Access Providers (APs) to dynamically assign prices, and poses new and interesting challenges to the regulatory function. The paper also discusses a framework for the integration of heterogeneous technologies and management policies based on the network context that make up this emerging, hybrid wireless landscape, and describes the economic characteristics of new markets likely to arise.

DOI: 10.4018/978-1-4666-2026-1.ch012

INTRODUCTION

When Carlitos was confronted with the harsh conditions his cellular telephone company would apply to his desire for contract termination, he wondered: "there has to be a more rewarding way to deal with a telecommunications service provider." In fairness, Carlitos' cellular provider did let him know by the time he signed up what would have happened had he decided not to continue his commercial relationship before a two-year period. What really attracted Carlitos to become its customer was the seemingly unlimited texting amount he could do. Texting had become "huge" according to the popular press and Internet reports; more people were texting every day, with teen-agers being the most fanatic in almost every country (Lenhart, 2010). The estimate that 2.5 trillion text messages were sent by consumer of texting services around the world in 2008 was another impressive piece that revealed the growing importance to the big cellular providers of services other than voice (Stross, 2008). Similarly it is becoming clear that mobile broadband devices are transforming the way users access the Web and access personal content at home. Even when someone like Carlitos is at home, he increasingly likes to use his connected devices and gadgets over WiFi and 3G networks for mobile entertainment (Sandvine, 2010).

One day, Carlitos came across yet another report on the state of wireless telecommunications around the world. As someone who really needs to communicate for business and leisure purposes, Carlitos would not really care much about the many facts regarding the cellular voice markets. After all, he reckoned, he was getting something really fantastic: the benefits of an invention turned into one of the most successful and profitable markets at the turn of the 21st century. The report highlighted the fact that it has taken the cellular industry only 26 years to reach almost 50% of the world's population (Belic, 2007), that is, about 3.3 billion people. It also said the market has continued to show encouraging signs of expansion, in spite of the world turmoil brought in by the catastrophic financial crisis of 2008.

To his amazement Carlitos learned that 1 bit of information encoding his voice would cost the company about 0.000015 cents, whereas a bit encoding the text messages he likes sending so much would cost 0.018 cents, that is, roughly 1200 times the cost of one voice bit (Kang, 2008). Carlitos could hardly believe it. Honestly anyone would hardly believe it. Cellular companies have been able to expand the range of services they provide, which originally only consisted of voice, directory and other minor information services, to a large range of new Internet mobile services (real-time communications, real-time entertainment, social networking, Web Browsing P2P file sharing, gaming, etc.) which are now supported by their third generation (3G) networks. However, it is not only the direct provision of services that provides them with huge revenues. Roaming charges seem unjustifiably large with companies relying on the inconveniences and difficulties associated with changing providers for a short period of time (say, while traveling abroad) to effectively lock customers in. On a report footnote Carlitos has just learned that, in fact, since March 1 2010, European mobile phone operators are obliged under European Union (EU) roaming rules to offer their customers (users) a cut-off limit facility to protect them from bill shocks while traveling in other EU countries (European Commission, 2010). In spite of such a lukewarm directive Carlitos can see that the big players seek not only to keep but also to strengthen the long-term commercial relationship with their customers. Their proprietary access technologies serve their business plans all too-well even if sometimes someone like him has to carry two different phones or two different access cards, to be able to use different services from different providers. Carlitos is going to have a hard time cancelling his cellular service before the contract termination date, so he wonders: "is there another way?"

SETTING THE CONTEXT

Carlitos likes to try new electronic communications gadgets. As many other users, he is quite aware of the possibilities those new devices might offer. But in spite of their technological virtues, Carlitos has a hard time when it comes to finding who would allow his newly acquired communication devices access to information, communication and entertainment (ICE) services. The Internet is now the main source of ICE services, and telecommunications companies engage in competition for users who seek reliable access paths. Mobile communications devices can engage in active search for access to wireless networks operators who provide access to the Internet. One of Carlitos' devices can choose among a number of wireless access providers; the built-in multimodal access technology allows the device to actively seek as many options as possible. Not being already engaged in any long-term commercial relation, of the kind cellular companies maintain with their customers, Carlitos could, through his device, purchase access on a short-term basis.

Carlitos is not completely new to accessing the Internet via a Wi-Fi provider as he has sometimes used his credit card to activate an Internet access for his laptop for a short time while waiting for his connecting flight in an international air hub. He has even been able to compare what five different operators would have in store for travelers just like him-even though it took so long to do this manual comparison that by the time he had made a choice it was too late to do any useful work and he had to rush to his gate.

Besides accessing the Internet Carlitos likes to use Skype to make voice and video calls, to engage in chat sessions with friends and colleagues, and to have access to his company's network using a virtual private connection. Sometimes he finds hot-spots that provide free Internet access but typically after a few minutes he notices a degradation of quality of service on such free-access networks. He is also concerned about performing any job-related tasks over such an unreliable connection.

It seems to him that the current mobile broadband options are designed to favor businesses and not individual users. It is not only what he experiences as a user but what he notices with other customers who are affected by limited competition

Although Carlitos is excited about these new proposals, many concerns appear about the feasibility of these new services. How can real competition be introduced into the market? It is his opinion that real competition means that several network operators (hopefully more than two) are offering attractive services and giving users the flexibility to pick and choose among those services, without being unnecessarily shackled to a provider by means of an onerous contractual relationship. Figure 1 and Figure 2 illustrate the current way of handling contracts (long-term contracts) and the envisioned approach for mobile services operations (short-term contracts). How is this achievable if the traditional operators are dominant in the wireless access network market? Is it possible for traditional operators to change their vision on service offers or will new operators become effective competitors? In the latter case, are there new alternatives to the current wireless access networks? Is it wishful thinking to yearn for a user-centric approach where the services' needs of the individual customers are at the front and center of any emerging service proposal?

Figure 1 shows the current situation of mobile services characterized by several service providers operating together in a geographical area and serving their respective customers. If a user is contractually bound to an Access Provider (AP) he is unable to consume services from other providers except when he establishes another contract with a different AP or until that contract is terminated. When a customer of provider nA temporarily leaves his geographical influence area, this new AP has no technical means to grant access to the customer and therefore it needs the mediation of another service provider, aB, with whom the former has established roaming agreements, even though the customer still maintains a long-term contract with nA. Figure 2 depicts the vision

Figure 1. Current "wallet garden" long-term contract for mobile services

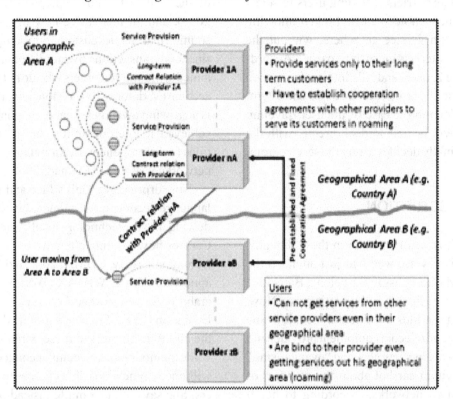

Figure 2. Short-term contract for mobile services

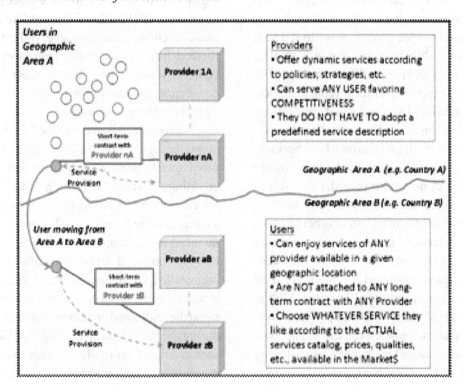

for this article: barriers impeding users to select the AP of their choice can be broken allowing them to obtain service anywhere, without the unnecessary intervention of third parties. According to Figure 2, users and APs interact in an open market of services offered through short-term contracts. Even in the case of the user traveling abroad, he will be able to deal directly with the AP that he finally decides to buy the service from.

CASE DESCRIPTION

While Carlitos was immersed in these thoughts his good friend Gail, who had just attended the Mobile World Congress in Barcelona, Barcelona 2010, came to visit with enthusiastic news. Now, Gail is what Carlitos considers a "techie". She works for a large telecom equipment provider and is constantly testing new gear and "evangelising" to anyone within earshot about the wonders of next-generation networks. According to her it was now clear that with the increasing demand for mobile broadband access and Internet applications and services, emerging entrepreneurs are beginning to understand the need to move to the next generation of mobile networks, not only to offer higher data rates and more efficient systems, but to allow broadband Internet access able to support innovative multimedia services and applications using novel business models in all-IP networks. Enthusiastically, Gail told Carlitos how business travellers, using their mobile devices, would send their travel plans to a provider that would automatically create an itinerary for them, sending real time alerts in case of delays or other troubles or clever text services that would let a user see the sender and content details of text messages without having any pre-stored information on their mobile phones or opening their inboxes (Mobile Nordic, 2009). She also learned about a mobile advertising platform where "subscribers become the advertising channel themselves by assigning audio advertisements on incoming calls instead

of the standard beep-beep tone" (TonlaKazan, 2009), and an innovative new mobile payment solution that enables customers to complete simple financial transactions by mobile phone in Kenya aimed at mobile customers who do not have a bank account (Vodafone, 2007). More importantly, there is a growing awareness that these goals would be achieved if interoperability and roaming functions for heterogeneous terminals across different networks is assured (Etemad, 2008).

Not surprisingly, Gail's face and entire body language become quite animated when she starts delving into the technology itself. She explains to Carlitos how existing alternatives to 3G cellular technologies (say, CDMA, 2000 and UMTS) are appearing such as WiMAX (Worldwide interoperability for Microwave Access) and Long Term Evolution (LTE). Most new mobile devices have the ability to connect to these wireless networks while maintaining their cellular connections. This will open up new possible choices to mobile users. She says: "for example instead of calling at premium rates, you could use wireless broadband, either WiFi or WiMAX, to make voice calls using voice-over-IP (VoIP) applications like Skype; instead of sending a text message, you could choose to send free e-mail; rather than buying mobile content, you can use your wireless broadband connection to watch mobile content (YouTube) from a mobile phone browser."

Gail reckons it is not only the fact that governments throughout the world are addressing regulatory issues but a range of industry initiatives that contribute towards the erosion of the traditional telecommunications operators' hold on users. For example, in the Barcelona'09 congress Nokia announced an agreement with Skype in which its new N97 phone, the rival of the iPhone, will have preinstalled the popular VoIP application. Soon it will be even easier to call other users without using the traditional operators. And more recently, during the Barcelona 2010 congress, Skype, long seen as a threat to mobile voice revenues, was being embraced by some providers as a competitive differentiator as was the case of Verizon unveiling a partnership with Skype (Verizon Wireless, 2010). The wireless arena, Gail reminded Carlitos, is the most competitive segment of the telecommunications industry. It continues to grow with wireless service providers upgrading their networks from older to newer technologies. In this competitive environment, she said, the issue of standards could play a fundamental role in the development of future technologies (Wang et al., 2008). Fixed WiMax, Wi-Fi and Mobile WiMax access points are becoming abundant in many cities' commercial districts (Tedeschi, 2008) and other locations that congregate consumers in rather large numbers (PCWorld, 2009).

Gail is aware that WiMAX has suffered delays in implementation and in product certification. Standardization bodies such as WiMax Forum frenetically work to unveil a new standard that will offer 100Mbps to enable mobility and 1Gbps for fixed applications, as early as 2012 (Vaughan-Nichols, 2008). Another development that caught Gail's attention is the IEEE 802.20 standard. (Greenspan, 2008; Bolton, 2007). The purpose of this standard is the deployment of cost effective, spectrum efficient, ubiquitous, always–on and interoperable multi-vendor mobile broadband wireless access. This is addressed to end-user markets that include access to Internet, intranet and enterprise applications by mobile users and access to "infotainment" sources (Greenspan, 2008). Wireless operators will have the opportunity to deploy systems that can achieve very high rates and aggregate data capacity within a minimum amount of spectrum, so they will have to reduce the number of cells sites required in the network. The latter implies that the cost of deploying and operating such 802.20 networks will be reduced and the consumers will have access to high speed data services at more affordable prices. The IEEE 802.20 standard will fill the gap between cellular networks (low bandwidth and high mobility) and the IEEE 802 standard for wireless networks (high bandwidth and low mobility) and it will provide seamless integration among work, home

and mobile usage, offering transparent support of real-time and non-real-time applications.

Carlitos can't help but ask Gail "Are the big guys quiet? What are they planning?" Gail knows the large wireless providers are usually less dynamic in adopting new challenges, but they are also developing the new generation of their wireless access technologies. In that sense, they are preparing their current third generation (3G) networks for the transition to fourth generation (4G) systems, or their dreamed LTE, driven by proposals to reach 300Mbps downstream and 100Mbps upstream. With these fast speeds they promise the provision of television, telephone, and Internet services. Other proposals aligned with the existing third generation (3G) cellular technologies (CDMA) (Code Division Multiple Access, 2000), which together with the UMTS are predominant in the market, plan to establish themselves as the preferred option for future access technologies. In this space Ultra Mobile Broadband (UMB) (Vaughan-Nichols, 2008), which is based on TCP/IP, builds on CDMA 2000 and offers theoretical rates of 280 Mbps, is now projected. The work of standardization is expected to be completed in 2010, appearing commercially in 2012. Figure 3 exhibits a view of several standards aimed to be used for wireless access.

In spite of the promissory future Carlitos suspects the road ahead for integration between dissonant technologies and evermore heterogeneous customers is not going to be an easy one so he asks Gail: "Who is going to provide the means to harmonize this complex heterogeneous scenario? How can the future wireless broadband operators integrate their proposed solutions?".

CHALLENGES AND PROBLEMS

Despite the promising developments in the field of devices and high-speed access technologies, it was clear, even to someone as optimistic in the future of the telecommunications industry as Gail, that supporting systems and applied concepts is

Figure 3. A heterogeneous broadband wireless access landscape (Source: Beltran et al., 2010)

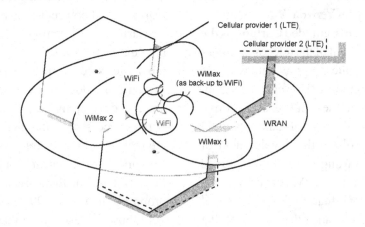

necessary to deploy the kind of solutions Carlitos is dreaming about. The wireless communications of the future will have to integrate multiple wireless access technologies in a seamless manner. Gail offers three concepts that Carlitos finds perplexing: dynamic pricing, policy-based management and cognitive wireless networks. She will have to do some explaining so that Carlitos can grasp the full potential of such techniques.

1. Dynamic pricing schemes

"Fundamentally" – says Gail - "the APs could offer short- term contracts to their users; furthermore, by using a suite of pricing schemes the price offered to the users may vary depending on some internal and as well as external selected context variables. In one word: prices won´t remain fixed for long". The increasing interest in wireless services and the necessity of the customers to have access to emergent technologies that can offer new services at reasonable cost, forces the Wireless Service Providers (WSPs) to find flexible and appropriate ways to price the services they offer. Carlitos wonders how is it possible to get other plan than a Flat-Rate pricing plan or, as a friend of his puts it, "all bits you can eat". Gail explains that wireless providers may now be trying new schemes such as Parameter-based pricing which

either sets the prices in a static way and users are charged in a predefined price for the service they use, as in Static pricing, or prefers to adopt a flexible way to pricing, as in Dynamic pricing (Gizelis & Vergados, 2010) .

Carlitos can see now that pricing, as known in other contexts, may now be plausible in the wireless market. In fact, users may be expected to discover the price of a service as is the case when auctions are used. In fact, Gail points out "in an auction the price of a service has not a standard value; this value has to be discovered through a bidding process. An auction is basically a negotiation process between the WSP and the users or between the WSPs themselves". The auctioned items may extend beyong provisioning the service; it may include ensure Quality of Service (QoS) to the subscribers by a Priority Call Admission Control (PCAC) mechanism (Yaipairoj & Harmantzis, 2006), or a Service Level Agreement (SLA) with de WSP that includes QoS parameters (Garg & Randhawa, 2002). Auctions may not be the only way to go. Another family of dynamic pricing schemes includes Priority pricing, where distinct services are characterized into different priority classes, which are defined by the WSP or are selected by the subscribers. In any case they can be modified during the service usage as in (Ozianyi, Ventura, & Golovins, 2008) whereby the WSPs allow their customers to specify their preferences on tariff structures according to their budgets.

And if multiple entities objectives have to be considered, Gail indicates to Carlitos' amazement, some researchers have developed pricing techniques based on the application of game theory. In game theoretic pricing, suitable for systems with multiple entities where each entity has its own objective (to maximize its profit), entities called agents differ in the amount of information they know about the system with users usually knowing better than the WSPs. Such asymmetry allows users to behave strategically forcing the WSPs to take such moves into consideration when setting up their pricing plans.

As the scenario where the services are offered, it is necessary periodical evaluations of the associated changes in this context. This predictable situation will force the WSPs, to constantly vary their predetermined rules (policies) that they use to assign prices each time in the most appropriate way for them. Consequently these prices will be changing dynamically. Prices and services are negotiated through agents that could use protocols such as the Resource Negotiation and Pricing Protocol, RNAP (Wang & Schulzrinne, 1999). In that sense the mode that WSPs assign prices under our vision is different from the short, but representative, research results presented in this section.

2. Policy-based management

Network's capability has to be continuously adapted to the variable environmental conditions and has to possess self-management functionality, requiring advances in reconfigurable elements (Demestichas et al., 2006). The self-management functionality is associated in recent research with the autonomic management of communications paradigm (Jennings et al., 2007). Autonomic communications address many problems; one of the most important is to reduce the complexity associated to managing large scale communications

networks. Autonomic communications address many problems; one of the most important is to reduce the complexity associated to managing large scale communications networks. Policy-based management is a critical facilitator for this vision that must be coordinated with the efficiency and scalability of the policy conflict analysis processes to cope with the dynamicity of such communications networks (Davy et al., 2008) and to enable flexible control of self-governed systems.

Carlitos is a little bit overwhelmed and wants to go back to his main train of thought so he asks Gail, once more, about the relationship between all these huge technological promises and the short-term contract? Accordingly, as the systems are more and more complex, policy based management demands a well-structured approach to policy rules and policy applications (Cox et al., 2008). "Well," says Gail, "I strongly believe that policy rules could be applied in many fields and of course, in the dynamic allocation of prices to the services that are requested by the users." In that sense these policies further to being focused on management functionality, could also exploit the knowledge they have about users' behavior and past usage and the offered services context to promote the dynamic allocation of prices, consequently facilitating the emergence of short-term contracts.

"How would that exactly happen?" interjects Carlitos. Gail explains that each provider should be able to manage its own pricing rules independently and it will be desirable that these rules be developed over open platforms that guarantee, not only the interoperability among the providers, which would facilitate the cooperation of providers to carry out services, but the implementation of their individual business strategies. Consequently, AP pricing policies could then be defined using the policy manager tool so that when a potential clients "walks" into the provider's coverage area a basic exchange can inform the client about the active policies for accessing the network facilities. Figure 4 shows how AP's information is presented to potential customers (users).

Figure 4. AP's information presented to potential customers

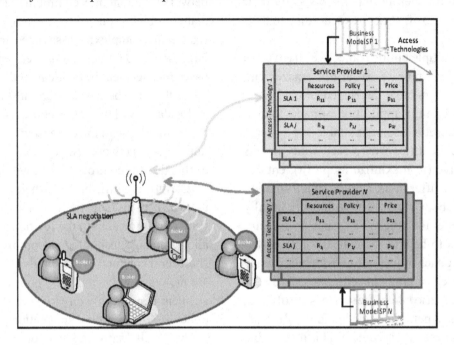

The depicted scenario is not currently possible due, aside the non-technical reasons, to the lack of service platforms (i.e., the instruments for service delivery) equipped with appropriate technology. New APs have to evolve the way service contracts have traditionally been offered, supporting "connection-as-you-go" or "spot contracts" as well as fine grained access services. This implies a technological evolution in their service platforms (OSS/BSS)[1] as well. The new service platforms should be equipped with a set of functionalities where APs describe the services they offer using different notations and formats. It is clear that the scenarios that we are envisaging should allow the concurrence of all imaginable types of service in terms of size, target market, type of offer and so on.

Therefore it wouldn't be realistic to assume such a unified way of using presentation formats, but it is necessary to maintain semantic interoperability between the offered services, which could be presented in different notations and formats. This a difficult problem that requires deep research

efforts to guarantee that different APs with different services and access technologies are able to use an open market, homogeneous structure which finally allows their potential customers to understand the different notations and formats which could be used in the depicted scenario.

Carlitos looks at Gail in disbelief: he needs examples. Gail smiles back and says "let's say a provider is able to keep track of the rate at which mobile users join its service in a given coverage area; under general market conditions such provider would possibly find it profitable to decrease its price if there are few users and the users are switching off at a low rate; it may also find it profitable if, on the contrary, there are many users and new users are switching on to the network at a rather high rate". But this is not the only example Gail uses to bring Carlitos' disbelief in line with what technology and autonomic communications might offer. She goes on to depict a situation in which two or more providers compete on a coverage area; their business strategies are supported by monitoring functions that allow them to know, minute to minute, the changing access prices being offered by their competitors. The application of policy-based management ideas would then allow a provider to decrease its price, at a controlled pace, if a competitor is setting lower or higher prices and its change rate is slow or fast (Baliosian, 2008). In fact, policies may include price structures (tariffs), security restrictions (who is allowed in), and resource allocation schemes (e.g., bandwidth). Carlitos still wants to have some concrete examples. Gails proceeds to present some scenarios that could further convince his friend about the feasibility of using policy-based techniques.The potential client (or an agent on her behalf) would analyze those policies which could be expressed on open formats (such as XML) and technologies (such as J2EE and Web services; Agrawal et al., 2005) and decide whether she would like to use the services. Figure 7 in the Appendix displays two examples of (pseudo)-coding pricing policies.

Carlitos can see now the enormous possibility opening for the market. He can foresee such dynamic mobile market scenario, if only, contrary to his current condition, short-term customer-provider relations are widely adopted. Of course, as a result of the expected vibrant competition among the services providers and the more flexible conditions on resources' availability and users' demand, service prices will be likely to change more dynamically. In spite of Gail's display of up-to-date technological knowledge, the optimistically technology-oriented Carlitos is less optimistic about the wisdom of markets; to satisfy his increasing curiosity he questions Gail again: "how far are these wonderful dreams from the harsh realities of the market?"

3. Cognitive wireless networks

As Gail really enjoys learning about trends and new developments in the industry, she tells Carlitos of a very active research field that has recently proposed new strategies that could be applied to solving the problem of lack of spectrum for emerging services. She talks about adaptive, reconfigurable wireless networks, also known as cognitive networks (Thomas et al., 2007), which can become the technology that facilitates the transition "beyond the 3G (B3G)" (Xie et al., 2008). In cognitive wireless networks (Sun et al., 2006; Ghandi et al., 2007; Xing et al., 2007), licensed users can offer dynamic sharing spectrum opportunities to unlicensed users or service providers, thus improving the efficiency in spectrum usage. Gail would expect that the battle for sharing the spectrum derives in competitive prices, which in turn would be a facilitator of new access opportunities to secondary (unlicensed) users (Niyato & Hossain, 2008b).

What really has Gail pondering about the future success of cognitive networks is their capability of continuously adapting to changing environmental conditions and users' needs. In fact, elements and terminals are reconfigurable and possess the intelligence to choose the best configuration, adapting themselves to environmental conditions. The same principles, though, translate quite well to the day-to-day operational realities of the telecommunications scenarios envisioned by Carlitos: organisations operating in a dynamic business landscape have thus 'the ability to integrate, build, and reconfigure internal and external competencies to address rapidly-changing environments' (Teece et al., 1997).

Complementary to the idea of a cognitive wireless networks concept, the network operator could select the best among the "cooperating networks", which operate with different access technologies, to guarantee the best service offer to its customers. In modern wireless networks, the service providers dynamically will compete with each other to offer wireless service to mobile users in a very dynamic scenario.

In general cognitive networks establish their behavior in different ways; using external triggers (based on the environment, context, etc.) as well as others principles (based on policies, rules, etc.), experience and knowledge. Cognitive networks need "cognitive terminals" to dynamically match the best technology in a seamless, transparent and reliable manner through appropriate management functionality that takes into account the context, goals and policies as well as the experience and knowledge of the user.

4.   Heterogeneous access

Gail is also convinced that heterogeneous wireless access networks should provide seamless services to the end user and freedom of movement between different geographical areas. The network management systems that currently support these facilities need to be dramatically improved to obtain a new architecture, which enables the users to accomplish their tasks independently of the device being used, the chosen media or the underlying technology. A novel autonomic architecture could dynamically synthesize the context knowledge, the environment and other characteristics (capabilities, constraints, etc) in order to adapt its network functionality to that which will be required. Every time the systems are more complex, thus policy based management mechanisms demand a well structured approach to their policy rules. In that sense, these rules should exhibit the knowledge that the APs have about users' behavior to assign dynamically prices, what facilitates the emergence of short-term contracts. Finally, the efficient allocation of resources becomes even more critical for success. In particular, given the seemingly scarce radio spectrum, radio resource allocation and competitive spectrum sharing rise as key issues in the provision of new and advanced services at high rates in a cost-efficient manner (Niyato & Hossain, 2007). Figure 8 in the Appendix shows the envisioned multi-provider/multi-technology access scenario for users and APs using short-term contracts.

POSSIBLE SOLUTIONS: A CASE FOR A NEW MARKET STRUCTURE

The news coming from Barcelona made it clear to Carlitos that the battle for technological supremacy in the next generation of wireless networks has two main players: WiMax and LTE. WiMax is promising many things and many players, especially in the computer industry, are happy to listen to those promises and become their advocates. LTE, on the other hand, is being endorsed by the gigantic wireless telephony companies.

As Carlitos watches the TV-news, he listens to an expert claim: "LTE is still in very early stages" or yet another announcing: "*t*he whole city of Portland, Oregon, US, is covered with WiMax". He is not done yet wondering what would become of this and other investments given the financially troubled world of the end of the first decade of the XXI century, when he sees another headline: "Motorola's executive says the current economic conditions may give WiMax more foothold in the market in the longer term" (Palmer, 2008). Experts gathered in Barcelona forecast the adoption of LTE to be commercialized in the mid/long term (Vaughan-Nichols, 2008) given that LTE is being built on existing infrastructure, and the companies expect to see first deployments working as of 2015 attracting more customers than rivals such as WiMAX (Palmer, 2008).

If WiMax and LTE were the only two developments in the forefront of the mobile telecommunications new wave, a picture could emerge in which new entrants could offer mobile services in competition with established operators. Carlitos would be keen on finding a way to connect his always-changing electronic communication gadgets to any provider who offers him an attractive service package. As he really dislikes long-term commitments to service providers, he would like to do business with any provider capable of accommodating his demand on a very short-term basis, or perhaps, just "on the spot". After all, credit and billing systems have been developed to a point whereby transactions and approvals don't take long.

As for device intelligence WiFi-enabled phones automatically use WiFi connections before using cellular connections for internet usage, showing that phones are somewhat intelligent and seem to be selective about using the cheapest connection. "What if" - Carlitos wonders - "while I walk or wait for my train, I can browse these new providers that promise so many things, and while browsing I can also learn about their services and prices?" Even more challenging is the thought of some kind of automated decision maker – well, call it software – that, once installed on his mobile device, acts on his behalf to decide which provider to get connected to. Such software piece would have to be fed with personal information that basically identifies who Carlitos is, or at least who he is when it comes to purchasing telecommunications services.

One thing seems obvious at this stage: Carlitos is still a potential customer of the fat cat. Large telcos and their mobile subsidiaries will try to keep him locked-in to their service packages. Increasingly telecommunications providers see in next-generation networks the sources of the promised service and network convergence, which in turn promise cost reductions. But their expectations do not stop there; Carlitos will see that service packets will include not only traditional voice services but also video, possibly TV service, Internet access and others, all fully or partially produced by the same company that owns the pipes.

On the other hand, new and traditional providers (Sprint, 2009) are pushing their way into the market. Let's take WiMax as an example. Carlitos might soon be running into quite a few of those new providers who decided to give WiMax a go and deployed urban and suburban access networks, sometimes being also the back up to WiFi hotspots. Such hybrid facilities could erect themselves as alternatives to those new mobile LTE deployments, in fact competing with them in a market hungry for bandwidth. Contrary to the non-open, proprietary

characteristics of mobile networks, WiMax operators might find it to their advantage to cooperate to offer users' devices a common language that devices and access points can speak to ease the process by which users become their customers for the time they need it.

Wonderful! Carlitos only needs a few key strokes here and there to describe his requirements to the decision-making software; such information would inform the software of his preferred services, how much he would be willing to pay at a given time of the day for a minute or so of connection, and perhaps his preferred call destinations. Actually, Carlitos will have to spend quite a bit of time feeding the desired requirements to his device, and even before that, he would have to learn the twists and tricks of relating to the system. In the end, if operators managed to agree on a standardized way for users' devices to treat the pricing and condition information about the operators' plans, then Carlitos would probably have cleverly invested his time as eventually he would not have to worry about price comparisons, price search, better deals and the like. Such scenario is going to demand a serious thought by the new providers who would certainly benefit to the extent that they can successfully challenge the established operators and their new technology. Carlitos would probably wonder "does this means that the prices I pay would be clearly cheaper that they used to be?" At any rate it was becoming clear that the role of the different actors (users, network providers, content providers) will dramatically change in the near future. Figure 5 informs how to match the needs of the users to the AP's offers.

Users may have heterogeneous devices with a minimum set of capabilities or more sophisticated ones in terms of support of different access capabilities, and different media. Naturally, users will be restricted to the functional capabilities of their terminals. Users don't need to be concerned with the negotiation process carried out with the APs. We have to admit that in these complex

Figure 5. Mapping of user's needs to AP's offers

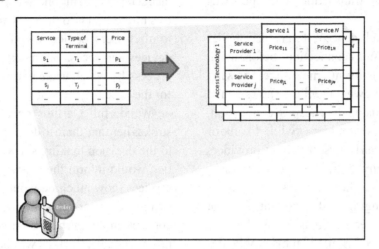

scenarios we can encounter users with a varied level of expertise. Therefore we assume that potential customers of APs would only need a few key strokes here and there to describe their requirements to embedded system intelligence (software agent); that is an access mechanism capable to support the user in their interactions with the APs. The information the user provides to the software agent or broker would help to draft a consumption profile (Sandvine, 2010, pp. 22-23) in which preferred services, willingness to pay, and preferred call destinations, among others, are specified.

Thanks to the possibility of comparing access capabilities users will have the service that best fits their needs. Conceptually the idea is that the access support is entrusted to adapt the user's needs represented in the table on the left side to the service offers represented in the tables on the right side of the diagram. The broker functionality shown represents the capabilities of the access support we have described. In this multi-provider competitive concurrence scenario, it is also fundamental to have mechanisms to allow users and providers to know and to enforce the terms of the short-term contract. It is necessary to regulate the service provisioning and to pro-

vide assurance for this process by means of the appropriate service level agreements (SLAs) and enforcement techniques in a dynamic short-term contract environment.

What Carlitos has been used to see out there is two or three mobile operators displaying all their advertising might everywhere he goes. He would not walk a few blocks before watching a large add on the back of a bus announcing a new mobile phone and a new service deal or he would only need to look up to some of the building tops to see huge billboards telling him to join them with no entry fee. Carlitos knows that once he signs up, he is "in", that is, locked-"in".

As networks are upgraded, transitioning towards all-IP networks, operators start resembling more like platforms that convey multiple types of users. Carlitos knows he is a primary consumer of services produced "on the other side" of the network. His technological knowledge allows him to realize that, even though his network operator is providing the basic services for him, he is also able to use such connection to get access to services provided by other, non-related sources. In other words, his mobile provider is not his entertainment provider. In fact, Carlitos is now becoming part of a market built on a platform that serves two sides: providers of content and other services and consumers (Rochet & Tirole, 2004).

Does Carlitos really care whether now some people think of this as a new market structure? Well, the point is that Carlitos has been able to carry on with many of his everyday activities because he can access his free e-mail account and do Internet searches at no cost. Service providers make sure they make money while providing such free services over the Internet. With Internet access also possible through his present and future wireless connections, Carlitos is part of a market that does no longer resemble the one-provider, one-service market of the past but instead a platform that attracts sellers and buyers with no unified or single revenue model. In fact, sometimes one service is for free, but sometimes Carlitos has to pay for another. Figure 6 depicts cross-layer management: an architecture that links together business objectives with configuration parameters of the underlying networks.

In this mixed scenario a key enabling factor is the capability to set prices. This means dynamic prices adapted to the context of the service. When the price of a service is based on static flat rates an unbalance is created between providers and users. Such a situation doesn't stimulate improvements in the quality of the services or the creation of a clear competitive market that allows significantly reduced prices for these services. A static solution does not take into account the service context and particularly the availability of resources and, of course, it does not include ways to keep users informed about the evolution of the current prices.

In this sense, policy rules can facilitate the dynamic setting of prices for the services requested. Policy-based management techniques can therefore be used as a promoter of dynamic price allocation and a facilitator of short-term contracts. These polices can't be manually created by system administrators, instead, policies have to be derived (refined) from business/revenue level objectives. The authoring mechanism of such policies has to be supported by a management model that establishes relationships between regulatory indicators, business indicators, SLA indicators, network and service management objectives and enforceable

Figure 6. Cross-layer management models

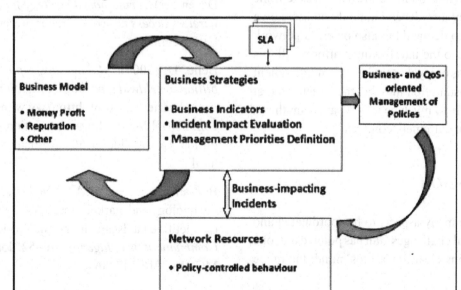

policies. *In other words, it is desirable to have a cross-layer management, which links together business objectives with configuration parameters of the underlying networks. This cross-layer management would be of vital importance for APs, because it would be a fundamental revenue management tool.*

One characteristic of such two-sided market structure is that the market is essentially affected by cross network effects between the two sides. This just describes the external effect over one group, for instance Carlitos and millions like him, when the size of the other group increases (Yoo, 2006). In just one example, an increasing number of service providers use the Internet to sell services such as VoIP, traditionally the domain of telephone companies. Consumers use their connection to their access provider to have access to services and contents. Determining the allocation of prices becomes a complex issue. In fact, as (Yoo, 2006) asserts: "the theory of two-sided markets implies that the retail prices charged to consumers and websites, whether in the form of fixed fees or variables fees, need not reflect the benefits or costs of either side by itself", we should expect subscription and usage fees to probably be more difficult to determine because they also depend not only on users own sensitivity to demand but also on cross-network effects, due to the interlinking platform. All this shows that as enjoyable as Carlitos entertainment service consumption may be, the structures that determines how much he would pay, if anything, is becoming extremely complex.

CONCLUSION

Despite the many aspects to be coordinated and the technical challenges Gail has pointed out, one thing remains clear in Carlitos' mind: the range of emerging networking services facilitated by broadband wireless access technologies are very promising; new enabling technologies which also include cognitive networks, policy-based network management, and crucially, dynamic pricing mechanisms will push both customers and APs towards short-term relationships that will evolve into new business and market structures. A completely new way of doing business, necessarily compatible with existing ways of accessing wireless access services, will emerge: Carlitos' way.

ACKNOWLEDGMENT

We want to acknowledge Farhaan Mirza for valuable input that improved the timeliness of some data and facts presented in this paper.

REFERENCES

Agrawal, D., Lee, K. W., & Lobo, J. (2005). Policy-based management of networked computing systems. *IEEE Communications Magazine*, 69–75. doi:10.1109/MCOM.2005.1522127

Baliosian, J., Borba, M., & Serrat, J. (2008, December). *A rule-based strategy for pricing in wireless access networks*. Paper presented at the UPC Seminar.

Belic, D. (2009). *Mobile subscriptions hit 3.3 billion worldwide or 50% of global population*. Retrieved from http://www.intomobile. com/2007/12/03/mobile-subscriptions-hit-33- billion- worldwide-or-50-of-global-population. html

Beltran, F., Gutierrez, J. A., & Melus, J. L. (2010). Technology and market conditions towards a new competitive landscape in mobile services. *IEEE Communications Magazine*, 46–52. doi:10.1109/ MCOM.2010.5473864

Bolton, W., Yang, X., & Guizani, M. (2007). IEEE 802.20: Mobile broadband wireless access. *IEEE Wireless Communications, 14*(1), 84–95. doi:10.1109/MWC.2007.314554

Cox, G. S., Strassner, J., Neuman de Souza, J., Raymer, D., Samudrala, S., Jennings, B., & Barrett, K. (2008). An enhanced policy model to enable autonomic communications. In *Proceedings of the Fifth IEEE Workshop on Engineering of Autonomic and Autonomous Systems* (p. 184).

Davy, S., Jennings, B., & Strassner, J. (2008). Efficient policy conflict analysis for autonomic network management. In *Proceedings of the Fifth IEEE Workshop on Engineering of Autonomic and Autonomous Systems* (p. 16).

Demestichas, P., Dimitrakopoulos, G., & Strassner, J. (2006). Introducing reconfigurability and cognitive network concepts in the wireless world. *IEEE Vehicular Technology Magazine, 1*(2), 32–39. doi:10.1109/MVT.2006.283572

Etemad, K. (2008). Overview of mobile WiMAX technology and evolution. *IEEE Communications Magazine, 46*(10), 31–40. doi:10.1109/MCOM.2008.4644117

European Commission. (2010). *Telecoms: Mobile phone customers entitled to protection from data-roaming "bill-shock" as from 1st March 2010.* Brussels, Belgium: European Commission.

European Union. (2007). *EU regulation on roaming.* Retrieved from http://ec.europa.eu/information_society/ activities/roaming/roaming_regulation/index_en.htm

Gandhi, S., Buragohain, C., Lili, C., Zheng, H., & Suri, S. (2007, April). A general framework for wireless spectrum auctions. In *Proceedings of the IEEE International Symposium New Frontiers Dynamic Spectrum Access Networks* (pp. 22-33).

Garg, R., & Randhawa, R. S. (2002). A SLA framework for QoS provisioning and dynamic capacity allocation. In *Proceedings of the 10th International Workshop on Quality of Service* (pp. 129-137).

Gizelis, C. A., & Vergados, D. D. (2010). A survey of pricing schemes in wireless networks. *IEEE Communications Surveys and Tutorials, 13*(1), 126–145. doi:10.1109/SURV.2011.060710.00028

Greenspan, A., Klerer, M., Tomcik, J., Canchi, R., & Wilson, J. (2008). IEEE 802.20: Mobile broadband wireless access for the twenty-first century. *IEEE Communications Magazine, 46*(7), 56–63. doi:10.1109/MCOM.2008.4557043

Jennings, B., van der Meer, S., Balasubramaniam, S., Botvich, D. O., Foghlu, M., Donnelly, W., & Strassner, J. (2007). Towards autonomic management of communications networks. *IEEE Communications Magazine, 45*(10), 112–121. doi:10.1109/MCOM.2007.4342833

Kang, C. (2008). *Do text messages cost too much?* Retrieved from http://voices.washingtonpost.com/posttech/2008/09/lawmaker_consumer_group _demand.html

Kumar, K. R., & Renjish, K. V. Y. H. (2008). Techno-economic analysis of international mobile roaming. *IEEE Wireless Communications, 15*(3), 73–80. doi:10.1109/MWC.2008.4547526

Lawson, S. (2009). *Clearwire WiMax coming to 10 cities on Sept. 1.* Retrieved from http://www.pcworld.com/businesscenter/article/169511/clearwire_wimax_coming_to _10_cities_on_sept_1.html

Lenhart, A., Ling, R., Campbell, S., & Purcell, K. (2010). *Teens and mobile phones.* Retrieved from http://www.pewinternet.org/Reports/2010/Teens-and- Mobile- Phones.aspx

Mobile Nordic. (2009). *Press release.* http://www.nordicid.com/en/press-centr/press- relizy.html

Niyato, D., & Hossain, E. (2007). Integration of WiMax and WiFi: Optimal pricing for bandwidth sharing. *IEEE Communications Magazine*, *45*(5), 140–146. doi:10.1109/MCOM.2007.358861

Niyato, D., & Hossain, E. (2008). Competitive pricing in heterogeneous wireless access networks: Issues and approaches. *IEEE Network*, *22*(6), 4–11. doi:10.1109/MNET.2008.4694168

Niyato, D., & Hossain, E. (2008). Spectrum trading in cognitive networks: A market- equilibrium-based approach. *IEEE Wireless Communications*, *15*(6), 71–80. doi:10.1109/MWC.2008.4749750

Ogren, E. (2009). *Sprint announces major WiMax expansion*. Retrieved from http://www.informationweek.com/blog/main/archives/2009/08/sprint_announce. html;jsession id=R45ED233R MONZQE1GHPCKHWATMY32JVN

Ozianyi, G. V., Ventura, N., & Golovins, E. (2008). A novel pricing approach to support QoS in 3G networks. *Computer Networks*, *52*(7), 1433–1450. doi:10.1016/j.comnet.2007.12.011

Palmer, J. (2008). *Mobile broadband next-gen battle*. Retrieved from http://news.bbc.co.uk/2/hi/technology/7896686.stm

Rochet, J.-C., & Tirole, J. (2004). *Two-sided markets: An overview*. Retrieved from http://faculty.haas.berkeley.edu/hermalin/rochet_tirole.pdf

Sandvine. (2010). *Intelligent broadband networks: Mobile Internet phenomena report*. Retrieved from http://www.sandvine.com

Stross, R. (2008). *What carriers aren't eager to tell you about texting*. Retrieved from http://www.nytimes.com/2008/12/28/business/28digi.html?_r=2&ref=technology

Sun, J., Modiano, E., & Zheng, L. (2006). Wireless channel allocation using an auction algorithm. *IEEE Journal on Selected Areas in Communications*, *24*(5), 1085–1096. doi:10.1109/JSAC.2006.872890

Tedeschi, B. (2008). *Taking your wi-fi cafe with you, but not everywhere*. Retrieved from http://www.nytimes.com/2008/10/23/technology/personaltech/23 smart.html?_r=2&pagewanted=1&8dpc

Teece, D. J., Pisano, G., & Shuen, A. (1997). Dynamic capabilities and strategic management. *Strategic Management Journal*, *18*(7), 509–533. doi:10.1002/(SICI)1097-0266(199708)18:7<509::AID-SMJ882>3.0.CO;2-Z

Thomas, R., Friend, D., DaSilva, L., & MacKenzie, A. (2007). Cognitive networks. In Arslan, H. (Ed.), *Cognitive radio, software defined radio, and adaptive wireless systems* (pp. 17–41). New York, NY: Springer. doi:10.1007/978-1-4020-5542-3_2

TonlaKazan. (2009). *TonlaKazan a new mobile advertising platform*. Retrieved from http://www.slideshare.net/anafikir/tonlakazan-a-new-mobile-advertising-platform- presentation

Vaughan-Nichols, S. J. (2008). Mobile WiMAX: The next wireless battle ground. *IEEE Computer*, *41*(6), 16–18. doi:10.1109/MC.2008.201

Verizon Wireless. (2010). *Version Wireless with Skype Mobile*. Retrieved from http://phones.verizonwireless.com/skypemobile/

Vodafone. (2007). *Safaricom and Vodafone launch M-PESA, a new mobile payment service*. Retrieved from http://www.vodafone.com/content/index/press/group_press_releases/2007/safaricom_and_ vodafone.html

Wang, F., Ghosh, A., Sankaran, C., Fleming, P., Hsieh, F., & Benes, S. (2008). Mobile WiMAX systems: Performance and evolution. *IEEE Communications Magazine*, *46*(10), 41–49. doi:10.1109/MCOM.2008.4644118

Wang, X., & Schulzrinne, H. (1999, June). RNAP: A resource negotiation and pricing protocol. In *Proceedings of the International Workshop on Network and Operating System Support for Digital Audio and Video*, Basking Ridge, NJ (pp. 77-93).

Xie, B. M., Kumar, A., & Agrawal, D. P. (2008). Enabling multiservice on 3G and beyond: Challenges and future directions. *IEEE Wireless Communications*, *15*(3), 66–72. doi:10.1109/MWC.2008.4547525

Xing, Y., Chandramouli, R., & Cordeiro, C. M. (2007). Price dynamics in competitive agile spectrum access markets. *IEEE Journal on Selected Areas in Communications*, *25*(3), 613–621. doi:10.1109/JSAC.2007.070411

Yaipairoj, S., & Harmantzis, F. C. (2006). Auction-based congestion pricing for wireless data services. In *Proceedings of the IEEE International Conference on Communications*, Istanbul, Turkey (pp. 1045-1050).

Yoo, C. S. (2006). Network neutrality and the economics of congestion. *The Georgetown Law Journal*, *94*(6), 1847–1900.

ENDNOTES

[1] Operation Support Systems/Business Support Systems

APPENDIX

This is an example of some intuitive market rules that deal with supply and demand and are a proof of the usefulness of policy-based techniques (Figure 7 and Figure 8):

- *if few_users and users_decreasing_slow then decrease_price_slow*
- *if lots_users and users_increasing_fast then increase_price_fast*

And this is another example that focuses on competition among a number of providers (Baliosian et al, 2008):

- *if competitor_price_lower and competitor_price_decreasing_slow then decrease_price_slow*
- *if competitor_price_higher and competitor_price_increasing_fast then increase_price_fast*

Figure 7. Two examples of policy-based pricing decision

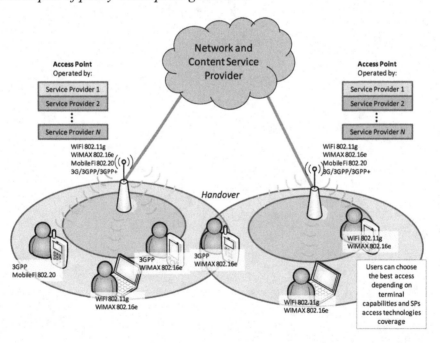

Figure 8. Envisioned multi-provider/multi-technology access services scenario

As in the case of virtual mobile operators, several APs share the same infrastructure location and possibly some systems as well. The ability to offer different access technologies allows the AP to offer different access services to specific targets, widening the potential number of customers. Different users equipped with different types of terminals that are under the coverage area of the shared service space (common access point) select one among the different APs. The integration of heterogeneous wireless access network technologies allow multimode wireless devices, equipped with multiple interfaces, to use appropriate networks that meet their service and cost requirements in any location and under any context circumstance.

The competition among APs sharing the same access area has beneficial side effects. In fact, from an environmental point of view, the use of a common location for the radio frequency front-end reduces the visual impact that causes the proliferation of antennas. On the other hand, a site which is no longer pre-assigned to a given provider allows fair competition among providers, since anyone can use the same "strategic location" without any special advantage. This is especially attractive for new virtual operators, since the cost of new incumbents is clearly reduced and consequently the prices to users could be lower. In this scenario the reconfiguration of the available resources should happen in a much faster time scale to address the immediacy of the multi-provider challenge.

This work was previously published in International Journal of Business Data Communications and Networking, Volume 7, Issue 3, edited by Varadharajan Sridhar and Debashis Saha, p.p 51-69, copyright 2011 by IGI Publishing (an imprint of IGI Global)

Chapter 13
Secure Video Transmission Against Black Hole Attack in MANETs

M. Umaparvathi
Anna University of Technology, India

Dharmishtan K. Varughese
Karpagam College of Engineering, India

ABSTRACT

Mobile Adhoc Networks (MANETs) are open to a wide range of attacks due to their unique characteristics like dynamic topology, shared medium, absence of infrastructure, and resource constraints. Data packets sent by a source node may reach destination through a number of intermediate nodes. In the absence of security mechanism, it is easy for an intermediate node to intercept or modify the messages, thus attacking the normal operation of MANET. One such attack is Black hole attack, in which, a malicious node called Black hole node attracts all the traffic of the network towards itself, and discards all the packets without forwarding them to the intended recipients. This paper evaluates the performance of Adhoc on-demand Distance Vector (AODV) and its multi-path variant Adhoc On-demand Multi-path Distance Vector (AOMDV) routing protocols under black hole attack. Non-cryptographic solutions Secure Blackhole AODV (SBAODV) and Secure Blackhole AOMDV (SBAOMDV) have been proposed to mitigate the effect of black hole attack. Through NS-2 simulations, the performance of the proposed protocols with video streaming is analyzed. The results show that the proposed solutions provide better performance than the conventional AODV and AOMDV.

1. INTRODUCTION

A Mobile Ad Hoc Network (MANET) is an autonomous system of mobile nodes connected by wireless links to form a communication network. The challenge in the design of protocol architec-

tures for MANETs is to provide a certain level of Quality of Service (QoS) in information transfer using the limited network resources. This design goal is further constrained by the unreliable physical channel, the mobility of the nodes, and the lack of infrastructure for network coordina-

DOI: 10.4018/978-1-4666-2026-1.ch013

tion. To meet the QoS requirements for real-time data communication, some coordination of the channel is needed, but centralized coordination is not feasible in MANETs. Furthermore, since a MANET is a dynamic and distributed entity, the optimal control of MANET should also be dynamic and adaptive.

In a MANET, there are no basic network devices, such as routers or access points. Data transfer among nodes is realized by means of multiple hops. Every node in MANET is not only serving as a single terminal but also acts as a router to establish a route. When a source node intends to transfer data to a destination node, packets are transferred through the intermediate nodes. Thus, searching for and quickly establishing a route from a source to a destination node is an important issue for MANETs. The currently available routing protocols are mainly categorized into proactive routing protocols and reactive routing protocols.

In a proactive routing protocol, every node proactively searches for routes to other nodes. The nodes, periodically, exchange routing messages, in order to ensure the correctness and freshness of the information in the routing table. DSDV (Destination Sequence Distance Vector) and OLSR (Optimized Link State Routing Protocol) are two popular proactive routing protocols for MANETs. Each node in a MANET is limited to a certain power and bandwidth, thus, continuous transmission of routing messages would lead to congestion of the network.

In a reactive routing protocol, a route is searched and established only when two nodes intend to transfer data; and therefore, it is also called an on-demand routing protocol, such as Ad hoc On-Demand Distance Vector (AODV) (Perkins et al., 2003) or Dynamic Source Routing(DSR) (Johnson et al., 2004). A source node generally broadcasts a route request message to the entire network by means of flooding, in order to search for and establish a route to the destination node.

The multi-path extension to the well-defined single path routing protocol AODV is referred as Ad hoc On-demand Multi-path Distance Vector (AOMDV). This protocol computes multiple loop-free and link-disjoint paths. Loop freedom is guaranteed by using a notion of "advertised hop-count" in AOMDV.

Most of these routing protocols rely on cooperation between nodes due to the lack of a centralized administration and assume that all nodes are trustworthy and well-behaved. However, in a hostile environment, a malicious node can launch routing attacks to disrupt routing operations. Thus, MANETs often suffer from security attacks because of their specification such as open medium, dynamic topology, lack of central monitoring and management, cooperative algorithms and no clear defense mechanism.

One such active Interruption attack in MANET on-demand routing protocol is the black hole attack, in which, the malicious node waits for the neighbors to initiate a Route Request (RREQ) packet. As the node receives the RREQ packet, it will immediately send a false Route Reply (RREP) packet with a modified higher sequence number. So, the source node assumes that the malicious node is having the fresh route towards the destination. The source node ignores the RREP packet received from other nodes and begins to send the data packets through the malicious node. Thus, the malicious node takes all the routes towards itself. It does not allow forwarding any packet anywhere. This attack is called a black hole as it swallows all data packets (Dokurer, 2006).

This paper analyses the effect of black hole attack on the reactive routing protocol, AODV and its multi-path variant AOMDV through simulation. And a non-cryptographic solution is proposed to reduce the impact of black hole attacks in the routing protocols AODV and AOMDV. The paper is organized as follows: In the next following section, Section 2, the previous work related to the black hole attack on AODV routing protocol is discussed. Section 3 describes the background of the protocol AODV, and Section 4 describes the multi-path on-demand routing protocol AOMDV, This follows Section 5, which discusses the characteristics of black hole attack. Section 6 details about the tool kit for the evaluation of Video transmission in MANET. The proposed method is provided with pseudo codes in Section 7. The analyses the effects of black hole attack in the two routing protocols AODV and AOMDV through simulations is given in Section 8. The future scope of this proposed work is given in Section 9.

2. RELATED WORK

In literature many solutions were proposed to counter-measure the black hole attack in MANETs. Some of the solutions are discussed.

The solution proposed in, "DPRAODV: A dynamic learning system against black hole attack in AODV based MANET" (Payal et al., 2009; Sen et al., 2011) detects and prevents the black hole attack in AODV routing protocol. Here, the black hole is prevented by comparing the sequence number in the RREP with a threshold value. If the sequence number is higher than the threshold value, then, the node which has sent the RREP is considered as the malicious node. The value of the threshold value is dynamically updated in the time interval. The node that is detected as the anomaly is black listed and ALARM packet is sent so that the further RREP packet from that malicious node is discarded. This solution increases the average end to end delay and normalized routing overhead.

In Lee (2002), the authors introduced a solution against black hole attack, which is independent on the sequence number of the RREP. In this approach, when an intermediate node receives the RREP it not only sends RREPs to the source node but also sends Route Confirmation Requests (CREQ) to its next-hop node towards the destination node. After receiving the CREQ, the next-hop node looks up

its cache for a route to the destination. If it has the route, it sends the Route Confirmation Reply (CREP) to the source. Upon receiving the CREP, the source node can confirm the validity of the path by comparing the path in RREP and the one in CREP. If both are matched, the source node decides that the route is correct. One drawback of this approach is that it cannot avoid the black hole attack in which two consecutive nodes work in collusion, that is, when the next-hop node is a colluding attacker sending CREPs that support the incorrect path. Similar solution is provided in Zhang et al. (2009).

Subathra (2010) proposed a solution to prevent the same black hole attack in another reactive routing protocol, Dynamic Source Routing (DSR). In Al-Shurman (2004), the author proposed a solution that requires a source node to wait until a RREP packet arrives from more than two nodes. Upon receiving multiple RREPs, the source node checks whether there is a shared hop or not. If there is, the source node decides that the route is safe. The main drawback of this solution is that it introduces time delay, because it must wait until multiple RREPs arrive.

In Kurosawa et al. (2006), the authors analyzed the black hole attack and showed that a malicious node must increase the destination sequence number sufficiently to convince the source node that the route provided is sufficiently enough. Based on this analysis, the authors propose a statistical based anomaly detection approach to detect the black hole attack, based on differences between the destination sequence numbers of the received RREPs. The key advantage of this approach is that it can detect the attack at low cost without introducing extra routing traffic, and it does not require modification of the existing protocol. However, false positives are the main drawback of this approach due to the nature of anomaly detection.

The paper Deng, Li, and Agrawal (2002) proposed a solution for single blackhole node detection. This method is almost similar to the method proposed in Leo (2002). When the source node receives the reply message, it does not send the data packets right away, but extracts the next hop information (NHN) from the reply packet and then sends a 'Further- Request' to the next hop. By receiving it, the node sends back the 'Further Reply' message, indicating that, it has a route to the destination node. Limitation of this proposal is that it would not be able to identify that NHN works cooperatively with the black hole node and sends back false 'Further Reply'.

Tamilselvan and Sankaranarayanan (2007) proposed a solution with the enhancement of the AODV protocol which avoids multiple black holes in the group. A technique is given to identify multiple black holes cooperating with each other and discover the safe route by avoiding the attacks. It was assumed in the solution that nodes are already authenticated and therefore can participate in the communication. It uses Fidelity table, where, every node, that is participating, is given a fidelity level that will provide reliability to that node. Any node having '0' value is considered as malicious node and is eliminated. A valid route is selected among the received RREP based on the threshold value. After getting the acknowledgement the fidelity level of the node is updated proving it safe and reliable.

The solution proposed in Dokurer (2007) uses a RREP caching mechanism. This assumes that, as the black hole sends the RREP message without checking its routing table, it is more likely the first RREP to arrive the source. So, the solution simply ignores the first RREP and selects the next RREP with highest sequence number. But, this decision may not be true always. For instance, the first RREP may be from a good node which is nearer to the source and the second RREP may be from the black hole node, which is far away from the source node. In this case, the solution ignores the correct RREP and selects the incorrect RREP.

Cai et al. (2010) provided a solution to black hole attack based on cross layer design based on

DSR routing protocol. A cryptographic based solution for black hole attack is given in Zhao and Zhou (2009), which consumes much of the computation power of the MANET nodes.

Thus, all the proposed solutions in the literature, either considers the RREP sequence number or the multiple RREPs. So, they will be suitable only for particular situations. They may produce false decisions in some other situations. Thus, this paper proposes a protocol which considers both the sequence number in the RREP and the arrival time of the RREP to choose the correct path without much overhead in the routing.

3. OVERVIEW OF AODV

AODV (Perkins et al., 2003) is a reactive routing protocol designed for a mobile ad hoc network. AODV is a state-of-the-art routing protocol that adopts a purely *reactive* strategy. It sets up a route on-demand at the start of a communication session, and uses it till it breaks, after which a new route setup is initiated (Gianni, 2008). In AODV, when a source node S wants to send a data packet to a destination node D and does not have a route to D, it initiates route discovery by broadcasting a route request (RREQ) to its neighbors. The immediate neighbors (I, J, K, L and M) who receive this RREQ rebroadcast the same RREQ to their neighbors. This process is repeated until the RREQ reaches the destination node. Upon receiving the first arrived RREQ, the destination node sends a route reply (RREP) to the source node through the reverse path where the RREQ arrived. The same RREQ that arrives later will be ignored by the destination node. The route discovery process of this protocol is shown in Figure 1.

In addition, AODV enables intermediate nodes that have sufficiently fresh routes (with destination sequence number equal or greater than the one in the RREQ) to generate and send an RREP to the source node. For example, if the intermediate

Figure 1. Route discovery process of AODV routing protocol

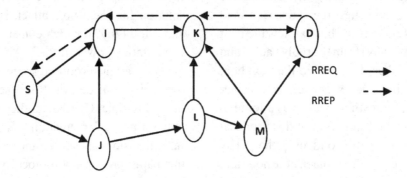

node K has the fresh route with highest sequence number to the destination, upon receiving the RREQ, it sends the RREP to the source. This situation is shown in Figure 2.

4. OVERVIEW OF AOMDV

The main idea in AOMDV (Samir et al., 2006) is to compute multiple paths during route discovery. It is designed primarily for highly dynamic ad hoc networks where link failures and route breaks occur frequently. When single path on-demand routing protocol such as AODV is used in such networks, a new route discovery is needed in response to every route break. Each route discovery is associated with high overhead and latency. This inefficiency can be avoided by having multiple redundant paths. Now, a new route discovery is

needed only when all paths to the destination break. To keep track of multiple routes, the routing entries for each destination contain a list of the next-hops along with the corresponding hop counts. All the next hops have the same sequence number. For each destination, a node maintains the advertised hop count, which is defined as the maximum hop count for all the paths. This is the hop count used for sending route advertisements of the destination. Each duplicate route advertisement received by a node defines an alternate path to the destination. To ensure loop freedom, a node accepts an alternate path to the destination if it has a lower hop count than the advertised hop count for that destination. AOMDV can be used to find node-disjoint or link-disjoint routes. To find node-disjoint routes, each node does not immediately reject duplicate RREQs. Each RREQ arriving via a different neighbor of the source defines a

Figure 2. Route reply process Of AODV routing protocol

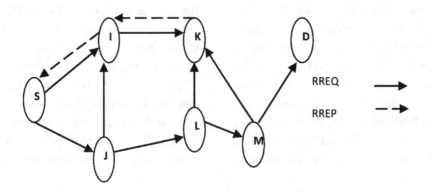

node-disjoint path. This is because nodes cannot broadcast duplicate RREQs, so any two RREQs arriving at an intermediate node via a different neighbor of the source could not have traversed the same node. In an attempt to get multiple link-disjoint routes, the destination replies to duplicate RREQs regardless of their first hop. To ensure link-disjoint-ness in the first hop of the RREP, the destination only replies to RREQs arriving via unique neighbors. After the first hop, the RREPs follow the reverse paths, which are node disjoint and thus link-disjoint. The trajectories of each RREP may intersect at an intermediate node, but each takes a different reverse path to the source to ensure link-disjoint-ness.

The performance study of AOMDV relative to AODV under a wide range of mobility and traffic scenarios reveals that AOMDV offers a significant reduction in delay, often more than a factor of two (Samir et al., 2006). It also provides reduction in the routing load and the end to end delay.

5. BLACKHOLE ATTACK

In MANET, during the route discovery phase of the AODV routing protocol, the malicious node, that is, black hole node, sends the false routing information (RREP), claiming that, it has the optimum route in terms of freshness and the number of hop counts. Thus, the source node selects the route through the black hole node and sends all

its packets through the blockhole node. Upon receiving the packets from the source, the black hole simply discards all the packets instead of forwarding to the destination. Thus, the packets sent by the source node never reach the destination.

Figure 3 shows the black hole attack, where S is the source node, D is the destination node, A is the black hole node and I,J,K and L are intermediate nodes. Here, attacker A sends a fake RREP to the source node S, claiming that it has a sufficiently fresher route than other nodes.

Since the attacker's advertised sequence number is higher than other nodes' sequence numbers, the source node S will choose the route that passes through node A and sends all its data packets to the destination through the black hole node A. But, the attacker A drops all the packets sent by the source node S. This is shown in Figure 4.

So, there must be a solution to identify the black hole node in the routing path and isolates the black hole node for further transactions.

6. OVERVIEW OF EVALVID

A novel and complete tool-set for evaluating the delivery quality of MPEG video transmissions in simulations of a network environment is given in Heng et al. (2008). This tool-set is known as EvalVid (Evaluation of Video) framework. The structure of the EvalVid framework is shown in Figure 5.

Figure 3. RREP from a black hole node(A)

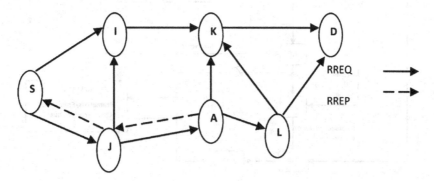

Figure 4. Packet drops at black hole node

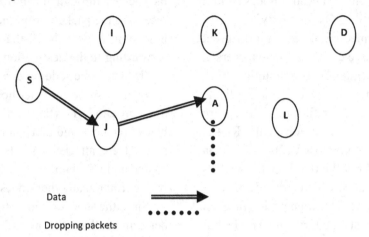

This integrated tool environment consists of an *MPEG-4 encoder, video sender, n*etwork *Simulator* (NS-*2*), *MPEG-4* (Moving Picture Experts Group) *decoder, evaluate trace* program, *PSNR*(Peak Signal to Noise Ratio) program and *MOS* (Mean Opinion Score) program. Figure 5 depicts the relationship between the different components, input video files and generated output files of the integrated tool environment. The integrated environment methodology was proposed and developed within the framework of EvalVid (Klaue, 2003) and extended the environment to include NS-2. A video clip, which is usually stored in YUV format, is fed to an MPEG-

4 encoder which in turn generates an encoded video stream. An open-source MPEG-4 encoder and decoder (ffmpeg) was used.

The encoded video stream is read by *Video Sender* (VS) to generate a *trace* file, which contains information such as frame type, size, etc. for each video frame. The trace file is then fed to the streaming server in the NS-2 simulator to produce video streams over MANET. The effect of streaming video over MANET is captured in a streaming client *log* file which is generated by NS-2. The log file contains information such as timestamp, size and identity of each packet. Note that, NS-2 also generates a similar log file for the

Figure 5. Structure of Evalvid framework

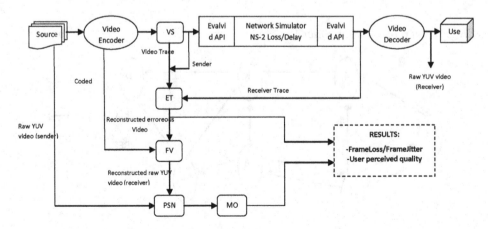

streaming server. The trace file and the log files are used by the *Evaluate Trace* (ET) program to generate possibly corrupted video files as a result of transmission over MANET. The corrupted video file is needed by *Peak Signal to Noise Ratio* (PSNR) programs to evaluate end-to-end video quality.

7. PROPOSED WORK

Though there are many solutions to avoid black hole nodes, which are based either on the sequence number in the RREP or on the time of arrival of RREP to the source. These solutions may not be efficient for all the scenarios of MANETs. Thus, there is a need for a solution against black hole node, considering both sequence number and the RREP arrival time.

This paper proposes two routing protocols Secure AdHoc On Demand Distance Vector Routing protocol against Black hole (SBAODV) and Secure AdHoc On Demand Multipath Distance Vector Routing protocol against Black hole (SBAOMDV) based on the well known routing protocols AODV and AOMDV respectively. In these protocols, the caching mechanism at the

source node is introduced to collect the RREPs for a particular RREQ arrived (Mistry et al., 2010) within a particular period of time, namely WAIT-TIME.

In the original AODV protocol, by default, the source node accepts the first fresh enough RREP coming to it. In this proposal, the caching mechanism stores all the RREPs in the newly created table viz. Cache_RREP_Tab until the time, WAIT_TIME. Based on the heuristics, initially, WAIT_TIME is set to be half the value of RREP_WAIT_TIME – the time for which source node waits for RREP control messages before regenerating RREQ.

In this solution, the source node after receiving first RREP control message waits for WAIT_TIME. For this time, the source node will save all the coming RREP control messages in Cache_RREP_Tab table. Subsequently, the source node analyses all the stored RREPs from Cache_RREP_Tab table, and discard the RREP having presumably very high destination sequence number. As before, the node that sent this RREP is suspected to be the malicious node. Once, such malicious node is identified, this solution selects a reply having highest destination sequence number

Box 1.

```
Pre_ReceiveReply (Packet P)   {
    t_0 = get(current time value)
    t_1= t_0 + WAIT_TIME
    while(CURRENT_TIME <= t_1)        {
      Store Dest_Seq_No in RREP and NODE_ID in  Cache_RREP_Tab table
    }
     while (Cache_RREP_Tab is not empty)  {
       Select Dest_Seq_No from table
       ReceiveReply(Packet q)   }
}
Where   Dest_Seq_No --- Destination Sequence Number
           Src_Seq_No ----- Source Sequence Number
```

from Cache_RREP_Tab table. It does so, by calling the method viz. the *Pre_ReceiveReply()* method.

The pseudo code for the same is given in Box 1.

For the RREP selected from Pre_RecieveReply, the source node compares the sequence number in the RREP with the threshold value, where this threshold value is dynamically updated in the time interval as in Satoshi (2007). As the value of the sequence number in RREP from a black hole node is found to be higher than the threshold value, the node is suspected to be malicious and it adds the node to the black list. After detecting the node as a black hole node, the source node will send a new control packet to its neighbors to indicate the presence of the black node and its identity. Further, if any node receives the RREP packet, it looks over the list, if the reply is from the blacklisted node; no processing is done for the same. It simply ignores the node and does not receive reply from that node again. In this way, the malicious node is isolated from the network.

The continuous replies from the malicious node are blocked, which results in less Routing overhead. The threshold value is dynamically updated using the data collected in the particular time interval. The threshold value is the average of the difference of destination sequence number in each time slot between the sequence number in the routing table and the RREP packet. The formula for the threshold at each time slot is given in Box 2.

$$Th = \frac{1}{N} \sum_{i=1}^{N} dS_i \qquad (1)$$

The time interval to update the threshold value is as soon as a node receives a RREP packet. As a node receives a RREP for the first time, it gets the updated value of the threshold. So, the proposed routing protocol not only detects the black hole attack, but tries to prevent it further, by updating the threshold value which reflects the real changing environment. And other nodes are also updated about the malicious act, and they react to it by isolating the malicious node from the network.

The method of detecting the Black hole nodes based on the sequence number in the proposed SBAODV and SBAOMDV are same and it is given as presented in Box 3.

Thus, in all situations, the black hole will be identified and it is isolated for further route update process. Thus, the effect of black hole nodes is reduced throughout the MANET.

8. SIMULATION

The performances of the routing protocols AODV, AOMDV, AODV with Black Holes(BAODV), AOMDV with black holes(BAOMDV), SBAODV and SBAOMDV under the presence of black hole attack were evaluated using Network Simulator NS-2 under a wide range of mobility and traffic scenarios.

In this, four new routing agents have been implemented with the basis of AODV and AOMDV like:

1. BAODV - AODV with black hole reception,
2. BAOMDV- AOMDV with black hole reception,

Box 2.

```
Let  S    - Destination sequence number in the routing table.
      rt
        S   -  Destination sequence number in the RREP Packet.
         rp
        dS  = Difference(S  ,S  ) at a time slot 'i'
          i                rt  rp
```

Box 3. At Source Node

```
ReceiveReply (Packet P)
{
    if (the source of the RREP is not in Black List)
    {
        if (P has an entry in Route Table)
        {
            if(Dest_Seq_No in RREP > Threshold)
            {
                Node is suspected as a Black hole
                Discard RREP
                Add the node in the black list
                Update threshold value using equation (1)
            }
            else
            {
              if(Dest_Seq_No in RREP > Dest_Seq_No in the Routing table)
                {
                    Update entry of P in routing table
                    Unicast data packets to the route specified in RREP
                }
                else
                {
                    Discard RREP
                }   }    }
    else
    {
        if ((Dest_Seq_No in RREP >= Source_Seq_No)
               &&(Dest_Seq_No in RREP <  Threshold))
        {
            Make entry of P in routing table
        }
        else
        {
            Node is suspected as a Black hole
            Discard RREP
            Add the node in the black list
        }   }     }
else
{
    Discard RREP // reply is from black hole node
}   } // End of ReceiveRREP
```

3. SBAODV-AODV with caching mechanism and sequence number comparison
4. SBAOMDV-AOMDV with caching mechanism and sequence number comparison.

All these implementations are based on the work described in Ros (2005) "Implementation of a New MANET Unicast Routing Protocol in NS-2".

The entire simulations were carried out using NS 2.34 network simulator which is a discrete event driven simulator developed at UC Berkeley as a part of the VINT (Virtual InterNetwork Testbed) project. The goal of NS2 is to support research and education in networking. It is suitable for designing new protocols, comparing different protocols and traffic evaluations. NS2 is developed as a collaborative environment. It is distributed as open source software. The propagation model used in this simulation study is based on the two-ray ground reflection model. The simulation also includes an accurate model of the IEEE802.11 Distributed Coordination Function (DCF) wireless MAC protocol.

Here the black hole attack takes place after the attacking node receives RREQ for the estimation node that it is going to impersonate. To succeed in the black hole attack, the attacker must generate its RREP with sequence number greater than the sequence number of the destination (AlShurman, 2004). Upon receiving RREQ, the attacker set the sequence number of RREP as a very high number, so that the attacker node can always attract all the data packets from the source and then drop the packets (Dokurer, 2007).

For the performance analysis of the network, a regular well-behaved AODV network was used as a reference. Then black holes were introduced into the network. Simulations were carried out for the MANET with one and more black holes. Then using the same set of scenarios, the simulation was carried out with the other protocols AOMDV, SBAODV and SBAOMDV. The simulation parameters are tabulated in Table 1.

About twenty scenarios with different node positions, mobility and speed have been simulated and tested. The network parameters were measured with the presence of zero, one, two, three, four and five black holes.

The simulations have been carried out by transmitting encoded video streams. The encoding technique used in this proposal is MPEG-4. And the network parameters Packet delivery ratio, Throughput, End-to-End delay, Jitter, Network Routing Overload and PSNR of the received video stream have been taken as evaluation parameters.

One of the sample simulation scenarios from 'nam' animator of NS2 with five block holes is shown in Figure 6. The following screen shot shows the packet drops around Black holes.

Figure 7, Figure 8, Figure 9, Figure 10, and Figure 11 show the comparison of various parameters with all these routing protocols.

Figure 7 shows the comparison of routing protocols AODV, AOMDV, SBAODV and SBAOMDV in terms of packet delivery ratio. With zero black hole, the packet delivery ratio is same for all the routing protocols. Whereas, when black holes are increased, the packet delivery ratio is reduced in all the protocols. But, this reduction is very high in AODV, next to that

Table 1. Simulation parameters

Parameter	Value
Simulator	NS-2 (ver 2.34)
Simulation Time	500 sec
Number of mobile nodes	50
Topology	1000 m X 1000 m
Transmission range	250 m
Routing Protocol	AODV & AOMDV
Traffic Model	MPEG-4 Video Streams
Maximum Speed	20 m/s
Source destination pairs	22
Packet Size	512
Mobility Model	Random Way point
Data Rate	10 Mbps

Figure 6. Sample scenario from NS-2

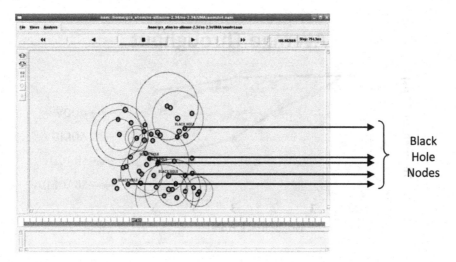

Black
Hole
Nodes

AOMDV. And the packet delivery ratio is reduced with a minimum amount in the case of SBAODV and SBAOMDV. For example, with the presence of five black holes, the packet delivery ratio is reduced by 13% in SBAOMDV, 33% in SBAODV, 70% in AOMDV and 81% in AODV.

The comparison of average throughput, that is, the number of packets communicated in one second, is shown in Figure 8. This graph shows that only in SBAOMDV and SBAODV, there is less reduction in average throughput in the pres-

ence of black holes. As an example, the average throughput is reduced by 10% in SBAOMDV, 31% in SBAODV, 69% in AOMDV and 80% in AODV.

Figure 9 shows the comparison of average end-to-end delay of all the four routing protocols. Here the reduction of average end-to end delay is almost same for all the protocols in the presence of black holes. For five black holes, the end to end delay is reduced by a factor of 0.17 in SBAOMDV, 0.25 in SBAODV, 0.24 in AOMDV and 0.256 in AODV from its actual end-to-end delay, which

Figure 7. Comparison on packet delivery ratio

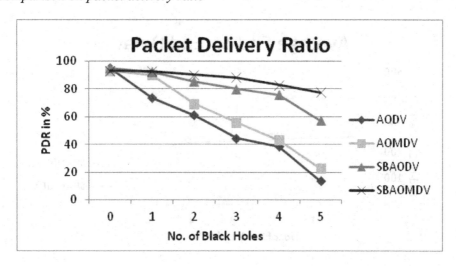

Figure 8. Comparison on average throughput

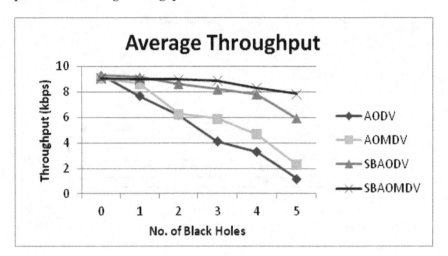

is the delay without any black holes. In all the cases the average end-to-end delay of SBAODV is the highest among all other routing protocols.

Figure 10 shows the comparison of average jitter in all the four routing protocols. Here also, the jitter is reduced almost equally in all the routing protocols. With the presence of five black holes, the average jitter is reduced by a factor of 0.28 for AODV, 0.21 for AOMDV, 0.31 for SBAODV and 0.25 for SBAOMDV.

The comparison of normalized routing load for the four routing protocols is shown in Figure 11.

From the presence of zero black hole to five black holes, the normalized routing load is increased by 49% in AODV, 44% in AOMDV, 30% in SBAODV and 36% in SBAOMDV.

From the comparisons, it is clear that, with the non-cryptographic solution incorporated with the routing protocols, that is, SBAODV and SBAOMDV, the effect of degradation of the performance of the MANET is reduced than that of the actual protocols AODV and AOMDV. And further, the effect is less in SBAOMDV in compared with SBAODV.

Figure 9. Comparison on average end-to-end delay

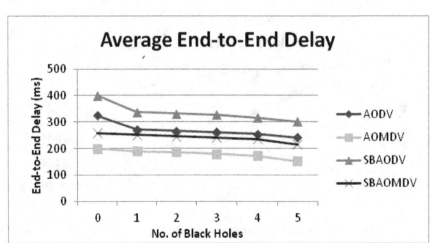

Figure 10. Comparison on average jitter

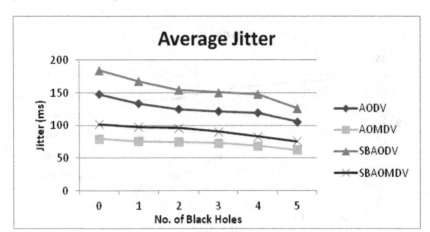

- **PSNR (Peak Signal Noise Ratio)**: PSNR is one of the most widespread objective metrics to assess the application-level Quality of Service (QoS) of video transmissions. This metric is computed by the Evalvid tool. The PSNR values of the routing protocols were measured and are compared in Figure 12.

This figure shows that, even with an increase in number of black holes, the PSNR of the routing protocol SBAOMDV is reduced only by a smaller amount.

Figure 13 shows the comparison of received video frame quality for a particular frame 110 in the standard video stream foreman_qcif.yuv.

The simulations have also been carried out with the solutions proposed in Dokurer (2007) namely, IDSAODV (Intrusion Detection System AODV), which uses Caching mechanism and in Payal et al. (2009), named as DPRAODV (Detection, Prevention and Reactive AODV) which uses sequence number comparison with threshold. The comparison of SBAODV with IDSAODV and DPRAODV is given in the figures.

Figure 11. Comparison on normalized routing load

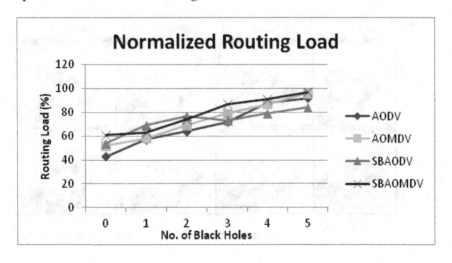

Figure 12. Comparison on received video PSNR

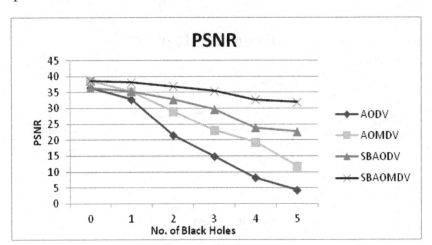

The comparison of Simulation parameters Packet delivery ratio, Average Throughput, Average End-to-end Delay, Average Jitter and Normalized Routing Load are given in Figure 14, Figure 15, Figure 16, Figure 17, and Figure 18. By comparing all these protocols, it is clear that the proposed protocol SBAODV performs well in all aspects, whereas the performance of SBAOMDV is the highest in terms of Packet delivery ratio, Average Throughput, Average End-to-end Delay and Average Jitter but with little increase in normalized routing load.

9. FUTURE SCOPE

The solution proposed in this paper provides solution for mitigating independent black holes. In future, this solution may be enhanced for mitigating cooperative black holes. The same proposed method can be implemented for other on-demand single path and multi path reactive routing protocols such as DSR. This solution simply ignores the identified block hole in route discovery. In future, the false acquisition and recovery of malicious nodes can be performed.

Figure 13. Received video frame with black holes

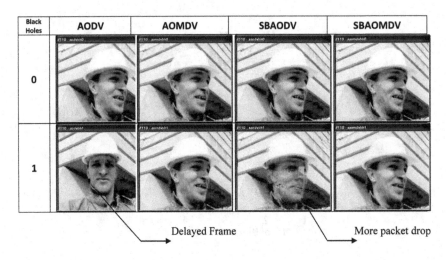

Figure 14. Comparison of packet delivery ratio

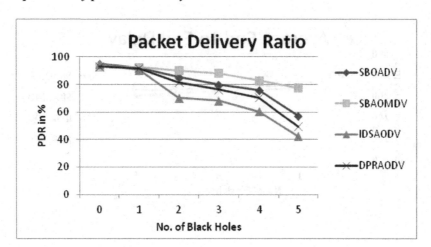

10. CONCLUSION

This paper analyses the effect of black hole nodes in MANET using the protocols AODV, its multi-path variant AOMDV, the proposed secure routing protocols SBAODV and its multi-path variant SBAOMDV. The simulation results shows that, the effect of black hole nodes on the network parameters packet delivery ratio, average throughput, average end-to-end delay, average jit-ter and normalized routing overload are reduced by an significant amount both in SBAODV and SBAODV. And further, the reduction is more in SBAOMDV than that of SBAODV. And these protocols were compared for video streaming with Evalvid Tool. In video streaming, the secure routing protocol SBAOMDV outperforms well. In future, the solution provided in this paper may be enhanced with cryptographic means, so that, the effect of black hole attack can be negligible.

Figure 15. Comparison of average throughput

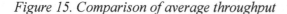

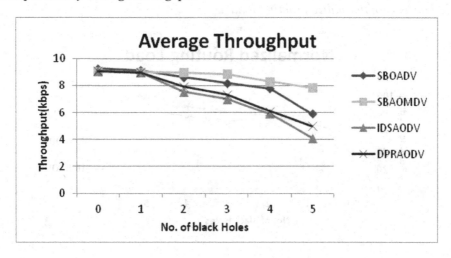

Figure 16. Comparison of average end-to-end delay

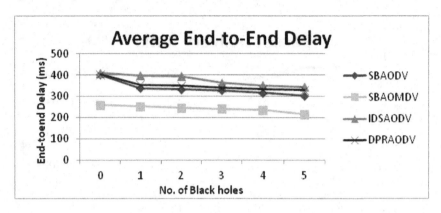

Figure 17. Comparison of average jitter

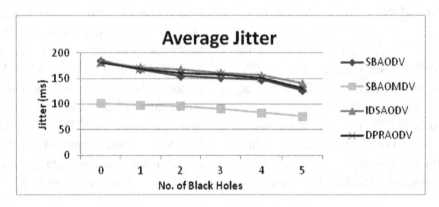

Figure 18. Comparison of normalized routing load

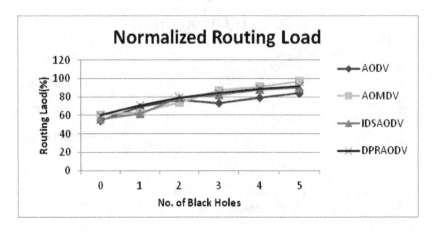

REFERENCES

Al-Shurman, M., Yoo, S. M., & Park, S. (2004). Black hole attack in mobile ad hoc networks. In *Proceedings of the 43nd Annual Southeast Regional Conference*.

Cai, J., Yi, P., Chen, J., Wang, Z., & Liu, N. (2010). An adaptive approach to detecting black and gray hole attacks in ad hoc network. In *Proceedings of the 24th IEEE International Conference on Advanced Information Networking and Applications* (pp. 275-280).

Deng, H., Li, W., & Agrawal, D. P. (2002). Routing security in wireless ad hoc network. *IEEE Communications Magazine*, *40*(10), 70–75. doi:10.1109/MCOM.2002.1039859

Di Caro, G. A., Ducatelle, F., & Gambardella, L. M. (2008). A simulation study of routing performance in realistic urban scenarios for MANETs. In M. Dorigo, M. Birattari, C. Blum, M. Clerc, T. Stützle, & A. F. Winfield (Eds.), *Proceedings of the 6th International Workshop on Ant Algorithms and Swarm Intelligence* (LNCS 5217, pp. 211-218).

Dokurer, S. (2006). *Simulation of black hole attack in wireless ad-hoc networks*. Unpublished master's thesis, Atılım University, Ankara, Turkey.

Dokurer, S., Ert, Y. M., & Acar, E. (2007, March 22-25). Performance analysis of ad hoc networks under black hole attacks. In *Proceedings of the IEEE Southeast Conference* (pp. 148-153).

Gong, W., You, Z., Chen, D., Zhao, X., Gu, M., & Lam, K.-Y. (2009). Trust based malicious nodes detection in MANET. In *Proceedings of the International Conference on E-Business and Information System Security* (pp. 1-4).

Johnson, D. B., Maltz, D. A., & Hu, Y. C. (2004). *The dynamic source routing protocol for mobile ad-hoc network (DSR)*. Retrieved from http://www.ietf.org/rfc/rfc4728.txt

Ke, C.-H., Shieh, C.-K., Hwang, W.-S., & Ziviani, A. (2008). An evaluation framework for more realistic simulations of MPEG video transmission. *International Journal of Information Science and Engineering*, 425-440.

Klaue, J., Rathke, B., & Wolisz, A. (2003). EvalVid – A framework for video transmission and quality evaluation. In *Proceedings of the 13th International Conference on Modeling, Techniques and Tools for Computer Performance Evaluation*, Urbana, IL. Retrieved January 20, 2011, from http://www.tkn.tu-berlin.de/research/evalvid

Kurosawa, S., Nakayama, H., Kato, N., Jamalipour, A., & Nemoto, Y. (2007). Detecting blackhole attack on AODV-based mobile ad hoc networks by dynamic learning method. *International Journal of Network Security*, *5*(6), 338–346.

Lee, S., Han, B., & Shin, M. (2002). Robust routing in wireless ad hoc networks. In *Proceedings of the International Conference on Parallel Processing ICPP Workshop*, Vancouver, BC, Canada (pp. 73-78).

Mistry, N., Jinwala, D. C., & Zaveri, M. (2010, March 17-19). Improving AODV protocol against blackhole attacks. In *Proceedings of the International Multiconference of Engineers and Computer Scientists*, Hong Kong (Vol. 2).

Perkins, C. E., Royer, E. M., & Das, S. R. (2003). *Ad hoc on-demand distance vector (AODV) routing*. Retrieved July 12, 2008, from http://www.ietf.org/rfc/rfc3561.txt

Raj, P. N., & Swadas, P. B. (2009). DPRAODV: A dynamic learning system against black hole attack in AODV based manet. *International Journal of Computer Science Issues*, *2*(3), 54–59.

Ros, F. J., & Ruiz, P. M. (2005). *Implementing a new manet unicast routing protocol in NS2.* Retrieved from http://imtl.skku.ac.kr/~hjlim99/ns2/%5B%BB%F5%B7%CE%BF%EE%20%B6%F3%BF%EC%C6%C3%20%C7%C1%B7%CE%C5%E4%C4%DD%20%B1%B8%C7%F6%5D/Implementing%20a%20New%20Manet%20Unicast%20Routing%20Protocol%20in%20ns2.pdf

Samir, M., Das, R., & Mahesh, K. (2006). On-demand multipath distance vector routing in ad hoc networks. *International Journal Wireless Communication and Mobile Computing, 6*(7), 969–988. doi:10.1002/wcm.432

Sen, J., Koilakonda, S., & Ukil, A. (2011). A mechanism for detection of cooperative black hole attack in mobile ad hoc networks. In *Proceedings of the IEEE International Conference on Intelligence Systems, Modelling and Simulation* (pp. 338-343).

Subathra, P., Sivagurunathan, S., & Ramaraj, N. (2010). Detection and prevention of single and cooperative black hole attacks in mobile ad hoc networks. *International Journal of Business Data Communications and Networking, 6*(1), 38–57. doi:10.4018/jbdcn.2010010103

Tamilselvan, L., & Sankaranarayanan, V. (2007). Prevention of blackhole attack in MANET. In *Proceedings of the 2nd International Conference on Wireless Broadband and Ultra Wideband Communications* (pp. 21-27).

Zhang, X. Y., Sekiya, Y., & Wakahara, Y. (2009). Proposal of a method to detect black hole attack in MANET. In *Proceedings of the International Symposium on Autonomous Decentralized Systems* (pp. 1-6).

Zhao, M., & Zhou, J. (2009). Cooperative black hole attack prevention for mobile ad hoc networks. In *Proceedings of the International Symposium on Information Engineering and Electronic Commerce* (pp. 26-30).

This work was previously published in International Journal of Business Data Communications and Networking, Volume 7, Issue 4, edited by Varadharajan Sridhar and Debashis Saha, p.p 1-17, copyright 2011 by IGI Publishing (an imprint of IGI Global)

Chapter 14
Enhancing Clustering in Wireless Sensor Networks with Energy Heterogeneity

Femi A. Aderohunmu
University of Otago, New Zealand

Jeremiah D. Deng
University of Otago, New Zealand

Martin K. Purvis
University of Otago, New Zealand

ABSTRACT

While wireless sensor networks (WSN) are increasingly equipped to handle more complex functions, in-network processing still requires the battery-powered sensors to judiciously use their constrained energy so as to prolong the elective network life time. There are a few protocols using sensor clusters to coordinate the energy consumption in a WSN, but how to deal with energy heterogeneity remains a research question. The authors propose a modified clustering algorithm with a three-tier energy setting, where energy consumption among sensor nodes is adaptive to their energy levels. A theoretical analysis shows that the proposed modifications result in an extended network stability period. Simulation has been conducted to evaluate the new clustering algorithm against some existing algorithms under different energy heterogeneity settings, and favourable results are obtained especially when the energy levels are significantly imbalanced.

1. INTRODUCTION

Wireless communication technologies continue to grow in diverse areas to provide new opportunities for business data networking and services. One fast-moving area is wireless sensor networks (WSN). With the advances in micro-electro mechanical systems, sensor devices can be built as small as lightweight wireless nodes. Wireless sensor networks (WSN) are highly distributed networks of such kind of sensor nodes, and have been deployed in large numbers to monitor produc-

DOI: 10.4018/978-1-4666-2026-1.ch014

tion systems, and natural or social environments. There is a growing need for the nodes to handle more complex functions in data acquisition and processing, and energy saving solutions remains a major requirement for these battery-powered sensor nodes.

A sensor node consists of three sensor subsystems (Qing et al., 2006): the environment sensor; the data processor that performs local computations on the data sensed, and the communicator that performs information exchange between neighbouring nodes. Each sensor is usually limited in their energy capacity, processing power, memory capacity and sensing capabilities. However, a network of these sensors gives rise to a robust, reliable and accurate network.

Many studies on WSNs have been carried out (Akyildiz et al., 2002a, 2002b; Baronti et al., 2007; Younis & Fahmy, 2004). WSN technologies are continuously finding new applications in various areas, such as in battle field surveillance, patient monitoring in hospital wards, and environmental monitoring in disaster prone areas. Although these sensors are not as reliable or as accurate as the expensive macro-sensors, their small size and low cost have enabled applications to network hundreds and thousands of these micro-sensors to achieve greater performance (Heinzelman et al., 2002). It is noted that, to maintain a reliable information delivery, data aggregation and information fusion are necessary for efficient and effective communication between these sensor nodes. Only processed and concise information should be delivered to the sinks or 'actuators' to reduce communications energy and to prolong the effective network lifetime. More in-depth discussions on the design issues of in-network processing and data aggregation can be found in Karl and Wilig (2007).

However, one of the key issues that merit attention is the energy heterogeneity in sensor networks (Mhatre & Rosenberg, 2004). To some extent energy heterogeneity among WSN nodes is inevitable. It occurs when there is significant energy difference between an individual sensor and its neighbours, either caused by the introduction of new sensors or re-energization of sensor nodes, or by network settings which may be necessary for some applications, e.g., different nodes having different sensor functions and hence different batteries. An inefficient use of the available albeit heterogeneous energy among the nodes will lead to poor performance and short lifecycle of the network. Despite some progress made in solving this problem, energy heterogeneity remains a challenge to WSNs. We present a modified algorithm for properly distributing sensor energy and ensuring prolonged network life time. Our algorithmic approach operates in a WSN under a modelling of three-level energy heterogeneity that controls the probability of conducting data transmission. Simulation results show an improvement in the effective network life time, and increased robustness of performance in the presence of energy heterogeneity.

The remainder of this paper is organized as follows. We briefly review related work in Section 2. The network model and the cluster formation mechanism are presented in details in Section 3 and the pattern of energy consumption within the clusters is examined. We then present our proposed clustering protocol in Section 4. The simulation results are presented in Section 5. Finally, we conclude the paper and highlight some future directions for further research.

2 RELATED WORK

Clustering techniques have been employed to deal with energy management in WSNs. Low Energy Adaptive Clustering Hierarchy (LEACH) (Heinzelman et al., 2002) is a pioneering work in this respect. LEACH is a clustering-based protocol, using randomized election and rotation of local cluster base station (so-called 'clusterheads' for transferring data to the sink node) to evenly preserve the energy among the sensors in the network. The rotation of cluster heads can also be a means of fault tolerance (Abbasi & Younis, 2007). However, the LEACH protocol is not heterogeneity-aware, in the sense that when there is an energy difference to some extent between sensor nodes in the network, the sensors die out faster than a more uniform energy setting (Smaragdakis & Bestavros, 2004). In real life situation it is difficult for the sensors to maintain their energy uniformly, which makes energy imbalance between nodes to occur easily. LEACH assumes that the energy usage of each node with respect to the overall energy of the system or network is homogeneous. Conventional protocols such as Minimum Transmission Energy (MTE) and Direct Transmission (DT) (Shepard, 1996) do not assure a balanced and uniform use of the sensors' residual energy as the network evolves. In Distributed Energy-Efficient Clustering algorithm (DEEC) (Qing et al., 2006), a probability based clustering algorithm was proposed. DEEC elects cluster heads based on the knowledge of the ratio between residual energy of each nodes and the average energy of the network. It however requires additional energy consumption to share the information among the sensor nodes. The Stable Election Protocol (SEP) (Smaragdakis & Bestavros, 2004) is another heterogeneity-aware protocol. It does not require energy knowledge sharing, but is based on assigning weighted probabilities for cluster head election according to each node's respective energy. This approach improves the random selection of cluster heads, therefore assuring a uniform use of the nodes energy. In SEP, two types of nodes (two tier in-clustering) and two level hierarchies were considered.

For a wider range of discussions, a survey of clustering algorithm was presented in (Abbasi & Younis, 2007); the proper distribution of sensors in clusters so that load balancing can be achieved is another objective of clustering when designing a robust protocol for WSNs (Al-karaki & Kamal, 2004; Younis & Fahmy, 2004). The clustering issue

was also discussed in a review on wireless multimedia sensor networks (Akyildiz et al., 2007).

We focus on the clustering optimisation in heterogeneous energy settings. The contribution of this work is a SEP extension that considers a three-tier node classification in a two-level hierarchical network. The new node type for the purpose of this study is referred to as "intermediate nodes", which serves as a bridge between the advanced nodes and the normal nodes. We analyse the energy consumption pattern of sensor nodes and reveal the importance of customised control on sensor cluster head election for heterogeneous energy settings. Our goal is to achieve a robust self-configured WSN that maximizes its lifetime.

3. THE NETWORK MODEL

Hereafter we introduce the network model with its radio and energy settings, the energy dissipation model, and the cluster head election mechanism.

3.1. Radio Channel and Energy Dissipation

Let us consider a radio energy dissipation model used in a number of previous studies (Heinzelman et al., 2002; Qing et al., 2006; Smaragdakis & Bestavros, 2004) as shown in Figure 1. Assume that for each bit energy dissipation is $E_{elec} = 50nJ$ to run the transmitter or receiver circuit. To transmit the data bits over a distance (d) with an acceptable SNR, amplification energy is expended to overcome either the free space (fs) or multipath (mp) loss, depending on the transmission distances d.

To transmit k bits, the energy to be expended is:

$$E_{Tx}\left(k,d\right) = E_{Tx-elec}\left(k\right) + E_{Tx-amp}\left(k,d\right)$$

Figure 1. Network model diagram

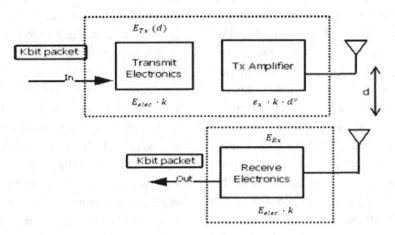

$$= \qquad (1)$$

Here d_0 is the distance threshold for swapping amplification models. It can be calculated as

$$d_0 = \sqrt{\frac{\varepsilon_{fs}}{\varepsilon_{mp}}} \; .$$

To receive a k-bit message, the radio will consume:

$$E_{Rx}\left(k\right) = E_{elec}k \; . \qquad (2)$$

We further assume a symmetric radio channel, i.e., the same amount of energy is required to transmit a k-bit message from node A to B and vice versa.

3.2. Cluster Formation and Data Aggregation

To form clusters, a distributed algorithm is used similarly to Heinzelman et al. (2002) and Smaragdakis and Bestavros (2004). The main idea is for the sensor nodes to elect themselves with respect to their energy levels autonomously. By clustering, sensor nodes save on communication cost as the transmission distance is reduced and much lower energy consumption is needed. Each node transmits its data to the closest cluster head, and the cluster heads performs data aggregation (Heinzelman et al., 2002; Smaragdakis & Bestavros, 2004), further reducing data transmission.

Now we proceed to our indicator function of choosing a cluster head. Assume an optimal number of clusters c in each round. It is expected that as a cluster head, more energy will be expended than being a cluster member. Each node can become cluster head with a probability P_{opt}, and every node must become cluster head once every $\frac{1}{P_{opt}}$ rounds. Intuitively, it means we have nP_{opt} clusters and cluster heads per round. Let the non-elected nodes form a set G in the past $\frac{1}{P_{opt}}$ round.

For Round r, a sensor node chooses a random number between 0 and 1. If this is lower than a threshold for node i, the sensor node becomes a cluster head. The threshold $T(i)$ is given by:

$$T(i) = \begin{cases} \dfrac{P_{opt}}{1 - P_{opt}\left[r \; mod\left(\dfrac{1}{P_{opt}}\right)\right]} & if \quad i \epsilon G; \\ \\ 0 & Otherwise. \end{cases} \qquad (3)$$

Assume nodes are uniformly and randomly distributed in a square area of $M \, \text{m}^2$. On average there would be $\dfrac{n}{c}$ nodes per cluster, one cluster head (CH) and $\dfrac{n}{c} - 1$ non-CH nodes. Each cluster head must dissipate energy receiving k bits of data packet from associated cluster members and transmitting to the sink. Also, data aggregation prior to transmission will also cost energy, which per bit is denoted as E_{DA}. In total, the energy dissipated by each cluster head is:

$$E_{CH} = kE_{elec}\left(\frac{n}{c} - 1\right) + kE_{DA}\frac{n}{c} + E_{Tx}\left(k, d_{to \, Sink}\right),$$

(4)

where d_{toSink} is the distance from cluster head node to the sink.

For a non-CH node, the energy expended will be to transmit k bits to the respective CHs, while a free space power loss d^2 is adopted since normally $d_{toCH} < d_0$ in Equation(1):

$$E_{non-CH} = kE_{elec} + k\epsilon_{fs}d_{to \, CH}^2,$$

(5)

where d_{toCH} is the distance from each node to their respective cluster heads.

The average value of d_{toCH} can be estimated as $M / \sqrt{2\pi c}$ (Heinzelman et al., 2002). The energy dissipated in a cluster per round can be estimated as

$$E_{cluster} \approx E_{CH} + \frac{n}{c} E_{non-CH}$$

(6)

And the total energy dissipation in the network per round will be the sum of the energy dissipated by all clusters, i.e.,

$$E_{total} = cE_{cluster}$$

(7)

If the average of d_{toSink} is greater than d_0, the total energy can be calculated as:

$$E_{total} =$$
$$c[kE_{elec}\left(\frac{n}{c} - 1\right) + kE_{DA}\frac{n}{c} + kE_{elec} + k\epsilon_{mp}d_{to \, Sink}^4]$$
$$+ (kE_{elec} + k\epsilon_{fs}M^2 / 2\pi c).$$

(8)

Otherwise, when $d_{toSink} < d_0$ applies, the total energy dissipation becomes

$$E_{total} = k[2nE_{elec} + nE_{DA} + \epsilon_{fs}\left(cd_{toSink}^2 + nd_{toCH}^2\right)].$$

(9)

Here the number of clusters (c) is an important parameter that controls the level of data aggregation (within clusters) and communication within and without clusters. The bigger c is, the smaller is the cluster sizes, hence lesser is energy consumption for data aggregation and within-cluster transmission; however, more CH nodes will be doing longer-distance transmission to the sink. As discussed in Heinzelman et al. (2002) and Smaragdakis and Bestavros (2004), the optimal number of clusters can be found by letting $\dfrac{\delta E_{total}}{\delta c} = 0$. The different forms of the E_{total} calculation will lead to different optimal c solutions. We consider the situation when the sink is located at the centre of the monitoring area and $d_{toSink} < d_0$ applies. It is shown $c_{opt} = 2.614\sqrt{\dfrac{n}{2}}$ (Smaragdakis & Bestavros, 2004). In a typical setting (details given later in Section 5), the energy consumption on average by each individual non-CH sensor and CH sensor, and the total energy consumed in each round, are plotted out in

Figure 2. Energy consumption pattern when the number of clusters (c) changes. Energy values in log-scale are in the unit of Joules

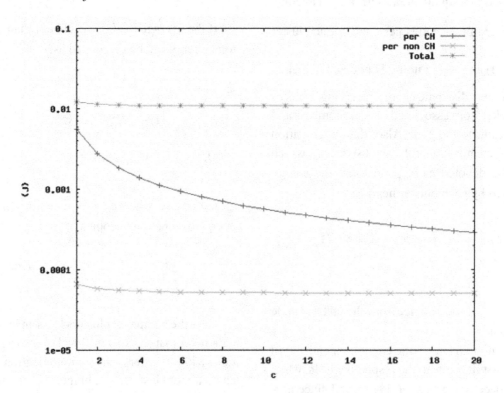

Figure 2 against varying numbers of clusters (c). While the total energy hits the bottom with $c_{opt} = 10$, it is not too sensitive to the setting of c as shown on the log-scale plot. However, it is clearly shown that for each node the energy consumption as a CH is much more significant than a non-CH node – more than 10 times as much over a wide range of c values.

The energy consumption pattern given in Figure 2 has a clear implication. For the network to operate over a long lifetime, the election of cluster heads hence is crucial, as inadequate control of the election process may lead to unduly over-consumption of energy, resulting in early death of nodes especially when a node with very low energy is chosen to be a CH. When energy heterogeneity exists, this issue becomes even more serious.

3.3. Energy Heterogeneity

Here we briefly discuss the intuition behind SEP and its improvement on LEACH. SEP improves the stable region of the system using a clustering hierarchy, making an efficient use of the extra energy introduced into the system that serves as a source of heterogeneity. Two energy levels are considered. SEP deals with the heterogeneous setting by extending the epoch of the sensor network to the LEACH protocol in proportion to the energy increment. For optimization of the stable region, SEP proposed a new epoch equal to

$$\frac{1}{P_{opt}} (1 + m\alpha) \text{(Smaragdakis \& Bestavros, 2004)}.$$

SEP uses an election probability based on the initial energy of each node to elect the cluster heads by assigning a weight equal to the initial energy of each node divided by initial energy of the normal nodes. The weighted probabilities for normal and advanced nodes in SEP are chosen to reflect the extra energy introduced into the network system. These probabilities and the total initial energy are given below respectively:

$$P_{nrm} = P_{opt} / (1 + m\alpha),$$

$$P_{adv} = P_{opt}(1 + \alpha) / (1 + m\alpha), \qquad (10)$$

$$E_{Init} = nE_o(1 + m\alpha),$$

where P_{nrm} is the election probability for normal nodes, P_{adv} is the probability for the advanced nodes, m is the proportion of advanced nodes (with α times more energy than the normal nodes), and finally E_{Init} is the total initial energy of the network.

4. EXTENDING SEP

4.1. The New Model

In this section we present our proposed solution as an extension to the SEP protocol, called 'SEP-E', by considering three energy levels in two hierarchy settings as an intended improvement to SEP and LEACH. We intend to optimize the stable region of the network system by further increasing the epoch to accommodate the additional energy introduced to the system. In our approach we introduce an additional type of nodes called the 'intermediate nodes', with an intention to accommodate and cater for multi-nodes diversity. This can be very important for some application specific settings such as continuous re-energization of nodes throughout the data retrieval process, by deploying new nodes to replace dead ones.

The intermediate node is chosen as fraction of energy between the limits of both the fractions of energy of advanced node as the upper bound and the normal node as the lower bound. As in SEP, the initial energy for normal nodes is E_o, and for advanced nodes, $E_{adv} = (1 + \alpha)E_o$. Assuming for intermediate nodes, $E_{int} = (1 + \mu)E_o$. For simplicity we set $\mu = \alpha / 2$.

Figure 3 demonstrates the heterogeneous settings we used. The new heterogeneous setting with the 3-tier node energy has no effect on the spatial density of the network. We keep P_{opt} the same. The total initial energy of the system is increased by the introduction of intermediate nodes:

$$E_{Init} =$$
$$nE_o(1 - m - b) + nmE_o(1 + \alpha) + nbE_o(1 + \mu)$$

$$= nE_o(1 + m\alpha + b\mu), \qquad (11)$$

where n is the number of nodes, m is the proportion of advanced nodes to the total number of nodes n and b is the proportion of intermediate nodes. Proceeding from similar analysis in Smaragdakis and Bestavros (2004), the following conditions must be satisfied:

C1: The advanced nodes must be cluster head exactly $(1 + \alpha)$ times within an epoch;

C2: The intermediate nodes must be cluster head exactly $(1 + \mu)$ times within an epoch;

C3: Every normal node must also become cluster head once every epoch;

C4: The average number of cluster in the network should be nP_{opt}.

Figure 3. A WSN with a 3-tier energy heterogeneity among sensor nodes

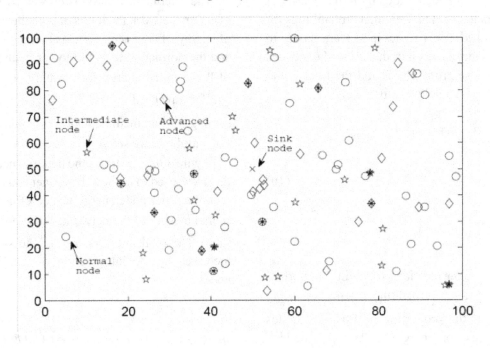

This translates into a probability problem that we can solve mathematically, giving a new set of election probabilities, with P_{int} introduced for intermediate nodes:

$$P_{nrm} \tag{12}$$

$$P_{int} = (P\_opt \ (1+\mu)) / (1 + m\alpha + b\mu), \tag{13}$$

and

$$P_{adv} = P_{opt}(1+\alpha) / (1 + m\alpha + b\mu). \tag{14}$$

To guarantee that the sensor nodes become cluster heads according to these probabilities as given above, we must define new thresholds for the election processes, modifying Equation(3). The threshold $T(n_{nrm})$, $T(n_{int})$, $T(n_{adv})$ for normal, intermediate and advanced nodes respectively, becomes:

$$T_{nrm}\left(n\right) =$$

$$\begin{cases} \dfrac{P_{nrm}}{1 - P_{nrm}\left[r \ mod\left(\dfrac{1}{P_{nrm}}\right)\right]} & if \ n_{nrm} \ \epsilon G\text{'}; \\ \\ 0 & Otherwise, \end{cases}$$

$$\tag{15}$$

where G' is the set of normal nodes that has not become cluster head in the past $1 / P_{opt}$ rounds. Hence we have $n(1 - m - b)$ normal node, meeting exactly Condition C3. The same applies to the conditions C2 and C1 for intermediate and advanced nodes, controlled by the following thresholds respectively:

$$T\left(n_{int}\right) =$$

$$\begin{cases} \dfrac{P_{int}}{1 - P_{int}\left[r \ mod\left(\dfrac{1}{P_{int}}\right)\right]} & if \ n_{int} \ \epsilon G\text{''}; \\ \\ 0 & Otherwise, \end{cases}$$

$$\tag{16}$$

where G'' is the set of intermediate nodes that have not become cluster head in the past $1/P_{int}$ rounds, and

$$T\left(n_{adv}\right) =
\begin{cases}
\dfrac{P_{adv}}{1 - P_{adv}\left[r \bmod \left(\dfrac{1}{P_{adv}}\right)\right]} & if \ n_{adv} \epsilon G'''; \\
0 & Otherwise,
\end{cases}
\tag{17}$$

with G''' being the set of advanced nodes that has not become cluster head in the past $1/Padv$ rounds.

From Equation (12) - (14), the average total number of cluster heads per round will be:

$$n\left(1 - m - b\right)P_{nrm} + nbP_{int} + nmP_{adv} = nP_{opt}. \tag{18}$$

This gives us the same number of cluster heads compared with the original LEACH setting. Therefore, while using new thresholds to ensure that conditions C1-C3 hold, C4 is also satisfied. On the other hand, energy dissipation is better adapted to energy heterogeneity in our approach, as we will illustrate as follows by examining the theoretical average lifetime of the sensor nodes.

4.2. Lifetime Analysis

Here we provide a mathematical analysis of the lifetime of SEP-E and show that compared with LEACH, SEP-E extends the lifespan of its all three types of nodes.

First, we concentrate on the normal nodes as they are the energy bottleneck of the network. It can be safely assumed that energy consumption at each node is largely caused by being elected as cluster head and having to conduct data aggregation and transmission. The lifetime of a normal node, in a LEACH setting, can then be roughly estimated as:

$$L = \frac{E_0}{E_{CH}P_{opt}} \tag{19}$$

In SEP-E, the nodes' election probabilities are modified, hence, according to Equation (12) - Equation (14), their lifetime is also changed. For normal nodes, we have

$$L' = \frac{E_0}{E_{CH}P_{nrm}} = \left(1 + m\alpha + b\mu\right)L, \tag{20}$$

which indicates an extended lifetime compared with LEACH.

For intermediate and advanced nodes (note that they have elevated initial energy), similarly we can work out the relevant lifetimes for SEP-E:

$$L'_i = \frac{\left(1 + \mu\right)E_0}{E_{CH}P_{int}} = \left(1 + ma + b\mu\right)L, \tag{21}$$

$$L'_a = \frac{\left(1 + a\right)E_0}{E_{CH}P_{adv}} = \left(1 + ma + b\mu\right)L,$$

suggesting both $L'_i = L'_a = L' > L$. Clearly the advanced nodes and intermediate nodes enjoy the same prolonged average lifetime. The stability period in SEP-E is therefore extended.

5. SIMULATION

5.1. Simulation Settings

For simulation we used a $100m \times 100m$ region of 100 sensor nodes scattered randomly. MATLAB is used to implement the simulation. To have a fair comparison with LEACH, we introduced advanced and intermediate nodes with different energy levels as in our SEP-E protocol. Likewise, to have a fair comparison with SEP in two node scenario, we introduced additional energy so that the total initial energy of the network system becomes the same as in SEP-E and LEACH in three node settings. The notion is for us to be able to assess the performance of these protocols in the presence of energy heterogeneity.

By changing the parameter values such as α, μ, m and b, we can simulate different scenarios of energy heterogeneity among the sensor nodes. Specifically, suppose we let 20% and 30% of the nodes be advanced nodes and intermediate nodes with additional energy levels: $\alpha = 3$ and $\mu = 1.5$ respectively. The epoch for the heterogeneous setting becomes $\frac{1}{P_{opt}}(1 + m\alpha + b\mu)$. Since $P_{opt} = 0.1$, on average we should have 10 nodes becoming cluster head per round. This means by our new heterogeneous epoch we should have, on average $n(1 - m - b)P_{nrm} = 2$ normal nodes becoming cluster head per round. Similarly, we should have $nbPint = 4$ intermediate nodes as cluster heads per round and $nmPadv = 4$ advanced nodes as cluster heads per round. Other parameters used in our simulation are shown in Table 1.

5.2. Performance Metrics

The following metrics are adopted to access the performance of all clustering protocols involved:

1. Stability period, the period from the start of the network operation and the first dead node.
2. Instability period, the period between the first dead node and last dead node.
3. Number of alive and dead nodes per round.
4. Spatial distribution and uniformity of alive and dead nodes per round in the network region under consideration.

As explained in Smaragdakis and Bestavros (2004), the larger the stability period and the smaller the instability period are, the better the reliability of the clustering process of the network system is. However, we need to note the trade-off between the reliability and lifetime of the network system. In some cases the last alive node can still provide feedback, but this could in most cases be unreliable. Therefore when assessing the performance of the three protocols we look for a good balance between the stability and instability periods.

5.3. Simulation Results

We compare the result of our simulation with both LEACH and SEP in dealing with different levels of energy heterogeneity: high, moderate, and low. Figure 4 shows the number of live nodes over time when using SEP-E, LEACH and SEP respectively in the presence of energy heterogeneity. The stability of SEP-E compared with LEACH increases from 995 rounds to 1450 rounds, and the instability is reduced from 4585 rounds to 3751 rounds. Also the stability in SEP-E is slightly better than SEP, and the instability is much lower than SEP. This is due to the introduction of intermediate nodes to SEP-E, which acts as a bridge between

Table 1. Parameter settings

Parameter	Values
$Eelec$	50nJ/bit
EDA	5nJ/bit/message
Eo	0.5J
k	4000
$Popt$	0.1
ϵ_{fs}	10pJ/bit/m2
ϵ_{mp}	0.0013pJ/bit/m4
n	100

the advanced nodes and the normal nodes, thus lowering the instability region. For an application with loose reliability requirements, for instance, it allows node death up to 50%, SEP-E will still outperform both SEP and LEACH, maintaining operation up till around Round 2500, compared with Round 1800 and 1500 respectively.

In scenarios with moderate or low level of energy heterogeneity as shown in Figure 5 and Figure 6, the stability region of SEP-E gain is reduced, yet SEP-E maintains the same stability period as SEP. In general, LEACH performs very poorly in the presence of energy heterogeneity compared with SEP-E. While the heterogeneity setting gives extra energy for LEACH to extend its stability period, the effect is negated by the lack of adaptiveness in LEACH, i.e., there is no mechanism in allowing normal nodes (with lower energy levels) get less chance of being elected as cluster heads. This results in unnecessary early death of normal nodes, leading to a prolonged instability period.

Figure 7 summarizes the spread of SEP-E, SEP and LEACH stability data in the presence of high energy heterogeneity. The box plots were generated by running each protocol under the

same randomized setting for 10 runs. The stability period length of the three protocols is very distinct from each other. It is observed that SEP-E achieved a clear advantage over both SEP and LEACH.

The superiority of SEP-E compared with LEACH can also be observed from the aspect of energy dissipation rates. Figure 8 compares the average energy dissipation pattern for three types of nodes under LEACH and SEP-E. For normal nodes, clearly SEP-E's energy dissipation slope is flatter than that of LEACH, therefore achieving a prolonged stability period approaching 2000 rounds. Interestingly, energy dissipation for intermediate nodes and advanced nodes are more aggressive in SEP-E than in LEACH, which suggests that these nodes take more turns in serving as cluster heads and reduces the potentially hazardous energy consumption on low-end normal nodes. LEACH on the other hand have rather similar energy dissipation pattern across three types of nodes the three corresponding curves are almost parallel to each other. Clearly, SEP-E achieves better utilization of energy heterogeneity introduced into the system compared with

Figure 4. Performance comparison under high energy heterogeneity: SEP-E (m=0.2, b=0.3, α=3 and μ=1.5), LEACH (m=0.2, b=0.3, α=3 and μ=1.5) and SEP (m=0.3, b=0, α=3.5 and μ=0); E_{Init} =102.5J

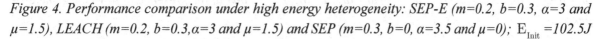
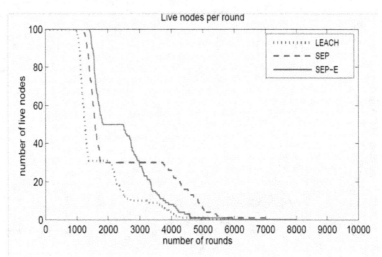

Figure 5. Performance comparison under moderate energy heterogeneity: SEP-E (m=0.1, b=0.2, α=2 and μ=1), LEACH (m=0.1, b=0.2, α=2 and μ=1) and SEP (m=0.3, b=0, α=1.3 and μ=0); E_{Init} =70J

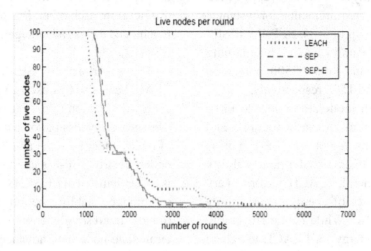

LEACH, confirming our design objective for the new protocol.

To sum up, in our simulation we have obtained a prolonged stability period and a reduction in the instability region in all trials. Ideally the advanced nodes become cluster heads more than both the intermediate and normal nodes. The intermediate nodes take up the role of cluster head more fre-quently than the normal nodes, also as expected according to our model design.

6. CONCLUSION

We present an enhanced clustering algorithm for WSNs in the presence of energy heterogeneity.

Figure 6. The performance of SEP-E (m=0.1, b=0.2, α=1 and μ=0.5), LEACH (m =0.1, b=0.2, α=1 and μ=0.5) and SEP (m=0.3, b=0, α=0.7 and μ=0); E_{Init} = 60J in the presence of low energy hetero-geneity

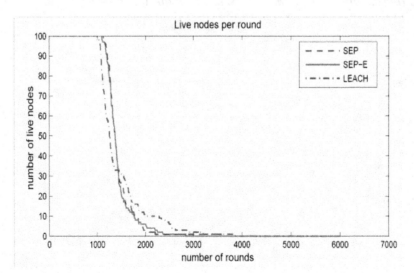

Figure 7. The behaviour of SEP-E and LEACH for 10 trials in the presence of heterogeneity. We have m = 0.2, b = 0.3, α = 3 and ¼= 1.5.

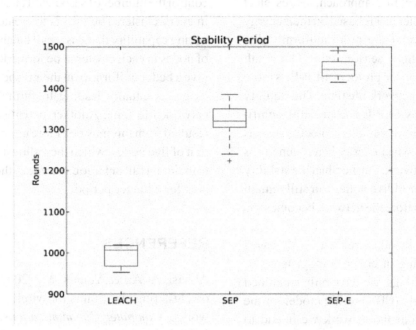

Figure 8. Shows the rate of energy dissipation of SEP-E and LEACH nodes the presence of energy heterogeneity. We have m = 0.2, b = 0.3, α = 2 and ¼= 1

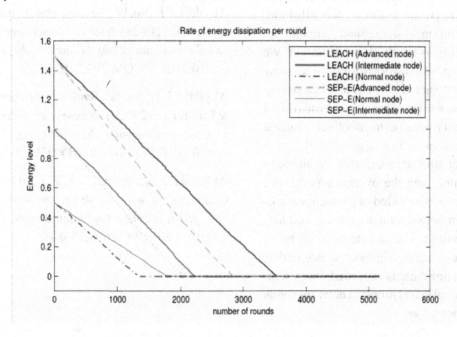

Using a heterogeneous three-tier node setting in a clustering algorithmic approach, nodes elect themselves as cluster heads based on their energy levels, therefore retaining more uniformly distributed energy among sensor nodes. Our result shows that the enhanced protocol, SEP-E, is more robust in terms of network life time. The stability period produced by SEP-E is especially significantly improved from previous protocols such as LEACH and SEP when energy heterogeneity is high within the network. Further than the stability period, the number of live nodes can still remain relatively higher before the network becomes too unreliable to use.

The same as in other related work based on sensor clustering in either homogeneous or heterogeneous settings, we have only examined the constant-bit-rate (CBR) traffic model for the sensor nodes. In our future work we intend to consider variable bit rate (VBR) traffic pattern which is necessary for some specific applications, for example to deal with compressed video streams that are bursty in nature. Sensoring modality can also be extended into a multi-modal scenario where information fusing can contribute to better local decision-making, which implies potentially more energy consumption for storage and computation. Nevertheless, this is worth of consideration. We also intend to extend our work to a multi-hierarchy scenario, by making use of multi-level clustering techniques where some of the cluster heads might take up different roles so as to effectively manage the available resources in a large network.

Another potential approach that we intend to explore for improving the overall network life cycle is to employ some kind of protocol switching mechanism between homogeneous and heterogeneous settings. The parameter might be an energy variance among neighbour sensor nodes, so that when a threshold is exceeded, the system triggers a protocol that is robust in heterogeneous settings and vice versa.

Finally, we are investigating how we can best control the number of associated cluster members in every cluster. The idea is to create a load balancing capability that ensures a balanced number of nodes in each cluster to be formed. This would give a better uniformity in their respective energy usage, eventually leading to further prolonged network life time. Another potential advantage resulted from this may be a more uniform distribution of live nodes, which then allows the network to maintain full or large coverage of the monitored area for a longer period.

REFERENCES

Abbasi, A. A., & Younis, M. (2007). A survey on clustering algorithms for wireless sensor networks. *Computer Communications*, *20*(14-15), 2826–2841. doi:10.1016/j.comcom.2007.05.024

Akyildiz, I. F., Melodia, T., & Chowdhury, K. R. (2007). A survey on wireless multimedia sensor networks. *Computer Networks*, *51*(4), 921–960. doi:10.1016/j.comnet.2006.10.002

Akyildiz, I. F., Su, W., Sankarasubramaniam, Y., & Cayirci, E. (2002a). A survey on sensor networks. *IEEE Communications Magazine*, *40*, 102–114. doi:10.1109/MCOM.2002.1024422

Akyildiz, I. F., Su, W., Sankarasubramaniam, Y., & Cayirci, E. (2002b). Wireless sensor networks: a survey. *Computer Networks*, *38*, 393–422. doi:10.1016/S1389-1286(01)00302-4

Al-karaki, J. N., & Kamal, A. E. (2004). Routing techniques in wireless sensor networks: A survey. *IEEE Wireless Communications*, *11*, 6–28. doi:10.1109/MWC.2004.1368893

Baronti, P., Pillai, P., Chook, V. W. C., Chessa, S., Gotta, A., & Hu, Y. F. (2007). Wireless sensor networks: A survey on the state of the art and the 802.15.4 and ZigBee standards. *Computer Communications*, *30*(7), 1655–1695. doi:10.1016/j.comcom.2006.12.020

Heinzelman, W. R., Chandrakasan, A., & Balakrishnan, H. (2002). An application-specific protocol architectures for wireless networks. *IEEE Transactions on Wireless Communications*, *1*, 660–670. doi:10.1109/TWC.2002.804190

Karl, H., & Wilig, A. (2007). *Protocols and architectures for wireless sensor networks*. New York, NY: John Wiley & Sons.

Mhatre, V., & Rosenberg, C. (2004). Homogeneous vs. heterogeneous clustered sensor networks: A comparative study. In *Proceedings of the IEEE International Conference on Communications* (Vol. 6, pp. 3646-3651).

Qing, L., Zhu, Q., & Wang, M. (2006). Design of a distributed energy-efficient clustering algorithm for heterogeneous wireless sensor networks. *Computer Communications*, *29*(12), 2230–2237. doi:10.1016/j.comcom.2006.02.017

Shepard, T. J. (1996). A channel access scheme for large dense packet radio networks. *ACM SIGCOMM Computer Communications Review*, *26*(4), 219–230. doi:10.1145/248157.248176

Smaragdakis, G., Matta, I., & Bestavros, A. (2004). A stable election protocol for clustered heterogeneous wireless sensor networks. In *Proceedings of the International Workshop on SANPA*.

Younis, O., & Fahmy, S. (2004). HEED: A hybrid, energy-efficient, distributed clustering approach for ad hoc sensor networks. *IEEE Transactions on Mobile Computing*, *3*(4), 366–379. doi:10.1109/TMC.2004.41

This work was previously published in International Journal of Business Data Communications and Networking, Volume 7, Issue 4, edited by Varadharajan Sridhar and Debashis Saha, p.p 18-31, copyright 2011 by IGI Publishing (an imprint of IGI Global)

Chapter 15
New Strategies and Extensions in Kruskal's Algorithm in Multicast Routing

Mohamed Aissa
University of Nizwa, Oman

Rion Murray
University of Trinidad and Tobago, Trinidad and Tobago

Adel Ben Mnaouer
Dar Al Uloom University, Saudi Arabia

Abdelfettah Belghith
HANA Research Group University of Manouba, Tunisia

ABSTRACT

Multimedia applications are expected to guarantee end-to-end quality of service (QoS) and are characterized by stringent constraints on delay, delay-jitter, bandwidth, cost, and so forth. The authors observe that Kruskal's algorithm is limited to minimal (maximal) spanning unconstrained tree. As such, the authors extend Kruskal's algorithm to incorporate the delay bound constraint. Consequently, a novel algorithm is proposed, called EKRUS (Extended Kruskal), for constructing multicast trees. The EKRUS' distinguishing features consists of a better management of Kruskal's priority queues, and in the provision of edge priority aggregation. Preliminary results show that the proposed EKRUS algorithm performs as well as the best-known algorithms (such as the DDMC, DMCTc algorithms) while exhibiting reduced complexity. The authors conducted an intensive analysis and evaluations of different strategies of assigning edges into the classes of the queue as well as edge selection. As a result, the EKRUS algorithm was further extended with different edge assignment and selection strategies. Through extensive simulations, the authors have evaluated various versions of the EKRUS and analyzed their performance under different load conditions.

DOI: 10.4018/978-1-4666-2026-1.ch015

INTRODUCTION

Minimum spanning tree algorithms find applications in diverse areas such as: least electrical wiring, minimum cost connecting communication and transportation network, network reliability problems, minimum stress networks, clustering and numerical taxonomy, etc.

The problem of finding a spanning subtree of a given connected network which has minimum total length was first solved by Kruskal (1956). Shortly thereafter, Prim (1959) and Dijkstra (1959) suggested another algorithm which appeared to be more efficient. So far, all the problems relating to spanning trees are solved using either Prim or Dijkstra's algorithm.

However, recent works suggest that a suitable implementation of Kruskal's algorithm is computationally more efficient in a number of interesting cases, in particular when the network under consideration is sparse.

Navneet and Jianer (2002) showed that maximum bandwidth paths can be constructed by a modified Kruskal's algorithm. They demonstrate that their approach is simpler, easier in implementation, more flexible, and faster than using a modified Dijkstra's algorithm.

For complex communication network architecture, communication network architecture has a heavy workload in the process. If we constructed it in the traditional way, it will result in a great waste of resource. Consequently, we need to ensure good efficiency and increase economic efficiency. Only by using rational design, we can get the best results, otherwise, the workload will be large, and the efficiency will be low (Chenghui & ChuanJun, 2010).

Kershenbaum and Van (1972) observed that for sparse networks a dramatic reduction in execution time can be obtained by the use of Kruskal's algorithm.

The motivation for the present work is threefold. First, we have identified a weakness in the classical Kruskal's algorithm. It consists in the fact that the priority queue contains all the edges in only one class. In this class, all the edges in the priority queue are sorted either in increasing order to form a maximal spanning tree or in decreasing order to find the minimal spanning tree. Second, in most cases found in the literature, the extraction of edges from the priority queue, in the classical Kruskal's algorithm, is done according to one single criterion, which is the priority of that edge in the queue. Third, in most cases, Kruskal's algorithm is used without considering constraints.

The contributions of our work are as follows. At first, we propose to organize the priority queue of the original Kruskal's algorithm into multiple classes. These classes are formed by the edge containing the source node, the edges containing destination nodes and the edges containing relay nodes respectively. Then, we introduce a new strategy in edge selection, giving priority to edges containing one or two destination nodes to be selected. Finally, based on these two strategies, we address the problem of constructing the delay constrained multicast tree using a fast and simple heuristic algorithm named the *Extended Kruskal's (EKRUS)* algorithm. Furthermore, the assignment strategy of edges into the classes of the queue, as well as the edge selection process are investigated. As a result, of this investigation, the EKRUS algorithm was divided into different variants depending on different edge assignment and selection strategies. These strategies are subjected to extensive simulation in order to assess their performances and their suitability under different load conditions.

In the remainder of this paper, the next section provides an overview of some related work. The network model is then presented. The formal definition of the EKRUS algorithm and its analysis are given. A comparative study of the various variants of the EKRUS algorithm against some well-known algorithms from the literature is also provided. We prove the correctness and time complexity analysis of the EKRUS algorithm and discuss simulation results. Concluding remarks are provided in the last section.

RELATED WORK

Prim's algorithm is easy to implement and is very fast for large nearly complete graphs (Kershenbaum & Van, 1972). Unfortunately, for sparse graphs, Prim's algorithm becomes considerably more complex and some speed is lost in analyzing such graphs (Kershenbaum & Van, 1972). Dijkstra algorithm assures a rapid and correct dissemination of topological information (McDonald, 1997). Unfortunately, the algorithm suffers from scalability problem (Alpert et al., 1993), and the written programs are long and complicated (Navneet & Chen, 2002). For constructing a maximum bandwidth path in a network, Kruskal's algorithm is always at least three times (up to five times, in some cases) as fast as Dijkstra's algorithm (Navneet & Chen, 2002). The written program is short and simple (Navneet & Chen, 2002). It works better than Prim's algorithm for sparse graphs (Kershenbaum & Van, 1972).

In Guttoski et al. (2007), it is declared that Kruskal's algorithm presents some advantages like its simplified code, its polynomial-time execution and the reduced search space to generate only one query tree, that will be the optimal tree. In most experiments, Kruskal's algorithm got the expected results in almost the same time as the results achieved by default PostgreSQL's optimization algorithms. The results confirm that Kruskal's algorithm is a feasible method for query optimization. Kruskal and Prim are Greedy algorithms and their implementation is simple due to their reduced code size. They are polynomial-time algorithms, presenting lower complexity than Dynamic Programming. On the other hand, greedy algorithms take the best immediate solution in each step, without regarding future consequences, and sometimes produce a solution that may not be the best one. Guttoski et al. (2007) declared that comparing Kruskal's and Prim's algorithms, Kruskal's algorithm presents the most adequate way to build the final solution in the query optimization process, because when the most profitable joins are performed first, the joins that will be formed after are going to have their cost reduced, mainly joins between tables with high number of tuples.

Pan et al. (2009) used a tree structure called Union-find sets (UFS) used to deal with the issue of merging and inquiring of disjoint sets. UFS is used in Kruskal's algorithm to determine whether the selected edge has formed a loop with other identified edges. Based on their results, they concluded that in Kruskal's algorithm UFS using in "select edge and judge loop" is about 10 times faster than common way. They have obtained a good result in the algorithm's time complexity $O(ElogE)$, where E is the set of edges.

In Chenghui and ChuanJun (2010), the authors concluded that using the Prim Algorithm can effectively reduce the waste of resources, improve computing speed, and have important significance both in theory and practice.

Unfortunately, many works relating to Kruskal's algorithm are delay unconstrained. Consequently, we address the problem of extending Kruskal's algorithm to construct delay bounded multicast trees. We extend previous works by providing an EKRUS algorithm based on the extended version of Kruskal's algorithm. Our extensive simulation results prove the efficiency of our algorithm.

SOME QOS PARAMETERS ANALYSIS OF WELL KNOWN ALGORITHMS

The Kruskal's algorithm (Kruskal, 1956) builds an optimal spanning tree from scratch by adding one edge at a time. All the edges are first sorted in nondecreasing order of their costs. Then a STACK is defined to store the set of edges which is part of a minimum spanning tree. Initially the STACK is empty. A stack is a dynamic set in which the element removed from the set by a DELETE operation is prespecified (Cormen et al., 2001). The edges in the sorted order one by one is examined and checked whether adding the edge to STACK creates a cycle with the edges already in STACK. If it does not, the edge is added to the STACK, otherwise it is discarded. The process is terminated when the number of elements of STACK is (n-1). At termination, the edges in STACK constitute a minimum spanning tree.

Focusing on the cost and delay QoS metrics, we apply Kruskal's, Prim's and Dijkstra's algorithms on the graph of Figure 1. We have pruned all non-destination leaf nodes for some of their resulting graphs. In the original graph, each pair *c/d* of numbers along any edge, represent the cost *(c)* and the delay *(d)* for that edge. The source node is F. The nodes {B, D, E, H} shown in boldface represent the multicast group *Z* (of destination nodes). The resulting minimal cost trees (MCT) and the least delay trees (LDT) are presented in Figure 2 and Figure 3 respectively. The branches added to the tree are shown in boldface on the network diagram.

To investigate and compare these execution algorithms, we introduce the following definitions:

Total Cost (Total Delay): By Total Cost (Delay) of a multicasting tree *T*, we mean the summation of the cost (delay) of all the paths starting from the source *s* and ending at every destination node. For Total Cost, common links are calculated only once.

$$TotalCost_{max}\left(T\right) = \sum_{e \in T} C\left[e\right] \qquad (1)$$

$$TotalDelay_{max}\left(T\right) = \sum_{e \in P(s,v)} D\left[e\right] \qquad (2)$$

In all these definitions, the path is the unique and shortest route from the source *s* to *v* (a leaf or destination node) in *T*.

Applying these definitions and these algorithms on the original graph provided in Figure 1, we generated the resulting graphs depicted in Figure 2 and Figure 3. Based on these graphs, we have built Table 1 which provides a comparison of the three algorithms. We give next the network model used in our analysis.

THE PROPOSED EXTENDED KRUSKAL'S TRADEOFF ALGORITHM (EKRUS)

Network Model

Given a directed asymmetric, acyclic graph *G* = *(V, E)* with *V* as the set of vertices (i.e., the network nodes) and *E* as the set of edges representing physical or logical connections between nodes, we define the following weight functions on the edges, for any edge *e*:

Figure 1. Original graph

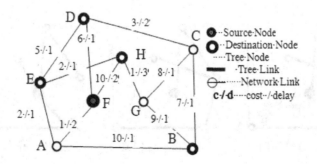

Figure 2. Minimal cost trees

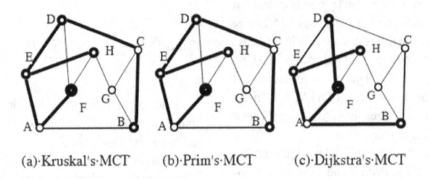

(a)·Kruskal's·MCT   (b)·Prim's·MCT   (c)·Dijkstra's·MCT

$C(e): E \to \mathbb{R}^+,$

a positive real edge cost function, and

$D(e): E \to \mathbb{R}^+,$

a positive real delay edge function.

The cost of a link can be associated with the utilization of the link. The delay of a link is the sum of the perceived queuing delay, transmission delay, and propagation delay over that link. The nodes represent routers or switches and edges represent the communication links between them. An edge e $\in$ E from $u \in$ V to $v \in$ V is represented by e = *(u,v)*.

Each link is bi-directional, i.e., the existence of a link e = *(u,v)* from node u to node v implies the existence of another link e' = *(v, u)* for any

$u, v \in V$. As the network is asymmetric, it is possible that $C(e) \neq C(e')$ and $D(e) \neq D(e')$.

On this graph, we designate a source node $s \in V$ and a set of destination nodes Z, called the multicast group members such that $Z \subseteq V - \{s\}$. Given a delay tolerance (delay bound) Δ, the delay-constrained multicast routing problem can be stated as follows. Find a tree T $(T \subseteq G)$ rooted at s and spanning all nodes in Z, such that for each node v in Z, the delay on the path from s to v is bounded above by Δ.

$$Delay[v] = \sum_{e \in P(s,v)} D[e] < \Delta \qquad (3)$$

Here $P(s, v)$ is the unique path in T from s to v, such that

Figure 3. Least delay trees

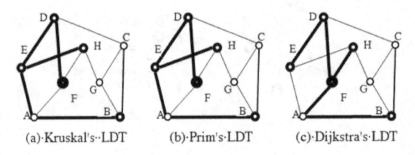

(a)·Kruskal's··LDT   (b)·Prim's·LDT   (c)·Dijkstra's·LDT

$$Cost\left(T\right) = \sum_{e \in T} C\left[e\right] \ is\ minimized \qquad (4)$$

Motivated by the results provided in Kershenbaum and Van (1972) and Navneet and Chen (2002), we propose the extended Kruskal's algorithm (EKRUS) to construct multicast trees. Below, we propose a method used in our algorithm.

EKRUS and the Delay Constraint

In Li et al. (1997), it is claimed that a network is stable if and only if all the packets experience bounded delay within the network. The delay bound (Δ) is a parameter reflecting the fact that a packet delivered more than Δ time units after its transmission at the source is of no value to the receiver (e.g., because it has missed its play out instant). Furthermore, in Salama (1996), it is mentioned that the upper bound on the end-to-end delay from any source to any receiver in real time session is the main QoS parameter considered during their investigation of various routing problems. Again in Salama (1996), it is mentioned that a guaranteed upper bound on the end-to-end delay must be provided to certain distributed multimedia applications and especially for high-speed networking. It is necessary and sufficient for the network to satisfy the given bound, i.e., there is no need to minimize the end-to-end delay (Salama, 1996). For these reasons stated, a delay bound constraint was introduced in the EKRUS algorithm.

EDGE PRIORITY AGGREGATION

Another aspect that had also motivated our construction of the EKRUS algorithm is the profit gains identified for Prim-Dijkstra tradeoff algorithm in Alpert et al. (1993) and Mohamed and Adel (2004), where a greedy strategy based on the shortest-path and minimal spanning trees

was applied. This greedy strategy combines the minimum cost and the minimum radius objectives by combining respectively the optimal Prim's and Dijkstra's algorithms. The adopted strategy in Alpert et al. (1993) and Mohamed and Adel (2004) biases routes selection through destinations.

In this regard, our contribution extends these works by incorporating Prim-Dijsktra tradeoff advantages in Kruskal's algorithm. Consequently, here we address the problem of investigating new methods in Kruskal's algorithm to give edges formed by one or two destination nodes the priority to be selected, during the tree construction process.

PRIORITY QUEUE ENHANCEMENT

Our present work addresses the problem of improving Kruskal's algorithm to incorporate the delay bound as a QoS constraint. The delay constraint, i.e., the upper bound to-end delay, is an important QoS requirement, because most real-time applications are delay-sensitive. This information must be received within some delay bound.

Therefore, one of our tasks is to improve the classical structure of the priority queue in Kruskal's algorithm. In most of the cases where Kruskal's algorithm is mentioned in the literature, all the edges are sorted either in increasing order to form a maximal spanning tree or in decreasing order to form a minimal spanning tree.

Table 1. Comparison between Prim's, Dijkstra's and Kruskal's algorithms on the original graph of Figure 1

Algorithm	Minimal Cost Tree	Least Delay Tree
	Total Cost	Total Delay
Prim	20	24
Dijkstra	24	17
Kruskal	20	24

However, in Alpert et al. (1993) and Mohamed and Adel (2004), the authors proposed a technique, where priority is given to destination nodes to be selected. To take advantage of this technique to improve the performance of Kruskal's algorithm, we need to modify and enhance the handling of the priority queues in Kruskal's algorithm. For this purpose, we were inspired by the priority queue management of the SCTF algorithm (Ramanathan, 1996). Indeed, in the SCTF, vertices already in the tree (terminals and non-terminals) are arranged in a priority queue such that (presented in Box 1):

No ordering is performed among any two terminals or any two non-terminals. We modify and adapt this priority queue handling scheme to fit in our proposed algorithm.

In our case, the priority queue is composed of three classes organized as follows: *the first class* contains only one edge linking the source node s to a given node v such that the edge (s, v) has the minimal cost among all edges connected to the source node. The remaining edges, which are linked to the source node, but having higher costs, are either added to the second class if they contain destination nodes, or they are added to the third class otherwise.

The second class contains all edges (u, v) sorted by cost values in increasing order and such that one node u or v (or both) is (are) *destination node*(s). *The third class* contains all the remaining relay links, sorted by increasing cost values. For two edges having equal cost values at the second priority class, the priority is given to the edge having two destination nodes or containing the source node. There is no difference between any two edges having equal cost values at the third

priority class containing relay edges. Hence, we have (presented in Box 2).

ALGORITHM DESCRIPTION

The pseudo-code of the proposed EKRUS algorithm is depicted in Figure 4. The operation *Make_Set(u)* creates a new set whose only member (and thus representative) is u. The operation *Find_Set(u)* returns a representative element from the set that contains u. Thus we can determine whether two vertices u and v belong to the same tree by testing whether *Find_Set(u)* equals *Find_Set(v)*. The combining of trees is accomplished by the Union procedure (Cormen et al., 2001). The algorithm repeatedly selects from the priority queue the vertex with the minimum key value. The key represents the least cost path estimate from either the source or the destinations found so far. The selected vertex is inserted into S, which is a subset of the vertices whose path from the source has already been determined. We maintain a priority queue Q that initially contains E class edges as discussed earlier. After the extraction operation, Q will contain all the vertices in $E - S$. To move from one class to another, the edges of the last class must be already considered.

From the first priority class, we extract the first edge containing the source node and having the least cost among all the remaining links starting from the source. It is added to the tree. This edge constitutes the first sub-path added to the tree. Subsequently, from the second priority class, we select the next edge. In this paper, we will not deal with partial added trees but rather with

Box 1.

```
priority(source)>priority(terminal)>p
riority(non-terminal).
```

Box 2.

```
Priority of edge with source
node>priority of edges with destina-
tion node(s)>priority of edges with
relay nodes.
```

Figure 4. The pseudo-code of the EKRUS algorithm

```
EKRUS(G, Z, D)
Input
        G(V, E) = graph, s = source node, D( )= positive real delay edge function
        Z = set of destination nodes,  Δ = Application specified delay bound
        /* P(s,v) is the unique path in T from s to v (as mentioned earlier) */
Output
        A minimum spanning tree T
                                    T ← ∅
for each node v ∈ V do
                    MAKE _ SET(v)
sort the links E of G in terms of link cost in increasing order E = {e₁,e₂,....eₙ,}
        in proposed priority queue Q as discussed earlier;
/* After sorting E = {u₁,v₁},{u₂,v₂},{u₃,v₃},...., {u|E|, v|E|}   */

for each edge (u,v) ∈ E , taken from the priority Q do

1.          {
                if  Find _ Set(uᵢ) ≠ Find _ Set(vᵢ)
2.                          {
                    case 1:  uᵢ.=s :
                                    {Delay[vᵢ]=D(s, vᵢ), Flag=1}
                    case 2:  (uᵢvᵢ) ∈ P(s,vᵢ) :
                                    {Delay[vᵢ]=Delay[uᵢ]+D(u, vᵢ),  Flag=1}
                    case 3:  (uᵢvᵢ) ∉ P(s,vᵢ) (isolated):
                                    {(u, vᵢ) not validated, Flag=0 }

                        if  Flag=1 AND (Delay[vᵢ]<Δ)
3.                                              {
                                                T ← T∪{uᵢ,vᵢ}
                                                Union (uᵢ,vᵢ)
                                                Q ← Q−{e}
                                                S ← S+{e}
4.                                              }
5.                          }
6.              }
7.  Return T
```

added edges. Table 2 summarizes the situations that an edge undergoes during the sub-tree construction process. A validated subpath or edge is directly added to the tree.

A temporary not yet validated subpath or edge is taken to the end of the class queue to which it belongs (destination or relay classes). If, at a working stage of the algorithm, some reported subpaths or some edges from the second class

Table 2. Situation of sub-graphs and edge types during tree construction

Edge Membership	Edge State
$(u_i, v_i) \in P(s, v_i)$	*Validated*
$(u_i, v_i) \notin P(s, v_i)$	*Not validated*
$u_i = s$ ((u_i, v_i) connected directly with the source node).	*Validated*

cannot be connected, then we move on to the third priority class containing relay edges (not containing any destination nodes). If all destination edges are connected, then there is no need to investigate the third priority class. Table 3 provides a comparison of our algorithm against a set of others well-known ones.

The EKRUS Algorithm

EKRUS Algorithm Operation

A detailed example in Figure 5 is provided to show how the EKRUS algorithm works on the original graph depicted in Figure 1. Figure 5 (a–e) shows the progression of the algorithm, with each branch added to the tree shown in boldface on the network diagram. The resulting multicast tree is shown in Figure 5(e). In the original graph, each pair *c/d* of numbers along any edge, represent the cost *(c)* and the delay *(d)* for that edge. *F* is the source node. The delay bound Δ is set to 5 and the set of destination nodes *Z* is set to: Z={B, D, E, H}. The edges are arranged in the priority queue as mentioned in Table 3.

Initially, the queue *Q =*{*(F,A), (H,G), (A,E), (E,H), (C,D),(D,E), (B,C), (B,G),(F,D),(F,H), (A,B), (C,G)*}. So the edge *(F,A)* is taken from the priority queue and added to the tree *T* as its delay is less than the delay bound. The edge *(H,G)* is taken from *Q*. As it is not connected to a subpath containing the source node, it is taken to the end of the 2nd priority queue. *Q* becomes *{(A,E), (E,H), (C,D), (D,E), (B,C), (B,G), (F,D),(F,H), (A,B), (H,G), (C,G)}*. The edge *(A,E)* is taken from *Q*. It is connected to a subpath containing the source

Table 3. Priority Queue arrangement

Source Edge	Destination Edges	Relay Edges
(F,A)	*(H,G), (A,E), (E,H), (C,D), (D,E), (B,C), (B,G),|(F,D),(F,H), (A,B)*	*(C,G)*

node. Its delay $Delay[E] = Delay[A]+D(A,E)=2+1=3< \Delta$. It is added to the tree. *Q* becomes *{(E,H), (C,D), (D,E), (B,C), (B,G), (F,D),(F,H), (A,B), (H,G), (C,G)}*. Next, the edge *(E,H)* is taken from *Q*. It is connected to the newly formed subpath *(FE)* containing the source node. Its delay from the source node is calculated as follows $Delay[H]= Delay[E]+D(E,H)=3+1=4< \Delta$. Then it is added to the tree *T*. *Q* becomes *{(C,D),(D,E),(B,C),(B,G), (F,D),(F,H), (A,B),(H,G),(C,G)}*. The edge *(C,D)* is taken from *Q*. As it is not connected to a subpath containing the source node, it is taken to the end of the 2nd priority queue. *Q* becomes *{(D,E),(B,C),(B,G), (F,D),(F,H), (A,B),(H,G), (C,D),(C,G)}*. Next, the edge *(D,E)* is taken from *Q*. It is connected to a subpath containing the source node. Its delay $Delay[D]= Delay[E]+D(E,D)= 3+1=4<\Delta$. So it is added to the tree *T*. *Q* becomes *{(B,C), (B,G), (F,D),(F,H), (A,B), (H,G), (C,D), (C,G)}*. Next, the edge *(B,C)* is taken from *Q*. It is not connected to a subpath containing the source node, so it taken to the end queue of the second class. *Q* becomes *{(B,G), (F,D),(F,H),(A,B),(H,G), (C,D), (B,C), (C,G)}*. Next, the edge *(B,G)* is taken from *Q*. It is not connected to a subpath containing the source node, so it is taken to the end queue of the second class. *Q* becomes *{(F,D),(F,H), (A,B),(H,G), (C,D),*

Figure 5. EKRUS algorithm execution method

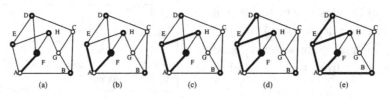

(B,C),(B,G), (C,G)}. Next, the edge *(F,D)* is taken from *Q*. As it is in the same tree, it is discarded. *Q* becomes *{(F,H), (A,B),(H,G), (C,D), (B,C),(B,G), (C,G)}*. Next, the edge *(F,H)* is taken from *Q*. As it is in the same tree, it is also discarded. *Q* becomes *{ (A,B),(H,G), (C,D), (B,C),(B,G), (C,G)}*. Next, the edge *(A,B)* is taken from *Q*. It is connected to a subpath containing the source node. Its delay *Delay[B]=Delay[A]+D(A,B)= 2+1=3< Δ*. So it is added to the tree *T*. *Q* becomes *{(H,G), (C,D), (B,C),(B,G), (C,G)}*.

The final tree *T* is shown in Figure 5(e). The other edges left in the second and third priority class are omitted because all destination nodes contained in edges have been already connected. If all destination nodes are connected, there is no need for further processing even though the priority queue was not yet empty.

Observation 1

Our obtained tree (Figure 5(e)) has the same total cost (equal to 21) as the least cost tree obtained by the classical Kruskal's algorithm depicted in Figure 2(a) after trimming non leaf nodes. Furthermore our tree is delay bounded.

Comparison with Other Algorithms

In Table 4, we compare the execution of the mentioned algorithms on the original graph depicted in Figure 1. The delay bound Δ is set to 5, and the set of destination nodes Z is set to Z={B,D,E,H}. All the algorithms mentioned in Table 4 (except QDMR) (Guo & Matta, 2000) and AHHK (Alpert et al., 1993) have used the same original graph of Figure 1 as a model withsimilar data (source node*s=F*, cost, delay, delay bound Δ=5), on which they applied their algorithms. For *QDMR* and AHHK, it was applied to the graph depicted in Figure 1. It can be noted that the *EKRUS* tree is similar to the best well-known trees indicated in Table 4 and Figure 6.

Correctness Proof and Time Complexity Analysis of the EKRUS Algorithm

Correctness Proof

The correctness of the algorithm EKRUS results from the following two theorems:

Theorem 1

The path generated by the EKRUS algorithm is loop-free.

Table 4. Comparison between EKRUS and other algorithms by costs and delays

Algorithm	COST	DELAY
	Total Cost	Total Delay
EKRUS, DMCTc (Kompella et al., 1993), DDMC (Shaikh & Shin, 1997)	20	14
EPDT (Mohamed and Adel, 2004), QDMR((Guo & Matta, 2000), DMCTcd (Kompella et al., 1993), CSOC (Pasquale et al., 1998), CCET (Meylan et al., 1999)	21	11
AHHK (Alpert et al., 1993)	21	12
CBT (Pasquale et al., 1998)	29	14
CSOD (Pasquale et al., 1998)	32	8

CBT: Core based Tree, CSOC: Combined Separate Optimal Cost, CSOD: Combined Separate Optimal Delay, CCET: Constrained Cheapest Edge Tree, DDMC: Destination-Driven Multicast, QDMR: QoS Dependent Multicast Routing, EEPDT: Extended Prim-Dijkstra Tradeoff.

Figure 6. Some trees to compare with the EKRUS tree

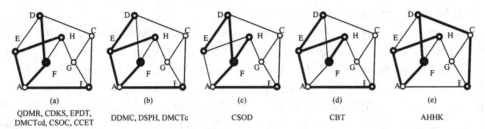

(a)	(b)	(c)	(d)	(e)
QDMR, CDKS, EPDT, DMCTcd, CSOC, CCET	DDMC, DSPH, DMCTc	CSOD	CBT	AHHK

Proof

The proof is obvious and results from the fact that Kruskal's algorithm (used in the EKRUS algorithm) is loop free. Any edge from the graph G is added to the tree T only if it does not create a cycle. This operation is satisfied by the condition in line 7 ($if\ Find\_Set\left(u_i\right) \neq Find\_Set(v_i)$).

Theorem 2

The algorithm EKRUS always constructs a delay-bounded multicast tree if such a tree exists.

Proof

As all edges are initially put in the priority queue Q, so all of them will be treated individually. If some edges were not selected at some steps of the EKRUS algorithm execution due to their high delay bound, then they will be selected and connected during some other coming steps through other paths. Their cost may be higher. However, if at the end of the algorithm execution, some edges are still unconnected, then we can conclude that the initial delay bound value (Δ) is too tight and must be relaxed. Thus, the execution of the EKRUS algorithm always leads to a delay-bounded multicast tree.

Time Complexity Analysis

In the following, we analyze the time complexity of our proposed EKRUS algorithm.

Theorem 3

The time complexity of EKRUS is $O\left(\left|E\right| log \left|E\right|\right)$.

Proof

The initialization in line 1 takes $O\left(1\right)$ time. The operation in line 2 takes $O(\left|V\right|)$. The operation in line 3 takes $O(\left|E\right| log \left|E\right|)$. The time to sort the edges in E in increasing order by cost weight takes $O(\left|E\right| log \left|E\right|)$. The operation in line 5 takes $O log n)$. Then with a proper implementation of Union-Find, EKRUS algorithm has a running time $O(\left|E\right| log \left|E\right|)$.

Table 5 shows that our EKRUS algorithm has a complexity that is superior to others well-known algorithms.

Variants of EKRUS

As mentioned previously, one of the main attributes of the EKRUS algorithm is the management of the priority queue. The strategy of assigning edges into the classes of the queue as well as edge selection can be further investigated. As a result, the EKRUS algorithm can be further divided into different edge assignment and selection strategies to investigate which strategy gives optimal performance. Four different strategies (scenarios) were formulated and summarized in Table 6 and Table 7. For each scenario number (S) corresponds an EKRUS version (EKRUS1, EKRUS2, EKRUS3 and EKRUS4).

Table 5. Algorithm complexities

Algorithms	Time Complexities
EKRUS	$O(|E| \log |E|)$
EPDT, QDMR, DDMC	$O(|E| \log |V|)$
AHHK (ALG1)	$O(|V^2|)$
DMCT$_c$ & DMCT$_{CD}$	$O(|V^3|)$

PERFORMANCE EVALUATION

In this section, the performance of the proposed EKRUS1, EKRUS2, EKRUS3 and EKRUS4 algorithms were compared against other well known multicast routing algorithms such as the QoS dependent multicast routing algorithm, QDMR (Guo & Matta, 2000), the distributed shortest path heuristic algorithm DSPH (Jia, 1998), the Constrained Dijkstra's algorithm CDKS (Sun & Langendorfre, 1995). The aim was to observe the performances of these algorithms in sparse and dense networks. Hence the simulation environ-ment was setup to allow for comparisons for varying destination group sizes, varying node degrees in the constructing the network, varying network sizes and varying delay bound parameters. The multicast routing simulator (MCRSIM) (Salama et al., 1995) was used to compare these algorithms.

Comparison with Destination Set Size Parameter

This simulation attempted to compare the tree cost and delay as the destination group size varied. The size of the entire network and the delay bound values were constant. The number of nodes in the entire network was 64 with an average node degree of 4. This simulation varied the destination group size from 4 group members or nodes to 56 nodes in intervals of 4. The aim was to assess the cost and delays as the network is densely populated with destination group nodes. The value of delay bound at each interval remained constant for all multicast routing algorithms reviewed in the simulation. The values for the cost of the constructed multicast tree and the delay were then recorded. The results obtain from the simulation of the total tree cost against the destination group size (mul-

Table 6. EKRUS scenarios: edge assigning strategies

S	Source Class Content	Relay Class Content
1 & 2	This class consists of ONLY ONE edge with the lowest cost. This edge MUST consist of the source node.	This class consists of all other edges sorted in ascending order of cost, and not containing destination nodes.
3 & 4	This class consists of ALL edges containing the source node. These edges are sorted in ascending order of cost.	

	Destination Class Content
1	This class consists of all edges sorted in ascending order of cost. Each edge in this class must consist of at least one destination node. Any edge that consists of both a destination node and a source node is not included in this class. If two edges have the same cost, priority is given to an edge consisting of two destination nodes than to an edge that consists of only one destination node.
2	This class consists of all edges sorted in ascending order of cost. Each edge in this class must consist of at least one destination node. Any edge that consists of both a destination node and a source node is included in this class. If two edges have the same cost, priority is given to an edge consisting of two destination nodes than to an edge that consists of only one destination node.
3 & 4	This class consists of ALL edges containing at least one destination node. These edges are sorted in ascending order of cost. If two edges have the same cost, priority is given to an edge consisting of two destination nodes than to an edge that consists of only one destination node.

Table 7. EKRUS scenarios: edge selection strategies

S	Priority Queue Handling Method
1 & 2	The ONLY edge in the Source Class is used to construct tree, followed by edges in the destination class. If edges in the destination class cannot be connected to the tree, then the edges in the Relay Class are considered. If an edge is found in the Relay Class, the next edge is selected from the Destination Class. This process is repeated until the tree is constructed.
3	The edge with the minimum cost is first selected from the Source Class to construct the tree. This is followed by selection of edges in the Destination Class. If all edges are considered in the Destination Class and the tree is not completed, then edges are considered in the Relay Class. If an edge can be selected from the Relay Class then the next edge to be considered will be from the Destination Class. If an edge cannot be selected from both the Relay Class nor the Destination Class then the least cost validated edge is considered from the Source Class.
4	The edge with the minimum cost is first selected from the Source Class to construct the tree. This is followed by selection of edges in the Destination Class. If all edges are considered in the Destination Class and the tree is not completed, then edges are considered in the Source Class. If an edge can be selected from the Source Class then the next edge to be considered will be from the Destination Class. If an edge cannot be selected from both the Source Class nor the Destination Class then the least cost validated edge is considered from the Relay Class.

ticast group size) were plotted in Figure 7. The delay of the same multicast tree obtained against that multicast group size is shown in Figure 8. The results from Figure 7 graph clearly showed that as the multicast group size increased all versions of the EKRUS algorithms were more costly than the other multicast algorithms. DSPH had the cheapest cost as the destination size increased but was closely contested by QDMR. EKRUS2 and EKRUS4 showed the cheapest cost among all the other versions of EKRUS algorithms with EKRUS2 having a slight edge over EKRUS4. It was seen that EKRUS2 and EKRUS4 had

lower costs over EKRUS1 and EKRUS3 for small destination sizes until the destination group size was 20 to 24 nodes. It was at those values that EKRUS2 seemed to have a cheaper cost than the other EKRUS versions. The results from Figure 8 showed that minimum spanning tree constructed by all EKRUS algorithms had a better delay than DSPH algorithm for any multicast group size. CDKS algorithm showed the best delay results as the destination group size increased. EKRUS2 showed the second best delay results bypassing QDMR, DSPH and the other versions of EKRUS shown.

Figure 7. Graph of tree cost against the number of destination nodes in a 64 node network

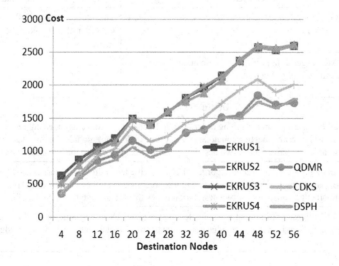

Figure 8. Graph of delay in ms against the number of destination nodes in a 64 node network

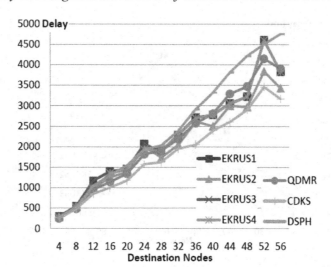

Comparison with Network Size Parameter

The aim of this simulation is to assess the cost and delay performances of the algorithms in sparse networks. To simulate this, the number of members in the multicast destination group was set to a constant value of 10 nodes, while the total number of nodes in the entire network varied. The total network size started at 20 and increased by 10 for each stage of the simulation until the network size reached the value of 100. The average node degree to construct the network graph was 4 and the value of the delay bound was constant for each multicast routing algorithm. In Figure 9 the total tree cost against the total network size was plotted. The tree delay against the total network size is shown in Figure 10. The results on Figure 9 showed that DSPH had the best tree cost among all multicast algorithms as the network size increased. EKRUS2 and EKRUS4 showed to be the best competing algorithms among all

Figure 9. Graph of total cost against network size in a destination group Set of 10

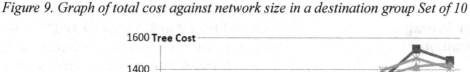

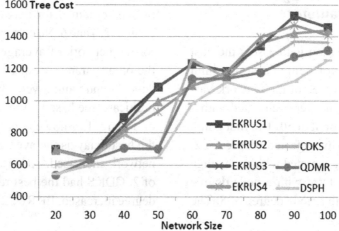

Figure 10. Graph of delay (ms) against total network size in a destination group Set of 10

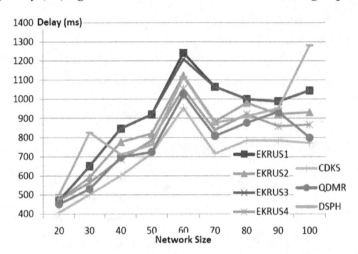

other EKRUS algorithms. As the network size increased to around 60 nodes, EKRUS4 proved to have the best cost of all the EKRUS versions.

However, as the network size increased past 60 nodes, the EKRUS2 algorithm showed better cost as compared to the other EKRUS versions. The results on Figure 10 showed that EKRUS1 and EKRUS3 have the worse delay values as the network size increased. CDKS showed the best delay as the network became sparser. EKRUS2 and EKRUS4 competed well with QDMR and DSPH, with EKRUS4 showing more stability than DSPH. EKRUS4 proved to be the best of the EKRUS algorithm in sparser networks.

Comparison with Average Node Degree Parameter

The aim of this simulation is to assess the cost and delay performances of the multicast algorithm as the average node degree of the network varies. Four network graphs were generated with a network size or node count of 50. The first graph was generated with an average node degree of 2, the second graph was generated with an average node degree of 4, the third with a node degree of 6 and the fourth with a node degree of 8. The

multicast group on each graph was set to 25 and the delay bound values were constant for each multicast routing algorithm. In Figure 11 the values obtained for the total tree cost were plotted against the average node degree of the tree. The delay values of the multicast tree were also plotted against the average node degree and are displayed in Figure 12. The results on Figure 11 showed that the total costs of the multicast trees formed by all versions of the EKRUS algorithm were much higher than those formed by the other multicast algorithms. As the average node degree increases for the network, the tree cost decreases for multicast algorithms. QDMR algorithm has the best tree cost as the average node degree increased from 2 to 8. Values for DSPH could only be obtained for networks of average node degrees 2, 4 and 6. No cost value could be obtained for the network of average node degree 8 since the other parameters of destination size 25 and delay bound values were not sufficient to form a multicast tree based on its algorithm. The graph of Figure 12 showed that EKRUS2 produced the best delay as the average node degree of the network increased. At an average node degree of 2, CDKS had the best results but as the node degree increased, EKRUS2 proved to be margin-

Figure 11. Graph of total tree cost vs. average node degree of the network of size 50

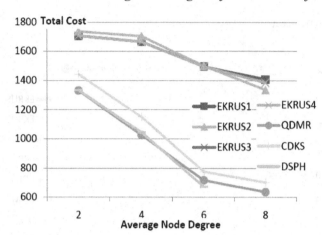

ally better than CDKS. EKRUS1, EKRUS3 and EKRUS4 showed to be very competitive against both QDMR and DSPH. They proved to be much better in average node degrees between 3 and 7 against QDMR.

Comparison with Delay Bound Parameter

The effect of the tree cost and delay as the delay bound increases is examined in this simulation. The size of the entire network and the destination group size were constant. The number of nodes in the entire network was set to 50 with

an average node degree of 4.The destination or multicast group size was set to 10. This simulation varied the delay bound value from 70ms to 310ms in intervals of 30ms. Tree cost and delay values were recorded at each interval when the multicast tree was constructed. In Figure 13, the values obtained for the total tree cost against the delay bound of the multicast tree were plotted. The delay values obtained from the multicast trees of the various algorithms were plotted against the delay bound values and are shown in Figure 14. Figure 13 showed that the DSPH multicast algorithm maintained the best tree cost as the delay bound was relaxed. The EKRUS algorithms have

Figure 12. Graph of delay (ms) vs. average node degree of the network of size 50

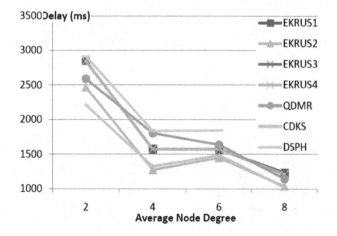

Figure 13. graph comparing the tree cost against the delay bound (ms) in a 50 node network

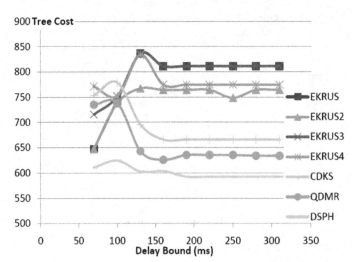

shown that the tree cost increased for low values of delay bound until it reached a specified delay bound value. When this value was reached, the tree costs remained constant for other subsequent delay bound values. The graph also showed that EKRUS2 algorithm had the better tree cost as compared to EKRUS1, EKRUS3 and EKRUS4. The tree costs of all the EKRUS algorithms proved to be very competitive against all other algorithms for delay bound values below 100ms. Figure 14 showed that as the delay bound values were

relaxed all delay values of respective multicast algorithms increased until threshold values for the delay bound were reached. The QDMR algorithm proved to have the best delay values as the delay bound of the network was relaxed. EKRUS2 and EKRUS4 had the best delay values among all EKRUS algorithms and the DSPH algorithm.

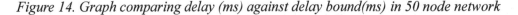

Figure 14. Graph comparing delay (ms) against delay bound(ms) in 50 node network

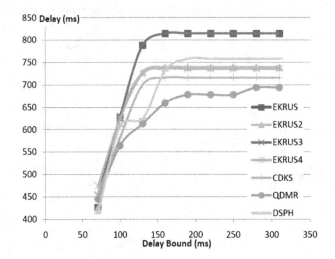

Simulation Results' Analysis

EKRUS2 algorithm was found to be the most efficient of the EKRUS algorithms in the simulations. The results showed that as the number of destination nodes increased and as the average node degree increased, EKRUS2 exhibits better delays than the QDMR and CDKS algorithms. This is as a result of the possibility of more edges for selection in the source class and destination class. The probability of more edges selected containing source node, destination nodes, or both, increases as the average node degree and the number of destination nodes increases The priority queue arrangement and edge selection process of EKRUS2 have proven to give this algorithm the edge over the other EKRUS algorithms. This is because the Destination Class in the priority queue contains edges that can include both a destination node and a source node. This allows for a selection of a wider pool of edges that can begin at the source node and go through the destination node. This is quite different from EKRUS1 where the Destination Class can only contain edges with destination nodes and not inclusive of source edges. The EKRUS4 algorithm proves to be the second best performing EKRUS algorithm. This algorithm has generated competitive delays in all simulated models performed. The EKRUS4 has a priority queue arrangement where the Source Class contains all edges, consisting of a source node, sorted in increasing order of cost. The Destination Class has all edges containing destination nodes and the Relay Class contains all other nodes. This algorithm uses edge selection by first considering the Source Class then the Destination Class. If there are no edges in the Destination Class that can form a validated path, then the Source Class is then visited. Therefore, the Relay Class is considered if and only if a validated path cannot be formed from both the Source Class and the Destination Class. This allows for constructing a tree that is mainly dependent on source and destination nodes to hopefully minimize cost and delay. The simulations show that the delays are competing against well known algorithms such as QDMR and CDKS but at a higher cost. EKRUS4 proves to be a very good algorithm in sparse networks. This can be contributed to the Source Class consisting of sorted edges of containing at least one source node. This means that an edge with a source node and a relay node has a higher possibility of being considered which allows for construction of destination nodes that are sparsely distributed in a network.

CONCLUSION

We have considered the problem of determining multicast trees that guarantee certain bounds on the overall cost, and end-to-end delays from the source to each of the destination nodes. We have presented a simple algorithm, for multicast routing in arbitrary topology networks. Furthermore we have developed two important strategies. The first one deals with the organization of the priority queue in Kruskal's algorithm, and the second one concerns edge priority aggregation. Four scenarios were developed for these two strategies. As a result, the EKRUS algorithm was divided into different edge assignments and selection strategies, yielding to four different algorithms EKRUS1, EKRUS2, EKRUS3 and EKRUS4. Based on our simulation results, EKRUS2 proved to have the best performance.

Through our extensive simulation results it was shown that our proposed algorithm performs similar to the best well-known algorithms (such as the QDMR, CDQS, DSPH). In addition we believe that *EKRUS* is well suited to actual implementation in networks requiring support for multicast communication.

REFERENCES

Alpert, C. J., Hu, T. C., & Huang, J. H. (1993). A direct combination of the Prim and Dijkstra constructions for improved performance-driven global routing. In *Proceedings of the IEEE International Symposium on Circuit and Systems*, Chicago, IL (pp. 1869-1872).

Chenghui, Y., & Chunanjun, R. (2010). Simulation research of communication networks based on Prim algorithm. In *Proceedings of the International Forum on Information Technology and Applications.*

Cormen, T. H., Leiserson, C. E., Rivest, R. L., & Stein, C. (2001). *Introduction to algorithms* (2nd ed.). Cambridge, MA: MIT Press.

Dijkstra, E. W. (1959). A note on two problems in connection with graphs. *Numerische Mathematik*, *1*, 269–271. doi:10.1007/BF01386390

Guo, L., & Matta, I. (2000). QDMR, an efficient QoS dependent multicast routing algorithm. *Journal of Communications and Networks, 2*(2).

Guttoski, P. B., Sunye, M. S., & Silva, F. (2007). Kruskal's algorithm for query tree optimization. In *Proceedings of the 11th International Database Engineering and Applications Symposium.*

Jia, X. (1998). A distributed algorithm of delay-bounded multicast routing for multimedia applications in wide area networks. *IEEE/ACM Transactions on Networking, 6*, 823–837.

Kershenbaum, A., & Van Styke, R. (1972). Computing minimum spanning trees efficiently. In *Proceedings of the ACM Annual Conference* (Vol. 1, pp. 518-527).

Kompella, V. P., Pasquale, J. C., & Polyzos, G. C. (1993, June). Two distributed algorithms for multicasting multimedia information. In *Proceedings of the International Conference on Computer Communications and Networks*, San Diego, CA (pp. 343-349).

Kruskal, J. B. (1956). On the shortest spanning subtree of a graph and the traveling salesman problem. *Proceedings of the American Mathematical Society, 7*, 48–50. doi:10.1090/S0002-9939-1956-0078686-7

Li, C., Raha, A., & Zhao, W. (1997), Stability in ATM networks. In *Proceedings of the 16th Annual Joint Conference of the IEEE Computer and Communications Societies Driving the Information Revolution* (pp. 160-167).

McDonald, A. B. (1997). *Survey of adaptive shortest-path routing in dynamic packet-switched networks.* Pittsburgh, PA: University of Pittsburgh.

Meylan, F., Kiatake, L. G. G., Santos, M. Z., Kofuji, S. T., & Courtiat, J. P. (1999). Comparative analysis of multicast routing algorithms for multimedia communication over ATM networks. In *Proceedings of the IEEE Latin American Network Operations and Management Symposium*, Rio de Janeiro, Brazil.

Mohamed, A., & Adel, B. (2004). A new delay-constrained algorithm for multicast routing tree construction. *International Journal of Communication Systems*, 985–1000.

Navneet, M., & Chen, J. A. (2002). Note on practical construction of maximum bandwidth paths. *Information Processing Letters, 83*, 175–180. doi:10.1016/S0020-0190(01)00323-4

Pan, D., Liu, Z.-B., Ding, X.-F., & Zheng, Q. (2009). The application of union-find sets in Kruskal algorithm. In *Proceedings of the International Conference on Artificial Intelligence and Computational Intelligence* (pp. 159-162).

Pasquale, J. C., Polyzos, G. C., Xylomenos, G. V., & Kompella, V. P. (1998). The multimedia multicasting problem. *Multimedia Systems, 6,* 43–59. doi:10.1007/s005300050075

Prim, B. C. (1959). Shortest connecting networks and some generalizations. *The Bell System Technical Journal, 36,* 1389–1401.

Ramanathan, S. (1996). Multicast tree generation in networks with asymmetric links. *IEEE/ACM Transactions on Networking, 4*(4), 558–568. doi:10.1109/90.532865

Salama, H. F. (1996). *Multicast routing for real-time communication on high-speed networks* (Doctoral dissertation). Raleigh, NC: North Carolina State University.

Salama, H. F., et al. (1995). *MCRSIM simulator source code and users' manual.* Raleigh, NC: North Carolina State University. Retrieved from http://ftp.csc.ncsu.edu:/pub/rtcomm

Shaikh, A., & Shin, K. (1997). Destination-driven routing for low-cost Multicast. *IEEE Journal on Selected Areas in Communications, 15,* 373–381. doi:10.1109/49.564135

Sun, Q., & Langendoerfre, H. (1995). Efficient multicast routing for delay-sensitive applications. In *Proceedings of the 2nd Workshop on Protocols for Multimedia Systems* (pp. 452-458).

This work was previously published in International Journal of Business Data Communications and Networking, Volume 7, Issue 4, edited by Varadharajan Sridhar and Debashis Saha, p.p 32-52, copyright 2011 by IGI Publishing (an imprint of IGI Global)

Chapter 16
Emerging Areas of Research in Business Data Communications

Debashis Saha
Indian Institute of Management Calcutta, India

Varadharajan Sridhar
Sasken Communication Technologies, India

Much like the financial crisis that precipitated a new world order, a quiet revolution of some sorts is happening in the telecom industry worldwide. The bankruptcy of stalwarts such as Nortel and the impregnation of Google and Apple into the mobile phone space at an amazing alacrity are changing the world order once dominated by the likes of biggies such as AT&T. What are these changes and what can we expect in the future? We explore in this article, the emerging technologies, market evolution, business models and regulatory interventions and indicate possible research directions in the area of data communications and networking in the coming days.

We begin with the Web as it has now become part and parcel of all businesses. Everything else depends on how good your web utilization is.

WEB

When Tim Berners-Lee, then a graduate of Oxford University, invented the World Wide Web at CERN circa 1990 as an internet-based hypermedia initiative for global information sharing, little did he think that after 20 years it would become such a hyper-phenomenon. In its early days, Web was a read only- traffic was always one way, from web to readers. There was no possibility of adding new content or modifying the content. Eric Schmidt, CEO of Google, now defines Web as a set of "applications that are pieced together - with the characteristics that the apps are relatively small, the data is in the cloud, the apps can run on any device (PC or mobile), the apps are very fast and very customizable, and are distributed virally

DOI: 10.4018/978-1-4666-2026-1.ch016

(social networks, email, etc.)". Evidently, WWW has travelled a long way from what it started with. It has come of age by breaking the digital divide and making the information available for everyone out there looking for it. The move from information to interaction has changed the web from read-only to and read-n-write. From a developer's perspective the web moved from html based web to more sophisticated Ajax platform.

Since the web now is more about the users content, it makes all the more about users preferences, user likes and user dislikes. As far as the ownership over the resources was concerned, the individual has gained in terms of democracy as he has every right to express freely on the web. The flow of information changed drastically with the emergence of social networks. You are connected the friends, acquaintances and relatives through the virtual communities and are constantly fed with what they want to share. The scalability of the mobile platform from phone devices to communication devices for both data and voice was critical on the diffusion of the web services and applications.

The emergence of Internet-based social media has made it possible for one person to communicate with hundreds or even thousands of other people in the network. Social media encompasses a wide range of online, word-of-mouth forums including blogs, discussion boards and chat rooms, consumer-to-consumer e-mail, consumer product or service ratings websites and forums, Internet discussion boards and forums, moblogs (sites containing digital audio, images, movies, or photographs), and social networking websites, to name a few (Mangold & Faulds, 2009). An important disruption we have been seeing is that the high-speed access networks and Smartphones enable users to access and use these social media through mobile phones, any time any where. These many-to-many group forming transactional communication networks and the associated exponential value generation in such networks was characterized way back in 2001 by Reed (Reed,

2001). The analysis of communication patterns in such social media and peer-to-peer networks will throw a light on their impact on network capacity, topology and routing.

NETWORKS

Ever since mobile wireless networks have taken the centre stage, wired networks have gone into the background just as they have been pushed to the core by the wireless access. It all began with voice in the wireless domain, but now data as usual is surging ahead as the killer service. In a recent research study, it has been pointed out that mobile data traffic will grow at a Compound Annual Growth Rate of 92 percent from 2010 to 2015, reaching 6.3 Exabytes per month by 2015. The study also points out "The mobile-only Internet" population will grow 56-fold from 14 million at the end of 2010 to 788 million by the end of 2015 (Cisco, 2010). These trends clearly indicate the possible exponential growth in the use of mobile devices to access Internet and bandwidth intensive application. Though technologies such as Long Term Evolution (LTE), LTE-Advanced, WiMAX, mobile WiMAX (IEEE 802.16e) are gaining ground in different geographical areas and being actively adopted by the mobile operators worldwide to provide enhanced user experience, spectrum crunch is evident. In tune with these trends, we see two active research areas in networking. One is Cognitive Radio (CR) that enables flexible and dynamic spectrum usage with cognitive capabilities for opportunistically seizing vacant Radio Frequency spectrum blocks in both licensed and unlicensed bands (Chapin & Lehr, 2007). In a major breakthrough to the proponents of CR technologies, IEEE released 802.22 standards earlier this year that defines the unlicensed use of frequencies between TV channels in the Very High Frequencies (VHF) and Ultra High Frequency (UHF) bands. However, there are still evolving research problems on interference management, frequency allocation algorithms and power management that need to be addressed. Wireless technology is also in the midst of an important stage in its technical commercial evolution from radios with behavior fixed in hardware to radios with behavior determined by software. The flexibility demanded by the radio systems can potentially be embedded best in software rather than hardware and hence the development of Software Defined Radios (SDR) (Partridge, 2011). Though the SDRs on their own could not stand on its own commercially, the CR combined with SDRs to provide flexible spectrum management provides an enlarged space for wireless researchers. Research is also needed in ways to allow software radios to use the spectrum appropriately.

In the core network, through IP multimedia sub systems are being deployed currently, research on next generation core network protocols, addressing schemes, routing methods and dealing with more sophisticated and bandwidth intensive edge networks require substantial attention in the years to come.

As more and more devices get networked, need for managing these heterogonous devices on the network is challenging. The Digital Living Network Alliance (DLNA) comprising of leading consumer electronics, computing industry and mobile device companies envisions a wired and wireless network of interoperable consumer electronics, personal computers and mobile devices in the home and on the road, enabling a seamless environment for sharing and growing new digital media and content services. This provides a fertile ground for researchers to work on issues relating to addressability, routing of multimedia content, protocol optimization, radio access network problems, content security and authorization.

To take care of the burgeoning demand for the Internet bandwidth, scientists are turning to optoelectronic technology – transmitting data using light. However, research question remains on its capacity to handle huge bandwidth demand at

low cost in an energy efficient way. As the Internet paves way for people across the globe to engage in intense collaborative activity, need for efficient, scalable and energy efficient Internet architecture and technologies are required and research questions in this domain remain abundant.

Mobile ad-hoc networks continue to generate interesting research problems in the area of connectivity, routing, security and power management. Dynamic topologies, bandwidth constraints, energy-constrained operations, wireless vulnerabilities, and limited physical security are among the characteristics that differentiate mobile ad hoc networks from fixed multihop networks. These networks when connected to high-bandwidth wireless backhaul networks require efficient hand-off mechanisms, and bandwidth shaping rules. The field of sensor and mesh networking is reemerging amid unprecedented growth in the scale and diversity of Machine to Machine (M2M) networking. M2M enables one device to communicate its status continually or sequentially to another device, often linked to a central management system. People and vehicles can be internetworked in areas without a pre-existing communication infrastructure, or when the use of such infrastructure requires wireless extension. Therefore, such networks are designed to operate in widely varying environments, from military networks (with hundreds of nodes) to low-power sensor networks and other embedded systems.

Topology control is one of the fundamental research topics in wireless ad hoc and sensor networks. There are a variety of means to perform topology control such as turning on/off network nodes, changing transmission power of network nodes, and building hierarchical network topologies. When designed properly, topology control can improve the operation of wireless ad hoc and sensor networks in terms of energy efficiency, mobility resilience, network capacity increase, interference reduction, etc. Nevertheless, many aspects need to be addressed when designing suitable topology control mechanisms for wireless ad hoc and sensor networks. For instance, both the gains by means of topology control and the drawbacks (e.g., relevant overhead on communication & management) from it need to be taken into account. In addition, the realistic networking environments (such as homogeneous & heterogeneous devices, stationary or mobile nodes, QoS requirements, traffic patterns) pose challenges on topology control to work together with other networking tasks. Moreover, topology control has interactions with other layers in the protocol stack such as MAC (Medium Access Control) and routing mechanisms. Hence, comprehensive research efforts on topology control techniques are necessary to meet the various requirements in wireless ad hoc and sensor networks.

Sensor networks and grid computing are being deployed to better manage public utilities such as electricity, water and transport. Smart grids improve the efficiency of electricity grids through active monitoring and reducing reliance on centralized electricity production. Smart city networks monitor traffic, carbon emission, energy usage and help reduce traffic congestion and help earn cities earn carbon credit. Smart M2M communications are a growing area in wireless telecommunications and are expected to be behind 80% of the total carbon savings. Research issues abound in this area relating to optimization of sensor network topologies, performance improvement, energy, and power optimization.

Historically, telecom service providers were focused on supplying connectivity based on the concept of Virtual Private Networks (VPNs). Over the years, these services have evolved to facilitate outsourcing of advanced functionalities such as routing and even security (L3 IP VPNs, security as a service, etc.). Soon VPN service providers started to offer dynamic access (through VPNs) to their own skeleton cloud services and also to 3rd party cloud services; e.g., the "VPN gallery service" of Orange Business Services. Recently, advances in distributed systems technology have made it easy for the provisioning of services on

an unprecedented scale and with increasing flexibility. At the same time, businesses have started to embrace a model wherein 3rd party services that can be acquired with minimal service provider interaction, replace or complement those that are managed internally. Organizations have only started to grasp the economic implications of this evolution where service and cloud computing enable resource to be employed in utility-based fashion.

CLOUD COMPUTING

Cloud Computing is probably the biggest revolution that IT industry is witnessing since the dot com era (Armbrust et al., 2010). Not without reason, the IT infrastructure is becoming diverse, complex, expensive and difficult to maintain. For instance, in the current decade, we have witnessed huge data explosion driven by new types of applications and devices. Currently, petabyte-scale archives are no longer a rare occurrence. Even traditional application domains have become data intensive. Fostering capabilities to extract value from large data sets is no longer the problem and desire of the big companies alone; government agencies, small and medium-sized enterprises and even individuals perceive value in data. Among other things, this shift is driven by the cost, scalability and availability benefits coming with the emergence and rapid adoption of massively parallel processing paradigms. Further, firms needs only a portion of the big whole, and that too when needed (i.e., on-demand). Thus, the investment in computing resources needs to be optimal and matched with the demand. In this background, cloud computing is fast transforming itself from a distant vision to a near reality because of the recent significant advances in several of its component technology and management areas, spanning from grid/virtualization/utility computing to Web 2.0 and Service Oriented Computing (SOC). It aims to provide secure and reliable, on demand QoS guaranteed computing facilities for the end-users. Cloud computing services usage in both academia and industry has changed the way of thinking on how users' needs can be satisfied by computational infrastructures. Customers (enterprises or individuals) can provision and deploy services in a 'pay-as-you-go' fashion and in a convenient way, saving huge capital investment in their own IT infrastructures. Workflow automating business and scientific processing in step by step can be executed in service and cloud computing environments in the benefit of deploying resources for execution in that fashion. As a global market for infrastructure, platform and software services emerges, efforts are going on with the final goal to make cloud technologies and services more mature so to enable and boost a more widespread industrial uptake of cloud systems.

The Internet and Virtualization have together complemented the cloud computing paradigm. Nobody knows or need to know exactly where server side applications like such as email, web servers, and databases are located or how many users are sharing it. Several companies are now moving to the cloud due to its advantages of cost, flexibility and scalability. However, despite several successful commercial provisioning of cloud systems recently, it is still unclear whether current solutions will be able to withstand the abrupt and unpredictable changes imposed by the emergent cloud application scenarios, where services will activate (or deactivate) dynamically on a continuous basis. The whole hardware and/or software stacks (from the kernel upward) have to scale up and down resiliently and quickly by exploiting highly distributed and heterogeneous virtualized resources. With the increase of data transferred among different places, it became critical how to support distributed computing resources with advanced network infrastructure services.

These developments pose interesting problems to researchers ranging from optimization of storage spaces, bandwidth and routing to efficient allocation of resources amongst users, providing

secured reliable access. In near future, it will be important to include risks associated with cloud computing as part of the risk assessment for your business. Accordingly, at the current stage, after the initial hype of enthusiasm is slowly giving way to more practical techno-managerial issues, several research efforts need to focus deeply on the closed/open management aspects of the Cloud, such as interoperability, scalability, reliability, power management, and confidentiality/auditability. The need to understand and deal with these implications is quickly growing. In addition, a multitude of new challenges arises. It is envisioned that network infrastructure services provisioned on-demand could be managed and reconfigured dynamically by cloud operators and user applications to achieve optimal usage criteria. Such dynamic infrastructures reveal new aspects in network virtualization, service delivery automation and general infrastructure resources management that should be supported by well-defined information models and related middleware. Cloud services are usually deployed over the Internet. More recently, companies are deploying their own private cloud solutions and we see a need for portability and interoperability of public and private clouds, making brokering a key component in such future solutions. Future will enable dynamic mapping of cloud services over existing VPNs, hence allowing the VPN service provider to become a broker of cloud-based infrastructure and services. In the meantime, a new generation of brokers that will dynamically select from among various available cloud providers and orchestrate both network and cloud services to answer dynamically specific client's requirements. Moreover, cloud resources that are controlled by service providers will move out of large datacenters to be located in various other points, including telecom service providers, networking Points of Presence, and even customers locations (e.g., in CPEs). Security issues should addressed as a part of the general service delivery framework/workflow and support both infrastructure provisioning process and secure virtualized services/infrastructures operation. Another related issue is how to green the cloud when it becomes increasingly challenging and extremely important in terms of global energy efficiency and environmental sustainability. New components of the required network infrastructure for cloud services and applications should create an integrated self-management environment that can react to changes in workloads and other events with minimal human interference. These issues are inherently multi-disciplinary and relate to aspects such as the operation and structure of the services market, the alignment of cost, revenue and quality-related objectives when taking on a service consumer or provider role, and the creation of innovative business models and value chains.

APPLICATIONS

The demand for wireless broadband continues due to exponential growth of Smartphone adoption. The Smartphone growth has also fuelled intense competition in mobile platform technologies and associated business models. Apple's iOS, Microsoft's Windows Platform 7/8, Google's open source Android, and RIM's Blackberry have sparked interesting research problems theories and applications. These multiple platforms have also resulted in the need to look at the importance of Intellectual Property (IP) and patents.

The growth of mobile Internet, Smartphones and the mobile operating platforms has renewed research interest in two and multi-sided markets (Cusumano, 2011). The interaction between mobile network operators, mobile device manufacturers, mobile application providers enable strong cross-side network effects. The success or failure of a platform and hence the associated ecosystem depends on the magnitude of this effect and hence pose challenging research problems in the area of network economics (Basole & Karla, 2011)

The availability of multiple platforms and devices has provided users with tremendous choice. This has necessitated the IT infrastructure in organizations to be more flexible in accommodating the diverse needs of the users in terms of device support and management. Research problems in the area of converging IT infrastructure, optimization of organization policies do become important.

Business communication has undergone sea change lately, thanks to mobile telepresence that connect virtual meeting rooms to smart phones via wireless broadband networks. Using wireless telecommunications products, organizations create virtual offices that enable employees to work remotely and from home, reducing travel and office space. However, these throw up challenges in the management of remote offices, collaborative tools for enabling efficient knowledge sharing, and effective configuration systems for communication of work artifacts.

While the newer technologies in networking and applications are getting diffused through the society, the dire need of applications and solutions for addressing the digital divide continues to increase. Innovative applications that use less energy and memory, at the same time capable of scaling up to provide the desired economies continue to pose interesting research problems.

As bandwidth intense applications and networks diffuse, the need for effective security management not only within organizations but also across national infrastructure continue to increase. As each country is creating equivalence of Homeland Security, the need for providing surveillance, monitoring and management are increasing.

Besides security, the biggest weakness in today's Internet and Intranet is the lack of built-in network management techniques. Among the ideas under consideration are automated ways to reboot systems, self-diagnosing protocols, finer grained data collection and better event tracking. All of these tools will provide better information about the health and status of networks so that security, availability and reliability of networks can be improved.

REGULATION AND POLICY

The ubiquitous wireless networks demand efficient allocation of scare resources, namely spectrum. While regulators all over the world have been looking at methods such as spectrum refarming, digital dividend, spectrum pooling, and spectrum trading, policy research still lags behind the technology evolution. Policy questions on optimal spectrum allocation and competition management still remain.

Due to the above convergence in technologies and service provisioning, there are challenges for telecom regulations and policy. While most of the countries have migrated to technology agnostic policy and licensing, legacies and political economies clearly dichotomize the communication space in to (i) the traditional Public Switched Telephone Network/ Public Land Mobile Network, and (ii) the Internet. While the former enjoys the privileges of legacy inheritance, the latter is armed with unprecedented technology evolution. This is the basis of the much debated *Net Neutrality* principles advocated by the Internet firms and opposed by the telcos (Economides, 2008). While the proponents of net neutrality want no prohibition or priority of applications, services and content to encourage innovation, the opponents cite limited bandwidth, especially in wireless access as the reason for prioritization and blocking.

Though the Federal Communications Commission (FCC) came up with a partial regulation on net neutrality, a number of issues need to be addressed. While the FCC regulation poses the wire-line service providers strict adherence to network neutrality, it is lenient towards wireless broadband service providers. Access-tiering, bundling of content, and vertical integration remain important issues to be addressed.

Regulation on cloud computing is in an infant stage. The biggest regulatory challenge is to categorize the different entities in cloud computing so that it fits within the extant regulatory framework. Research is needed to synthesize the regulatory framework for all associated entities in cloud computing including wireless providers, infrastructure providers, content and storage providers. Since cloud computing revolves around the provisioning of services, regulation needs to focus on service management, quality of service, security, privacy, reliability and pricing of services.

REFERENCES

Armbrust, M., Fox, A., Griffith, R., Joseph, A. D., Katz, R., & Konwinski, A. (2010). A view of cloud computing. *Communications of the ACM, 53*(4), 50–58. doi:10.1145/1721654.1721672

Basole, R., & Karla, J. (2011). On the Evolution of Mobile Platform Ecosystem Structure and Strategy. *Business & Information Systems Engineering, 5*, 313–322. doi:10.1007/s12599-011-0174-4

Chapin, J. M., & Lehr, W. H. (2007). Cognitive radios for dynamic spectrum access-the path to market success for dynamic spectrum access technology. *IEEE Communications Magazine, 45*(5), 96–103. doi:10.1109/MCOM.2007.358855

Cisco. (2010). *Cisco Visual Networking Index: Global Mobile Data Traffic Forecast Update, 2010–2015*. Retrieved March 15, 2011, from http://www.cisco.com

Cusumano, M. (2011). The platform leader's dilemma. *Communications of the ACM, 54*(10), 21–24. doi:10.1145/2001269.2001279

Economides, N. (2008). Net Neutrality: Non-Discrimination and Digital Distribution of Content Through the Internet. *I/S. Journal of Law and Policy, 4*(2), 209–233.

Mangold, W. G., & Faulds, D. (2009). Social media: The new hybrid element of the promotion mix. *Business Horizons, 52*, 357–365. doi:10.1016/j. bushor.2009.03.002

Partridge, C. (2011). Realizing the Future of Wireless Data Communications. *Communications of the ACM, 54*(9), 62–68. doi:10.1145/1995376.1995395

Reed, D. (2001, February). The law of the pack. *Harvard Business Review*, 23–24.

This work was previously published in International Journal of Business Data Communications and Networking, Volume 7, Issue 4, edited by Varadharajan Sridhar and Debashis Saha, p.p 52-59, copyright 2011 by IGI Publishing (an imprint of IGI Global)

Compilation of References

2007 *Attorney General Cuomo cracks down on Internet auction fraud* (p. 4). New York: Beacon.

ABB AG. (2009). Ganzheitlich gut: Generations. *Kontakt, 5,* 21.

Abbasi, A. A., & Younis, M. (2007). A survey on clustering algorithms for wireless sensor networks. *Computer Communications, 20*(14-15), 2826–2841. doi:10.1016/j.comcom.2007.05.024

Abdulai, J., Ould-Khaoua, M., & Mackenzie, L. (2007). Improving probabilistic route discovery in mobile ad hoc networks. In *Proceeding of the 32nd IEEE Conference on Local Computer Networks (LCN '07),* Dublin, Ireland (pp. 739-746). Washington, DC: IEEE Computer Society.

Abdulrazak, B., Chikhaoui, B., Gouin-Vallerand, C., & Fraikin, B. (2010). A standard ontology for smart spaces. *International Journal of Web and Grid Services, 6*(3), 244–268. doi:10.1504/IJWGS.2010.035091

Abowd, G. D., Dey, A. K., Brown, P. J., Davies, N., Smith, M., & Steggles, P. (1999). Towards a better understanding of context and context-awareness. In *Proceedings of the 1st international Symposium on Handheld and Ubiquitous Computing,* Karlsruhe, Germany.

Ackermann, R., Schumacher, M., Roedig, U., & Steinmetz, R. (2001). Vulnerabilities and Security Limitations of Current IP Telephony Systems. In *Proceedings of the Conference on Communications and Multimedia Security* (pp. 53–66).

Adabi, S., Rezaee, A., Jabbehdari, S., & Adabi, S. (2008). Distributed fuzzy score-based clustering algorithm for mobile ad-hoc networks. In *Proceedings of the IEEE Asia Pacific Services Computing Conference* (pp. 193-198).

Adams, H. (2001). *Best practices for web services: Web services performance considerations, Parts 1 & 2.* Retrieved from http://www.ibm.com/developerworks/library/ws-best9/ and http://www.ibm.com/developer-works/library/ws-best10/

Adams, D. A., Nelson, R. R., & Todd, P. A. (1992). Perceived usefulness, ease of use, and usage of information technology: a replication. *Management Information Systems Quarterly, 16*(2), 227–247. doi:10.2307/249577

Aggelou, G. (2005). *Mobile ad hoc networks.* New York, NY: McGraw-Hill.

Agostini, A., Bettini, C., & Riboni, D. (2005). Loosely coupling ontological reasoning with an efficient middleware for context-awareness. In *Proceedings of the Second Annual International Conference on Mobile and Ubiquitous Systems: Networking and Services.*

Agrawal, D., Lee, K. W., & Lobo, J. (2005). Policy-based management of networked computing systems. *IEEE Communications Magazine,* 69–75. doi:10.1109/MCOM.2005.1522127

Ahmed, A., Zairi, S., & Alwabel, S. (2006). Global benchmarking for Internet and e-commerce applications. *Benchmarking International Journal, 13*(2), 68–80. doi:10.1108/14635770610644583

Akyildiz, I. F., Melodia, T., & Chowdhury, K. R. (2007). A survey on wireless multimedia sensor networks. *Computer Networks, 51*(4), 921–960. doi:10.1016/j.comnet.2006.10.002

Akyildiz, I. F., Su, W., Sankarasubramaniam, Y., & Cayirci, E. (2002). A survey on sensor networks. *IEEE Communications Magazine, 40,* 102–114. doi:10.1109/MCOM.2002.1024422

Akyildiz, I. F., Su, W., Sankarasubramaniam, Y., & Cayirci, E. (2002). Wireless sensor networks: a survey. *Computer Networks, 38,* 393–422. doi:10.1016/S1389-1286(01)00302-4

Al-Bahadili, H., & Jaradat, Y. (2007). Development and performance analysis of a probabilistic flooding in noisy mobile ad hoc networks. In *Proceedings of the 1ˢᵗ International Conference on Digital Communications and Computer Applications (DCCA'07),* Irbid, Jordan (pp. 1306-1316).

Al-Bahadili, H. (2009). On the use of discrete-event simulation in computer networks analysis and design . In Abu-Taieh, E. M. O., & El-Sheikh, A. A. (Eds.), *Handbook of Research on Discrete-Event Simulation Environments: Technologies and Applications* (pp. 414–442). Hershey, PA: Information Science Reference. doi:10.4018/978-1-60566-774-4.ch019

Al-Bahadili, H., & Jaradat, R. (2010). Performance evaluation of an OMPR algorithm for route discovery in noisy MANETs. *International Journal of Computer Networks and Communications, 2*(1), 85–96.

Al-Bahadili, H., & Kaabneh, K. (2010). Analyzing the performance of probabilistic algorithm in noisy MANETs. *International Journal of Wireless & Mobile Networks, 2*(3), 83–95. doi:10.5121/ijwmn.2010.2306

Aldridge, A., White, M., & Forcht, K. (1997). Considerations of doing business via the internet: Cautions to be considered. *Internet Research: Electronic Networking Applications and Policy, 7*(1), 9–15. doi:10.1108/10662249710159809

Aleksy, M., & Stieger, B. (2009). Challenges in the development of mobile applications in industrial field service. In *Proceedings of the 12th International Conference on Network-Based Information Systems* (pp. 586-591). Washington, DC: IEEE Computer Society.

Aleksy, M., Stieger, B., & Fantana, N. (2010). Utilizing mock-ups in the development of distributed information systems for semantic data federations. In *Proceedings of the 4th International Conference on Complex, Intelligent and Software Intensive Systems* (pp. 307-312). Washington, DC: IEEE Computer Society.

Aleksy, M., Stieger, B., & Vollmar, G. (2009). Case study on utilizing mobile applications in industrial field service. In *Proceedings of the 11th IEEE Conference on Commerce and Enterprise Computing* (pp. 333-336). Washington, DC: IEEE Computer Society.

Aletheia. (2009). *Semantische Föderation umfassender Produktinformationen.* Retrieved from http://www.aletheia-projekt.de/

Al-karaki, J. N., & Kamal, A. E. (2004). Routing techniques in wireless sensor networks: A survey. *IEEE Wireless Communications, 11,* 6–28. doi:10.1109/MWC.2004.1368893

Alpert, C. J., Hu, T. C., & Huang, J. H. (1993). A direct combination of the Prim and Dijkstra constructions for improved performance-driven global routing. In *Proceedings of the IEEE International Symposium on Circuit and Systems,* Chicago, IL (pp. 1869-1872).

Al-Shurman, M., Yoo, S. M., & Park, S. (2004). Black hole attack in mobile ad hoc networks. In *Proceedings of the 43nd Annual Southeast Regional Conference.*

Altinel, M., Luo, Q., Krishnamurthy, S., Mohan, C., Pirahesh, H., Lindsay, B. G., et al. (2002). DBCache: Database caching for web application servers. In *Proceedings of the ACM SIGMOD International Conference on Management of Data* (p. 612).

Ambrose, P., & Johnson, G. (1998). A Trust Model of Buying Behavior in Electronic Retailing, Association for Information Systems. In *Proceedings of the Americans Conference,* Baltimore, MD (pp. 263-265).

Amiri, K., Park, S., & Tewari, R. (2002). A self-managing data cache for edge-of-network web applications. In *Proceedings of the Eleventh ACM CIKM International Conference on Information and Knowledge Management* (pp. 177-185).

Amiri, K., Park, S., Tewari, R., & Padmanabhan, S. (2003). DBProxy: A dynamic data cache for web applications. In *Proceedings of the 19ᵗʰ IEEE ICDE International Conference on Data Engineering* (pp. 821-831).

Amza, C., Soundararajan, G., & Cecchet, E. (2005). Transparent caching with strong consistency in dynamic content web sites. In *Proceedings of the 19ᵗʰ Annual ACM ICS International Conference on Supercomputing* (pp. 264-273).

Anbazhagan, M., & Nagarajan, A. (2002). *Understanding quality of service for Web services*. Retrieved from http://www.ibm.com/developerworks/webservices/library/ws-quality/index.html

Andreolini, M., Casalicchio, E., Colajanni, M., & Mambelli, M. (2001). *QoS-aware switching policies for a locally distributed web system*. Retrieved from http://www2002.org/CDROM/poster/141.pdf

Andreolini, M., Casalicchio, E., Colajanni, M., & Mambelli, M. (2004). A cluster-based web system providing differentiated and guaranteed services. *Cluster Computing*, 7, 7–19. doi:10.1023/B:CLUS.0000003940.34740.be

Angele, J., & Gesmann, M. (2006). Data integration using semantic technology: A use case. In *Proceedings of the* Second International Conference on Rules and Rule Markup Languages for the Semantic Web (pp. 58-66). Washington, DC: IEEE Computer Society.

Anton, J., & Petouhoff, N. (2002). *Customer Relations Management: the Bottom Line to Optimizing Your ROI*. Upper Saddle River, NJ: Prentice Hall.

Apache HTTP Server. (2011). *Caching guide*. Retrieved from http://httpd.apache.org/docs/2.2/caching.html

Aperture. (2010). *A java framework for getting data and metadata*. Retrieved from http://aperture.sourceforge.net/

Armbrust, M., Fox, A., Griffith, R., Joseph, A. D., Katz, R., & Konwinski, A. (2010). A view of cloud computing. *Communications of the ACM*, 53(4), 50–58. doi:10.1145/1721654.1721672

Armes, D. (2006). Online auctions prove their staying power. *Strategic Direction*, 22(7), 6–7. doi:10.1108/02580540610669008

Armstrong, J. (2007). *Programming Erlang, software for a concurrent world*. Raleigh, NC: Pragmatic Bookshelf.

Baker, D. J., & Ephremides, A. (1981). The architectural organization of a mobile radio network via a distributed algorithm. *IEEE Transactions on Communications*, 29, 1694–1701. doi:10.1109/TCOM.1981.1094909

Baliosian, J., Borba, M., & Serrat, J. (2008, December). *A rule-based strategy for pricing in wireless access networks*. Paper presented at the UPC Seminar.

Bani-Yassein, M., & Ould-Khaoua, M. (2007). Applications of probabilistic flooding in MANETs. *International Journal of Ubiquitous Computing and Communication*, 1(1), 1–5.

Bani-Yassein, M., Ould-Khaoua, M., Mackenzie, L., & Papanastasiou, S. (2006). Performance analysis of adjusted probabilistic broadcasting in mobile ad hoc networks. *International Journal of Wireless Information Networks*, 13(2), 127–140. doi:10.1007/s10776-006-0027-0

Baronti, P., Pillai, P., Chook, V. W. C., Chessa, S., Gotta, A., & Hu, Y. F. (2007). Wireless sensor networks: A survey on the state of the art and the 802.15.4 and ZigBee standards. *Computer Communications*, 30(7), 1655–1695. doi:10.1016/j.comcom.2006.12.020

Barrett, C., Eidenbenz, S., Kroc, L., Marathe, M., & Smith, J. (2005). Parametric probabilistic routing in sensor networks. *Journal of Mobile Networks and Applications*, 10(4), 529–544. doi:10.1007/s11036-005-1565-x

Ba, S., & Pavlou, P. A. (2002). Evidence of the effect of trust building technology in electronic markets: price premiums and buyer behavior. *Management Information Systems Quarterly*, 26(3), 243–268. doi:10.2307/4132332

Basagni, S. (1991, June). Distributed clustering for ad hoc networks. In *Proceedings of the International Symposium on Parallel Architectures, Algorithms and Networks* (pp. 310-315).

Basole, R., & Karla, J. (2011). On the Evolution of Mobile Platform Ecosystem Structure and Strategy. *Business & Information Systems Engineering*, 5, 313–322. doi:10.1007/s12599-011-0174-4

Basu, P., Khan, N., & Little, T. D. C. (2001). Mobility based metric for clustering in mobile ad hoc networks. In *Proceedings of the Workshop on Distributed Computing Systems* (pp. 413-418).

Battelle, J. (2009). *Comparing Twitter's growth to Facebook and Google*. Retrieved from http://www.businessinsider.com/comparing-twitters-growth-to-facebook-and-google-2009-3

Beaumont, C. (2010, January 16). *New York plane crash: Twitter breaks the news, again*. Retrieved from http://www.telegraph.co.uk/technology/twitter/4269765/New-York-plane-crash-Twitter-breaks-the-news-again.html

Bechhofer, S., Harmelen, F. v., Hendler, J., Horrocks, I., McGuinness, D., Patel-Schneijder, P., et al. (2004). *OWL web ontology language reference*. Retrieved from http://www.w3.org/TR/owl-ref/

Behrendt, W., Gangemi, A., Maass, W., & Westenthaler, R. (2005). Towards an ontology-based distributed architecture for paid content. In Proceedings of the Second European Semantic Web Conference (pp. 257-271).

Belic, D. (2009). *Mobile subscriptions hit 3.3 billion worldwide or 50% of global population*. Retrieved from http://www.intomobile.com/2007/12/03/mobile-subscriptions-hit-33-billion-worldwide-or-50-of-global-population.html

Beltran, F., Gutierrez, J. A., & Melus, J. L. (2010). Technology and market conditions towards a new competitive landscape in mobile services. *IEEE Communications Magazine*, 46–52. doi:10.1109/MCOM.2010.5473864

Benjamin, K. (2009). Battle of the brands. *Revolution (Staten Island, N.Y.)*, 41–43.

Benjamins, V. R., Davies, J., Baeza-Yates, R., Mika, P., Zaragoza, H., & Greaves, M. (2008). Near-term prospects for semantic technologies. *IEEE Intelligent Systems*, 23(1), 76–88. doi:10.1109/MIS.2008.10

Berners-Lee, T., Chen, Y., Chilton, L., Connolly, D., Dhanaraj, R., Hollenbach, J., et al. (2006, November). Tabulator: Exploring and analyzing linked data on the semantic web. In *Proceedings of the 3rd Semantic Web User Interaction Workshop*.

Bettstetter, C. (2004). The cluster density of a distributed clustering algorithm in ad hoc networks. In *Proceedings of the 2004 IEEE International Conference on Communications (ICC'04)*, Paris (Vol. 7, pp. 4336-4340). Washington, DC: IEEE Computer Society.

Bhagdev, R., Chapman, S., Ciravegna, F., & Lanfranchi, V. (2008, June). Hybrid search: Effectively combining keywords and ontology-based searches. In Proceedings of the 5th European Semantic Web Conference (pp. 554-568).

Birch, D. (1999). Mobile finance services: the Internet is not the only digital channel to consumers. *Journal of Internet Banking and Commerce*, 4(1), 20–29.

Bird, S., & Liberman, M. (1999, June). Annotation graphs as a framework for multidimensional linguistic data analysis. In *Proceedings of the Association for Computational Linguistics Workshop on Towards Standards and Tools for Discourse Tagging* (pp.1-10).

Birkinshaw, J., Morrison, A., & Hulland, J. (1995). Structural and competitive determinants of a global integration strategy. *Strategic Management Journal*, 16(8), 637–655. doi:10.1002/smj.4250160805

Bishop, C. M. (1995). *Neural Networks for Pattern Recognition*. Oxford, UK: Oxford University Press.

Bishop, M. (2002). *Computer Security: Art and Science*. Reading, MA: Addison-Wesley.

Bizer, C., & Cyganiak, R. (2006). Publishing relational databases on the web as SPARQL-endpoints. *International Journal on Semantic Web and Information Systems*, 5(3), 1–22. doi:10.4018/jswis.2009081901

Bizer, C., Heath, T., & Berners-Lee, T. (2009). Linked data–The story so far. *International Journal on Semantic Web and Information Systems*, 5(3), 1–22. doi:10.4018/jswis.2009081901

Black, G. (2005). *Socio-economic determinates of participation in on-line auctions*. Retrieved from http://reddog.rmu.edu:2079/pqdweb?index=32&did=994410521&SrchMode=1&sid=1&Fmt=6&VInst=PROD&VType=PQD&RQT=309&VName=PQD&TS=1194354264&clientId=2138

Bland, E., & Barrett, R. T. (2006). A measure of the factors impacting the effectiveness and efficiency of eBay in the supply chain of online firms. *The Costal Business Journal*, 18(2), 1–15.

Bolton, G. E., Katok, E., & Ockenfels, A. (2004). Trust among Internet traders: a behavioral economics approach. *Analyse & Kritik*, 26(1), 185–202.

Bolton, W., Yang, X., & Guizani, M. (2007). IEEE 802.20: Mobile broadband wireless access. *IEEE Wireless Communications*, 14(1), 84–95. doi:10.1109/MWC.2007.314554

Booker, E. (2000). Protect online brand from unauthorized use. *B to B.*, 85(18), 12-39.

Boyd, J. (2002). In community we trust: online security communication at eBay. *Journal of Computer-Mediated Communication, 7*(3).

Broekstra, J., Kampman, A., & Van Harmelen, F. (2002). A generic architecture for storing and querying RDF and RDF schema. In I. Horrocks & J. Hendler (Eds.), *Proceedings of the First International Conference on* the Semantic Web *(LNCS 2342, pp.* 54-68).

Brown, F., Divietri, J., Diaz, G., & Fernandez, E. (1999). The Authenticator Pattern. In *Proceedings of PLoP.*

Bruner, G. C. II, & Kumar, A. (2005). Explaining consumer acceptance of handheld internet devices. *Journal of Business Research, 58*(5), 553–558. doi:10.1016/j.jbusres.2003.08.002

Brunner, J.-S., Ma, L., Wang, C., Zhang, L., Wolfson, D. C., Pan, Y., et al. (2007). Explorations in the use of semantic web technologies for product information management. In Proceedings of the 16th International Conference on World Wide Web (pp. 747-756). New York, NY: ACM Press.

Bunt, R. B., Eager, D. L., Oster, G. M., & Williamson, C. L. (1999). Achieving load balance and effective caching in clustered web servers. In *Proceedings of the 4th International Web Caching Workshop*, San Diego, CA (pp. 159-169).

Burton-Jones, A., & Hubona, G. S. (2005). Individual differences and usage behavior: Revisiting a technology acceptance model assumption. *The Data Base for Advances in Information Systems, 36*(2), 58–77. doi:10.1145/1066149.1066155

Cai, J., Yi, P., Chen, J., Wang, Z., & Liu, N. (2010). An adaptive approach to detecting black and gray hole attacks in ad hoc network. In *Proceedings of the 24th IEEE International Conference on Advanced Information Networking and Applications* (pp. 275-280).

Caillaud, B., & Jullien, B. (2003). Chicken & egg: Competing matchmakers. *The Rand Journal of Economics, 34*(2), 309–328. doi:10.2307/1593720

Calvanese, D., Giacomo, G. D., Lembo, D., Lenzerini, M., Poggi, A., Rosati, R., et al. (2008). Data integration through DL-LiteA ontologies. In *Proceedings of the 3rd International Workshop on Semantics in Data and Knowledge Bases* (pp. 26-47).

Campiolo, R. (2007). On modeling for pervasive computing environments. In *Proceedings of the 10th ACM International Workshop on Modeling Analysis and Simulation of Wireless and Mobile Systems* (pp. 240-243).

Candan, K. S., Li, W.-S., Luo, Q., Hsiung, W.-P., & Agrawal, D. (2001). Enabling dynamic content caching for database-driven web sites. In *Proceedings of the ACM SIGMOD International Conference on Management of Data* (pp. 532-543).

Cardellini, V., Casalicchio, E., & Colajanni, M. (2001). A performance study of distributed architectures for the quality of web services. In *Proceedings of 34th IEEE Annual Hawaii International Conference on System Sciences*.

Cardellini, V., Casalicchio, E., Colajanni, M., & Mambelli, M. (2001). *Enhancing a web-server cluster with quality of service mechanisms.* Retrieved from http://www.ce.uniroma2.it/publications/ipccc2002.pdf

Cardellini, V., Casalicchio, E., Colajanni, M., & Mambelli, M. (2001). *Web switch support for differentiated services.* Retrieved from http://portal.acm.org/ft_gateway.cfm?id=572320&type=pdf

Cardellini, V., Casalicchio, E., Colajanni, M., & Tucci, S. (2001). Mechanisms for quality of service in web clusters. *Computer Networks, 37*(6), 761–771. doi:10.1016/S1389-1286(01)00252-3

Cardellini, V., Casalicchio, E., Colajanni, M., & Yu, P. S. (2001). The state of the art in locally distributed web-server systems. *ACM Computing Surveys, 34*(2), 263–311. doi:10.1145/508352.508355

Carlson, L., Marcu, D., & Okurowski, M. E. (2002). *RST discourse Treebank.* Retrieved from http://www.ldc.upenn.edu/Catalog/CatalogEntry.jsp?catalogId=LDC2002T07

Carson, N. (2008) *Yahoo employee twitters through layoff.* Retrieved from http://www.businessinsider.com/2008/12/twittering-the-yahoo-layoffs-yhoo

Casalicchio, E., & Colajanni, M. (2001, May 1-5). A client-aware dispatching algorithm for web clusters providing multiple services. In *Proceedings of the Conference on World Wide Web*, Hong Kong (pp. 535-544).

Casanova, M. A., Lauschner, T., Andre, L. L., Breitman, K. K., Furtado, A. L., & Vidal, V. M. (2009). A strategy to revise the constraints of the mediated schema. In *Proceedings of the 28th Conference on Conceptual Modeling*, Gramado, Brazil (pp. 265-279).

Challenger, J., Iyengar, A., & Dantzig, P. (1999). A scalable system for consistently caching dynamic web data. In *Proceedings of the Eighteenth IEEE INFOCOMM Annual Joint Conference* (pp. 294-303).

Challenger, J. R., Dantzig, P., & Iyengar, A. (2004). Efficiently serving dynamic data at highly accessed web sites. *IEEE/ACM Transactions on Networking*, *12*(2), 233–246. doi:10.1109/TNET.2004.826289

Chandy, K. M., & Lamport, L. (1985). Distributed snapshots: Determining global states of distributed systems. *ACM Transactions on Computer Systems*, *3*(1), 63–75. doi:10.1145/214451.214456

Chapin, J. M., & Lehr, W. H. (2007). Cognitive radios for dynamic spectrum access-the path to market success for dynamic spectrum access technology. *IEEE Communications Magazine*, *45*(5), 96–103. doi:10.1109/MCOM.2007.358855

Chau, P. Y. K. (1996). An empirical assessment of a modified technology acceptance model. *Journal of Management Information Systems*, *13*(2), 185–204.

Chen, G., Wang, C.-L., & Lau, F. C. M. (2003). P-Jigsaw: A cluster-based web server with cooperative caching support. *Concurrency and Computation*, *15*, 681–705. doi:10.1002/cpe.723

Chenghui, Y., & Chunanjun, R. (2010). Simulation research of communication networks based on Prim algorithm. In *Proceedings of the International Forum on Information Technology and Applications*.

Chetan, S., Ranganathan, A., & Campbell, R. (2005). Towards fault tolerance pervasive computing. *IEEE Technology and Society Magazine*, *24*(1), 38–44. doi:10.1109/MTAS.2005.1407746

Chiang, C. C., Wu, H. K., Liu, W., & Gerla, M. (1997, April). Routing in clustered multihop, mobile wireless networks with fading channel. In *Proceedings of the IEEE International Conference on Networks*, Singapore (pp. 197-211).

Ciampa, M. (2005). *Security+ Guide to network security fundamentals* (2nd ed.). Boston: Course Technology.

Cisco. (2010). *Cisco Visual Networking Index: Global Mobile Data Traffic Forecast Update, 2010–2015*. Retrieved March 15, 2011, from http://www.cisco.com

Colvin, G. (1997). The changing art of becoming unbeatable. *Fortune*, *136*(10), 299–300.

Core, M. G., & Allen, J. F. (1997). Coding dialogues with the DAMSL annotation scheme. In *Proceedings of the Working Notes of the AAAI Fall Symposium on Communicative Action in Humans and Machines* (pp. 28-35).

Cormen, T. H., Leiserson, C. E., Rivest, R. L., & Stein, C. (2001). *Introduction to algorithms* (2nd ed.). Cambridge, MA: MIT Press.

Coulson, G., Blair, G., Grace, P., Taiani, F., Joolia, A., & Lee, K. (2008). A generic component model for building systems software. *ACM Transactions on Computer Systems*, *26*(1), 1–42. doi:10.1145/1328671.1328672

Cox, G. S., Strassner, J., Neuman de Souza, J., Raymer, D., Samudrala, S., Jennings, B., & Barrett, K. (2008). An enhanced policy model to enable autonomic communications. In *Proceedings of the Fifth IEEE Workshop on Engineering of Autonomic and Autonomous Systems* (p. 184).

Creativity-online. (2010). *Old Spice: Responses case study*. Retrieved from http://creativity-online.com/work/old-spice-responses-case-study/20896

Crockford, D. (2006). *The application/JSON media type for JavaScript object notation (JSON)*. Retrieved from http://www.ietf.org/rfc/rfc4627.txt

Cross, M. (2001). Set strategy before selecting a web site host. *Internet Health Care Magazine*, 42-43.

Cruz, I. F., Xiao, H., & Hsu, F. (2004, July). An ontology-based framework for XML semantic integration. In *Proceedings of the International Database Engineering and Applications Symposium* (pp. 217-226).

Cuenca-Acuna, F. M., & Nguyen, T. D. (2001). Cooperative caching middleware for cluster-based servers. In *Proceedings of the 10th International Symposium on High Performance Distributed Computing* (pp. 303-314).

Cumming, S. (1993). Neural networks for monitoring of engine condition data. *Neural Computing & Applications*, *1*(1), 96–102. doi:10.1007/BF01411378

Cummings, L., & Bromiley, P. (1996). The Organizational Trust Inventory (OTI): Development and Validation . In Kramer, R. M., & Tyler, T. R. (Eds.), *Trust in Organizations: Frontiers of Theory and Research*. Thousand Oaks, CA: Sage.

Cusumano, M. (2011). The platform leader's dilemma. *Communications of the ACM, 54*(10), 21–24. doi:10.1145/2001269.2001279

Dance, S. (2010). *Can Twitter save the day?* Retrieved from http://www.continuitycentral.com/feature0762.html

Datta, A., Datta, K., Thomas, H. M., VanderMeer Suresha, D. E., & Ramamritham, K. (2002). Proxy-based acceleration of dynamically generated content on the World Wide Web: An approach and implementation. In *Proceedings of the ACM SIGMOD International Conference on Management of Data* (pp. 97-108).

Datta, A., Datta, K., Thomas, H. M., VanderMeer Suresha, D. E., Ramamritham, K., & Fishman, D. (2001). A comparative study of alternative middle tier caching solutions to support dynamic web content acceleration. In *Proceedings of the 27ᵗʰ Conference on Very Large Data Bases*, Rome, Italy.

Davy, S., Jennings, B., & Strassner, J. (2008). Efficient policy conflict analysis for autonomic network management. In *Proceedings of the Fifth IEEE Workshop on Engineering of Autonomic and Autonomous Systems* (p. 16).

Degenaro, L., Iyengar, A., Lipkind, I., & Rouvellou, I. (2000). A middleware system which intelligently caches query results. In *Proceedings of the IFIP/ACM International Conference on Distributed Systems Platforms* (pp. 24-44).

Dell. (2010). *Dell outlet twitter feed.* Retrieved from http://twitter.com/DELLOUTLETUK

Delort, J.-Y., Bouchon-Meunier, B., & Rifqi, M. (2003, August). Enhanced web document summarization using hyperlinks. In *Proceedings of the Fourteenth ACM Conference on Hypertext and Hypermedia*, Nottingham, UK (pp. 208-215).

Demestichas, P., Dimitrakopoulos, G., & Strassner, J. (2006). Introducing reconfigurability and cognitive network concepts in the wireless world. *IEEE Vehicular Technology Magazine, 1*(2), 32–39. doi:10.1109/MVT.2006.283572

Deng, H., Li, W., & Agrawal, D. P. (2002). Routing security in wireless ad hoc network. *IEEE Communications Magazine, 40*(10), 70–75. doi:10.1109/MCOM.2002.1039859

DeRose, S. J., Maler, E., Orchard, D., & Walsh, N. (2010, 3 6). XML linking language (XLink) Version 1.1. Retrieved from http://www.w3.org/TR/2010/REC-xlink11-20100506/

Dhillon, G. (2006). *Principles of information systems security: Texts and Cases*. Hoboken, NJ: Wiley.

Dholakia, U. M. (2004). The usefulness of bidders' reputation ratings to sellers in online auctions. *Journal of Interactive Marketing, 19*(1), 31–40. doi:10.1002/dir.20029

Dholakia, U. M., & Simonson, I. (2005). The effect of explicit reference points on consumer choice and online bidding behavior. *Marketing Science, 24*(2), 206–217. doi:10.1287/mksc.1040.0099

Dhurandher, S. K., & Singh, G. V. (2007, January). Stable clustering with efficient routing in wireless ad-hoc networks. In *Proceedings of the COMSWARE 2nd International Conference* (pp.1-12).

Di Caro, G. A., Ducatelle, F., & Gambardella, L. M. (2008). A simulation study of routing performance in realistic urban scenarios for MANETs. In M. Dorigo, M. Birattari, C. Blum, M. Clerc, T. Stützle, & A. F. Winfield (Eds.), *Proceedings of the 6th International Workshop on Ant Algorithms and Swarm Intelligence* (LNCS 5217, pp. 211-218).

Dijkstra, E. W. (1959). A note on two problems in connection with graphs. *Numerische Mathematik, 1*, 269–271. doi:10.1007/BF01386390

Dokurer, S. (2006). *Simulation of black hole attack in wireless ad-hoc networks*. Unpublished master's thesis, Atılım University, Ankara, Turkey.

Dokurer, S., Ert, Y. M., & Acar, E. (2007, March 22-25). Performance analysis of ad hoc networks under black hole attacks. In *Proceedings of the IEEE Southeast Conference* (pp. 148-153).

Drennan, J., & McColl-Kennedy, J. (2003). The relationship between internet use and perceived performance in retail and professional service firms. *Journal of Services Marketing, 17*(3), 295–311. doi:10.1108/08876040310474837

Duana, W., Gub, B., & Whinston, A. (2008). Do online reviews matter? An empirical investigation of panel data. *Decision Support Systems, 45*(3), 1007–1016. doi:10.1016/j.dss.2008.04.001

eBay's bid to win back buyers. (2007). *BusinessWeek.* Retrieved from http://www.businessweek.com/print/technology/content/sep2007/tc20070917_75070.htm

Economides, N. (2008). Net Neutrality: Non-Discrimination and Digital Distribution of Content Through the Internet. *I/S. Journal of Law and Policy, 4*(2), 209–233.

Economides, N., & Joacim, T. (2009). *Net neutrality on the Internet: A ywo-sided market analysis (Research Rep. 2451/26057).* New York, NY: New York University.

Emiliani, M. L. (2000). Business-to-business online auctions: key issues for purchasing process improvement. *Supply Chain Management, 5*(4), 176–193. doi:10.1108/13598540010347299

Ephremides, A., Wieselthier, J. E., & Baker, D. J. (1987). A design concept for reliable mobile radio networks with frequency hopping signaling. *Proceedings of the IEEE, 75,* 56–73. doi:10.1109/PROC.1987.13705

Er, I. I., & Seah, W. K. G. (2004). Mobility-based d-hop clustering algorithm for mobile ad hoc networks. In *Proceedings of the IEEE Conference on Wireless Communications and Networking* (pp. 2359-2364).

Etemad, K. (2008). Overview of mobile WiMAX technology and evolution. *IEEE Communications Magazine, 46*(10), 31–40. doi:10.1109/MCOM.2008.4644117

European Commission. (2010). *Telecoms: Mobile phone customers entitled to protection from data-roaming "bill-shock" as from 1st March 2010.* Brussels, Belgium: European Commission.

European Union. (2007). *EU regulation on roaming.* Retrieved from http://ec.europa.eu/information_society/activities/roaming/roaming_regulation/index_en.htm

Evans, P., & Wurster, T. (1997). Strategy and the new economics of information. *Harvard Business Review, 9*(10), 71–82.

Experian. (2009). *Top websites and search engines.* Retrieved from http://www.hitwise.com/uk/resources/data-centre

Facebook. (2010). *Facebook statistic.* Retrieved from http://www.facebook.com/press/info.php?statistics

Feki, M. A., & Mokhtari, M. (2006). Context aware and ontology specification for assistive environment. *International Journal of Human-friendly Welfare Robotic Systems, 4*(2), 29–32.

Ferrucci, D., & Lally, A. (2004). UIMA: An architectural approach to unstructured information processing in the corporate research environment. *Natural Language Engineering, 10*(3-4), 327–348. doi:10.1017/S1351324904003523

Fielding, R., Gettys, J., Mogul, J., Frystyk, H., Masinter, L., Leach, P., & Berners-Lee, T. (1999). *Hypertext transfer protocol--HTTP/1.1.* Retrieved from http://www.w3.org/Protocols/rfc2616/rfc2616.html

Forcht, K., & Richard, E. (1995). Security issues and concern with the internet. *Internet Research: Electronic Networking Applications and Policy of MCB, 5*(3), 23–31. doi:10.1108/10662249510104621

Fornell, C., & Larcker, D. (1981). Evaluating Structural Equation Models with Unobservable Variables and Measurement Error. *Management Science, 40*(4), 440–465.

Freitas, J., Correia, A., & Brito e Abreu, F. (2008). An ontology for IT services. In *Proceedings of the 13th Conference on Software Engineering and Databases.*

Gabrilovich, E., & Markovitch, S. (2007, January). Computing semantic relatedness using Wikipedia-based explicit semantic analysis. In *Proceedings of the International Joint Conference on Artificial Intelligence,* Hyderabad, India (pp.1606-1611).

Galindo-Legaria, C., Grabs, T., Kleinerman, C., & Waas, F. (2005). Database change notifications: Primitives for efficient database query result caching. In *Proceedings of the 31st International Conference on Very Large Data Bases,* Trondheim, Norway (pp. 1275-1278).

Gandhi, S., Buragohain, C., Lili, C., Zheng, H., & Suri, S. (2007, April). A general framework for wireless spectrum auctions. In *Proceedings of the IEEE International Symposium New Frontiers Dynamic Spectrum Access Networks* (pp. 22-33).

Garfinkel, S., & Spafford, G. (1997). *Web security & commerce*. Sebastopol, CA: O'Reilly & Associates.

Garg, R., & Randhawa, R. S. (2002). A SLA framework for QoS provisioning and dynamic capacity allocation. In *Proceedings of the 10ᵗʰ International Workshop on Quality of Service* (pp. 129-137).

Garrett, J. J. (2005). AJAX: A new approach to Web applications. Retrieved from http://www.adaptivepath.com/ideas/essays/archives/000385.php

Gaylord, C. (2007). Why we do what we do on eBay. *The Christian Science Monitor*, pp. 13-14. Retrieved from http://www.csmonitor.com/2007/0716/p13s02-wmgn.html

Gefen, D., Straub, D., & Boudreau, M. (2000). Structural Equation Modeling and Regression: Guidelines for Research Practice. *Communications of the Association for Information Systems*, 4(7), 1–70.

Gerla, M., & Tsai, J. T. C. (1995). Multicluster, mobile multimedia radio networks. In. *Proceedings of the Wireless Networks Conference, 1*, 255–265. doi:10.1007/BF01200845

Gerla, G. (2001). *Fuzzy logic: Mathematical tools*. Boston, MA: Kluwer Academic.

Gessler, S., Martin, M., & Weiss, S. (2005). Context awareness in future life scenarios: Impact on service provisioning platforms. *Applications and the Internet Workshops*, 144-147.

Ghidini, C., & Serafini, L. (2006). Reconciling concepts and relations in heterogeneous ontologies. In Y. Sure & J. Domingue (Eds.), *Proceedings of the 3ʳᵈ European Semantic Web Conference on the Semantic Web: Research and Applications* (LNCS 4011, pp. 50-64).

Ghorbel, M., Mokhtari, M., & Renouard, S. (2006). A distributed approach for assistive service provision in pervasive environment. In *Proceedings of the 4ᵗʰ International Workshop on Wireless Mobile Applications and Services on WLAN Hotspots* (pp. 91-100).

Gill, P., Arlitt, M., Li, Z., & Mahanti, A. (2007, October 24-26). Youtube traffic characterization: A view from the edge. In *Proceedings of the 7th ACM SIGCOMM Conference on Internet Measurement*, San Diego, CA.

Gizelis, C. A., & Vergados, D. D. (2010). A survey of pricing schemes in wireless networks. *IEEE Communications Surveys and Tutorials*, 13(1), 126–145. doi:10.1109/SURV.2011.060710.00028

Gong, W., You, Z., Chen, D., Zhao, X., Gu, M., & Lam, K.-Y. (2009). Trust based malicious nodes detection in MANET. In *Proceedings of the International Conference on E-Business and Information System Security* (pp. 1-4).

Gouin-Vallerand, C., & Giroux, S. (2007). Managing and deployment of applications with OSGi in the context of smart home. In *Proceedings of the Third IEEE International Conference on Wireless and Mobile Computing, Networking and Communications* (p. 70).

Gouin-Vallerand, C., Giroux, S., Abdulrazak, B., & Mokhtari, M. (2008). Toward the autonomous pervasive computing. In *Proceedings of the International Conference on Information Integration and Web-Based Applications & Services*.

Great tools to help eBay sellers; expert recommends five tools to determine what items to sell on eBay. (2007). *PS Newswire*. Retrieved from http://reddog.rmu.edu:2079/pqdweb?index=1&did=1195547291&SrchMode=1&sid=6&Fmt=3&VInst=PROD&VType=PQD&RQT=309&VName=PQD&TS=1193760199&clientId=2138

Green, D., Barclay, D., & Ryans, A. (1995). Entry strategy and long-term performance: conceptualization and empirical examination. *Journal of Marketing*, 59(4), 1–16. doi:10.2307/1252324

Greenspan, A., Klerer, M., Tomcik, J., Canchi, R., & Wilson, J. (2008). IEEE 802.20: Mobile broadband wireless access for the twenty-first century. *IEEE Communications Magazine*, 46(7), 56–63. doi:10.1109/MCOM.2008.4557043

Gruber, T. (1993). Model formulation as a problem-solving task: Computer-assisted engineering modeling. *International Journal of Intelligent Systems*, 8(1), 105–127. doi:10.1002/int.4550080108

Gruber, T. (1995). Towards principles for the design of ontologies used for knowledge sharing. *International Journal of Human-Computer Studies, 43*, 907–928. doi:10.1006/ijhc.1995.1081

Gu, Y., Lu, W., Prasad, R. V., & Niemegeers, I. (2007). Clustering in ad hoc personal network formation. In Y. Shi, G. Dick van Albada, J. Dongarra, & P. M. A. Sloot (Eds.), *Proceedings of the 7ᵗʰ International Conference on Computational Science, Part IV* (LNCS 4490, pp. 312-319).

Guha, R. V., McCool, R., & Miller, E. (2003). Semantic search. In *Proceedings of the Twelfth International World Wide Web Conference* (pp. 700-709). New York, NY: ACM Press.

Guo, L., & Matta, I. (2000). QDMR, an efficient QoS dependent multicast routing algorithm. *Journal of Communications and Networks, 2*(2).

Guttoski, P. B., Sunye, M. S., & Silva, F. (2007). Kruskal's algorithm for query tree optimization. In *Proceedings of the 11ᵗʰ International Database Engineering and Applications Symposium*.

Haas, L. M., Kossmann, D., Wimmers, E. L., & Yang, J. (1997, August 25-29). Optimizing queries across diverse data sources. In *Proceedings of the 23rd International Conference on Very Large Data Bases*, Athens, Greece (pp. 276-285).

Haas, Z. J., Halpern, J. Y., & Li, L. (2006). Gossip-based ad hoc routing. *IEEE/ACM Transactions on Networking, 14*(3), 479–491. doi:10.1109/TNET.2006.876186

Hair, T., Anderson, R., Tatham, R., & Black, W. (1998). *Multivariate Data Analysis* (5th ed.). Upper Saddle River, NJ: Prentice Hall.

Halliday, J. (2010) *Old Spice viral campaign a hit.* Retrieved from http://www.guardian.co.uk/technology/blog/2010/jul/14/old-spice-viral-video-campaign

Halpin, H. (2006). Identity, reference, and meaning on the web. In *Proceedings of the Workshop on Identity Meaning and the Web*.

Hanash, A., Siddique, A., Awan, I., & Woodward, M. (2009). Performance evaluation of dynamic probabilistic broadcasting for flooding in mobile ad hoc networks. *Journal of Simulation Modeling Practice and Theory, 17*(2), 364–375. doi:10.1016/j.simpat.2008.09.012

Hartig, O., Bizer, C., & Freytag, J.-C. (2009). Executing SPARQL queries over the web of linked data. In A. Bernstein, D. R. Karger, T. Heath, L. Feigenbaum, D. Maynard, E. Motta et al. (Eds.), *Proceedings of the 8ᵗʰ International Semantic Web Conference on the Semantic Web* (LNCS 5823, pp. 293-309).

Hart, P., & Saunders, C. (1997). Power and Trust: Critical Factors in the Adoption and Use of Electronic Data Interchange. *Organization Science, 8*(1), 23–41. doi:10.1287/orsc.8.1.23

Hebeler, J., Fisher, M., Blace, R., & Perez-Lopez, A. (2009). *Semantic web programming*. Indianapolis, IN: John Wiley & Sons.

Heinzelman, W. R., Chandrakasan, A., & Balakrishnan, H. (2002). An application-specific protocol architectures for wireless networks. *IEEE Transactions on Wireless Communications, 1*, 660–670. doi:10.1109/TWC.2002.804190

Hepp, M. (2008). GoodRelations: An ontology for describing products and services offers on the web. In A. Gangemi & J. Euzenat (Eds.), *Proceedings of the 16th International Conference on Knowledge Engineering and Knowledge Management* (LNCS 5268, pp. 329-346).

Higgins, C., Duxbury, L., & Irving, R. (1992). Work-family conflict in the dual-career family. *Organizational Behavior and Human Decision Processes, 51*(1), 51–75. doi:10.1016/0749-5978(92)90004-Q

Holmedahl, V., Smith, B., & Yang, T. (1998). Cooperative caching of dynamic content on a distributed web server. In *Proceedings of the Seventh IEEE International Symposium on High Performance Distributed Computing*, Chicago, IL (pp. 243-250).

Hong, X., Gerla, M., Pei, G., & Chiang, C. (1999, August). A group mobility model for ad hoc wireless networks. In *Proceedings of the 2ⁿᵈ ACM/IEEE International Workshop on Modeling, Analysis and Simulation of Wireless and Mobile Systems*, Seattle, WA (pp. 53-60).

Hongwei, W., Fu, J., & Wu, J. (2003). A study on a formal ontology model: Constructing a customer ontology in a CRM context. In *Proceedings of the Americas Conference on Information Systems* (pp. 1201-1212).

Horrocks, I., Patel-Schneider, P. F., Boley, H., Tabet, S., Grosof, B., & Dean, M. (2004). *SWRL: A semantic web rule language combining OWL and RuleML*. Retrieved from http://www.w3.org/Submission/SWRL/

Huang, X., Radkowski, P., & Roman, P. (2007). Computer crimes. *The American Criminal Law Review*, *44*(2), 285–335.

Hu, G., Wang, L., Fetch, S., & Bidanda, B. (2008). A multi-objective model for project portfolio selection to implement lean and Six Sigma concepts. *International Journal of Production Research*, *46*(23), 6611–6648. doi:10.1080/00207540802230363

Hulland, J. (1999). Use of partial least squares in strategic management research: a review of four recent studies. *Strategic Management Journal*, *20*(2), 195–204. doi:10.1002/(SICI)1097-0266(199902)20:2<195::AID-SMJ13>3.0.CO;2-7

Hull, R., & Yoshikawa, M. (1990). *ILOG: Declarative creation and manipulation of object identifiers* (pp. 455–468). San Francisco, CA: Morgan Kaufmann.

Hyun, J., Jung, I., & Maeng, S. (2003). Content sniffer based load distribution in a web server cluster. *IEICE Transactions on Information and Systems*, *86*(7), 1258–1269.

Indulska, J., & Sutton, P. (2003). Location management in pervasive systems. In *Proceedings of the ACSW Frontiers Workshop on Wearable, Invisible, Context-aware, Ambient, Pervasive and Ubiquitous Computing* (pp. 143-151).

International Organization for Standardization. (2011). *ISO WG21: Programming Language C++, Document Number: N3290*. Retrieved from http://www.open-std. org/jtc1/sc22/wg21/

International Telecommunication Union. (2005). *ITU Internet reports 2005: The Internet of things –Executive summary*. Geneva, Switzerland: ITU.

Iyengar, A., & Challenger, J. R. (1997). Improving web server performance by caching dynamic data. In *Proceedings of the USENIX Symposium on Internet Technologies and Systems* (pp. 49-60).

Jain, V., Benyoucef, L., & Deshmukh, S. G. (2008). What's the buzz about moving from 'lean' to 'agile' integrated supply chains? A fuzzy intelligent agent-based approach. *International Journal of Production Research*, *46*(23), 6649–6678. doi:10.1080/00207540802230462

Jansen, B., & Zhang, M. (2009). Twitter power: Tweets as an electronic word of mouth. *Journal of the American Society for Information Science and Technology*, *60*(11), 36–48. doi:10.1002/asi.21149

Jarrar, M., Verlinden, R., & Meersman, R. (2003). Ontology-based consumer complaint management. In R. Meersman & Z. Tari (Eds.), *Proceedings of the Workshop on Regulatory Ontologies and the Modeling of Complaint Regulations* (LNCS 2889, pp. 594-606).

Java, A., Song, X., Finin, T., & Tseng, B. (2007, August 12). Why we twitter: understanding microblogging usage and communities. In *Proceedings of the 9th WebKDD and 1st SNA-KDD Workshop on Web Mining and Social Network Analysis*, San Jose, CA (pp. 56-65).

Jennings, B., van der Meer, S., Balasubramaniam, S., Botvich, D. O., Foghlu, M., Donnelly, W., & Strassner, J. (2007). Towards autonomic management of communications networks. *IEEE Communications Magazine*, *45*(10), 112–121. doi:10.1109/MCOM.2007.4342833

Jessup, L., & Valacich, J. (2008). *Information Systems Today: Managing in the Digital World*. Upper Saddle River, NJ: Pearson Education.

Jetblue. (2010). *Jetblue Twitter feed*. Retrieved from http://twitter.com/jetblue

Jia, X. (1998). A distributed algorithm of delay-bounded multicast routing for multimedia applications in wide area networks. *IEEE/ACM Transactions on Networking*, *6*, 823–837.

Johansson, P., Larsson, T., Hedman, N., Mielczarek, B., & Degermark, M. (1999, August). Scenario-based performance analysis of routing protocols for mobile ad hoc networks. In *Proceedings of the 5th ACM/IEEE International Conference on Mobile Computing and Networking*, Seattle, WA (pp. 195-206).

Johnson, D. B., Maltz, D. A., & Hu, Y. C. (2004). *The dynamic source routing protocol for mobile ad-hoc network (DSR)*. Retrieved from http://www.ietf.org/rfc/rfc4728.txt

Johnson, D., & Maltz, D. (1996). Dynamic source routing in ad hoc wireless networks . In Imielinski, T., & Korth, H. (Eds.), *Mobile Computing* (pp. 153–181). Dordrecht, The Netherlands: Kluwer Academic Publishers. doi:10.1007/978-0-585-29603-6_5

Kang, C. (2008). *Do text messages cost too much?* Retrieved from http://voices.washingtonpost.com/posttech/2008/09/lawmaker_consumer_group_demand.html

Karl, H., & Wilig, A. (2007). *Protocols and architectures for wireless sensor networks*. New York, NY: John Wiley & Sons.

Kasneci, G., Ramanath, M., Suchanek, F., & Weikum, G. (2008). The YAGO-NAGA approach to knowledge discovery. *SIGMOD Record*, *37*(4), 41–47. doi:10.1145/1519103.1519110

Katsiri, E. (2002). Principles of context inferences. In *Proceedings of the International Conference on Ubiquitous Computing*, Gotenborg, Sweden.

Ke, C.-H., Shieh, C.-K., Hwang, W.-S., & Ziviani, A. (2008). An evaluation framework for more realistic simulations of MPEG video transmission. *International Journal of Information Science and Engineering*, 425–440.

Kennedy, F. A., & Widener, S. K. (2008). A control framework: insights from evidence on lean accounting. *Management Accounting Research*, *19*(4), 301–319. doi:10.1016/j.mar.2008.01.001

Kephart, J. O., & Chess, D. M. (2003). The vision of autonomic computing. *IEEE Computer*, *36*, 41–50. doi:10.1109/MC.2003.1160055

Kernchen, R., Bonnefoy, D., Battestini, A., Mrohs, B., Wagner, M., & Klemettinen, M. (2006). Context-awareness in MobiLife. In *Proceedings of the 15th IST Mobile Summit*, Mykonos, Greece.

Kershenbaum, A., & Van Styke, R. (1972). Computing minimum spanning trees efficiently. In *Proceedings of the ACM Annual Conference* (Vol. 1, pp. 518-527).

Khan, I., Javaid, A., & Qian, H. (2008). Coverage-based dynamically adjusted probabilistic forwarding for wireless mobile ad hoc networks. In S. Giordano, W. Jia, P. M. Ruiz, S. Olariu, & G. Xing (Eds.), *Proceedings of the 1st ACM International Workshop on Heterogeneous Sensor and Actor Networks (HeterSanet '08)*, Hong Kong, China (pp. 81-88).

Kiani, S. L., Riaz, M., Zhung, Y., Lee, S., & Lee, Y.-K. (2005). A distributed middleware solution for context awareness in ubiquitous systems. In *Proceedings of the 11th IEEE International Conference on Embedded and Real-Time Computing Systems and Applications* (pp. 451-454).

Kifer, M., & Lausen, G. (1989). F-logic: A higher-order language for reasoning about objects, inheritance, and scheme. *SIGMOD*, *18*(2), 134–146. doi:10.1145/66926.66939

Kim, J. S., Zhang, Q., & Agrawal, D. P. (2004). Probabilistic broadcasting based on coverage area and neighbor confirmation in mobile ad hoc networks. In *Proceedings of the IEEE Global Telecommunications Conference Workshops (GlobeCom '04)*, Dallas, TX (pp. 96-101). Washington, DC: IEEE Computer Society.

Kirk, T., Levy, A. Y., Sagiv, Y., & Srivastava, D. (1995). The information manifold. In Proceedings of the AAAI Spring Symposium on Information Gathering from Heterogeneous, Distributed Environments (pp. 85-91).

Kiss, J. (2009). *Twitter job service launched*. Retrieved from http://www.guardian.co.uk/media/2009/mar/17/digital-media-twitter

Klaue, J., Rathke, B., & Wolisz, A. (2003). EvalVid – A framework for video transmission and quality evaluation. In *Proceedings of the 13th International Conference on Modeling, Techniques and Tools for Computer Performance Evaluation*, Urbana, IL. Retrieved January 20, 2011, from http://www.tkn.tu-berlin.de/research/evalvid

Kompella, V. P., Pasquale, J. C., & Polyzos, G. C. (1993, June). Two distributed algorithms for multicasting multimedia information. In *Proceedings of the International Conference on Computer Communications and Networks*, San Diego, CA (pp. 343-349).

Korotkich, V., & Dimitrov, V. (2002). *Fuzzy logic: A framework for the new millennium.* Berlin, Germany: Physica-Verlag.

Kossmann, D. (2000). The state of the art in distributed query processing. *ACM Computing Surveys, 32,* 422–469. doi:10.1145/371578.371598

Ko, Y., & Vaidya, N. (2000). Location-aided routing (LAR) in mobile ad hoc networks. *Journal of Wireless Networks, 6*(4), 307–321. doi:10.1023/A:1019106118419

Krishna, P., Vaidya, N. H., Chatterjee, M., & Pradhan, D. K. (1997). A cluster based approach for routing in ad hoc networks. In *Proceedings of the Second ACM SIG-COMM Symposium on Mobile and Location-Independent Computing* (pp. 1-10).

Kruskal, J. B. (1956). On the shortest spanning subtree of a graph and the traveling salesman problem. *Proceedings of the American Mathematical Society, 7,* 48–50. doi:10.1090/S0002-9939-1956-0078686-7

kSOAP2. (2011). *A lightweight and efficient SOAP engine suitable for J2ME or constrained java devices.* Retrieved from http://ksoap2.sourceforge.net/

Kumar, R., Novak, J., & Tomkins, A. (2006, August 20-23). Structure and evolution of online social networks. In *Proceedings of the 12th ACM SIGKDD International Conference on Knowledge Discovery and Data Mining,* Philadelphia, PA.

Kumar, K. R., & Renjish, K. V. Y. H. (2008). Techno-economic analysis of international mobile roaming. *IEEE Wireless Communications, 15*(3), 73–80. doi:10.1109/MWC.2008.4547526

Kumar, R., Park, S., & Subramaniam, C. (2008). Understanding the value of countermeasures portfolios in information systems security. *Journal of Management Information Systems, 25*(1), 241–279. doi:10.2753/MIS0742-1222250210

Kundu, M. (2007). *An improved clustering algorithm for mobile ad-hoc network using fuzzy logic.* Unpublished master's thesis, Jadavpur University, Kolkata, India.

Kunz, S., Aleksy, M., Brecht, F., Fabian, B., & Wauer, M. (2010). ALETHEIA – Improving industrial service-lifecycle management by semantic data federations. In *Proceedings of the IEEE 24th International Conference on Advanced Information Networking and Applications* (pp. 1308-1313). Washington, DC: IEEE Computer Society.

Kunz, S., Brecht, F., Fabian, B., Aleksy, M., & Wauer, M. (2010). Aletheia–Improving industrial service lifecycle management by semantic data federations. In Proceedings of the 24th International Conference on Advanced Information Networking and Applications (pp. 1308-1314). Washington, DC: IEEE Computer Society.

Kurosawa, S., Nakayama, H., Kato, N., Jamalipour, A., & Nemoto, Y. (2007). Detecting blackhole attack on AODV-based mobile ad hoc networks by dynamic learning method. *International Journal of Network Security, 5*(6), 338–346.

Lane, C. (1998). Five essential steps to privacy. *PC World, 16*(9), 116–117.

Langegger, A., Woss, W., & Blochl, M. (2008). A semantic web middleware for virtual data integration on the web. In S. Bechhofer, M. Hauswirth, J. Hoffmann, & M. Koubarakis (Eds.), *Proceedings of the 5th European Semantic Web Conference* (LNCS 5021, pp. 493-507).

Lansing, P., & Hubbard, J. (2002). Online auctions: the need for alternative dispute resolution. *American Business Review, 20*(1), 108–115.

Laudon, K., & Traver, C. (2008). *E-commerce: Business, Technology, and Society.* Upper Saddle River, NJ: Pearson Education.

Lawson, S. (2009). *Clearwire WiMax coming to 10 cities on Sept. 1.* Retrieved from http://www.pcworld.com/businesscenter/article/169511/clearwire_wimax_coming_to_10_cities_on_sept_1.html

Lee, S., Han, B., & Shin, M. (2002). Robust routing in wireless ad hoc networks. In *Proceedings of the International Conference on Parallel Processing ICPP Workshop,* Vancouver, BC, Canada (pp. 73-78).

Lee, B.-H., Lim, S.-H., Kim, J.-H., & Fox, G. C. (2009). Lease-based consistency schemes in the web environment. *Future Generation Computer Systems, 25*(1), 8–19. doi:10.1016/j.future.2008.06.001

Lenhart, A., Ling, R., Campbell, S., & Purcell, K. (2010). *Teens and mobile phones.* Retrieved from http://www.pewinternet.org/Reports/2010/Teens-and- Mobile-Phones.aspx

Lenzerini, M. (2002, June 3-5). Data integration: A theoretical perspective. In *Proceedings of the Twenty-First ACM SIGMOD-SIGACT-SIGART Symposium on Principles of Database Systems*, Madison, WI (pp. 233-246).

Li, C., Raha, A., & Zhao, W. (1997), Stability in ATM networks. In *Proceedings of the 16th Annual Joint Conference of the IEEE Computer and Communications Societies Driving the Information Revolution* (pp. 160-167).

Li, H., Ward, R., & Zhang, H. (2007). Risk, convenience, cost and online payment choice: a study of eBay transactions. *Commerce Center od DuPree College of Management, 8*(4), 1-36.

Li, L., Zhou, K., Xue, G.-R., Zha, H., & Yu, Y. (2009, April). Enhancing diversity, coverage and balance for summarization through structure learning. In *Proceedings of the 18th International World Wide Web Conference*, Madrid, Spain (pp. 71-80).

Liang, S., Fodor, P., Wan, H., & Kifer, M. (2009). OpenRuleBench: An analysis of the performance of rule engines. In Proceedings of the 18th International Conference on World Wide Web (pp. 601-610). New York, NY: ACM Press.

Lim, S.-J., & Ng, Y.-K. (2001, April). An automated change-detection algorithm for HYML documents based on semantic hierarchies. In *Proceedings of the 17th International Conference on Data Engineering* (pp. 303-312).

Lin, L., & Daim, T. U. (2005). Platform strategy framework for internet-based service development: case of eBay. *International Journal of Services Technology and Management, 11*(4), 334–354. doi:10.1504/IJSTM.2009.024565

Lowery, J. C. (2001). Caching hierarchies: Understanding content distribution/delivery networks. *Dell Power Solutions, 1*, 91–94.

Luo, Q., Krishnamurthy, S., Mohan, C., Pirahesh, H., Woo, H., Lindsay, B. G., & Naughton, J. F. (2002). Middle-tier database caching for e-business. In *Proceedings of the ACM SIGMOD International Conference on Management of Data* (pp. 588-593).

Lutz, M. (2005). *Ontology-based discovery and composition of geographic information services.* Unpublished doctoral dissertation, Institute for Geoinformatics, University of Munster, Munster, Germany.

Makris, K., Bikakis, N., Gioldasis, N., Tsinaraki, C., & Christodoulakis, S. (2009). Towards a mediator based on OWL and SPARQL. In M. D. Lytras, E. Damiani, J. M. Carroll, R. D. Tennyson, D. Avison, A. Naeve et al. (Eds.), *Proceedings of the Second World Summit on Visioning and Engineering the Knowledge Society: A Web Science Perspective* (LNCS 5736, pp. 326-335).

Mangold, W. G., & Faulds, D. (2009). Social media: The new hybrid element of the promotion mix. *Business Horizons, 52*, 357–365. doi:10.1016/j.bushor.2009.03.002

Mani, I. (2001). *Automatic summarization.* Amsterdam, The Netherlands: John Benjamins Publishing.

Manola, F., & Miller, E. (2004). *RDF primer.* Retrieved from http://www.w3.org/TR/rdf-primer

McCann, J. A., Kristofferson, P., & Alonso, E. (2004). Building ambient intelligence into a ubiquitous computing management system. In *Proceedings of the International Symposium on Challenges in the Internet and Interdisciplinary Research*, Amalfi, Italy.

McDonald, A. B. (1997). *Survey of adaptive shortest-path routing in dynamic packet-switched networks.* Pittsburgh, PA: University of Pittsburgh.

McDonald, A. B., & Znati, T. F. (1999). A mobility-based framework for adaptive clustering in wireless ad hoc networks. *IEEE Journal on Selected Areas in Communications, 17*, 1466–1486. doi:10.1109/49.780353

McPherson, K. (2007). Using eBay as a collection development tool. *Teacher Librarian, 34*(5), 71–73.

Melnik, M. I., & Alm, J. (2005). Seller reputation, information signals, and prices for heterogeneous coins on eBay. *Southern Economic Journal, 72*(2), 305–315. doi:10.2307/20062113

Messmer, E. (2000). Security needs spawn services. *New World (New Orleans, La.)*, *17*(14), 81–100.

Meylan, F., Kiatake, L. G. G., Santos, M. Z., Kofuji, S. T., & Courtiat, J. P. (1999). Comparative analysis of multicast routing algorithms for multimedia communication over ATM networks. In *Proceedings of the IEEE Latin American Network Operations and Management Symposium*, Rio de Janeiro, Brazil.

Mhatre, V., & Rosenberg, C. (2004). Homogeneous vs. heterogeneous clustered sensor networks: A comparative study. In *Proceedings of the IEEE International Conference on Communications* (Vol. 6, pp. 3646-3651).

Miaou, S.-G., Shih, F.-C., & Huang, C.-Y. (2007). A smart vision-based human fall detection system for telehealth applications. In *Proceedings of the IASTED Telehealth Conference*, Montreal, QC, Canada.

Minack, E., Sauermann, L., Grimnes, G., Fluit, C., & Broekstra, J. (2008). *The Sesame LuceneSail: RDF queries with full-text search*. Retrieved from http://citeseerx.ist.psu.edu/viewdoc/summary?doi=10.1.1.125.9864

Mislove, A., Marcon, M., Gummadi, K., Druschel, P., & Bhattacharjee, B. (2007, October 24-26). Measurement and analysis of online social networks. In *Proceedings of the 7th ACM SIGCOMM Conference on Internet Measurement*, San Diego, CA.

Mistry, N., Jinwala, D. C., & Zaveri, M. (2010, March 17-19). Improving AODV protocol against blackhole attacks. In *Proceedings of the International Multiconference of Engineers and Computer Scientists*, Hong Kong (Vol. 2).

Mobile Nordic. (2009). *Press release*. http://www.nordicid.com/en/press-centr/press- relizy.html

Mogha, R., & Preetham, V. V. (2003). *Java web services programming*. New York, NY: Wiley Dreamtech.

Mohamed, A., & Adel, B. (2004). A new delay-constrained algorithm for multicast routing tree construction. *International Journal of Communication Systems*, 985–1000.

Mohan, C. (2001). Tutorial: Caching technologies for web applications. In *Proceedings of the Conference on Very Large Data Bases*.

Nadamoto, A., Ma, Q., & Tanaka, K. (2005). B-CWB: Bilingual comparative web browser based on content-synchronization and viewpoint retrieval. *World Wide Web (Bussum)*, *8*(3), 347–367. doi:10.1007/s11280-005-1316-8

Nakayama, K., Pei, M., Erdmann, M., Ito, M., Shirakawa, M., Hara, T., & Nishio, S. (2008, July). Wikipedia mining - Wikipedia as a corpus for knowledge extraction. In *Proceedings of the Annual Wikipedia Conference*, Alexandria, Egypt.

Navneet, M., & Chen, J. A. (2002). Note on practical construction of maximum bandwidth paths. *Information Processing Letters*, *83*, 175–180. doi:10.1016/S0020-0190(01)00323-4

Nelson, M. (2000). *Hacker school teaches security*. Information Week.

Neovius, M., Sere, K., Yan, L., & Satpathy, M. (2006). A formal model of context-awareness and context-dependency. *Software Engineering and Formal Methods*, 177-185.

Ni, S., Tseng, Y., Chen, Y., & Sheu, J. (1999). The broadcast storm problem in a mobile ad hoc network. *Journal of Wireless Networks*, *8*(2), 153–167.

Niyato, D., & Hossain, E. (2007). Integration of WiMax and WiFi: Optimal pricing for bandwidth sharing. *IEEE Communications Magazine*, *45*(5), 140–146. doi:10.1109/MCOM.2007.358861

Niyato, D., & Hossain, E. (2008). Competitive pricing in heterogeneous wireless access networks: Issues and approaches. *IEEE Network*, *22*(6), 4–11. doi:10.1109/MNET.2008.4694168

Niyato, D., & Hossain, E. (2008). Spectrum trading in cognitive networks: A market- equilibrium-based approach. *IEEE Wireless Communications*, *15*(6), 71–80. doi:10.1109/MWC.2008.4749750

Novak, T. P., Hoffman, D. L., & Yung, Y. F. (2000). Measuring the customer experience in on-line environment: a structural modeling approach. *Marketing Science*, *19*(1), 22–42. doi:10.1287/mksc.19.1.22.15184

Nunnally, J., & Bernstein, I. (1994). *Psychometric Theory*. New York: McGraw-Hill.

Ogren, E. (2009). *Sprint announces major WiMax expansion*. Retrieved from http://www.informationweek. com/blog/main/archives/2009/08/sprint_announce. html;jsession id=R45ED233RMONZQE1GHPCKHW ATMY32JVN

Oja, E. (1989). Neural networks, principal components, and subspaces. *International Journal of Neural Systems, 1*(1), 61–68. doi:10.1142/S0129065789000475

Oracle Corp. (2011). *Java ME: Java platform micro edition*. Retrieved from http://www.oracle.com/technetwork/ java/javame/overview/index.html

Oracle Corporation. (2010). *Oracle application server web cache 11g*. Retrieved from http://www.oracle.com/ technetwork/middleware/ias/webcache11goverview-128137.pdf

OSGi Alliance. (2009). *OSGi technology*. Retrieved from http://www.osgi.org/About/Technology

Oyegoke, A. (1999). Surfing Europe. *The Banker, 1*(2), 72–73.

Ozianyi, G. V., Ventura, N., & Golovins, E. (2008). A novel pricing approach to support QoS in 3G networks. *Computer Networks, 52*(7), 1433–1450. doi:10.1016/j. comnet.2007.12.011

Pai, V. S., Aron, M., Banga, G., Svendsen, M., Druschel, P., Zwaenepol, W., & Nahum, E. (1998). *Locality-aware request distribution in cluster-based network services*. Retrieved from http://www.research.ibm.com/people/n/ nahum/publications/asplos98-lard.pdf

Pakucs, B. (2003). SesaME: A framework for personalized and adaptive speech interfaces. In *Proceedings of the EACL Workshop on Dialogue Systems: Interaction, Adaptation and Styles of Management* (pp. 95-102).

Palmer, J. (2008). *Mobile broadband next-gen battle*. Retrieved from http://news.bbc.co.uk/2/hi/technology/7896686.stm

Pan, D., Liu, Z.-B., Ding, X.-F., & Zheng, Q. (2009). The application of union-find sets in Kruskal algorithm. In *Proceedings of the International Conference on Artificial Intelligence and Computational Intelligence* (pp. 159-162).

Paralic, J., & Kostial, I. (2003). Ontology-based information retrieval. In Proceedings of the 14th International Conference on Information and Intelligent Systems, Varaždin, *Croatia* (pp. 23-28).

Parekh, A. K. (1994). *Selecting routers in ad hoc wireless networks*. Paper presented at the Intelligent Tutoring Systems Conference.

Parker, C. (1999). E-mail use and abuse. *Work Study, 48*(7), 257–260. doi:10.1108/00438029910294135

Parker, G., & Van Alstyne, M. (2005). Two-sided network effects: A theory of information product design. *Management Science, 51*(10). doi:10.1287/mnsc.1050.0400

Parr, B. (2010). *Thousands of archived tweets mysteriously disappear*. Retrieved from http://mashable. com/2010/01/13/tweets-vanish/

Partridge, C. (2011). Realizing the Future of Wireless Data Communications. *Communications of the ACM, 54*(9), 62–68. doi:10.1145/1995376.1995395

Pasquale, J. C., Polyzos, G. C., Xylomenos, G. V., & Kompella, V. P. (1998). The multimedia multicasting problem. *Multimedia Systems, 6*, 43–59. doi:10.1007/ s005300050075

Pathak, J. (2003). Assurance and e-auctions: are the existing business models still relevant? *Managerial Auditing Journal, 18*(4), 292–294. doi:10.1108/02686900310474307

Patil, L., Dutta, D., & Sriram, R. (2005). Ontology-based exchange of product data semantics. *IEEE Transactions on Automation Science and Engineering, 2*(3), 213–225. doi:10.1109/TASE.2005.849087

Pérez, J., Arenas, M., & Gutierrez, C. (2009). Semantics and complexity of SPARQL. *ACM Transactions on Database Systems, 34*(16), 1–45. doi:10.1145/1567274.1567278

Perkins, C. E., Royer, E. M., & Das, S. R. (2003). *Ad hoc on-demand distance vector (AODV) routing*. Retrieved July 12, 2008, from http://www.ietf.org/rfc/rfc3561.txt

Perkins, C. E. (2001). *Ad hoc networking*. Reading, MA: Addison-Wesley.

Plesa, R., & Logrippo, L. (2007). An agent-based architecture for context-aware communication. In *Proceedings of the 21ˢᵗ IEEE Conference on Advanced Information Networking and Applications*, Niagara Falls, ON, Canada (pp. 133-138).

Potter, J. A., & Smith, A. D. (2010). Performance appraisals and the strategic development of the professional intellect within non-profits. *International Journal of Management in Education*, 3(2), 188–203. doi:10.1504/IJMIE.2009.025275

Prasad, N., Bryan, D., & Reeves, D. (2007). Pennies from eBay: the determinants of price in online auctions. *The Journal of Industrial Economics*, 25(2), 223–233.

Prim, B. C. (1959). Shortest connecting networks and some generalizations. *The Bell System Technical Journal*, 36, 1389–1401.

Prud'hommeaux, E., & Seaborne, A. (2007). *SPARQL query language for RDF (working draft)*. Retrieved from http://www.w3.org/TR/rdf-sparql-query/

Qayyum, A., Viennot, L., & Laouiti, A. (2002). Multipoint relaying for flooding broadcast messages in mobile wireless networks. In *Proceedings of the 35ᵗʰ Hawaii International Conference on System Sciences (HICSS'02)* (pp. 3866- 3875).

Qing, L., Zhu, Q., & Wang, M. (2006). Design of a distributed energy-efficient clustering algorithm for heterogeneous wireless sensor networks. *Computer Communications*, 29(12), 2230–2237. doi:10.1016/j.comcom.2006.02.017

Quilitz, B., & Leser, U. (2008). Querying distributed RDF data sources with SPARQL. In S. Bechhofer, M. Hauswirth, J. Hoffmann, & M. Koubarakis (Eds.), *Proceedings of the 5th European Semantic Web Conference* (LNCS 5021, pp. 524-538).

Raghunathan, A., & Murugesan, K. (2010). Schema-based cache validation of dynamic content to improve query performance of web services. *Journal of Web Engineering*, 9(2), 116–131.

Rahman, A., Olesinski, W., & Gburzynski, P. (2004). Controlled flooding in wireless ad hoc networks. In *Proceedings of the IEEE International Workshop on Wireless Ad Hoc Networks (IWWAN'04)*, Oulu, Finland.

Raj, P. N., & Swadas, P. B. (2009). DPRAODV: A dynamic learning system against black hole attack in AODV based manet. *International Journal of Computer Science Issues*, 2(3), 54–59.

Ramanathan, R., & Steenstrup, M. (1998). Hierarchically-organized multihop mobile networks for quality-of-service support. *Mobile Networks and Applications*, 3(1), 101–119. doi:10.1023/A:1019148009641

Ramanathan, S. (1996). Multicast tree generation in networks with asymmetric links. *IEEE/ACM Transactions on Networking*, 4(4), 558–568. doi:10.1109/90.532865

Ranganathan, A., Shankar, C., & Campbell, R. (2005). Application polymorphism for autonomic ubiquitous computing. *Multiagent Grid Systems*, 1, 109–129.

Reed, D. (2001, February). The law of the pack. *Harvard Business Review*, 23–24.

Reif, G., Groza, T., Scerri, S., & Handschuh, S. (2008). Final NEPOMUK architecture – Deliverable D6.2.B. Retrieved from http://nepomuk.semanticdesktop.org/xwiki/bin/view/Main1/D6-2-B

Reynolds, G. (2006). *An army of Davids: How markets and technology empower ordinary people to beat big media, big government, and other Goliaths*. Nashville, TN: Thomas Nelson.

Richins, M., & Root-Shaffer, T. (1988). The role of involvement and opinion leadership in consumer word-of-mouth: An implicit model made explicit. *Advances in Consumer Research. Association for Consumer Research (U. S.)*, 15, 32–36.

Riedel, T., Fantana, N., Genaid, A., Yordanov, D., Schmidtke, H., & Beigl, M. (2010). Using web service gateways and code generation for sustainable IoT system development. In *Proceedings of the Conference on the Internet of Things* (pp. 1-8).

Rocha, C., Schwabe, D., & Aragao, M. P. (2004). A hybrid approach for searching in the semantic web. In Proceedings of the 13th International Conference on World Wide Web (pp. 374-383). New York, NY: ACM Press.

Rochet, J.-C., & Tirole, J. (2004). *Two-sided markets: An overview*. Retrieved from http://faculty.haas.berkeley.edu/hermalin/rochet_tirole.pdf

Rodrigues, T., Costa, P., Cardoso, J., & Fernandes, J. (2006). JXML2OWL. Retrieved from http://jxml2owl.projects.semwebcentral.org

Roman, S. (2007). The ethics of online retailing: a scale development and validation from the consumers' perspective. *Journal of Business Ethics, 72*(2), 131–148. doi:10.1007/s10551-006-9161-y

Ros, F. J., & Ruiz, P. M. (2005). *Implementing a new manet unicast routing protocol in NS2.* Retrieved from http://imtl.skku.ac.kr/~hjlim99/ns2/%5B%BB%F5%B7%CE%BF%EE%20%B6%F3%BF%EC%C6%C3%20%C7%C1%B7%CE%C5%E4%C4%DD%20%B1%B8%C7%F6%5D/Implementing%20a%20New%20Manet%20Unicast%20Routing%20Protocol%20in%20ns2.pdf

Ross, T. J. (2010). *Fuzzy logic with engineering applications.* Chichester, UK: John Wiley & Sons. doi:10.1002/9781119994374

Roy, P., Abdulrazak, B., & Belala, Y. (2008). Approaching context-awareness for open intelligent space. In *Proceedings of the 6th International Conference on Advances in Mobile Computing and Multimedia* (pp. 422-426).

Royer, E., & Toh, C. (1999). A review of current routing protocols for ad hoc mobile wireless networks. *IEEE Personal Communication Magazine, 6*(2), 46-55.

Ryan, K. (2009). *Twitter study.* San Antonio, TX: Pear Analytics.

Sabri, A. (2009). *Development of a dynamic noise-dependent probabilistic route discovery algorithm in MANETs.* Unpublished PhD thesis, The Arab Academy for Banking & Financial Sciences, Amman, Jordan.

Sacramento, E. R., Ponte, V. M., Fernandes, J. A., Lóscio, B. F. R. F. L., & Casanova, M. A. (2010). Towards automatic generation of application ontologies. In *Proceedings of the 25st Brazilian Symposium on Databases*, Belo Horizonte, Brazil (pp. 535-550).

Saeed, K., Grover, V., & Hwang, Y. (2005). The Relationship of E-Commerce Competence to Customer Value and Firm Performance: An Empirical Investigation. *Journal of Management Information Systems, 22*(1), 223–256.

Saiedian, M., & Naeem, M. (2001). Understanding, and reducing web delays. *IEEE Computer Journal, 34*(12), 30–37.

Salama, H. F. (1996). *Multicast routing for real-time communication on high-speed networks* (Doctoral dissertation). Raleigh, NC: North Carolina State University.

Salama, H. F., et al. (1995). *MCRSIM simulator source code and users' manual.* Raleigh, NC: North Carolina State University. Retrieved from http://ftp.csc.ncsu.edu:/pub/rtcomm

Samir, M., Das, R., & Mahesh, K. (2006). On-demand multipath distance vector routing in ad hoc networks. *International Journal Wireless Communication and Mobile Computing, 6*(7), 969–988. doi:10.1002/wcm.432

Sandvine. (2010). *Intelligent broadband networks: Mobile Internet phenomena report.* Retrieved from http://www.sandvine.com

Sasson, Y., Cavin, D., & Schiper, A. (2003). Probabilistic broadcast for flooding in wireless mobile ad hoc networks. In *Proceedings of IEEE Wireless Communications and Networking (WCNC'03),* New Orleans, LA (Vol. 2, pp. 1124-1130).

Savage, M. (2000). *Attacks bring new security solutions.* Computer Reseller News.

Schenk, S., Saathoff, C., Baumesberger, A., Jochum, F., Kleinen, A., & Staab, S. (2009). Semaplorer–Interactive semantic exploration of data and media based on a federated cloud infrastructure. *Web Semantics, 7*(4), 298–304. doi:10.1016/j.websem.2009.09.006

Scherrer-Rathje, M., Boyle, T. A., & Deflorin, P. (2009). Lean, take two! Reflections from the second attempt at lean implementation. *Business Horizons, 52*(1), 79–85. doi:10.1016/j.bushor.2008.08.004

Schou, C., & Shoemaker, D. (2006). *Information assurance for the enterprise: A roadmap to information security.* New York: McGraw-Hill Irwin.

Schütz, T. (2008, Sep). D11.1.1.B concept and design of the integration framework. Retrieved from http://www.eclipse.org/smila/docs/ORDO_D.11.1.1.b_ConceptIntegrationFramework_V1.0.pdf

Scott, D., & Yasinsac, A. (2004). Dynamic probabilistic retransmission in ad hoc networks. In H. R. Arabnia, L. T. Yang, & C. H. Yeh (Eds.), *Proceedings of the International Conference on Wireless Networks (ICWN '04)*, Las Vegas, NV (Vol. 1, pp. 158-164). CSREA Press.

Segars, A. (1997). Assessing the Unidimensionality of Measurement: a Paradigm and Illustration within the Context of Information Systems Research. *Omega, 25*(1), 107–121. doi:10.1016/S0305-0483(96)00051-5

Sen, J., Koilakonda, S., & Ukil, A. (2011). A mechanism for detection of cooperative black hole attack in mobile ad hoc networks. In *Proceedings of the IEEE International Conference on Intelligence Systems, Modelling and Simulation* (pp. 338-343).

Shadbolt, N., Berners-Lee, T., & Hall, W. (2006). The semantic web revisited. *IEEE Intelligent Systems, 21*(3), 96–101. doi:10.1109/MIS.2006.62

Shah, R., Chandrasekaran, A., & Linderman, K. (2008). In pursuit of implementation patterns: the context of Lean and Six Sigma. *International Journal of Production Research, 46*(23), 6679–6698. doi:10.1080/00207540802230504

Shaikh, A., & Shin, K. (1997). Destination-driven routing for low-cost Multicast. *IEEE Journal on Selected Areas in Communications, 15*, 373–381. doi:10.1109/49.564135

Sharifian, S., Motamedi, S. A., & Akbari, M. K. (2009). Estimation-based load balancing with admission control for cluster web servers. *ETRI Journal, 31*(2).

Sharifian, S., Motamedi, S. A., & Akbari, M. K. (2010). A predictive and probabilistic load balancing algorithm for cluster-based web servers. *Applied Soft Computing, 11*(1), 970–981. doi:10.1016/j.asoc.2010.01.017

Shepard, T. J. (1996). A channel access scheme for large dense packet radio networks. *ACM SIGCOMM Computer Communications Review, 26*(4), 219–230. doi:10.1145/248157.248176

Sheshunoff, A. (2000). Internet banking, an update from the frontlines. *ABA Banking Journal, 92*(1), 51–55.

Smaragdakis, G., Matta, I., & Bestavros, A. (2004). A stable election protocol for clustered heterogeneous wireless sensor networks. In *Proceedings of the International Workshop on SANPA*.

Smith, A. A., Synowka, D. P., & Smith, A. D. (2010). Exploring fantasy sports and its fan base from a CRM perspective. *International Journal of Business Innovation and Research, 4*(1-2), 103–142. doi:10.1504/IJBIR.2010.029543

Smith, A. D. (2002). Loyalty and e-marketing issues: customer retention on the Web. *Quarterly Journal of E-commerce, 3*(2), 149–161.

Smith, A. D. (2005). Accountability in EDI systems to prevent employee fraud. *Information Systems Management, 22*(2), 30–38. doi:10.1201/1078/45099.22.2.20050301/87275.4

Smith, A. D. (2006). Supply chain management using electronic reverse auction: a multi-firm case study. *International Journal of Services and Standards, 2*(2), 176–189. doi:10.1504/IJSS.2006.008731

Smith, A. D. (2009). The impact of e-procurement systems on customer relationship management: a multiple case study. *International Journal of Procurement Management, 2*(3), 314–338. doi:10.1504/IJPM.2009.024814

Smith, A. D. (2009). Leveraging concepts of knowledge management with total quality management: case studies in the service sector. *International Journal of Logistics Systems and Supply Management, 5*(6), 631–653. doi:10.1504/IJLSM.2009.024795

Smith, A. D. (2010). Retail-based loyalty card programs and CRM concepts: an empirical study. *International Journal of Innovation and Learning, 7*(3), 303–330. doi:10.1504/IJIL.2010.031949

Smith, A. D., & Lias, A. R. (2005). Identity theft and e-fraud as critical CRM concerns. *International Journal of Enterprise Information Systems, 1*(2), 17–36. doi:10.4018/jeis.2005040102

Smith, A. D., & Potter, J. A. (2010). Loyalty card programs, customer relationships, and information technology: an exploratory approach. *International Journal of Business Innovation and Research, 4*(1-2), 65–92. doi:10.1504/IJBIR.2010.029541

Snijders, C., & Zijdeman, R. (2004). Reputation and Internet auctions: eBay and beyond. *Analyse & Kritik, 26*(1), 158–184.

Soga, S., Hiroshige, Y., Dobashi, A., Okumura, M., & Kusuzaki, T. (1999). Products lifecycle management system using radio frequency identification. In Proceedings of the IEEE International Conference on Emergent Technologies and Factory Automation (pp. 1459-1467). Washington, DC: IEEE Computer Society.

Song, E. Y., & Lee, K. (2008). Understanding IEEE 1451-networked smart transducer interface standard. *IEEE Instrumentation & Measurement Magazine, 11*(2), 11–17. doi:10.1109/MIM.2008.4483728

Sprovieri, J. (2008). A Modest Increase. *Assembly, 51*(13), 22–41.

Srinivasan, V., Lämmer, L., & Vettermann, S. (2008). On architecting and implementing a product information sharing service. *Journal of Computing and Information Science in Engineering, 8*(1), 011006. doi:10.1115/1.2840775

Stepanov, A., & McJones, P. (2009). *Elements of programming*. Reading, MA: Addison-Wesley.

Stieger, B., Aleksy, M., & Vollmar, G. (2008). A method to identify mobile optimization opportunities in field service processes. In *Proceedings of the IADIS International Conference on e-Commerce* (pp. 255-259).

Stross, R. (2008). *What carriers aren't eager to tell you about texting*. Retrieved from http://www.nytimes.com/2008/12/28/business/28digi.html?_r=2&ref=technology

Stuckenschmidt, H., & van Harmelen, F. (2004). *Information sharing on the semantic web*. Berlin, Germany: Springer Verlag.

Stutzbach, D., Rejaie, R., Duffield, N., Sen, S., & Willinger, W. (2006, October 25-27). On unbiased sampling for unstructured peer-to-peer networks. In *Proceedings of the 6th ACM SIGCOMM Conference on Internet Measurement*, Rio de Janeriro, Brazil.

Subathra, P., Sivagurunathan, S., & Ramaraj, N. (2010). Detection and prevention of single and cooperative black hole attacks in mobile ad hoc networks. *International Journal of Business Data Communications and Networking, 6*(1), 38–57. doi:10.4018/jbdcn.2010010103

Suchanek, F. M., Kasneci, G., & Weikum, G. (2007, May). YAGO: A core of semantic knowledge unifying WordNet and Wikipedia. In *Proceedings of the 16th International World Wide Web Conference*, Banff, AB, Canada (pp. 697-706).

Summers, G. J., & Scherpereel, C. M. (2008). Decision making in product development: are you outside-in or inside-out? *Management Decision, 46*(9), 1299–1314. doi:10.1108/00251740810911957

Sun, J.-T., Shen, D., Zeng, H.-J., Yang, Q., Lu, Y., & Chen, Z. (2005, August). Web-page summarization using clickthrough data. In *Proceedings of the 28th Annual International ACM SIGIR conference on Research and development in information retrieval*, Salvador, Brazil (pp.194-201).

Sun, Q., & Langendoerfre, H. (1995). Efficient multicast routing for delay-sensitive applications. In *Proceedings of the 2nd Workshop on Protocols for Multimedia Systems* (pp. 452-458).

Sun. (2001). *The Java HotSpot™ Virtual Machine*. Retrieved from http://java.sun.com/products/hotspot/docs/whitepaper/Java_HotSpot_WP_Final_4_30_01.pdf

Sun, J., Modiano, E., & Zheng, L. (2006). Wireless channel allocation using an auction algorithm. *IEEE Journal on Selected Areas in Communications, 24*(5), 1085–1096. doi:10.1109/JSAC.2006.872890

Sun, J., & Song Dong, J. (2006). Design synthesis from interaction and state-based specifications. *IEEE Transactions on Software Engineering, 32*(6), 349–364. doi:10.1109/TSE.2006.55

Talwar, V., Milojicic, D., Wu, Q., Pu, C., Yan, W., & Jung, G. (2005). Approaches for service deployment. *IEEE Internet Computing, 9*(2), 70–80. doi:10.1109/MIC.2005.32

Tamilselvan, L., & Sankaranarayanan, V. (2007). Prevention of blackhole attack in MANET. In *Proceedings of the 2nd International Conference on Wireless Broadband and Ultra Wideband Communications* (pp. 21-27).

Tedeschi, B. (2008). *Taking your wi-fi cafe with you, but not everywhere*. Retrieved from http://www.nytimes.com/2008/10/23/technology/personaltech/23 smart.html?_r=2&pagewanted=1&8dpc

Teece, D. J., Pisano, G., & Shuen, A. (1997). Dynamic capabilities and strategic management. *Strategic Management Journal, 18*(7), 509–533. doi:10.1002/(SICI)1097-0266(199708)18:7<509::AID-SMJ882>3.0.CO;2-Z

Teo, Y. M., & Ayani, R. (2001). Comparison of load balancing strategies on cluster-based web servers. *Transactions of the Society for Modelling and Simulation, 77*(5-6), 185–195. doi:10.1177/003754970107700504

Thomas, R., Friend, D., DaSilva, L., & MacKenzie, A. (2007). Cognitive networks . In Arslan, H. (Ed.), *Cognitive radio, software defined radio, and adaptive wireless systems* (pp. 17–41). New York, NY: Springer. doi:10.1007/978-1-4020-5542-3_2

Tiwari, A., Lewis, F. L., & Ge, S. S. (2005). Wireless sensor network for machine condition based maintenance. In *Proceedings of the 8th IEEE* Control, Automation, Robotics and Vision Conference (Vol. 1, pp. 461-467). Washington, DC: IEEE Computer Society.

Toh, C. K. (1997). Associativity-based routing for ad-hoc mobile networks. *International Journal on Wireless Personal Communications, 4*(2).

Tolia, N., & Satyanarayanan, M. (2007). Consistency-preserving caching of dynamic database content. In *Proceedings of the ACM Conference on World Wide Web* (pp. 311-320).

Tombros, A., & Sanderson, M. (1998). Advantages of query biased summaries in information retrieval. In *Proceedings of the 21st Annual International ACM SIGIR Conference on Research and Development in Information Retrieval*, Melbourne, Australia (pp. 2-10).

TonlaKazan. (2009). *TonlaKazan a new mobile advertising platform*. Retrieved from http://www.slideshare.net/anafikir/tonlakazan-a-new-mobile-advertising-platform-presentation

Totty, P. (2001). Staying One Step Ahead of the Hacker. *Credit Union Magazine, 67*(6), 39–41.

Tran, D. T., Cimiano, P., Rudolph, S., & Studer, R. (2007). Ontology-based interpretation of keywords for semantic search. In K. Aberer, P. Cudré-Mauroux, K.-S. Choi, N. Noy, D. Allegmang, K.-I. Lee et al. (Eds.), Proceedings of the 6th International Semantic Web Conference and the 2nd Asian Semantic Web Conference Proceedings of the 6th International Semantic Web Conference (LNCS 4825, pp. 523-536).

Tran, T., Haase, P., Lewen, H., Garcia, O. M., Gomez-Perez, A., & Studer, R. (2007). Lifecycle-support in architectures for ontology-based information systems. In K. Aberer, P. Cudré-Mauroux, K.-S. Choi, N. Noy, D. Allegmang, K.-I. Lee et al. (Eds.), Proceedings of the 6th International Semantic Web Conference and the 2nd Asian Semantic Web Conference *(LNCS 4825, pp.508-522).*

Tran, T., Wang, H., & Haase, P. (2008). Search WebDB: Data web search on a pay-as-you-go integration infrastructure. Retrieved from http://academic.research.microsoft.com/Publication/5647448/searchwebdb-data-web-search-on-a-pay-as-you-go-integration-infrastructure

TRC. (2010). *Telecommunication Regularly Commission.* Retrieved January 5, 2010, from http://www.TRC.Jo

Trumler, W., Klaus, R., & Ungerer, T. (2006). Self-configuration via cooperative social behavior. In L. T. Yang, H. Jin, J. Ma, & T. Ungerer (Eds.), *Proceedings of the Third International Conference on Autonomic and Trusted Computing* (LNCS 4158, pp. 90-99).

Truong, H.-L., & Dustdar, S. (2009). A survey on context-aware web service systems. *International Journal of Web Information Systems, 5*(1), 5–31. doi:10.1108/17440080910947295

Tseng, T., Ni, S., Chen, Y., & Sheu, J. (2002). The broadcast storm problem in a mobile ad hoc network. *Journal of Wireless Networks, 8*(2), 153–167. doi:10.1023/A:1013763825347

Turaga, R., Cline, O., & Van Sickel, P. (2006). *WebSphere application server step by step*. Van Nuys, CA: MC Press.

Twestival. (2010). *What is twestival?* Retrieved from http://twestival.com/about-twestival-global-2010/

Twitter Blog. (2010). *Hello world.* Retrieved from http://blog.twitter.com/2010/04/hello-world.html

Twitter Counter. (2010). *The 1000 most popular Twitter users.* Retrieved from http://twittercounter.com/pages/100

Van Laerhoven, K. (2000). *Characteristics of context awareness.* Retrieved from http://www.teco.edu/tea/tea_vis.html

Vaughan-Nichols, S. J. (2008). Mobile WiMAX: The next wireless battle ground. *IEEE Computer, 41*(6), 16–18. doi:10.1109/MC.2008.201

Verizon Wireless. (2010). *Version Wireless with Skype Mobile.* Retrieved from http://phones.verizonwireless.com/skypemobile/

Verton, D. (2000). Co-op to certify tools to measure level of security. *Computerworld, 34*(49), 16.

Vidal, V. M., Sacramento, E. R., Macêdo, J. A., & Casanova, M. A. (2009). An ontology-based framework for geographic data integration. In C. A. Heuser & G. Pernul (Eds.), *Proceedings of the 3rd International Workshop on Semantic and Conceptual Issues in GIS in conjunction with the 28th International Conference on Conceptual Modeling* (LNCS 5833, pp. 337-346).

Vinodh, S., Sundararaj, G., Devadasan, S. R., & Maharaja, R. (2008). DESSAC: a decision support system for quantifying and analyzing agility. *International Journal of Production Research, 46*(23), 6759–6678. doi:10.1080/00207540802230439

Viswanath, K., & Obraczka, K. (2005). Modeling the performance of flooding in wireless multi-hop ad hoc networks. *Journal of Computer Communications, 29*(8), 949–956. doi:10.1016/j.comcom.2005.06.015

Vodafone. (2007). *Safaricom and Vodafone launch M-PESA, a new mobile payment service.* Retrieved from http://www.vodafone.com/content/index/press/group_press_releases/2007/safaricom_and_vodafone.html

W3C. (2004): *OWL web ontology language semantics and abstract syntax.* Retrieved from http://www.w3.org/TR/owl-semantics/

W3C. (2011). *Extensible markup language.* Retrieved from http://www.w3.org/XML/

Wache, H., Vögele, T., Visser, U., Stuckenschmidt, H., Schuster, G., Neumann, H., et al. (2001). Ontology-based integration of information - A survey of existing approaches. In *Proceedings of the Workshop on Ontologies and Information Sharing* (pp. 108-117).

Wang, C., Jing, F., Zhang, L., & Zhang, H.-J. (2007, November). Learning query-biased web page summarization. In *Proceedings of the 16th Conference on Information and Knowledge Management*, Lisbon, Portugal (pp. 555-562).

Wang, X., & Schulzrinne, H. (1999, June). RNAP: A resource negotiation and pricing protocol. In *Proceedings of the International Workshop on Network and Operating System Support for Digital Audio and Video*, Basking Ridge, NJ (pp. 77-93).

Wang, Y., Chen, H., Yang, X., & Zhang, D. (2007). WACHM: Weight based adaptive clustering large scale heterogeneous MANET. In *Proceedings of the International Symposium on Communications and Information Technologies*.

Wang, F., Ghosh, A., Sankaran, C., Fleming, P., Hsieh, F., & Benes, S. (2008). Mobile WiMAX systems: Performance and evolution. *IEEE Communications Magazine, 46*(10), 41–49. doi:10.1109/MCOM.2008.4644118

Wauer, M., Schuster, D., & Meinecke, J. (2010). Aletheia - An architecture for semantic federation of product information from structured and unstructured sources. In Proceedings of the 12th International Conference on Information Integration and Web-based Applications & Services (pp. 325-332). New York, NY: ACM Press.

Webster, T. (2010). *Twitter usage in America: 2010, The Edison Research/Arbitron Internet and multimedia study.* Somerville, NJ: Edison Research.

Weiser, M. (1993). Some computer science problems in ubiquitous computing. *Communications of the ACM,* 74–84.

Wiederhold, G. (1992). Mediators in the architecture of future information systems. *Computer, 25,* 38–49. doi:10.1109/2.121508

Wikipedia. (2011). *Neutral point of view.* Retrieved from http://en.wikipedia.org/wiki/Wikipedia:Neutral_point_of_view

Wilschut, A. N., & Apers, P. M. G. (1993). Dataflow query execution in a parallel main-memory environment. *Distributed and Parallel Databases, 1,* 103–128. doi:10.1007/BF01277522

Winograd, T. (2001). Architectures for context. *Human-Computer Interaction, 16*(2), 401–419. doi:10.1207/S15327051HCI16234_18

WIPO. (2008). *International classification of the figurative elements of marks under the Vienna agreement.* Retrieved from http://www.wipo.int/classifications/vienna/en/

Wold, H. (1985). Systems analysis by partial least squares . In Nijkamp, P., Leitner, L., & Wrigley, N. (Eds.), *Measuring the Unmeasurable* (pp. 221–251). Dordrecht, The Netherlands: Marinus Nijhoff.

Wolf, F., & Gibson, E. (2005). Representing discourse coherence: A corpus-based study. *Computational Linguistics, 31*(2), 249–287. doi:10.1162/0891201054223977

World Health Organization. (2001). *International classification of functioning, disability and health.* Retrieved from http://www.who.int/classifications/icf/en/

Wu, F., & Weld, D. S. (2008, April). Automatically refining the Wikipedia Infobox ontology. In *Proceedings of the 17th International World Wide Web Conference,* Beijing, China (pp. 365-644).

Xie, B. M., Kumar, A., & Agrawal, D. P. (2008). Enabling multiservice on 3G and beyond: Challenges and future directions. *IEEE Wireless Communications, 15*(3), 66–72. doi:10.1109/MWC.2008.4547525

Xing, Y., Chandramouli, R., & Cordeiro, C. M. (2007). Price dynamics in competitive agile spectrum access markets. *IEEE Journal on Selected Areas in Communications, 25*(3), 613–621. doi:10.1109/JSAC.2007.070411

Xiong, Z., & Yan, P. (2005). A solution for supporting QoS in web server cluster. In *Proceedings of the International Conference on Wireless Communications, Networking and Mobile Computing* (Vol. 2, pp. 834-839).

Yagoub, K., Florescu, D., Issarny, V., & Valduriez, P. (2000). Caching strategies for data-intensive web sites. In *Proceedings of the Conference on Very Large Data Bases* (pp. 188-199).

Yaipairoj, S., & Harmantzis, F. C. (2006). Auction-based congestion pricing for wireless data services. In *Proceedings of the IEEE International Conference on Communications,* Istanbul, Turkey (pp. 1045-1050).

Yaiz, R. A., Selgert, F., & den Hartog, F. (2006). On the definition and relevance of context-awareness in personal networks. In *Proceedings of the 3rd Annual International Conference on Mobile and Ubiquitous Systems* (pp. 1-6).

Yang, S. J., & Chou, H. C. (2009). Design issues and performance analysis of location-aided hierarchical cluster routing on the MANET. In *Proceedings of the International Conference on Communications and Mobile Computing.*

Yoo, C. S. (2006). Network neutrality and the economics of congestion. *The Georgetown Law Journal, 94*(6), 1847–1900.

Younis, O., & Fahmy, S. (2004). HEED: A hybrid, energy-efficient, distributed clustering approach for ad hoc sensor networks. *IEEE Transactions on Mobile Computing, 3*(4), 366–379. doi:10.1109/TMC.2004.41

Zaslavsky, A. (2004). Mobile agents: Can they assist with context awareness? In *Proceedings of the IEEE International Conference on Mobile Data Management* (pp. 304-305).

Zhang, X. Y., Sekiya, Y., & Wakahara, Y. (2009). Proposal of a method to detect black hole attack in MANET. In *Proceedings of the International Symposium on Autonomous Decentralized Systems* (pp. 1-6).

Zhang, Q., & Agrawal, D. P. (2005). Dynamic probabilistic broadcasting in MANETs. *Journal of Parallel and Distributed Computing, 65*(2), 220–233. doi:10.1016/j.jpdc.2004.09.006

Zhao, C. X., & Wang, G. X. (2004, June 15-19). Fuzzy-control-based clustering strategy in MANET. In *Proceedings of the 5th World Congress on Intelligent Control and Automation.*

Zhao, M., & Zhou, J. (2009). Cooperative black hole attack prevention for mobile ad hoc networks. In *Proceedings of the International Symposium on Information Engineering and Electronic Commerce* (pp. 26-30).

Zhuang, S.-Y., & Yeh, Y.-C. Chiang, & M.-L. (2008). Locality-aware request distribution with frequency-based replication in web server clusters. In *Proceedings of the International Computer Symposium*, Taipei, Taiwan.

Ziegler, P., & Dittrich, K. R. (2004). Three decades of data integration - All problems solved? In *Proceedings of the 18th IFIP World Computer Congress* (Vol. 12, pp. 3-12).

Zoliat, A., Ibrahim, A., & Farooq, A. (2009). A Study on the Internet Security and its Implication for e-Commerce in Yemen. In *Proceedings of the Conference on Knowledge Management and Innovation in Advancing Economies* (pp. 911-922).

About the Contributors

Varadharajan Sridhar is a Professor in Information Management at the Management Development Institute (India) and is currently a visiting research fellow at Sasken Communication Technologies (Bangalore, India). He received his BE from the University of Madras (India), Post Graduate Diploma in Industrial Engineering from the National Institute for Training in Industrial Engineering (Mumbai, India), and PhD in MIS from the University of Iowa (USA). He had taught at Ohio University and American University in the US; University of Auckland in New Zealand, and at the Indian Institute of Management (Lucknow, India). Dr. Sridhar's primary research interests are in the area of telecommunication management and policy and global software development. He has published many research articles, business cases, and chapters in edited books in his area of research. Dr. Sridhar is a member of the Committee on Allocation and Pricing of Spectrum for Access Services set-up by the Indian Government. He was the recipient of the Nokia Visiting Fellowship awarded by the Nokia Research Foundation. He is on the editorial board of the *Journal of Global Information Management* and is a member of ACM and AIS.

Debashis Saha is a professor with the MIS Group, Indian Institute of Management (IIM)-Calcutta. Previously, he was with CSE Department at Jadavpur University (Kolkata, India). He received his BE (Hons) degree from Jadavpur University (Kolkata, India), and the MTech and PhD degrees from the Indian Institute of Technology (IIT-Kharagpur, India) all in electronics and telecommunications engineering. His research interests include pervasive communication and computing, network operations, management and security, wireless networking and mobile computing, ICT for development, and network economics. He has supervised thirteen doctoral theses, published about 230 research papers in various conferences and journals, and directed four funded research projects on networking. He has co-authored several book chapters, a monograph, and five books including Networking Infrastructure for Pervasive Computing: Enabling Technologies and Systems (Norwell, MA: Kluwer, 2002) and Location Management and Routing in Mobile Wireless Networks (Boston, MA: Artech House, 2003). Dr. Saha is the recipient of the prestigious career award for Young Teachers from AICTE, Government of India, and is a SERC Visiting Fellow with the Department of Science and Technology (DST), Government of India. He is a Fellow of West Bengal Academy of Science and Technology (WAST), Senior Life Member of Computer Society of India, Senior Member of IEEE, member of ACM, member of AIS, and member of the International Federation of Information Processing Working Group's 6.8 and 6.10. He was the founding Chair of Calcutta Chapter of IEEE Communications Society (2003-2008).

* * *

Bessam Abdulrazak, PhD, is an Assistant Professor of Computer Science and director of the Research Center on Intelligent Habitats at the University of Sherbrooke, Canada. His research interests include ubiquitous and pervasive computing, Ambient-Intelligence, Smart-Environments, Assistive Technologies and Rehabilitation Robotics.

Takeshi Abekawa is a research assistant professor at National Institute of Informatics. His research interests include natural language processing and information retrieval, especially information extraction from various data. He received Doctor of Engineering from Tokyo Institute of Technology in 2006.

Femi A. Aderohunmu obtained First Class BS in applied mathematics from the University for Development Studies, Ghana, in 2007, and MS from the University of Otago, New Zealand, in 2010. He is currently a PhD candidate at the Department of Information Science, University of Otago. His research interests focus on wireless sensor networking and its application.

Mohamed Aissa received the engineering diploma, MEng in computer Engineering in 1988 from Kiev Polytechnic Institute. In 1992, he received the PhD in computer networks from the same institute. In September 1996, he joined Sur College, Oman, to serve as assistant professor and as head of computer section. From 2004 to 2009, he worked at Al-Imam M. Ibn Saud Islamic University, where he served as head of computer department at the Community College. In 2009, he joined University of Nizwa, Oman, where he is serving as Assistant professor. His the author of many research papers in multicast routing and quality of service (QoS) provisioning in wired and wireless networks.

Hussein Al-Bahadili is an associate professor at Petra University, Jordan. He received his PhD and M.Sc degrees from University of London (Queen Mary College) in 1991 and 1988, respectively. He received his B.Sc in Engineering from the University of Baghdad in 1986. He is a visiting researcher at the Centre of Wireless Networks and Communications (WNCC) at the School of Engineering, University of Brunel (UK). He has published many papers in different fields of science and engineering in numerous leading scholarly and practitioner journals, and presented at leading world-level scholarly conferences. He recently published two Chapters in two prestigious books in IT and Simulations. He is also a reviewer for a number of books, and currently, he is engaged in edition a book titled Simulation in Computer Network Design and Modeling: Use and analysis. His research interests include computer networks design and architecture, routing protocols optimizations, parallel and distributed computing, cryptography and network security, data compression.

Markus Aleksy received the Management Information Systems Degree in 1998, and the Doctorate Degree in 2002 from the University of Mannheim, Germany, and the Doctorate Degree in Information Science in 2007 from Tokyo Denki University, Japan. He lectured in University of Mannheim, Germany, and Queen's University, Canada. Markus is the author or coauthor of more than 80 research papers published in international journals and conference proceedings. He was / is involved in the organization of several conferences as member of the steering committee, general (co-)chair, program (co-)chair, workshop (co-)chair etc as well as was / is a member of various program committees. His current research focuses on distributed systems, mobile computing, and life cycle science.

Markus Aleksy received the Management Information Systems Degree in 1998, and the Doctorate Degree in 2002 from the University of Mannheim, Germany, and the Doctorate Degree in Information Science in 2007 from Tokyo Denki University, Japan. He lectured in University of Mannheim, Germany, and Queen's University, Canada. Markus is the author or coauthor of more than 80 research papers published in international journals and conference proceedings. He was / is involved in the organization of several conferences as member of the steering committee, general (co-)chair, program (co-)chair, workshop (co-)chair etc as well as was / is a member of various program committees. His current research focuses on distributed systems, mobile computing, and life cycle science.

Eiji Aramakii is a senior researcher of the University of Tokyo Japan.He leads the research of medical Natural Language Processing projects(MEDNLP). His research interests lie in both NLP and medical informatics. He received his Ph.D. in informatics degree from the University of Tokyo in 2005.

Yacine Belala is a senior research scientist at SAP Labs, Montreal, Canada. His research interests include design, performance, and security issues related to adaptive mobile multimedia applications and service architectures. He received a M.Sc. degree in Electronics from Pierre et Marie Curie University in Paris and a PhD degree in Computer Science (Artificial Intelligence) from the University of Paris-Sud Orsay (France).

Fernando Beltrán is currently a Senior Lecturer in the Information Systems and Operations Management Department, University of Auckland Business School, New Zealand, where he leads the Pricing in Next-Generation Networks (PING) research group. He received a B.S. degree in Electrical Engineering from the Universidad de Los Andes, Bogotá, Colombia, and a Ph.D. in Applied Mathematics from SUNY, Stony Brook, NY. His research focuses on pricing in Next-Generation networks. He has been a visiting scholar at the FCC and the CITI Columbia Business School.

Marco A. Casanova has a BSc in Electronic Engineering from the Military Institute of Engineeruing (1974), a MSc in Computer Science from the Pontifícia Universidade Católica do Rio de Janeiro (1976), and a PhD in Applied Mathematics from the Havard University (1979).

Kevin Curran BSc (Hons), PhD, SMIEEE, FBCS CITP, SMACM, FHEA is a senior lecturer in Computer Science at the University of Ulster. His achievements include winning and managing UK & European Framework projects and Technology Transfer Schemes. He has published over 600 published works to date. He is the Editor in Chief of the International Journal of Ambient Computing and Intelligence (IJACI). Dr Curran is a Fellow of the Higher Education Academy, a Fellow of the British Computer Society and is listed by Marquis in their prestigious Who's Who in Science and Engineering. He is also listed in the Dictionary of International Biography and by Who's Who in the World.

Jeremiah D. Deng obtained the BEng degree from the University of Electronic Science and Technology of China in 1989, and the MEng and PhD both from the South China University of Technology in 1992 and 1995 respectively. He is now a Senior Lecturer at the Department of Information Science, University of Otago. Dr. Deng's research interests include wireless communications, machine learning and multimedia data mining.

José Antonio Fernandes de Macêdo has a graduate in Processamento de dados from the Universidade Católica do Rio de Janeiro (1997), an MSc in Informática from the Pontifícia Universidade Católica do Rio de Janeiro (2000), an PhD at Informática from the Pontifícia Universidade Católica do Rio de Janeiro (2005) and Postdoctorate from the Polytechnique Fédéral de Lausanne (2009).

Sylvain Giroux, PhD, is a professor at the University of Sherbrooke, Canada. He co-founded DOMUS laboratory of the University of Sherbrooke in 2005. His main research interests are mobile computing, pervasive computing, distributed artificial intelligence, multi-agent systems, user modeling and intelligent tutoring systems.

Charles Gouin-Vallerand, MSc, is a Ph.D. candidate in computer science at the University of Sherbrooke, Canada, jointly with the Institut Telecom /University of Pierre and Marie Curie, France. His main research interests are Pervasive Computing, Distributed Computing, Smart Spaces, Context Awareness and Assistive Technologies.

Jairo A. Gutiérrez is a Full Professor with the Systems Engineering Department, Universidad Tecnológica de Bolívar (UTB), Cartagena, Colombia. He is also the Director of Research and Innovation at UTB, and was the Editor-in-Chief of the International Journal of Business Data Communications and Networking (2004–2008). He received his Systems and Engineering degree from the Universidad de Los Andes, a Masters degree in Computer Science from Texas A&M University, and a Ph.D. in Information Systems from the University of Auckland. His current research is on network management systems, viable business models for mobile commerce, and quality of service in Internet protocols.

Thomas Janke holds a master's degree in computer science from the Technische Universität Dresden. In 2009 he joined SAP Research as a PhD student. His research work mainly focuses on ontology engineering as well as on the application of semantic technologies in real world business applications. Moreover, Thomas has many years of experience as a software engineer working for various companies. He has a strong background in the field of model driven development (MDD), service oriented architectures and mobile application development.

Andreas Konzag is a doctorate researcher at the Chair for Industrial Information Technology at the BTU Cottbus, Germany and employee at BMW AG. He received his engineer degree in industrial engineering and management at the same university in 2009 for the research on a methodology to provide customer related product features for quality controls of vehicles. Since 2009 he works on a methodology for providing context sensitive information for the development of vehicle concepts. His advisor is Prof. Uwe Meinberg. He is team leader of the German BMBF project Aletheia considering semantic federation of product information.

Mousumi Kundu got her Bachelor of Engineering (B.E.) degree in ETCE in 2005 and Master of Engineering (M.E.) degree in ETCE in 2007, both from JU, Kolkata. She got a total of two Gold Medals for standing first in the order of merit at M.E. (ETCE) Exam., and for securing the top position among all the courses of M.E. Exam. of JU, both in 2007. She also got the Third Prize in IEEE All India M. V. Chauhan Students Paper Contest in 2007. She got the Ministry of Human Resource Development

(MHRD), Govt. of India Scholarship in Engineering for the year 2005 – 2007. She is at present working as a Design Engineer with Society for Applied Microwave Electronics Engineering and Research (SAMEER) – Kolkata Centre since 2007.

Johannes Meinecke is a researcher at the Business Intelligence Practice at SAP Research Dresden, SAP AG. Before joining SAP, he worked for 5 years as a research associate at the University of Karlsruhe as well as at the University of Chemnitz, where he received a PhD in Computer Science. His research at that time has been concerned with Web Engineering, Federated Identity Management and Semantic Web. He is currently working on architectural issues of semantic information systems and question- answering in a Business Intelligence context. He is also a founding-member and treasurer of the International Society for Web Engineering e.V. and coauthor of over 25 research papers.

José Luis Melús is a Full Professor at the Polytechnic University of Catalonia in the Telecommunications Engineering Department. He holds both a B.S. degree and a Ph.D. degree in telecommunications from Escuela Técnica Superior de Ingenieros de Telecomunicación, Barcelona, Spain. His present research interests include network management, quality of service, planning and evaluation of networks of computers, and security and pricing telecommunications services.

Adel Ben Mnaouer received his BS degree in computer science from the "Ecole Supérieure des communications (SUP'COM)" of Tunisia in 1985 and the Meng and PhD degrees in electrical and computer engineering from the University of Fukui and from Yokohama National University, Japan, in 1993 and 1997 respectively. From 1997 to 2010 he served as an academic staff in several Universities such as Yokohama National University (1997-1999), CS dept of Sultan Qaboos University, Oman (1999 - 2002), School of Computer Engineering at Nanyang Technological University, Singapore, (2002-2005), the "Ecole Supérieure de Technologie et d'Informatique", 7th November university, Tunisia (2005-2008). Dr. Ben Mnaouer served in the Centre of Information and Communication technologies of the University of Trinidad and Tobago (UTT) as an associate professor (2008-2010). Since September 2010, he is an associate professor with the college of computer engineering and information technology of Dar Al Uloom University, Saudi Arabia. His research interests are in the areas of protocol design and analysis of wired and wireless (4G, MANETs, VANETs, Sensor and Mobile) networking and in cluster and grid computing. He served/serving in the TPC of scores of international conferences, such as the IEEE ICC, GLOBECOM, LCN, and WCNC. He organized and chaired workshops, and technical sessions in several international conferences. He offers regular peer review services to several international journals on computer science and networking. Dr. Ben Mnaouer is a senior member of the IEEE Communication Society.

Yohei Murakami is a senior researcher of National Institute of Information and Communications Technology, Japan. He currently leads the research and development of Service Grid platform, the purpose of which is to share various resources as Web services and enable users to create new services. His research interests lie in services computing and multiagent systems. He founded the Technical Committee on Services Computing in the Institute of Electronics, information and Communication Engineers (IEICE) in 2009. He received his Ph.D. in informatics degree from Kyoto University in 2006.

Rion Murray received his associate degree in information systems management in 1999 from the National Institution of Higher Education, Research, Science and Technology of Trinidad. In 2002, he acquired a bachelor of science in computer science from the University of the West Indies in Trinidad and Tobago. He graduated from the University of Trinidad and Tobago in 2010 with a master of science in information communications and technology where he received an award for the most outstanding student of his department from the student's guild. His research interests are in the areas of protocol design of wired and wireless networking.

K. Murugesan is working as an Associate Professor in the Department of Mathematics, National Institute of Technology, Tiruchirappalli, Tamil Nadu, India. He has 20 years of teaching and research experience. He has also visited several countries for delivering lectures and presenting papers at Conferences. He was a Visiting Research Professor in the Department of Mathematics, Pusan National University, Pusan, South Korea during 2003-04. His research interests are Numerical Techniques, Cellular Neural Networks, Web services and Data mining and he has published around 45 papers in various International Journals related to Numerical Methods and Computer Applications.

Akiyo Nadamoto is a professor of Konan University, Japan. Her research interests lie in Web computing and database, especially search system, web mining and ser generated Content analysis. She received her Doctor of Engineering from Kobe University in 2002.

Rabindranath Nandi is a Professor in the Dept. Of ETCE, JU, Kolkata, India. His areas of interest are Analog Signal Processing (ASP), DSP and Computer Communication. He has authored more than 110 research papers in National / International Journals and some in Conferences / Seminars. He served as the Head of ETCE Dept., JU during 1999-2001 and served as the Chair of IEEE Calcutta Section during 2003-2005. He has taught in various Institutes abroad.

Sean O'Brien is an undergraduate student studying Computer Science at the University of Ulster. His research interests include web programming and e-business.

Kevin O'Hara is an undergraduate student studying Computer Science at the University of Ulster. His research interests include Internet Technologies and the World Wide Web.

Kanika Orea is pursuing her B.E. Degree in ETEC from JU, Kolkata. Her field of research is Wireless Communication Networks which includes Mobile Ad hoc networks, 3G and UMTS technology. She presented a research paper entitled " Simulation and Performance Analysis of OLSR Protocol under Identity Spoofing Attack in Mobile Ad-Hoc Networks" in the Second International Conference on Advances in Communication, Network and Computing (CNC 2011), during March 2011 in Bangalore, India. The Proceedings of CNC 2011 was published by Springer-Verlag Berlin Heidelberg in CCIS 142 (pp. 308-310).

João C. Pinheiro has a BSc in Computer Science from the Universidade Federal do Maranhão (1999), an MSc in Computer Science from the Universidade de São Paulo (2001), and I'm currently a PhD student from thet Computer Science from Universidade Federal do Ceará (2011).

Fabio Porto has a BSc in Matemática Modalidade Informática from the Universidade do Estado do Rio de Janeiro (1987), an MSc in Informática from the Pontifícia Universidade Católica do Rio de Janeiro (1996), and a PhD in Informática from the Pontifícia Universidade Católica do Rio de Janeiro (2001), and Postdoctorate from the Polytechnique Fédéral de Lausanne (2006).

Martin Purvis, BS (Yale), MFA (Columbia), MS, PhD, Massachusetts) is a professor of information science, and also the director of both the Telecommunications and Software Engineering programmes in Applied Science at the University of Otago. Prof. Purvis has been the principal investigator on a number of externally-funded research projects. His teaching and research activities include both mobile telecommunications and software engineering.

A. Raghunathan is Deputy General Manager, Informatics Centre, Bharat Heavy Electricals Ltd., Tiruchirappalli, India. He has a B.E. degree in Electrical Tech and Electronics from the Indian Institute of Science, Bangalore, India and an M.E. degree in Computer Science from the National Institute of Technology, Tiruchirappalli, India. He has over 25 years of experience in Software Design and Development, Database Management, Server Administration, Web services and ERP. He also serves as External Faculty and Examiner at leading Engineering and Management Institutes. His research interests include Databases, Data mining, Information Integration and Web services. He has published and presented several papers in journals, conferences and IT Conventions. He is currently pursuing PhD in Computer Science at the National Institute of Technology, Tiruchirappalli, India in the area of Web Services.

Till Riedel is a researcher at the TecO at the Karlsruhe Institute of Technology. He received a diploma degree in computer science from the University of Karlsruhe in 2005. Since 2005 he has been actively contributing to a number of national and international research projects that work on augmenting real world business processes with internet of things technology. His research interests include the design and modeling of software for ubiquitous computing systems. He is coauthor of over 40 peer-reviewed publications in the area of ubiquitous computing, internet of things and wireless sensor networks.

Patrice Roy is a senior lecturer and a PhD candidate at the University of Sherbrooke, Canada. He has been teaching Computer Science in college since 1998, and has been a lecturer at Université de Sherbrooke since 2001. His research gravitates around Context-aware autonomous agents and open intelligent spaces.

Alia Sabri is an assistance professor at the Applied Sciences Private University, Jordan. She received her PhD and M.Sc in Computer Information Systems from the Arab Academy for Banking & Financial Sciences (Jordan) in 2009 and 2005, respectively. She received her B.Sc degree in Computer Science from Jordan University of Science and Technology (Jordan) in 2002. Her current research interests are in developing efficient dynamic routing protocols for mobile ad hoc networks, wireless networks management and security, and ad hoc networks modeling and simulation.

Daniel Schuster is a post-doc researcher and lecturer at the Professorship for Computer Networks at TU Dresden, Germany. His advisor is Prof. Alexander Schill. His research interests are in the areas of real-time collaboration (RTC) and semantic information retrieval. He is involved in the German-Brazilian project Mobilis that deals with mobile RTC and gives a lecture about RTC technologies and protocols. He is also team leader and work package leader of the German BMBF lighthouse project Aletheia considering semantic federation of product information from structured and unstructured sources. Daniel Schuster received a PhD in Computer Science from TU Dresden, Germany, in 2007 and a Master's Degree from the same university in 2004. During his master and doctoral studies he has been working in industry co-operation projects in the area of real-time collaboration (especially distribution of multimedia content).

Amin Shaqrah is currently Assistant Professor of Management Information Systems at Al Zaytoonah University of Jordan. He holds a PhD in MIS from Arab Academy for Banking and Financial Sciences, and received MA in MIS from Amman Arab University for Graduate Studies. He is a Certified e-business Consultants and a KM Professional. He is affiliated with a number of international professional societies on KM, E-business, and a member of editorial review boards for a number of International Journals. He had a leadership role in the design and implementation of MIS program at the undergraduate level. His research interests are mainly knowledge sharing and transfer, organizational knowledge theory, knowledge culture, CRM value strategies, data mining techniques, Innovative work environment, human and social implications of Enterprise systems (ERP, CRM, and SCM). His work appears in number International Journals and conferences.

Srishti Shaw is currently pursuing her B.E. Degree in ETCE from JU. Her field of research is the Performance Evaluation and Network Modeling for Mobile Ad-Hoc Networks. She presented a research paper entitled "Joint Optimization of 2-tier Dual-homing for NodeBs and RNCs in UMTS Meta-heuristic Techniques" in the Fifth Workshop on Intelligent Networks: Adaptation, Communication & Reconfiguration (IAMCOM 2011) during January 2011 in Bangalore, India. She was selected for the Internship in Federal University of Parana, Brazil under the Dept. of Science and Technology (DST), Govt. of India Scheme entitled "Summer Internship Programme for Students from India in Brazil" in 2011.

Alan D. Smith is presently University Professor of Operations Management in the Department of Management and Marketing at Robert Morris University, located in Pittsburgh, PA. Previously he was Chair of the Department of Quantitative and Natural Sciences and Coordinator of Engineering Programs at the same institution, as well as Associate Professor of Business Administration and Director of Coal Mining Administration at Eastern Kentucky University. He holds concurrent PhDs in Engineering Systems/Education from The University of Akron and in Business Administration (OM and MIS) from Kent State University, as well as author of numerous articles and book chapters.

Bernd Stieger studied Management Information Systems at the University of Mannheim, Germany, where he received his Master's degree in 2007. Afterwards, he joined the life cycle science group which belongs to the department of Industrial Software and Applications of ABB Corporate Research Center Germany. He is conducting research and is responsible for managing global projects in the areas of service process optimization as well as mobile and knowledge management applications and technologies.

M. Umaparvathi completed her BE(ECE) from Madras University in the year 1995. She completed her M.Tech (Communication Systems) from NIT, Trichirapalli in the year 2005. Currently she is doing PhD in Anna University of Technology, Coimbatore. Her research interests are wireless networks, Information security and Digital Signal Processing.

Dharmishtan K. Varughese completed his BS(Engg.) from College of Engineering, Trivandrum in the year 1972. He completed his MS(Engg.) from College of Engineering, Trivandrum in the year 1981. He completed his PhD from Indian Institute of Science, Bangalore in the year 1988. He was working as Senior Joint Director from the year 2003 to 2007. Currently he is working as a Professor in Karpagam College of Engineering, Coimbatore. His research interests are microstrip antennas, microwave theory, information theory and optical fiber communication.

P. Venkateswaran has been working as an Associate Professor in the Dept. of Electronics & Tele-Communication Engg. (ETCE), Jadavpur University (JU), Kolkata, India since October 2001. He has published over 40 papers in various National / International, Journal / Conference Proceedings. His fields of interest are Computer Communication, Microcomputer Systems and Digital Signal Processing (DSP). He is a Member of IEEE(USA), and the present Secretary of IEEE Communications Society Calcutta Chapter.

Vânia M. P. Vidal has a graduate degree in Engenharia Civil from the Universidade Federal do Ceará (1979), master's at Informática from the Pontifícia Universidade Católica do Rio de Janeiro (1982), PhD at Engenharia de Sistemas from the Universidade Federal do Rio de Janeiro (1994), and Postdoctorate from the Polytechnique Fédéral de Lausanne (2008).

Matthias Wauer is a doctorate researcher at the Chair for Computer Networks at TU Dresden, Germany. He received his Diplom Degree in Media and Computer Science at the same university in 2008 for research on dynamic resource management using REST based Web services at IBM Deutschland Research & Development GmbH, Germany. His advisor is Prof. Alexander Schill. He currently works on a system architecture and resource selection mechanisms for semantic product information federation for the Aletheia project, which is funded by the German BMBF. His research interests include distributed information retrieval, Web services, semantic resource representations, and information system architectures.

Index

A

Adhoc on-demand Distance Vector (AODV) 240
Adhoc On-demand Multi-path Distance Vector
  (AOMDV) 240
Aletheia project 70-71, 140, 147, 155, 163, 166
  Aletheia Service Hub (ASH) 74
Application Programming Interface (API) 170, 174
Authentication 40-41, 165, 181
autonomic communications 220, 227-228, 235
autonomic computing 117-119, 121, 131, 133-135,
  137
    self-configuration 121
    self-healing 123
    self-optimization 125
    self-protection 122
Autonomic Pervasive Computing 117-120
average latency 54

B

broadband wireless access technologies 220, 234
business-to-consumers (B2C) 1

C

Cloud Computing 297-298, 300
Code Division Multiple Access (CDMA) 225
Cognitive Radio (CR) 295
cognitive wireless networks 220, 226, 229
Content-Aware Policy (CAP) 188
context-awareness 117-129, 134-138
    macro context-awareness 118, 120-126, 128-
    129, 134
    micro context-awareness 117-118, 120-125,
    127, 129, 134-135
Cost Per Mile (CPM) model 176
Crawling Data Provider 153, 157
cross-functional team 2
Customer Relationship Management (CRM) 70
cyber law 44

D

data integration 98-100, 103, 106, 108, 113-116,
  153, 155, 166
Destination Sequence Distance Vector (DSDV) 241
Devices Profile for Web Services (DPWS) 154
Dialog Act Markup in Several Layers (DAMSL) 87
Digital Living Network Alliance (DLNA) 296
Distributed Energy-Efficient Clustering algorithm
  (DEEC) 261
Distributed Fuzzy Score-based Clustering Algorithm
  (DFSCA) 209
dynamic data chaching 186
    automatic cache invalidation 189, 192-195,
    197-198, 200-202
    cache revalidation 186-187
    cache validation methods 187
    cluster caching 188
    expiry-based cache invalidation 191, 194, 196,
    199-200
dynamic probabilistic algorithm 52, 58-59, 61, 64
dynamic routing protocols (DRPs) 53
Dynamic Source Routing (DSR) 53, 242

E

eBay pulse™ 6
electronic commerce competence 37
electronic Word Of Mouth (eWOM) 172
Encryption 40, 44
energy heterogeneity 259-260, 264, 266-272
Enterprise Resource Planning (ERP) 70
expanding online auction service provider (OASP)
  industry 2

F

Federal Communications Commission (FCC) 300
federated information systems 139, 144
feedback systems 1, 3, 9-10, 15-18, 23, 25, 30